THE MAKING OF FINANCE

Using a variety of theoretical frameworks drawn from the social sciences, the contributions in this edited collection offer a critical perspective on the dominant paradigms used in contemporary financial activities. Through a detailed study of the organisation and functioning of financial intermediaries and institutions, the contributors to this volume analyse 'finance in the making', by shedding light on the structuring of banking and financial systems, on their capacity to prescribe action and control, on their modes of regulation and, more generally, on the process of financialisation.

Contributions presented in this volume have been written by authors working within the 'social studies of finance' tradition, a research programme that emerged twenty years ago, with the aim of addressing a diversity of financial fieldworks and related theoretical questions. This book, therefore, sheds light on different areas that are representative of contemporary financial realities. Specifically, it first studies the work of financial employees: traders, salespeople, investment managers, financial analysts, investment consultants, etc. but also provides an analysis of a range of financial instruments: financial schemes and contracts, financial derivatives, socially responsible investment funds, as well as market rules and regulations. Finally, it puts into perspective the organisations contributing to this financial reality: those developing and selling financial services (retail banks, brokerage houses, asset management firms, private equity firms, etc.), and also those contributing to the regulation of such activities (banking regulators, financial market authorities, credit rating agencies, the State, to name a few).

Each text can be read without any specific knowledge of finance; the book is thus addressed to anyone willing to better understand the intricacies of contemporary financial realities.

Isabelle Chambost is Associate Professor in Management at the Conservatoire National des Arts et Métiers, Paris, France.

Marc Lenglet is Associate Professor in the Department of Strategy and Entrepreneurship at NEOMA Business School, Rouen, France.

Yamina Tadjeddine is Professor of Economics at the Université de Lorraine, Nancy, France.

THE MAKING OF FINANCE

Perspectives from the Social Sciences

Edited by Isabelle Chambost, Marc Lenglet and Yamina Tadjeddine

Routledge
Taylor & Francis Group

LONDON AND NEW YORK

First published 2019
by Routledge
2 Park Square, Milton Park, Abingdon, Oxon OX14 4RN

and by Routledge
711 Third Avenue, New York, NY 10017

Routledge is an imprint of the Taylor & Francis Group, an informa business

British Library Cataloguing-in-Publication Data
A catalogue record for this book is available from the British Library

Library of Congress Cataloging-in-Publication Data
Names: Chambost, Isabelle, editor. | Lenglet, Marc, 1978– editor. | Tadjeddine, Yamina, editor.
Title: The making of finance : conventions, devices, and regulation / edited by Isabelle Chambost, Marc Lenglet and Yamina Tadjeddine.
Description: 1 Edition. | New York : Routledge, 2018.
Identifiers: LCCN 2018011586 | ISBN 9781138498563 (hardback) |
ISBN 9781138498570 (pbk.) | ISBN 9781351016117 (ebook) |
ISBN 9781351016100 (web pdf) | ISBN 9781351016094 (epub) | ISBN 9781351016087
Subjects: LCSH: Finance. | Banks and banking. | Financial institutions—Law and legislation.
Classification: LCC HG173 .M273 2018 | DDC 332—dc23
LC record available at https://lccn.loc.gov/2018011586

ISBN: 978-1-138-49856-3 (hbk)
ISBN: 978-1-138-49857-0 (pbk)
ISBN: 978-1-351-01611-7 (ebk)

Typeset in Bembo
by codeMantra

CONTENTS

FIGURES

TABLES

CONTRIBUTORS

Michel Aglietta is Professor of Economics at the University of Paris – Nanterre, France, and a scientific counsellor at CEPII. From 1997 to 2003, he was a member of the Council of Economic Analysis for the French prime minister. He is one of the founders of the French regulation school of economics. He has published several books, translated into English, Spanish, Japanese and numerous articles. Among these are: *A Theory of Capitalist Regulation: The US Experience* (Paris: Calmann-Lévy, 1976; London: Verso books, 1979) and *La violence de la monnaie* (with André Orléan, Paris: PUF, 1982).

Isabelle Chambost is Associate Professor in Management (accounting studies) at the Conservatoire National des Arts et Métiers (CNAM), Paris, France. Her research focuses on financialisation, its development by financial intermediaries, its dissemination (especially through accounting standards), and its social consequences (especially on labour). She has published articles and edited collections in *La Nouvelle Revue du Travail* and *Economies et Sociétés* (formerly *Revue de l'ISMEA*) among others.

Jacques-Olivier Charron is Associate Researcher at the IRISSO research centre, Université Paris-Dauphine, PSL Research University, Paris, France. He holds a PhD in management, obtained in 2010 at the CNAM (Conservatoire National des Arts et Métiers) in Paris. He works on financial theory, financial regulation and the future of capitalism from a social studies of finance perspective. Between 2015 and 2017, he was President of the Social Studies of Finance Association (SSFA), where he is now Secretary.

Eve Chiapello is Professor at EHESS (School for Advanced Studies in Social Sciences), Paris, France, where she holds a chair on the 'sociology of the transformation of capitalism'. Her present work is about the financialisation of public policies, on which she has organised a series of international conferences with the University of Hamburg. She received the Anneliese Maier Research Award 2016 from The Humboldt Foundation.

Géry Deffontaines. After a career debut in investment banking, Géry conducted a thesis at the crossroads of urban studies, economic sociology, and the sociology of finance at Laboratoire Techniques Territoires Sociétés (Ecole Nationale des Ponts et Chaussées, Paris, France). His PhD focused on the construction of an institutional framework for Public Private Partnerships – that is, opening the market of public procurement to the project finance industry. He now works as a researcher at GERPISA, an international network of the automobile industry.

Laurent Deville is Associate Professor of Finance and director of the Financial Economics track at EDHEC Business School, France (on leave from CNRS). His research interests primarily lie in the field of market microstructure with applications to index products. His current research is mainly devoted to the analysis of Exchange Traded Funds. He investigates the impact of these innovative instruments from multiple perspectives: financial, sociological and ethical.

Marnix Dressen is Professor of Sociology at the University of Versailles-Saint-Quentin-en-Yvelines, France, and a member of the CNRS 'Printemps' laboratory. Since the early 1990s, he has published several articles or research reports on the dynamics of bank restructuring, focusing on human resource management and industrial relations. See for instance, Dressen, M. and Blaustein, E. (1993). *Décomposition, recomposition dans la banque (marché, profession, organisation, culture)*. Genève: Bureau International du Travail; Dressen, M. and Roux-Rossi, D. (1997). *Restructuration des banques et devenir des salariés*. Paris: La Documentation Française; or Dressen, M. (1999). French banks: Between deregulation and State control. In M. Regini, J. Kitay and M. Baeghte (Eds.), *From Tellers to Sellers: Changing Employment Relations in Banks* (pp. 187–222). Cambridge: The MIT Press.

Olivier Godechot is Research Professor in Sociology (Sciences Po and OSC-CNRS) and the Co-Director of MaxPo research centre, Paris, France. He is interested in the study of labour markets, especially finance and academic labour markets, as a means to understand the development of unequal exchange relations at work and their impact on the dynamics of inequality. He recently published *Wages, Bonuses and Appropriation of Profit in the Financial Industry* (London: Routledge, 2017).

Caroline Granier holds a PhD in economics from the University of Bordeaux and is currently Post-Doctoral Research Fellow at Sant'Anna School of Advanced Studies in Pisa, Italy. She participates in the Horizon 2020 project ISIGrowth aimed at developing tools and a policy agenda for an Innovation-fuelled, Sustainable and Inclusive Growth in Europe. Her research focuses on financial geography, financial regulation and the relationship between firm growth and market funding.

Isabelle Huault is Professor of Organization Studies at Université Paris Dauphine-PSL, France. Her research interests lie in the social studies of finance and critical management studies. She has published her work in a number of leading journals including *Organization Studies, Organization, Management Learning, M@n@gement, Technological Forecasting and Social Change,* and co-authored books and edited collections. One of her recent books is *Finance: The Discreet Regulator* (Basingstoke: Palgrave MacMillan, 2012, with Chrystelle Richard).

Franck Jovanovic is Full Professor in Economics and Finance at the School of Administrative sciences at TELUQ University, Canada. He was previously Associate Professor in Finance at University of Leicester School of Management (UK). His research focuses mainly on the influence of financial economics on financial markets and the links between econophysics and financial economics. He has published more than 40 articles and books, including *Econophysics and Financial Economics: An Emerging Dialogue* (Oxford: Oxford University Press, 2017).

Eileen Keller is Researcher, responsible for the research area on 'economic policy' at the Franco-German Institute (dfi), Germany. Her research focuses on the development of financial sectors and corporate financing in a comparative perspective. She holds a doctorate from Humboldt University, Berlin. She was a guest researcher at the MaxPo Center at Sciences Po in Paris and Max Weber Fellow at the European University Institute in Florence.

Paul Lagneau-Ymonet is Assistant Professor of Sociology at Paris-Dauphine University, Paris, France. He co-published with Angelo Riva 'Trading forward: The Paris Bourse in the nineteenth century' (*Business History*, 20[2], 2018), and *Histoire de la Bourse* (Paris: La Découverte, 2012).

Pierre de Larminat earned a PhD in sociology from the University of Reims in 2013. His dissertation focused on the assessment of the quality of asset managers by investment professionals living in a world of uncertainty. He translated Max Weber's classic work *Die Börse* (1894–1896) from German into French (*La Bourse*. Paris: Allia, 2010). He lives in Frankfurt (Germany) and works as a consultant in financial analysis at Morningstar.

Jeanne Lazarus is a Tenured CNRS Research Fellow at the CSO in Sciences Po (Paris, France). Her research has focused on relationships between bankers and customers in French retail banks. She published *L'Epreuve de l'argent* (Paris: Calmann-Lévy, 2012), and edited several journal special issues on banking, credit and money management. The latest was co-edited with Mariana Luzzi ('L'argent domestique: des pratiques aux institutions', *Critique Internationale*, 2015/4, n°69). She is currently studying the making of a 'responsible' financial market for individuals.

Benjamin Lemoine is Researcher in Political Science and Socio-Economics at CNRS (Paris, France), and member of IRISSO (Paris Dauphine University) since 2013. He mobilises a critical science and technology studies (STS) approach in order to analyse the materiality and the politics of sovereign debt. His current fieldwork includes sovereign debt diplomacy, the international politics of sovereign debt restructuring, and the redefinition of sovereignty by global financial law. He recently published *L'ordre de la dette. Enquête sur les infortunes de l'État et la prospérité du marché* (Paris: La Découverte, 2016) and "The politics of public debt financialisation: (Re)inventing the market for French sovereign bonds and shaping the public debt problem (1966–2012)" in M. Buggeln, M. Daunton and A. Nützennadel

(Eds.), *The Political Economy of Public Finance. Taxation, State Spending and Debt since the 1970s.* Cambridge: Cambridge University Press, 2017.

Marc Lenglet, PhD in management, is Associate Professor in the Department of Strategy and Entrepreneurship at NEOMA Business School, Rouen, France. His research focuses on regulation and how innovations such as algorithmic trading impacts norms, rules and practices within financial institutions. His work has been published in the *Journal of Financial Regulation and Compliance, Economy & Society, Theory, Culture & Society,* and *Research in the Sociology of Organizations* among others.

David Martin, PhD in sociology, is Assistant Professor in the Marketing department at Novancia Business School, Paris, France. His more recent contributions are on citizen-consumer efforts to transform the prevailing financial practices and culture.

Valentina Moiso is Postdoctoral researcher in Sociology at the University of Turin, Department of Cultures, Politics and Society, Italy. Her research interests include household finance and social vulnerability, innovation in money circuits, Islamic finance, mafia expansion and collusive relations. She published in several journals, such as *Stato e Mercato* and *Critique Internationale,* among others.

Sabine Montagne is Researcher in sociology and socio-economics at CNRS (Paris, France), and member of IRISSO (Paris-Dauphine University-PSL) since 2004. She published her PhD on the impact of legal rules (trusts, fiduciary duties, ERISA) on US pension funds governance, highlighting the passivity of workers and the empowerment of money managers. She then explored the institutional conditions of sustainable long-term investment policies in Europe. She is currently preparing a book on the history of investment norms of US asset managers since WWII.

Pascale Moulévrier is Professor of Sociology at University of Nantes, France, and Researcher at the CENS – CNRS. Banking or financial relations, observed in banks but also in the context of microcredit institutions or financial education of the poorest, constitute her main fieldworks for problematising the question of the social and moral frameworks of economic action. She co-published with Matthieu Hély *L'économie sociale et solidaire: de l'utopie aux pratiques* (Paris: La Dispute, 2013).

Horacio Ortiz is Researcher at Université Paris-Dauphine, PSL Research University, CNRS, IRISSO, France, and Associate Professor at Research Institute of Anthropology, East China Normal University, China. He researches the politics of the global financial industry. He is the author of *Valeur financière et vérité. Enquête d'anthropologie politique sur l'évaluation des entreprises cotées en bourse* (Paris: Presses de Sciences Po, 2014), and co-author of *Capitalization: A cultural guide* (Paris: Presses des Mines, 2017).

Mohamed Oubenal holds a PhD in sociology from Paris-Dauphine University. He is currently Researcher in Sociology at Institut Royal de la Culture Amazighe (IRCAM) in Rabat, Morocco. He studies the transformations of Amazigh society in Morocco, as well as economic elites in North Africa. His PhD has been published as a book, titled *La légiti-mation des produits financiers: le réseau de promotion des Exchange Traded Funds (ETF) en France* (Cormelles-le-Royal: Editions EMS, 2015).

Alexandra Ouroussoff is a social anthropologist specialising in political economies, and is currently Research Fellow at Brunel University, London, UK. Her book, *Wall Street at War: The Secret Struggle for the Global Economy* (London: Polity, 2010 and Paris: Fondation de la Maison des Sciences de l'Homme, 2013), identifies a fundamental and unprecedented shift during the late 1970s in investors' conception of risk and its crucial structural consequences. Her current research focuses on why these major transformational events remain hidden from public view.

Elise Penalva-Icher is Assistant Professor at Paris-Dauphine, PSL Research University, Paris France. She is a member of the IRISSO research centre, where, as she specialises in economic sociology and the social construction of markets, she animates the valuation and market process team. She is also a social network analyst, member of the ORIO team. She has recently published an article in *The American Sociologist* introducing the French School of Social Network Analysis.

Hélène Rainelli-Weiss is Professor of Finance and Organization Theory at the Management School of the University of Strasbourg, France. Her research interests focus on organisation studies within the context of financial services. She is author or co-author of books and articles on the role of financial theory in contemporary financial practices, the organisation of financial markets, the institutional work performed by financial actors and the marketisation of financial innovations. She has published her work in a number of leading journals including *Organization Studies*, and in books (recently in Du Gay, P., & Morgan, G. (Eds.).(2014), *New spirits of capitalism? Crises, justifications, and dynamics.* Oxford University Press).

Valérie Revest is Associate Professor in Finance and Economics at the University of Lyon 2 France, research centre Triangle. Her research focuses on the creation, the functioning and the dynamics of stock markets dedicated to SMEs and to innovation. She has published in *Small Business Economics*, *Socio-Economic Review* and *Industrial and Corporate Change* among other journals.

Angelo Riva is Professor of Finance and Dean of Research at the European Business School, Paris, France. He is also Affiliate Member at the Paris School of Economics. His research focuses on monetary and financial history, and he has published extensively on the history of Italian and French financial markets. His work has been published in *Business History*, *Economic History Review*, *Explorations in Economic History*, and *Journal of Monetary Economics*, among others.

Yamina Tadjeddine is Full Professor in Economics at the Université de Lorraine, Nancy, France, and Research Fellow Beta, UMR CNRS 7522. Her research focuses on financial practices and regulation. She has published in *International Economics*, *Bankers, Markets & Investors* and the *Journal of Financial Regulation & Compliance* among others.

Benjamin Taupin is Associate Professor of Organization Studies at Conservatoire National des Arts et Métiers (CNAM), Paris, France, and research member of LIRSA. Based on field research in the finance industry, his previously published works focused on delineating the features that characterise complex financial domination in credit rating and financial inter-mediation. For his research on credit ratings, Benjamin took part in the registration of the credit rating agencies pursuant to the European Regulation as an employee of the French Autorité des Marchés Financiers (AMF).

Anne EA van der Graaf is a researcher affiliated to Sciences Po, Paris, France. She works on the sociology of financial markets and organisations, including a focus on the insurance industry.

Christian Walter is a fully qualified actuary (CERA), Professor of Finance and History of Financial Thought at Kedge Business School and member of the Sorbonne Contemporary Philosophy Center (PHICO, Univ. Paris 1 Panthéon-Sorbonne). He holds the Chair 'Ethics and Finance' (Fondation Maison des sciences de l'homme, Paris, and PHICO). His work has focused on financial markets and risk modelling related issues (mathematical, economic, philosophical, and historical) with an emphasis on interplays between the history of science, the modern financial approaches to pricing, and ethical perspectives. He has published 60 articles and books on these topics and recently co-authored with Olivier Le Courtois *Extreme Financial Risks and Asset Allocation* (London: Imperial College Press, 2014), winner of the 2016 Kulp-Wright Book Award of the American Risk and Insurance Association.

ACKNOWLEDGEMENTS

The editors and authors acknowledge all who gave their support to this project, and thank the following institutions for their contribution to the present collection:

- Centre de Sociologie des Organisations (CSO), UMR 7116, Sciences Po, Paris
- Département de l'IUP Finance, Université de Lorraine, Nancy
- Département de Sciences Economiques, Université Paris Nanterre, Nanterre
- Laboratoire Interdisciplinaire de Recherches des Sciences de l'Action (LIRSA), EA4603, Conservatoire National des Arts et Métiers, Paris
- Laboratoire IRISSO, UMR 7170, Université Paris Dauphine, Paris
- Laboratoire TRIANGLE, UMR 5206, Université Lumière Lyon II, Lyon
- Max Planck Sciences Po Center on Coping with Instability in Market Societies (MaxPo), Paris

INTRODUCTION

Finance as social science

Isabelle Chambost, Marc Lenglet and Yamina Tadjeddine

For several decades, from the 1960s through to the 2000s, banking and financial activities were by and large approached via the dominant paradigm of modern finance, which in turn served to reinforce the dominance of this paradigm. The existence of a finance industry co-existing in close synergy with the financial markets is a phenomenon which was constructed and gradually institutionalised – in the United States from the 1960s onwards (Whitley, 1986) and in Europe from the 1980s onwards (Kleiner, 1999) – in close and constant parallel with the development of modern portfolio theory and hypotheses regarding the efficiency of financial markets. These theories, which have come to inform the way in which financial activities are regulated, are invoked to justify the role of financial markets as the defining economic reference point for wealth transfer over time, for the management of associated risks and, as such, for the ownership of future wealth.

Founded on an assumption of rational decision-making in a context of known risks, coupled with the principle of perfect competition, mainstream financial theories are based on the idea that financial markets exist in a state of general equilibrium. The informational and allocative efficiency of these markets is secured by the modelling of financial asset prices, based on the random walk hypothesis (Fama, 1965), and optimal investment decisions made possible by effective models for valuing financial assets (Markowitz, 1959; Sharpe, 1964). Market prices therefore reflect the 'true' value of financial assets, whether they are issued by companies or governments, and ensure the optimal allocation of resources.

In this context, the financial intermediation industry is understood in terms of its contribution to the 'smooth' functioning of financial markets. The industry is responsible for the operational deployment of financial theories, with reference to artefacts and organisations, but also by establishing a certain division of labour between different professions and operating rules. For example, in order to continue to function the stock markets rely on the miniaturised representations provided by the market indicators used as reference points (or benchmarks) for the profits to be expected from investments, and on a well-established division of labour between economists, strategists, analysts and investors (third-party asset managers and proprietary traders attached to investment banks, for example).

The regulation of financial markets, meanwhile, assumes the existence of genuine competition between investors, in particular via the principle of transparency of information.

Regulation also presupposes that the conflicts of interest inherent to the very structure of financial intermediation will be handled appropriately. In this context, financial crises are viewed as epiphenomena and the infiltration of finance into our economic, social, family and even intimate decision-making processes (Zelizer, 2005) is considered natural.

The financial crises of the early twenty-first century have acted as a catalyst to the development of research on the phenomenon of financialisation (or the colonisation of non-financial spheres of activity by ideas and thought processes derived from the financial sphere): above and beyond discussions regarding the exact definition of this concept, its multiple manifestations and irreversible consequences have been clearly demonstrated and used to question the legitimacy, at least in certain academic milieus, of the orthodox view of finance outlined above.

Sharing this heterodox perspective, the aim of our work is to demonstrate how the social sciences can help us to adopt a denaturalising approach to contemporary finance, changing the way we think about it. Building on the confrontations, exchanges and debates which have dominated social studies in the field of finance since the late 1980s, we aim to propose analytical perspectives based on the empirical practices applied by economists, sociologists, management scholars, anthropologists and historians. Drawing upon an array of techniques for data gathering, critical analysis of sources, research organisation, modelling and comparative analysis, the authors included here share a commitment to achieving a new understanding of financial phenomena which is not dictated by the dominant discourse (Haag and Lemieux, 2012). The proximity of these researchers to their subjects, achieved using different techniques of observation, allows for profound analyses which are clearly situated within their temporal and geographical contexts, paving the way for a deeper, cross-disciplinary understanding of the phenomena in question.

New approaches to finance via three critical subjects

We therefore propose a methodology designed to nurture a new conceptual approach to finance (Lemieux et al., 2017). The structure of our methodology is based on critical analysis of the three main phases in the development and institutionalisation of finance as presented in this introduction: a first section offering a 'Critical analysis of mainstream financial theory and its uses', a second section looking at 'Structural dynamics in the financial industry' and a third section focusing on 'Finance as a new system of accumulation'. In order to firmly establish the genealogy of these concepts, we include pioneering alternative research works in economics and sociology, which laid the groundwork for the researchers cited here: works which have inspired a variety of reactions and positions in subsequent generations of academics.

Critical analysis of mainstream financial theory and its uses

Research compiled in this first section demonstrates the existence of operational mechanisms differing from those recognised by mainstream financial theory. Convention theory, for example, seeks to *call into question, to a greater or lesser extent, the hypotheses and concepts on which mainstream financial theories are based*, particularly the rationality of individuals and decision-making under the influence of risk. By situating these concepts within a context of radical uncertainty (Knight, 1921), André Orléan's work (2012) explores the effects of mimetism and self-referentiality, demonstrating that market values are also influenced by information endogenous to the market.

The contributions cited here adopt an empirical stance, analysing the way in which different approaches to the reference concepts can develop. This includes the way in which prices are formed in the market, the oft-overlooked process of commensuration of financial derivatives (Chapter 7, Rainelli-Weiss and Huault), the statistical choices made when it comes to modelling market values (Chapter 8, Walter) and the fact that financial services are inevitably dependent on various non-market parameters which define or codify informal exchanges (Chapter 1, Tadjeddine).

This research, and particularly those works which demonstrate the performative nature of economic theories (Callon, 1998; MacKenzie and Millo, 2003), has also focused on the ways in which economic theories are used. *Financial theories are embodied in tools, rules and artefacts acting as vectors influencing and legitimising financial practices, justifying transfers of wealth within the field of intermediation but also in relation to different economic spheres.* We can thus tease out the political and moral assumptions at work behind the mathematical formulae which are supposed to work exclusively in favour of market efficiency, a façade of neutrality which helps to ensure that 'the relationships of power inherent to the distribution of credit' (Chapter 3, Ortiz) are neglected when it comes to analysing and explaining financial crises. Close analysis of the manner in which financial actors comprehend risk also reveals, at best, a patchwork system which overrides the supposed division of labour in this domain (Chapter 2, Larminat) or, in the worst cases, the existence of baseless assumptions underpinning supervisory systems which are themselves a source of considerable risk (Chapter 6, van der Graaf).

The role played by financial analysts, supposed to provide the whole financial community with analysis based on information drawn from outside the financial markets, is also called into question, not least in light of the importance of 'road shows' held to bring together company directors and investors (Chapter 4, Chambost). Close scrutiny has also been applied to the financial structuring of public–private partnerships, with their capacity to shelter their creators from the risks involved (Chapter 5, Deffontaines). Finally, Jovanovic (Chapter 9) has examined the way in which the hypothesis of market efficiency gives rise to fictional constructs which in turn inform judgements, contextualising these judgements with reference to a phenomenon he calls 'hyperreality'.

Structural dynamics in the financial industry

In the USA, as early as the late 1950s, Gurley and Shaw's work (1956 and 1960) highlighted, without renouncing their neo-classical affiliations, the gradual institutionalisation of the process of financial intermediation in the American economy. From a more sociological perspective, and with greater reference to the existing social studies in the field of finance, Adler and Adler (1984) and Abolafia and Kilduff (1988) set out to analyse the financial markets as social structures. In France, the work of François Morin (1998) on the transformation of ownership structures within French capitalism revealed the creeping structural influence of the financial industry.

Economic, political and social analysis of the financial industry and its modus operandi also extends to *studying the formal aspects of financial thought processes* and their cognitive referents via the *marshalling of different management tools but also, more broadly speaking, the over-arching institutional and organisational structures and their capacity to control and contain action. Analysis should also take into account the regulatory mechanisms at work, their origin, their level of effectiveness, the associated accountability processes and their development over time.* Studying the transformations observed in the financial industry, especially in different political and economic contexts, allows researchers to identify the phenomena in play, their characteristics and any potential differentiating factors.

The contributions collected in these chapters analyse the shifting geographical base of the financial industry, looking at its business models and connections with other industries (Chapter 13, Tadjeddine) as well as the processes of recruiting and training workers, highlighting the transition observed in French banks from a model based on internal mobility to a greater reliance on external recruitment (Chapter 14, Dressen). The positions adopted by banks in relation to the dominant model are also analysed in terms of their fidelity (or lack thereof) to their specific identities, for example the way in which mutual savings banks regard their cooperative heritage (Chapter 15, Moulévrier), or German banks and their specific attitudes to lending (Chapter 16, Keller).

These dynamics are also analysed with regard to the manner in which innovation challenges (or fails to challenge) existing positions and profit-sharing arrangements within the financial intermediation industry, including the impact of new markets such as socially responsible investing (Chapter 12, Penalva-Icher) or the Alternative Investment Market (Chapter 11, Revest). Such innovations are also analysed in terms of the risks they involve, and the ways in which these risks are transferred within and beyond the financial sphere (Chapter 10, Oubenal and Deville).

We also address the issue of regulation and the forms it takes: first, the manner in which regulation of practices actually works within financial organisations, through the medium of compliance managers who are responsible for deciding how the rules should be applied (Chapter 18, Lenglet). Another facet explored here is the viewpoint tacitly enshrined in regulation: that of investors, or taxpayers or the beneficiaries of investments (Chapter 19, Charron). What emerges from this analysis is the prioritisation of investors' interests over the other two groups and the accompanying failure, on the part of the financial markets, to take sufficient account of the broader societal consequences of the actions of businesses and governments. A third perspective is also offered here (Chapter 17, Lagneau-Ymonet and Riva): an attempt to put the unprecedented predominance of the financial markets into historical perspective. The authors falling within this current explore the dynamics at play in the privatisation of market data, the fragmentation of liquidity and the near-impossible task of effectively monitoring all behaviour on the markets.

A new system of accumulation

Gradually expanding the scope of our investigations leads us to a third level of critical analysis, approaching financialisation by studying new methods of regulation. Research in this domain draws on the pioneering work of authors such as Bourdieu, Boltanski and Chamboredon (1963) who demonstrated the social dimension of individuals' relationship to credit, as well as the work of Jean Labasse (1974) on the influence of monetary and financial flows on the structural development of regions, and of course Fernand Braudel's research (1981) highlighting the importance of financial and monetary structures to the functional dynamics of market exchanges and the development of capitalism. But perhaps the greatest influence here is the regulation school (Aglietta, 1979 and Boyer, 1986), with their emphasis on challenging Fordism, the pre-emptive colonisation of value added by finance and the essential role played by crises in the development of finance, laying the groundwork for further analysis of the mechanisms of financial domination.

Perhaps the best way to truly get to the root of financialisation is via the *denaturalisation of financial techniques* and modes of thought (particularly in terms of the colonisation of future wealth): this much emerges clearly from close analysis of derivative assets (Chapter 20, Martin) and methods of valuation (Chapter 21, Chiapello).

Analysing the *structural systems* which govern the private equity industry, focusing on their discursive, material and political dimensions, allows us to get to the heart of the *power relationships which define the structure of this field*, and to cast light on the *domination* imposed upon the employees of companies acquired in this manner (Chapter 25, Chambost). The same dimensions are also essential to understanding the way in which rating agencies have succeeded in maintaining their pre-eminent position in the financial sector (Chapter 24, Ouroussoff), despite regular criticism of their role (Chapter 23, Taupin). Taking client relations as our starting point also allows us to analyse the manner in which Italian mutual banks have survived the profound transformation of the European banking industry in the wake of the Basel reforms (Chapter 22, Moiso).

Putting the *legal framework* which governs the operations of mutual funds into *historical perspective* allows us to demonstrate the extent to which legal reforms have contributed to the international expansion of such funds and their development in Europe (Chapter 26, Granier). Legal analysis, with particular focus on standards of diligence, also allows us to study the effects of financialisation on wage relations, via the changes observed in the management of social protection assets (Chapter 27, Montagne). No institutional analysis of this kind would be complete without examining the role of money as a mode of coordination embodying both the inherent instability of finance and its constitutive unity (Chapter 30, Aglietta). Thinking of money as debt also helps to elucidate some of the internal contradictions of the financial system. Analysing the way the markets handle the sale of emblematic debts such as government bonds also allows us to get to the heart of those social mechanisms by which wealth is distributed and inequalities reinforced (Chapter 28, Lemoine). In conclusion, it is in the very *fabric of our daily lives* that the consequences of financialisation are most apparent: one clear example is the existence of credit ratings, capable of playing a decisive role in our job prospects, love lives and the other phenomena which define social inclusion and exclusion (Chapter 29, Lazarus).

Developing a new approach to finance operating at three different levels of observation

Social sciences, unlike purely mathematical or philosophical economic theories, are founded upon a process of 'give and take' between abstract theorising and observation drawn from reality. French sociologist Bernard Lahire has written extensively on this topic, particularly in *Monde pluriel. Penser l'unité des sciences sociales* (*Plural world. Intellectual unity in the social sciences*, 2012), a work from which we drew inspiration when structuring this collection. Lahire insists upon the dual implications of the empirical foundations of social theories. First and foremost, research is always rooted in a historical, spatial and cultural context. The observations which emerged from early twenty-first-century Europe are of a different nature to those recorded by nineteenth-century researchers such as Max Weber, Gabriel Tarde or Marcel Mauss. The importance of context is a recurring theme in pragmatic sociology: Lahire's approach is original in that it adds a scale of observation, selected by the researcher, to the existing contextual foundations.

In our view this second component is what makes the present collection original and useful, and the same can be said more generally of inter-disciplinary research of the kind conducted by the Social Studies of Finance Association and the researchers it has inspired (see the following 'Rethinking finance with input from social sciences' section). By recognising that the same social phenomenon can be analysed at multiple levels, divergences between disciplines – and between theories within these disciplines – melt away to reveal a continuous spectrum of complementary interpretations. Approaches adopting the perspective of individuals, tools, categories, classes, organisations, structures, fields, institutions and even nations are all legitimate, each making a complementary contribution to our understanding of the same phenomena. B. Lahire (2012, p. 228) sets out this vision of the social sciences using the metaphor of a folded and refolded piece of paper, where each fold constitutes an original social phenomenon whose observation and analysis contributes to our understanding of the whole. Accepting this pluralism can make the idea of a general social theory seem fancifully utopian, but that does not equate to an endorsement of theoretical nihilism because each level of observation and its corresponding theoretical interpretation have their own legitimacy.

This collection uses three levels of observation to unfold and probe the financial field: techniques, organisations and institutions. None of these levels takes precedence over the others in terms of our comprehension of finance; each level contributes its own legitimate interpretations. None of the levels is inextricably linked to any specific discipline or theory. Nevertheless, certain theories are only compatible with certain scales of analysis. For example, it should come as no surprise to find researchers operating at the 'techniques' level of observation drawing upon actor-network theory. Similarly, authors affiliated with French Regulation Theory will be more inclined to analyse subjects at institutional level. We now propose to look at each of these levels in turn: techniques, organisations and institutions.

The financial techniques approach

The first level at which researchers might choose to approach financial topics is via the observation of *techniques*, i.e. the tools, algorithms, theories and even contracts used by the financial sector. Contrary to the received wisdom still frequently encountered in the dominant economic discourse, financial instruments cannot be dismissed as mere neutral objects: not only do they play a role in shaping financial behaviour, they are also representative of shared ideologies. The task facing researchers is to examine the nature, content, origin and use of these instruments, in order to elucidate their social, political, economic and managerial implications. The work initiated by Callon (1998), followed by MacKenzie and Millo (2003) and Callon and Muniesa (2005), utilises the concept of marshalling knowledge, looking at how financial theories are transposed into action via calculation tools, and in doing so re-appropriating and redeploying the concept of performativity. The research included here does not all belong to the same theoretical corpus, but does incorporate and explore this theory. The topics covered include risk theories (Chapter 8, Walter), valuation models (Chapter 7, Rainelli-Weiss and Huault; Chapter 21, Chiapello), internal risk modelling (Chapter 6, van der Graaf), derivative contracts (Chapter 20, Martin) and ETFs (Chapter 10, Oubenal and Deville).

The financial organisations approach

Financial organisations represent the second potential level of analysis. We can define organisations as collections of individuals structured on the basis of a division of labour, a decision-making system and the existence of routines designed to deliver specific financial services. Social scientists' route into the world of finance almost always involves finding an organisation agreeing to host an observer. Once accepted into an organisation, the researcher still needs to make a clear decision to study its operations rather than focusing on techniques (internal valuation models, for example) or institutions (application of rules). All of the articles included in the 'organisation' category take as their subject a specific organisation, setting out to comprehend its internal workings. At this level we find numerous works rooted in the sociology of organisations, neo-institutionalist sociology and institutionalist economics.

The modern financial world is home to a myriad array of financial organisations. A recent study published by the FSB (2015) found that a standard loan securitisation operation involves an average of 40 intermediaries between the household and the investor. It would be possible to establish a full list of all such organisations, but there is not enough space in this introduction. Nonetheless, because the application of social sciences to finance provides an empirical base on which we can build, we now possess detailed and precise descriptions of organisations and the links which exist between them. We therefore feel that this introduction is the right place to offer a functionalist classification of financial intermediaries: following the example set by Merton (1995), we can divide these organisations into five classes based on their areas of specialisation:

- The investment of savings originating from households, pensions, insurance policies, companies or governments: asset management firms, mutual funds, pension funds, trusts, financial advisers, private equity funds, hedge funds;
- The financing of states and companies via the issuing of shares, debt bonds or financial derivatives combining shares and credit: corporate and investment banks, securities traders;
- The structuring or products for the coverage and transferral of risk: investment banks, SIV, SPV;
- The production of information to facilitate financial decision-making: rating agencies, financial analysts, brokerage firms;
- The transmission and execution of transactions. This group includes brokers, market makers and clearing houses.

Some of these functions are associated with independent entities, as is often the case in the United States. In mainland Europe, they are often performed by dedicated subsidiaries of major European banking and insurance groups, groups comprising a range of structures covering the whole spectrum of banking and financial activities. To these categories we must add the internal or delegated support functions involved, including back office (accounting and pricing), middle office (risk control) and internal monitoring (compliance, depositary).

In this collection, organisations from all five of these categories are studied. Given the importance of collective management, many of the chapters are devoted to the role played by intermediaries, particularly management firms (Chapter 1, Tadjeddine, Chapter 2, Larminat; Chapter 3, Ortiz; Chapter 12, Penalva-Icher; Chapter 10, Oubenal and Deville; Chapter 26, Granier), but also pension funds (Chapter 27, Montagne) and private equity firms (Chapter 25, Chambost). Figure 0.1 offers a schematic overview of these organisations: intermediaries in the true sense of the word are shown in the middle (sovereign

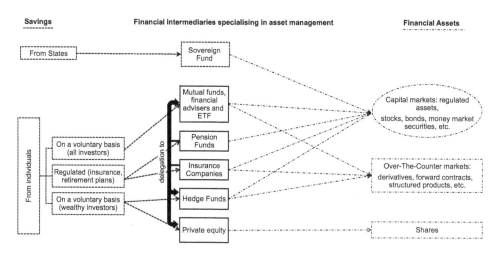

FIGURE 0.1 Financial intermediaries: from savings to financial portfolios

investment funds, mutual funds, pension funds, insurance companies, hedge funds, private equity). They receive money from governments, households and other household organisations who trust them to manage their investments (pension funds and insurance firms, primarily). They are therefore responsible for selecting securities on the regulated markets (shares, money liabilities), over-the-counter markets or directly with non-listed companies. While the activities of mutual funds, pension funds and insurance companies are subject to regulations requiring them to hold primarily regulated securities, hedge funds are free to invest in all available segments. Private equity firms prioritise investments in non-listed companies.

Banks are well-represented among these financiers (Chapter 14 Dressen; Chapter 15, Moulevrier; Chapter 16, Keller; Chapter 22, Moiso), but public finance organisations are also studied (Chapter 28, Lemoine; Chapter 5, Deffontaines). Figure 0.2 covers the three potential avenues of financing available: financing via lending from banks (method 1), financing via the financial markets (method 2) and financing operations which combine bank loans with the issuing of securities (method 3). There are few chapters here focusing on the organisations responsible for constructing risk coverage tools, but the techniques employed by these organisations are represented (Chapter 6, van der Graaf; Chapter 7, Rainelli-Weiss and Huault). Studying credit rating agencies (Chapter 23, Taupin; Chapter 24, Ouroussoff) and financial analysts (Chapter 25, Chambost) allows better understanding of the construction of financial information disseminated and utilised across the financial markets (Chapter 11, Revest; Chapter 17, Lagneau-Ymonet and Riva).

Finally, Figure 0.3 represents the different organisations which exert an influence over the financial decision-making process. The ultimate decision-maker is the party deciding to buy or sell securities, whether on their own behalf (proprietary traders) or on behalf of others (fund managers). These decisions are taken with the help of information provided by financial analysts, who issue recommendations regarding listed companies. These analysts may be working on the buy side (internal analysts within organisations) or the sell

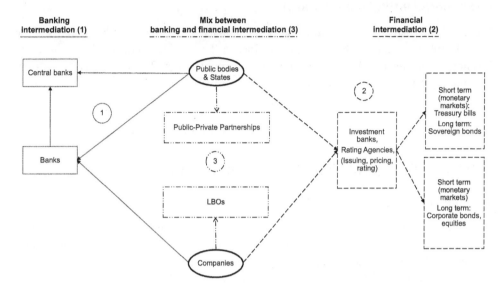

FIGURE 0.2 Financial intermediaries: financing of public or private investments

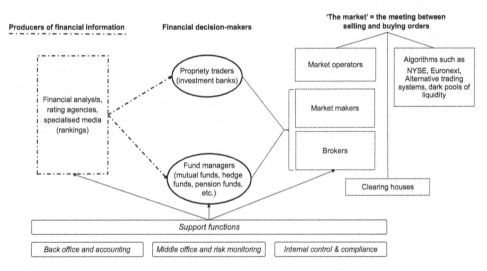

FIGURE 0.3 Financial intermediaries: financial market infrastructures

side (external analysts, generally employed by brokers). Rating agencies assess the risk that creditors will not repay their debts. Decision-makers, like all participants in the financial system, are obliged to abide by the various obligations enshrined in the systems, organisational routines and procedures which are developed, maintained and monitored by support services (internal monitoring, middle office, back office). Finally, the completion of financial transactions requires the involvement of various intermediaries: a broker to place the order, a market maker who holds the securities and offers them for sale at a given price, a clearing house which monitors the systematic compliance of securities transactions and financial flows, and finally the organisations responsible for handling negotiations (markets and alternative trading platforms).

The financial institutions approach

The third and final level is to analyse the *societal institutions*, which define the contours of the financial sphere, while also being shaped by finance. These include law, soft law (Chapter 9, Jovanovic; Chapter 18, Lenglet; Chapter 19, Charron; Chapter 26, Granier) and education (Chapter 29, Lazarus). We can also choose to scrutinise the institutional compromises which arise in the sector, with regard to the distribution of the social risk associated with pension commitments (Chapter 27, Montagne), public debt (Chapter 28, Lemoine) or, more broadly, the different prevailing forms of capitalism (Chapter 16, Keller; Chapter 30, Aglietta).

Rethinking finance with input from social sciences

Opening up to inter-disciplinarity

The inter-disciplinary scope of this collection was made possible by the pioneering work of a research association founded in France in the late 1990s, the Social Studies of Finance Association (or SSFA). The SSFA brings together researchers from across the social sciences – sociologists, economists, historians, anthropologists, management scientists, political scientists, geographers – whose work focuses on the world of finance. Theoretical and disciplinary diversity have played a fundamental role in the success and longevity of the association and its regular seminars (running since 1998), ensuring a constant influx of new members and studies. This inter-disciplinarity is also reflected in the diversity of the empirical and theoretical approaches represented, all united by a shared commitment to furthering our understanding of financial phenomena (Haag and Lemieux, 2012). Inter-disciplinarity requires us to share knowledge and concepts between disciplines: the SSFA seminar fulfils this role, obliging researchers to frame their problems and formulate their explanations in terms which are accessible to all participants.

Since its formation in 1998, the seminar has encouraged the comparison, discussion and exchange of methods, theories and points of view. The variety of theoretical frameworks put forward – economic sociology, convention economics, philosophy of norms, economic anthropology, neo-institutional sociology, sociology of work, financial geography, sociology of law, the regulation school, pragmatic sociology, institutional economics – has nurtured dialogue and fuelled vibrant debates centred around the scientific objectives shared by all members of the association. The social experience of participating in these seminars facilitates the transmission of concepts from one discipline to another, encouraging critical appropriation of concepts and detailed examination of their epistemic foundations. It has also permitted participants to discover new fields and ideas. We feel that this positive experience deserves to be acknowledged and emulated, embodying as it does something of the fundamental principles of social science. The matrix used to organise and present this collection is derived from our unique experience in the field of finance; nonetheless, this framework is by no means exclusive to finance and could easily be applied to other inter-disciplinary research projects.

A proposed analytical table

The chapters included in this inter-disciplinary collection are united by the fact that they all adopt one of the analytical angles enshrined in our three categories (criticism of classical financial theory, studying the structural dynamics of the industry, casting new light on a specific system of accumulation), all operate at one of the three levels of observation possible in the financial field (techniques, organisations and institutions) and all exist within an established disciplinary and theoretical corpus which is pertinent to the context of their analyses. The collection is structured around the categories set out above, with chapters grouped together into categories, each with its own introduction, then presented in ascending order based on the scale of their analysis (from micro, i.e. techniques, to meso, i.e. organisations, and finally to macro, i.e. institutions). For each contribution we identify the dominant theoretical stances, and some chapters draw upon different theoretical and disciplinary traditions.

This summary overview of the themes addressed in the present collection demonstrates the inter-disciplinary reach made possible by crossing three distinct critical approaches at three different levels of observation. But it is also possible to navigate through the collection based on the theoretical affiliations or empirical sources of the various authors.

By using Table 0.1, readers can easily pick out chapters based on the theories they invoke. We can note, for example, the large proportion of contributions with roots in economic sociology. It is also possible to select chapters based on their empirical objectives. For example, a reader with a particular interest in asset management can easily identify chapters with a focus on asset management firms.

Cross-referencing theoretical angles and empirical subject matter allows us to demonstrate the benefits of adopting an inter-disciplinary approach at different scales. Analysis of the same phenomena (laws, banks, risks, etc.) by researchers from different disciplines applying different theoretical approaches inevitably sheds new light on the subject in question. Far from producing divergent or contrasting findings, the resulting theoretical interpretations often converge, thus illustrating the influence of the SSFA seminar and its role as a catalyst for dialogue and shared reflection. This is certainly true of the contributions from anthropologist H. Ortiz, economist Y. Tadjeddine and sociologist P. de Larminat. All three look at asset management, and the difficulties inherent to selling such services. But while the anthropologist invokes representations, the economist prefers to focus on systems for resolving asymmetry of information, while the sociologist highlights the political influences of different components of the organisation.

Another example of fruitful cross-pollination comes from the field of *soft law*. One author analyses the consequences of European directives (Charron), another looks at the way that financial theory is interpreted by judges (Jovanovic), a third seeks to gauge the influence of the law in the structuring of the asset management industry in Europe (Granier), while a fourth scrutinises the legal practices at work in compliance monitoring (Lenglet).

One final illustration comes from the different perspectives on banks offered by three sociologists: Dressen looks at banker's training through the prism of professional sociology; Moulevrier studies mutual and cooperative banks in order to determine what makes them unique; last but not least, Moiso analyses the ways in which Italian mutual banks have resisted the structural regulatory changes imposed by the Basel committee.

Towards new analytical fields and challenges

This collection ends with an in-depth study by Olivier Godechot, analysing the phenomenon of financialisation via three structurally significant aspects: the depoliticisation of the markets, new forms of knowledge and a ruthless commitment to profit. He concludes by affirming the importance of making finance the subject of political debate again.

TABLE 0.1 Critical approaches and levels of observation

	Techniques	*Organisations*	*Institutions*
Critical analysis of classic financial theory	**(c.6) van der Graaf** *Sociology of quantification* (Risk models) **(c. 7) Rainelli–Weiss & Huault** *Organization studies* (Pricing models) **(c. 8) Walter** *History of financial theory* (Theory of risk)	**(c.1) Tadjeddine** *Convention economics* (Asset management) **(c.2) Larminat** *Economic sociology* (Asset management) **(c.3) Ortiz** *Anthropology of finance* (Asset management) **(c.4) Chambost** *Neo-institutionalist sociology* (Financial analysis) **(c.5) Deffontaines** *Economic sociology* (Public financing)	**(c.9) Jovanovic** *Economic sociology* (Financial law)
Structural dynamics in the financial industry	**(c.10) Oubenal & Deville** *Economic sociology* (ETFs)	**(c.11) Revest** *Institutional economics* (Market design) **(c.12) Penalva-Icher** *Economic sociology* (Asset management) **(c.13) Tadjeddine** *Geography of finance* (Asset management) **(c.14) Dressen** *Labour sociology* (Banking) **(c.15) Moulevrier** *Economic sociology* (Banking)	**(c.16) Keller** *Institutional economics* (Capitalisms) **(c.17) Lagneau-Ymonet & Riva** *Economic history* (Financial market regulation) **(c.18) Lenglet** *Philosophy of norms* (Soft laws and regulations) **(c.19) Charron** *Convention economics* (European laws and regulations)
A new system of accumulation	**(c.20) Martin** *Economic sociology* (Derivatives) **(c.21) Chiapello** *Sociology of quantification* (Pricing models)	**(c.22) Moiso** *Economic sociology* (Cooperative banks) **(c.23) Taupin** *Pragmatic sociology* (Rating agencies) **(c.24) Ouroussoff** *Anthropology of finance* (Rating agencies) **(c.25) Chambost** *Sociology of management* (Private equity)	**(c.26) Granier** *Institutional economics* (European law) **(c.27) Montagne** *French regulation theory* (Pension funds) **(c.28) Lemoine** *Political sociology* (Sovereign debt) **(c.29) Lazarus** *Economic sociology,* (Financial literacy) **(c. 30) Aglietta** *French regulation theory* (Capitalisms)

This collection is enriched by research of great depth and breadth, while remaining geographically and temporally consistent: the great majority of the chapters included here are derived from research conducted between 2000 and 2014 in a specific geographical context (Western Europe and, to a much lesser extent, the United States). The development of specialist forms of credit (such as Islamic finance or micro-credit) and new modes of financing (offered by nascent fintech firms) could prove to be fertile ground for further research.

On a more general level, there are huge swathes of the financial world still to be explored. Good examples include the supranational regulatory bodies (IMF, World Bank, BIS), as well as subjects which illustrate the rise of social inequality and the aggravating role of tax evasion, or how the dark side of finance (money laundering and the funding of terrorism) is able to operate via crowdfunding, crypto-currencies or the dark web. These topics have already been the subject of considerable journalistic investigation and fictional exploration, but they remain largely inaccessible to researchers.

We feel certain that the continuation of the SSFA seminar and the exciting new contributions it regularly attracts will provide ample material for a second volume of this collection a few years from now. Thank you for reading.

References

Abolafia, M. Y. and Kilduff, M. (1988). Enacting market crisis: The social construction of a speculative bubble. *Administrative Science Quarterly*, 33(2), 177–193.

Adler, P. and Adler, P. (Eds.) (1984). *The social dynamics of financial markets*. Greenwich: JAI Press.

Aglietta, M. (1979). *A theory of capitalist regulation. The US experience*. London: Verso.

Bourdieu, P., Boltanski, L. and Chamboredon, J.-C. (1963). *La banque et sa clientèle. Eléments d'une sociologie du crédit*, t. I. Paris: Centre de Sociologie Européenne de l'Ecole Pratique des Hautes Etudes, VIᵉ section.

Boyer, R. (1986), *La théorie de la régulation: une analyse critique*. Paris, La Découverte.

Braudel, F. (1981). *Civilization and capitalism, 15th–18th century*. Glasgow: William Collins Sons & Company Limited.

Callon, M. (1998). Introduction: The embeddedness of economic markets in economics. In M. Callon (Ed.), *The laws of the markets* (pp. 1–57). Oxford: Blackwell Publishers.

Callon, M. and Muniesa, F. (2005). Peripheral vision: Economic markets as calculative collective devices. *Organization Studies*, 26(8), 1229–1250.

Gurley, J. G. and Shaw, E. S. (1956). Financial intermediaries and the saving-investment process. *The Journal of Finance*, 11(2), 257–276.

Gurley, J. G. and Shaw, E. S. (1960). *Money in a Theory of Finance*. Washington, DC: Brookings Institution.

Fama, E. (1965). Random walk in stock market price. *Financial Analyst Journal*, 21(5), 55–59.

FSB (2015). *Global Shadow Banking Monitoring Report 2015*. Basel: Financial Stability Board.

Haag, P. and Lemieux, C. (2012). Critiquer, une nécessité. In P. Haag and C. Lemieux (Eds.), *Faire des sciences sociales, t. 1: Critiquer* (pp. 13–27). Paris: Editions de l'EHESS.

Kleiner, T. (1999). *The transformation of French asset management industry, 1984–1999*. Jouy-en-Josas: Les Etudes du Club.

Knight, F. H. (1921). *Risk, uncertainty and profit*. Boston: Houghton Mifflin.

Labasse, J. (1974). *L'espace financier, interprétation géographique*. Paris: Armand Colin.

Lahire, B. (2012). *Monde pluriel. Penser l'unité des sciences sociales*. Paris: Seuil.

Lemieux, C., Berger, L., Macé M., Salmon G. and Vidal, C., (2017). Rouvrir la bibliothèque des sciences sociales. In C. Lemieux (Ed.), *Pour les sciences sociales* (pp. 7–16). Paris : Editions de l'EHESS.

MacKenzie, D. and Millo, Y. (2003). Constructing a market, performing theory: The historical sociology of a financial derivatives exchange. *American Journal of Sociology*, 109(1), 107–145.

Markowitz, H. (1959). *Portfolio selection: Efficient diversification of investment*. New York: John Wiley & Sons.

Merton, R. C. (1995). A functional perspective of financial intermediation. *Financial Management*, 24(2), 23–41.

Morin, F. (1998). *Le modèle français de détention et de gestion du capital. Analyse, prospective et comparaisons internationales. Rapport pour le Conseil Analyse Economique*. Paris: Les éditions de Bercy.

Orléan, A. (2012). Knowledge in finance: Objective value versus convention. In R. Arena, A. Festré and N. Lazaric (Eds.), *Handbook of Knowledge and Economics* (pp. 313–338). Cheltenham: Edward Elgar.

Sharpe, W. (1964). Capital asset prices: A theory of market equilibrium under conditions of risk. *Journal of Finance*, 19(3), 445–442.

Whitley, R. (1986). The transformation of business finance into financial economics: The roles of academic expansion and changes in U.S. capital markets. *Accounting, Organization and Society*, 11(2), 171–192.

Zelizer, V. (2005). *The purchase of intimacy*. Princeton: Princeton University Press.

PART I

Critical analysis of mainstream financial theory and its uses

Introduction

Founded on an assumption of rational decision-making in a context of known risks, and the principle of perfect competition, mainstream financial theories are based on the idea that financial markets exist in a state of general equilibrium. The informational and allocative efficiency of these markets is secured by the modelling of financial asset prices, based on the random walk hypothesis (Fama, 1965), and optimal investment decisions made possible by effective models for valuing financial assets (Markowitz, 1959; Sharpe, 1964). Market prices therefore reflect the 'true' value of financial assets, whether they are issued by companies or governments, and ensure the optimal allocation of resources. The research cited in this first section questions the practical implications of these concepts, in terms of the way in which prices are formed in the market and the oft-overlooked importance of the process of commensuration of financial derivatives (Rainelli-Weiss and Huault), the statistical choices made when it comes to modelling market values (Walter) and the fact that financial services are inevitably dependent on various non-market parameters which shape exchanges (Tadjeddine).

The researchers cited here have also questioned the way in which these theories are embodied in the tools, rules and organisations which influence financial, economic and legal practices, and are used to legitimate certain professions, reinforce roles and delimit spheres of influence. Hence Ortiz explores the role played by the political and moral positions which tacitly underpin the selection and deployment of mathematical formulae in finance. Close analysis of the manner in which financial actors comprehend risk also reveals, at best, a patchwork system which overrides the supposed division of labour in this domain (Larminat) or, in the worst cases, the existence of baseless assumptions underpinning supervisory systems which are themselves a source of considerable risk (van der Graaf). The role played by financial analysts, supposed to provide the whole financial community with analysis based on information drawn from outside the financial markets, is also called into question, not least in light of the importance of 'road shows' held to bring together company directors and investors (Chambost). Close scrutiny has also been applied to the financial structuring of public–private partnerships, with their capacity to shelter their creators from the risks involved (Deffontaines). Finally, Jovanovic has examined the way in which the hypothesis

TABLE I.1 Critical analysis of classic financial theory – classification based on scale of observation

Techniques	*Organisations*	*Institutions*
(c.6) van der Graaf *Sociology of quantification* (Risk models)	**(c.1) Tadjeddine** *Convention economics* (Asset management)	**(c.9) Jovanovic** *Economic sociology* (Financial law)
(c. 7) Rainelli-Weiss & **Huault** *Organization studies* (Pricing models)	**(c.2) Larminat** *Economic sociology* (Asset management)	
(c. 8) Walter *History of financial theory* (Theory of risk)	**(c.3) Ortiz** *Anthropology of finance* (Asset management)	
	(c.4) Chambost *Neo-institutionalist sociology* (Financial analysis)	
	(c.5) Deffontaines *Economic sociology* (Public financing)	

of market efficiency gives rise to fictional constructs with real consequences for judgements, contextualising these judgements with reference to the phenomenon of hyperreality.

The complexity of these theories, of the financial dynamics in action and the financial derivatives involved acts as a barrier to entry and may prove to be off-putting (and understandably so) for researchers who do not consider themselves to be specialists in this field. In our opinion, a more accessible approach to understanding these financial processes is to begin by observing the organisations involved and the professionals who operate within them (cf. Table I.1). This is the approach adopted by Tadjeddine, Larminat and Ortiz, who have conducted research within asset management firms in order to produce studies focusing on managers, and thus address the practical side of investment processes. Similarly, Chambost visited brokers' offices to meet sell-side financial analysts and traders. The analysis offered by Deffontaines is also rooted in a detailed examination of the organisations and professions involved in the financial structures which underpin public–private partnerships. Focusing on techniques makes such studies easier to conduct, allowing researchers to address subjects such as interest rate coverage (van der Graaf) and how prices are established on the derivatives market (Rainelli-Weiss and Huault). Mastering the theoretical aspects of these techniques allows us to directly analyse their foundations (Walter), or even their origins in legal precedent as seen from an institutional perspective (Jovanovic). While reading this section you may also find it useful to refer to Figures 0.1 and 0.2 provided in the Introduction.

References

Fama, E. (1965). Random walk in stock market price. *Financial Analyst Journal*, 21(5), 55–59.

Markowitz, H. (1959). *Portfolio selection: Efficient diversification of investment*. New York: John Wiley & Sons.

Sharpe, W. (1964). Capital asset prices: A theory of market equilibrium under conditions of risk. *Journal of Finance*, 19(3), 445–442.

1

FINANCIAL SERVICES

A collection of arrangements

Yamina Tadjeddine

The role of financial organisations is to act as intermediaries providing a service targeted at either those who hold savings funds and wish to invest in the financial markets, or those who have a need for monetary resources. Thanks to the financialisation of the economy, the intermediation chain has become considerably strengthened. New services, roles, and organisations have appeared, notably in the area of risk hedging and asset management. Examining the hegemony of finance today means questioning the legitimacy of the economic rent received by financial intermediaries and in the same instance questioning the true nature of the financial services provided.

For those with savings, asset management proposes to turn to the expertise of an intermediary – the funds manager – in order to build up a portfolio of financial securities. The funds manager is considered to have a greater understanding of those entities issuing financial securities (governments, corporations) and of how the market works. He/she is also expected to have privileged access to information and rumours, and is therefore better informed as to how best to yield profit from capital. It is this enhanced knowledge concerning opportunities for speculative profit that justifies his/her fees. Appealing to the services of a funds manager means the saver can expect a higher profit than what he/she would have achieved without this mediation.

From the perspective of a canonical economic interpretation, a direct connection should exist between the quality of the service provided by the manager – namely the judicious selection of securities to include in a portfolio – and the capital yields paid out to the saver. The issue of the quality of financial services would therefore be resolved. Yet, the financial reality is marked by the uncertainty of price variations: financial hazard is not Gaussian, it follows more complex processes which render its prediction impossible both in the short and long term. As a result, speculative profit achieved over the short term is above all the result of good luck or of a bad turn. It provides little information regarding the value of the service provided by the manager and furthermore makes it impossible to determine his/her prospective ability to attain the same returns. This informational deficiency both *ex ante* and *ex post* creates suspicion and market failures (Akerlof, 1970). Nevertheless, in practice, the trade undoubtedly takes place as certain arrangements like signals or reputation are employed to resolve the market failure. The existence of such arrangements was revealed through socio-economic research examining the quality of services by Eymard-Duvernay (1989), Gadrey (2004) and Karpik (1989). Ortiz (2005) additionally proposed to assimilate these various socio-economic studies, in order to understand the nature of the relationship between funds manager and broker. He shows how the personalisation of the trades leads to the existence of various modes of qualification. We pursue this pathway within this chapter, basing our work upon another type of relationship (between sales personnel and institutional investors).

This chapter therefore proposes to examine the social and political construction of the quality of a particular financial service – asset management. The first section succinctly describes the activity of fund management delegation that takes place between institutional investors and asset management corporations. The second section focuses on the quality of the financial service. The financial relationship cannot singularly be reduced to the returns yielded; rather, it is built through a collection of social and political arrangements which will be presented in the final section of this chapter.

The relation between institutional investor and asset management companies

Asset management companies provide the service of portfolio management. In France, conducting fund management activities for third-party accounts is regulated by the AMF – *Autorité des marchés financières* (Financial Market Authority). According to a report on third-party account management published in 2012 by the AMF, in this same year there existed a total of 604 asset management companies which between them handled 2,867 billion euros. However, this elevated figure obscures a major imbalance: the subsidiary of large insurance and banking groups manage practically 90 per cent of the assets (AMF, 2012). We have monitored the case of one management firm, the subsidiary of a private Belgian bank, which declared in April 2013 that it had under its management 2.6 billion euros worth of assets. This private bank employs around a hundred employees and offers its services to private individuals, though also and more importantly to institutional investors. We were able to observe the work of the person responsible for customer relations with their institutional clients. The observation consisted of regular encounters with this person, within their firm, for over more than a year, in addition to the consultation of numerous commercial documents (prospectus presenting the company's products, contracts, calls for tender, reports).

The main institutional investors in France are insurance companies, private health insurance firms (*mutuelles*), pension funds, associations and foundations. The origin of funds could be private savings or regulated capital (insurance reserves or retirement funds), the management of which is controlled by public rules. In France, 69 per cent of managed assets are from institutional investors. Consequently, the relationship between institutional investor and asset management company is at the very core of current financial capitalism (Aglietta and Rigot, 2009). Certain institutional investors own the subsidiaries of fund management firms and hence invest their funds within them. This is the case with several insurance firms (AXA with AXA IM), but also with a number of private health insurance firms (EGAMO is a subsidiary of MGEN) and some pension funds (Pro BTP Finance). Institutional investors can also choose to invest with an external service provider, such as the private Belgian bank that I was able to observe. The service may be carried out in various juridical forms: share subscriptions for UCITS (undertakings for collective investment in transferable securities) or trust. It is common that institutional investors turn at the same time towards various competitor internal and external service providers. Decisions concerning the delegation of fund management involve numerous internal actors (financial directors, executive officers, lawyers, follow-up committees, etc.), but also external consultants who will be tasked with selecting the management firms. The representative for the management firm is generally the salesperson responsible for canvassing new clients and fulfilling their expectations.

The quality of the financial service

Within the collective management market, the client (here the institutional investor) must choose a producer (the manager). The production in this trade is the portfolio yield. This yield is furthermore the only market signal received by the client, yet it is impossible to infer from it the true quality of the manager.

We thus find ourselves confronted with a key debate within the informational economic theory, which concerns the consumer's knowledge about the quality of the provided service. Three types of services have been identified in economic literature. In the first instance, Nelson (1970) proposes to distinguish between services for which the quality can be discerned *ex ante* ('*search goods*') and services for which the quality will only be known once consumed ('*experience goods*'). Darby and Karni (1973) have added a third category, '*credence goods*', covering those services for which it is impossible even *ex post* to discern the quality. Yet none of these three categories are applicable to the circumstances of financial services due to the presence of financial uncertainty. The knowledge of past yields is not reliable enough to distinguish good managers either *ex ante* or *ex post*. The financial service therefore cannot be classified as either a *search good* or an *experience good*. Neither is it, on the other hand, a *credence good* in which the agent is able to use the information asymmetry in an opportunistic way to maximise his/her own interest. The existence of financial uncertainty harms equally the client (who may lose their money) and the portfolio manager (whose hard work may go unrecognised).

The financial service thus falls under the definition of a *unique good*, also known as 'singularities' (Karpik, 2010). The challenge of the trade is to overcome this lack of information by establishing a personal relationship based on the co-production of a service. To this end, the protagonists must back-up the commercial relation with measures that they will eventually define over time and which will allow the financial service to be qualified, framed and monitored.

The arrangements required for trading and legitimising financial services

Financial services cannot merely be summarised as a simple market exchange, as they involve a personal relationship which engages the co-exchangers. As such, it is not only the yield that is bought, and which must be taken into consideration by the client and the seller, but also a collection of practices, knowledge, rules, symbols and feelings which will bind together the protagonists (Ortiz, 2005). These non-commercial and co-constructed arrangements are precisely what constitute the essence of the financial trade. In these conditions, the characterisation of the good or bad manager, as well as any impending sanction, is dependent upon the nature of the relationship founded. We propose to illustrate this unique aspect of the financial service through three arrangements thus observed: membership with symbolic social networks (a *personal arrangement* according to Karpik, 2010), the standardisation of practices involving the use of predefined styles, benchmarks and classifications (*impersonal, significant or formal arrangements*, again according to Karpik, 2010), and finally framework agreement (the *contrat-cadre* according to Eymard-Duvernay, 1994).

Personal arrangements

Historically, calling upon a specialist to manage one's private fortune relied heavily upon the individual and personal trust built up between two protagonists. Personal knowledge, belonging to shared social networks or having family in common reassured the saver with regards to the correct moral standards of the person who was responsible for investing his/her savings. The commercial agreement is made possible thanks to the individuals' embeddedness in social structures that bring with them moral guarantees concerning the fund manager's good will. The commercial conclusion is nothing more than the outcome of these weak ties which initially allowed the seller and the client to enter into contact and to establish a connection across the long term. Any knowledge of embezzlement would give rise to social rupture, with the manager being banned from the group, and as a consequence commercial rupture would ensue. The research of Pinçon and Pinçon-Charlot (1998) has demonstrated the importance of private clubs within upper-class society and in particular within the financial sphere. Individuals who belong to the same social networks (Freemasons, clubs and religious communities) or who share similar activities (hunting, mountaineering) encourage trust.

Nevertheless, following the current liberalisation of society in which values such as transparency, avoiding conflict of interest and short-term competition dominate, this 'personal' form which relies on reciprocity, informality and opacity has been denounced. At present, it is impossible for the financial director of a private health fund, for example, to justify his/her choice of portfolio management uniquely on the basis of pre-existing social connections. Despite all this, weak ties still remain essential to building connections between actors. A *salesperson* is only valuable as long as the names in his/her address book are influential and loyal. As such the salesperson whom I observed had maintained a number of relations over several decades, even though the individual in question had changed companies several times.

Impersonal, significant and formal arrangements

The second grouping assembles together arrangements which aim to homogenise and characterise practices by establishing a reference point for judging and comparing the services provided (Vatin, 2009). As such, the service bought is no longer idiosyncratic, but can be compared to others which are equivalent in order to evaluate the fund manager's skills in the light of his/her peers. Moreover, the relationship is no longer strictly personal but involves the existence of recognised evaluation agencies. In asset management, this movement towards professional standardisation during the 1980s was based on classical financial theory following the naturalisation of 'benchmarks', and later in response to practitioners via the creation of a professional practices rating.

Traditional asset management developed in reference to the evaluation model of financial assets: the CAPM – Capital Asset Pricing Model. This model enabled a reference portfolio composed of a sample of assets that account for the global evolution of a market to be established. The market index thus acquired scientific legitimacy and naturalisation, and ever since all financial centres have been equipped with one or several indexes (the CAC40 in Paris, S&P500 in New York, etc.). Global, ethical, sector and mandatory indexes were developed in the wake. These indexes were defined and built by market firms responsible for listing and pairing together orders (such as Euronext) or financial companies (such as Standard & Poor's). The success of these indexes resulted for the most part from the fact that they provided a publicly accessible referent, which allowed the yield of a portfolio built up by the manager to be compared with the reference portfolio.

The existence of indexes also allowed portfolio management to become standardised. From the beginning of the 2000s, a new financial product, created and developed in the United States during the 1990s, the *Exchange Traded Fund* (or EFT) appeared in France. These products automatically reproduce the index, without involving any expert input from the fund manager. They were subject to an extremely strong buying craze, notably among institutional investors, who subsequently bought into an industrialised product (Gadrey, 2004), for which the yield remains risky yet perfectly correlated with the market index. As such the EFT enables any uncertainty concerning the quality of the manager to be eliminated and maintains only financial uncertainty.

There exists a second impersonal arrangement: classification by asset management style. The domination of passive index management signalled the death-knell for manager expertise, as all that was deemed necessary to obtain an optimal yield was a basket of 'scientifically' defined securities. From the 1980s, several professionals in asset management and financial econometricians discussed and wrote about the fact that certain managers who developed strategies for selecting securities, regularly and considerably obtained higher yields than those theoretically predicted (Aaron et al., 2005). This observation directly challenges the thesis of information efficiency, though it grants scientific legitimacy to employing a fund manager. Upon this basis, three strategies for securities selection gained prominence among both clients and practitioners: the sector, growth and value styles. The *sector* or geographical style aims to select securities in relation to their activity sector or geographical zone. The *growth* style consists of selecting companies that are predicted to experience high growth rates. The *value* style favours unlisted companies, abnormally affordable and predicted to undergo a hike in prices.

The categories unite together homogeneous practices in that they are all based on similar strategies for selecting securities. Allocation in one or the other of these categories can take place via public information, through studies carried out by specialised companies or by the manager declaring their preferred style.

These categories are currently employed as often by managers to explain their strategy, as they are by clients to choose. They contribute towards standardising practices by obliging managers to qualify their strategy through pre-determined categories. Consequently, the UCITS funds of the private Belgian bank are presented within the prospectus of the AMF, as they similarly are directly to clients, in accordance with whichever dominant style the manager happens to choose. Nevertheless, this categorising process leaves a wide berth of choice within a selection of securities, which explains the possibility of differentiated yields. Ratings based on styles are created and the quality of the manager is judged in the light of these categories.

The 'contract-cadre' or framework agreement

The final grouping is concerned with contractual arrangements which explain and frame the production process. These arrangements were put into place during the 1990s in the US and later on in France, during the shift towards the judicialisation of society. They were initiated by institutional investors to counterbalance the power held by asset managers in the delegation relationship. An initial set of rules enacted *ex ante* by the client or by an external consultant outlines the preferences and expectations of the institutional investor on the subject of funds investment. Two methods exist: either these rules are published during calls-for-tender and are communicated to the highest number of people possible; or they are communicated during individual encounters with select firms, and in this case we refer to *due diligence*. The management firm, if it wishes to trade with the client, must fulfil these expectations by answering detailed questionnaires about its practices concerning the selection of securities, its management style, its reference indexes, its risk management, its staff members, its internal organisation, its clients, performances, etc. It is only after having answered all these questions that the commercial relationship can begin through the competitive comparison of the various responses given by the managers. A selection and listing takes place on the basis of the responses given. Using this base, the client chooses one or several asset companies. It informs some of the non-selected firms that they may have an opportunity of being selected at a later date, if they change certain elements within their proposed service. Consequently, a historical account takes place which allows for the behavioural evolution of firms to be monitored. Once the selection is concluded, a contract then binds together the institutional investor and the chosen manager.

Strictly speaking, this commercial contract contains two elements: the first details the expectations of the client in terms of the management (market sectors, management styles, risks, reference indexes, and the freedom regarding this index, i.e. *'tracking error'*); the second outlines a set of rules targeted at reducing any moral hazard by framing the practices and obliging the manager to pass on regular information via *reporting* and during meetings. The information communicated explains the motivations behind the selection of securities, the reasons for the performances attained and the future directions. As such the institutional investor frames the work of the manager and obliges him/her to regularly disclose information. The manager's opportunism is much lower and the portfolio yield represents nothing more than a lone indicator among many others.

Conclusion

Financial services comprise a collection of co-assembled arrangements which qualify, define and frame the financial relation. Current arrangements are the product of private actors (fund managers and institutional investors) and target uniquely financial objectives (achieving profit across the short to medium term and attempting to control risks). With regards to what should be the economic, social and political utility of financial intermediation, no long-term perspectives are ever really considered within the social construction of the quality of a financial service.

References

Aaron, C., Bilon, I., Galanti, S. and Tadjeddine, Y. (2005). Les styles de gestion de portefeuille existent-ils? *Revue d'Economie Financière*, 81, 171–188.

Aglietta, M. and Rigot, S. (2009). *Crise et rénovation de la finance*. Paris: Odile Jacob.

Akerlof, G. (1970). The market for 'lemons': Quality, uncertainty and the market mechanism. *Quarterly Journal of Economics*, 84(3), 488–500.

AMF [Autorité des Marchés Financiers] (2012). *Rapport annuel sur la gestion d'actifs pour le compte de tiers en 2012*. Paris: AMF.

Darby, M. and Karni, E. (1973). Free competition and the optimal amount of fraud. *Journal of Law and Economics*, 16(1), 67–88.

Eymard-Duvernay, F. (1989). Conventions de qualité et formes de coordination. *Revue économique*, 40(2), 329–359.

Eymard-Duvernay, F. (1994). Coordination par l'entreprise et qualité des biens. In A. Orléan (Ed.), *Analyse économique des conventions* (pp. 307–334). Paris: PUF.

Gadrey, J. (2004). *Socio-économie des services*. Paris: La Découverte.

Karpik, L. (1989). L'économie de la qualité. *Revue française de sociologie*, 30(2), 187–210.

Karpik, L. (2010). *Valuing the unique: The economics of singularities*. Princeton: Princeton University Press.

Nelson, P. (1970). Information and consumer behavior. *Journal of Political Economy*, 78(2), 311–329.

Orléan, A. (2005). Réflexions sur l'hypothèse d'objectivité de la valeur fondamentale. In D. Bourghelle, O. Brandouy, R. Gillet and A. Orléan (Eds.), *Croyances, représentations collectives et finance* (pp. 21–39). Paris: Economica.

Ortiz, H. (2005). Évaluer, apprécier: les relations entre *brokers* et gérants de fonds d'investissement. *Économie rurale*, 286–287, 56–70.

Pinçon, M. and Pinçon-Charlot, M. (1998). *Les Rothschild, une famille bien ordonnée*. Paris: La Dispute.

Vatin, F. (Ed.) (2009). *Évaluer et valoriser. Une sociologie économique de la mesure*. Toulouse: Presses Universitaires du Mirail.

2

TAMING THE RISK BORNE BY FINANCIAL PRODUCTS

Pierre de Larminat

The realisation of human undertakings generally requires the collective action of many actors among whom there are those who contribute by way of financing, which ensures that the means required for success are brought together. In the case of economic ventures, success can be understood as the reproduction of the resources for undertaking future ventures, and it can be measured by the ventures' eventual profitability. The level of this profitability is subject to the same uncertainty that strikes all social and economic phenomena. This uncertainty, epistemic in nature, is conveyed *a posteriori* by the variability of profitability and constitutes a risk for a company's stakeholders when profitability becomes negative (absolute loss) or inferior to the profitability of another company (relative loss). Risk is the subjective side of the unpredictability of economic phenomena; the latter does not constitute an actual risk for social actors unless these phenomena cause undesirable outcomes. The social opportunities of these actors and their ability to engage in further ventures are thus weakened.

The capital driven by the actors of the contemporary financial system enables them to favour or to obstruct the most diverse ventures. They draw their legitimacy to do so from their ability to skilfully manage the risks that the uncertainty of success imposes upon the reproduction of the means to undertake – both from the perspective of the capitalists, who benefit directly from any profits, and from the perspective of all the social actors whose existence depends on trade. The succession of financial crises calls into question the credibility of such a claim, or at least the reality of finance professionals implementing this ability, nevertheless reaffirmed since the subprime mortgage crisis by the enhancing and refining of departments especially dedicated to risk management.

A widely accepted concept of risk that can be traced back at least as far as Frank Knight (1921), but which we do not share, regards risk as corresponding to a particular state of the world in which the variability of phenomena can be wholly expressed in measurable quantities, whereas uncertainty characterises those worlds in which the variability of phenomena cannot be reduced to a mathematical equation. The Knightian distinction at least reflects the efforts carried out over the centuries to develop the symbolic instruments that give form to the variability of economic phenomena, so as to create out of such variability an object capable of being handled and controlled (Brian, 2009). This chapter is dedicated to the way those instruments are used.

We first call to mind that financial risks constitute a particular type of social risk and that they therefore depend on a certain type of organisation of society. We then go on to retrace the production of the technologies that are today available for harnessing financial risks. Finally, we show that the social conditions in which these technologies are being implemented play a crucial role in the ability of economic actors to effectively protect themselves against the undesirable outcomes of financial uncertainty.

Financial risks are social risks

Financial asset prices are social facts to the largest extent of the term. On the one hand, they originate from the cognitive tools by which agents measure the value of goods. On the other hand, they result from competing valuations during market interactions. The economic uncertainty that results in variations in the profitability of financial products is therefore one expression of the uncertainty that spans across social interactions, and financial risks are thus social in nature. The production of institutions stabilises interactions and contributes towards reducing the uncertainty that results from their instability (Brian, 2009). The construction of a financial market, whether it be organised around a trading pit like the stock markets of centuries past or around digital telecommunication systems, constitutes such an institution. For example, the procedure of fixing opening and closing prices on the Paris Stock Market is a social technology that controls the ways in which exchange participants interact shortly before the opening and the closing of the Stock Market. This procedure ensures a less radical impact from the uncertainty weighing on prices that determine the decisions and successes of numerous economic actors (Muniesa, 2000).

Despite the efforts made by social agents to institutionalise their relations and stabilise their interactions, their behaviours and the ensuing outcomes remain imperfectly predictable. Stock market prices alternate between prolonged periods of growth and decline which are not always correlated or proportionate to the movements of other economic events that are said to belong to the 'real' economy because they appear to be more directly connected to satisfying needs. The use of the qualifying terms 'bubble' and 'frenzy' to refer to growth phases, expresses the awareness social actors have regarding the amplification of economic risks that market interactions provoke within the financial sphere. As we have just seen, the ways in which market participants are brought together and in which their interactions with each other are organised may reduce or amplify the risks borne by financial products. The amplification of such risks can also result from the degree of control exercised over those participating in the exchange as members of a social group that is more of less capable of controlling its members' actions (Abolafia, 1996; Lagneau-Ymonet and Riva, 2012; Weber, 1999). Furthermore, they could even be related to the self-referential dimension of stock market operations. Even the spread of risk management practices can shift and increase the risks that financial actors find themselves exposed to. For example, the widespread use of so-called portfolio insurance techniques right before the 1987 crash contributed towards amplifying the magnitude of the crash (MacKenzie, 2006). Such practices are the result of symbolic instruments elaborated in order to give form to financial uncertainty. We will therefore examine these instruments before moving on to consider how they have become embedded in the social context formed by financial professions.

Controlling risk in a stochastic framework

The methods for controlling financial risk that are taught as part of specialised finance curricula are based on a constituted body of knowledge, the foundations of which were laid in the 1950s and the synthesis of which was carried out at the turn of the 1960s and 1970s (MacKenzie, 2006; Walter, 2006). This synthesis integrated into the neoclassical theory of economic action first, the accounting practices carried out by financial analysts when assessing the fundamental value of businesses, and second, the stochastic calculation practised by statisticians. At the core of this synthesis, one finds the idea that random processes can represent the evolutions of stock market prices and that stochastic calculation therefore allows the assessment of the risks borne by investors.

The symbolic instruments introduced by the academic theory of finance transformed the way in which financial actors envisioned risk. These instruments have formed an interpretative framework in which risk is no longer considered to be an inherent feature of securities. From this point on, it is the correlation of price variations that investors take into account, as their investment theory has become a portfolio theory (Markowitz, 1959). A secure portfolio from herein is considered to be a well-balanced portfolio, in which the evolutions of an investment's return offset the return of other investments.

This paradigm is built upon assumptions pertaining to the choice of the phenomenon being represented: is the random process concerned with a price variation occurring between two units of calendar time or between a certain number of successive transactions? Following the stream of transactions means calculating at the pace of the exchange, while remaining in calendar time means remaining in contact with other social spheres that share at least the temporality of the clock with the exchange. Should the focus be on the price variation from one transaction to another or on the variation of the average price of a certain number of transactions? Should the focus be on the variation of a quote, or on the variation in the logarithm of the quote? Other assumptions include the choice of mathematical modelling tools. Should we choose Brownian processes based on the Laplace-Gauss distribution, or other Lévy processes that correspond to less specific cases but also less convenient ones in terms of calculation? These are not insignificant choices as they correspond to very different worlds. A Brownian model represents a symmetric world in which happy and unhappy events spin around the mean in equal proportions. Although the events closest to the mean occur the most frequently and surprise events are often encountered here, there are rarely any miraculous or catastrophic ones. To choose Lévy processes is to admit to the possibility of a world in which the course of events is generally monotone, even though it is interrupted by relatively frequent miracles or catastrophes, or the possibility of a world in which a countless number of petty irritations are counterbalanced by great joys. Such worlds lend themselves more or less well to calculation. In the Brownian case, it is mathematically legitimate to calculate an estimate of not only the expected value of a portfolio's return but also of the standard deviation of the return. In the second case, however, the result of the standard deviation calculation occasionally makes no sense from a mathematical point of view. Managing financial risks, once one has placed one's trust in a type of modelling, therefore means working with the calculations that are allowed in this frame.

The symbolic instruments of academic portfolio theory support investment practices that are compatible with a programme aimed at optimising the relationship between profitability and financial risks as they are modelled by this theory. Two emblematic practices are portfolio diversification and indexed portfolio management. (i) The traditional models of portfolio theory, which are based on a Brownian representation of the exchange, thus advocate for diversifying portfolios rather than concentrating them. Indeed, if stock market prices were represented as the outcome of Brownian stochastic processes, then the representation of risk is exhausted by the standard deviation of the distribution of returns and risk is minimised by maximal diversification. Investors are therefore invited to proceed to a large number of investments, with each one representing a very small fraction of the portfolio. Conversely, criticising the relevance of a Brownian representation of the stock market reality leads to contemplating the possibility of portfolios that are low risk, though also extremely concentrated (Brian and Walter, 2008). (ii) According to the capital asset pricing model (Sharpe, 1964), the optimal portfolio is not only diversified, but it also reproduces the proportions of the market portfolio, in other words it invests in each of the available securities on the market, in proportion to their stock market capitalisation. Market indexes reflect this proposition. Market indexes are fictional portfolios meant to offer an aggregate image of the value of all the securities traded on a market or of those securities that investors view as being the same class, or kind, of financial assets. Investors are therefore invited to allocate their capital, dividing it between the different asset classes, and fund managers are summoned, as part of this asset allocation, to measure their own performance against the index representing the asset class for which they are responsible. As such, indexes serve as a benchmark for analysts who evaluate the risk of the investments carried out by the asset fund managers, such as for example a deviation from the norm constituted by the indexes. The use of market indexes as comparison benchmarks is so widespread that regulatory standards require asset management firms to indicate which indexes they want their funds to be compared against. An index production industry has also surged, grouping together financial information firms, rating agencies and international banking groups. Together orthodox risk control theories, regulatory standards, and index providers institutionalise the indexed nature of contemporary asset management. (iii) The symbolic instruments made available to investors also induce a differentiation among financial organisations with regards to their risk monitoring practices and especially to the attention given to risk metrics. For those financial actors who consider their action in line with the Brownian paradigm, too much information kills information and it is advised to be careful that one does not enlist too many statistic indicators to estimate the incurred risks. Indeed, the extent of an unexpected loss remains limited and it has a strong chance of being compensated by a comparable profit; thus, it is considered useless to go overboard. For those who distance themselves from this paradigm, one can never be too cautious as a moment's inattention in the non-Brownian world can have fatal consequences from which it would be highly unlikely to recover, whereas a well-seized opportunity may indeed free you once and for all from want. The risks involved can therefore never be considered too carefully.

The social embeddedness of risk reduction practices

The procedures through which financial actors endeavour to tame the risks they are confronted with, owe just as much to the structuring of the social framework in which they act as they do to the nature of the phenomena they take as objects, because the methods for reducing financial risk are embedded within the society of which they are a product (Durkheim and Mauss, 1903).

For example, when investment professionals evaluate the quality of asset managers on the basis of their ability to make investments that procure high returns with modest variability for the portfolio being managed, their analysis is divided between what they call 'quantitative' and 'qualitative' analyses. From a risk control perspective, these two types of analysis maintain a functional relationship with each other (Larminat, 2013). The former provides a statistical assessment of past returns and it uses probability calculations to characterise the uncertainty burdening the profitability of investments carried out by asset managers. The latter analysis endeavours to identify the social interactions and practices that govern the production of the observed returns. Among other things, it focuses on the organisation of tasks, on procedural rules, and on the views on investing and the investment techniques which prevail among those asset managers evaluated. An analysis of the social conditions in which speculation is carried out allows analysts to judge whether those conditions that shaped past variations still exist and whether it is reasonable to use the statistical analysis of these variations as a basis for estimating the risks potentially associated to an investment decision. However, asset management actors distance themselves from this functional interpretation of the relationship between 'quantitative' and 'qualitative' analyses. They interpret these analyses as two bodies of heterogeneous though complementary knowledge. In their view, one provides access to facts of a quantitative nature which guarantees their indisputable reality, whereas the other springs from the personal, labile and not easily communicated intuition of practitioners, who are no doubt shrewd but whose emotions are likely to mislead them. The classification of these types of analysis according to their alleged nature is being reflected in the classification of job positions and of people who specialise in practising them. One axis of differentiation separates workers who pursue careers dedicated to one or the other of these analyses, where such careers match the symbolic capital brought by the workers: psychological sensitivity, computing and mathematical brilliance, up-to-date knowledge of the art of speculation, accredited by diplomas, by certifications or by a list of previously occupied positions. Following a secondary line of differentiation, 'quantitative' analysis tends to be entrusted to younger workers or those the furthest away from positions of power. Effectively, 'quantitative' analysis puts to use knowledge related to statistical methods taught as part of specialised financial curricula. On the other hand, the length of service and the responsibility for making end decisions impart an experience that is recognised as the source of intuition required for 'qualitative' analysis. Therefore, there clearly exists an affinity between the classification of activities and the division of labour, which solidifies an interpretation of the practices of analysing financial risk which is not as much adapted to uncertain phenomena as it is to the organisation of the society of those who are exposed to these phenomena. The interaction between collective representations, professional pathways and the division of work related to risk analysis, masks the connection between risk control practices in the asset management industry and the uncertain phenomenon to which they are applied. Risk control practices and risks are being decoupled by the social structure of the asset management industry. The overshadowing of this divide undermines the effectiveness of the control that laypersons can exercise over asset management professionals. The analysis of the uncertainty related to the returns provided by asset managers thus demonstrates that the techniques used to tame financial uncertainty are embedded in a social context which can either favour or damage their efficiency.

Conclusion

Considering the social nature of financial risks in all seriousness not only involves a close examination of the genesis of symbolic forms that agents use to consolidate their perception of these risks, but also necessitates a careful study of the integration of associated techniques within a social organisation that structures their use. An assessment of the control that financial agents wield over the risks they take or that they impose upon the society they belong to, must therefore also examine the social context in which their actions are carried out and, in particular, analyse the division of labour and the professional career pathways present in the financial field. It is a task that the social sciences of finance take on by combining the genealogy of financial representations (Brian, 2009; MacKenzie, 2006; Walter, 2013) with a study into the effects that the division of labour (Honegger et al., 2010) or the mechanisms of socialisation (Ho, 2009) have on diminishing the accountability of financial actors.

References

Abolafia, M. (1996). *Making markets. Opportunism and restraint on Wall Street*. Cambridge: Harvard University Press.

Brian, E. (2009). *Comment tremble la main invisible. Incertitude et marchés*. Paris: Springer.

Brian, E. and Walter, C. (2008). *Critique de la valeur fondamentale*. Paris: Springer.

Durkheim, E. and Mauss M. (1903). De quelques formes primitives de classification. Contribution à l'étude des représentations collectives. *L'Année sociologique*, 6, 1–72.

Ho, K. (2009). *Liquidated: An ethnography of Wall Street*. Durham: Duke University Press.

Honegger, C., Magnin, C. and Neckel, S. (Eds.) (2010). *Strukturierte Verantwortungslosigkeit. Berichte aus der Bankenwelt*. Berlin: Suhrkamp Verlag.

Knight, F. (1921). *Risk, uncertainty and profit*. Boston: Houghton Mifflin.

Lagneau-Ymonet, P. and Riva, A. (2012). *Histoire de la Bourse*. Paris: La Découverte.

Larminat (de), P. (2013). Entre 'quantitatif' et 'qualitatif': comment les investisseurs professionnels évaluent les gérants d'actifs financiers. *L'Année sociologique*, 63(1), 77–105.

MacKenzie, D. (2006). *An engine, not a camera. How financial models shape markets*. Cambridge: MIT Press.

Markowitz, H. (1959). *Portfolio selection: Efficient diversification of investment*. New York: John Wiley & Sons.

Muniesa, F. (2000). Un robot walrasien. Cotation électronique et justesse de la découverte des prix. *Politix*, 52, 121–154.

Sharpe, W. (1964). Capital asset prices: A theory of market equilibrium under conditions of risk. *Journal of Finance*, 19(3), 425–442.

Walter, C. (2006). Les martingales sur les marchés financiers. Une convention stochastique? *Revue de synthèse*, 127(2), 379–391.

Walter, C. (2013). *Le modèle de marche au hasard en finance*. Paris: Economica.

Weber, M. (1999) [1894]. *Die Börse*. In *Gesamtausgabe, Abteilung I: Schriften und Reden, Börsenwesen (1893–1898)*, Teilband 5/1. Tübingen, Mohr Siebeck.

3

THE POLITICAL AND MORAL IMAGINARIES OF FINANCIAL PRACTICES

Horacio Ortiz

Anthropology and sociology have shown that within economic transactions, the hierarchy between the objects being exchanged is often accompanied by a hierarchy between the participants exchanging. Social identities are thus in part determined by the rights and duties of the individuals involved in such transactions. The 'economic' meaning of a price, a contract or a negotiation often characterises a moral, political or religious meaning linked to whatever social act it constitutes. These analyses have been developed to account for situations in which local, national and global currencies meet (Guyer, 2004), in addition to accounting for the emotional component of monetary transactions (Zelizer, 2005) and for the formation of political and national identities through monetary policy (Hart, 1986). Standardised methods used within the global bureaucratic space that today constitutes the financial industry must also be analysed through the prism of the moral and political meanings they possess in their everyday application.

Professional financial practices are today extremely standardised. In most jurisdictions, financial regulation establishes the category of the 'qualified', 'sophisticated' or simply 'professional' investor, defined by its (the *investor's*) command of a shared corpus of financial methodology and thanks to its (*idem.*) material capacity to apply it.[1] Concretely, this regulation thereby describes the employees of the financial industry, whose social space is thus characterised as a meeting place for investors, which would give rise to markets in which efficiency should enable prices to reflect the true value of the objects traded, thus functioning as signals for the optimal allocation of credit for the whole of society. As several authors have shown, and as we will see in more detail below, financial methodology is the product of an intellectual, academic and industrial history that takes on categories of liberal philosophy located in neo-classical economic theory and the results of over a hundred years of research in statistics (cf. for example De Goede, 2005; MacKenzie, 2006). In these spaces, financial theory has obtained an aura of scientificity reinforced by the Nobel prizes awarded to its most well-known authors since the 1990s.

This methodology establishes a circular logic. According to this logic, when investors apply techniques modelled within financial theory they are able to attain the market efficiency presupposed by this same theory. In a manner highlighted by the Foucauldian reading of the neo-liberal project (Foucault, 2004), the political aim of the optimal allocation of monetary resources for the whole of society should result from the application of a series of techniques that would be neither political, nor moral. Policy would therefore be the result of practices, the purely technical nature of which should guarantee the truth that would result from them. This truth of prices would also represent the true hierarchy of the social value of those activities judged suitable to be financed, and therefore would be a foundation for the justice of this hierarchy (Ortiz, 2013a, 2014a). These discourses do not only concern financial regulation or formalisation in standard theory. They are also fundamental in determining the procedures used by employees in the financial industry to distribute credit on an everyday basis, with regards to both the actual details of these transactions and the ways in which such transactions make sense for those who carry them out.[2]

Political and moral imaginaries of financial methodologies

The concepts of efficient markets and the independent, maximising investor are fundamental to the definition of valuation and investment methods modelled in standard financial theory.[3] All calculation formulas, for example the definition of the weighted average cost of capital, or formulas defining the value of listed shares, bonds, non-listed companies, futures, options and swaps, and even formulas established to determine an optimal investment portfolio in accordance with Modern Portfolio Theory, are in fact formulated from the perspective of the figure of the investor. Moreover, most of the variables used in these calculations come from financial asset prices, and are either a price established at a given moment or through the statistical processing of a price series. These prices are considered to be in some way representative, notably with regard to the value of the objects they are meant to refer to, which stems from the notion that the markets that produce them are efficient. Otherwise, it would not make sense to take them into account.

At the same time, numerous calculation formulas and methods of valuation and investment are punctured by a type of tension, or at times a contradiction, which is also formalised in standard financial theory. According to this theory, market efficiency is dependent on the independent valuations of investors who seek out the 'true value' of the objects traded, and whose interactions lead to this truth being reflected into a price. Yet, if markets are efficient, then prices reflect all the available information and investors can only yield to their 'truth', unable to 'beat' them by finding a truer value. Thus, according to this theory, for efficiency to be possible, there needs to be investors who consider markets to be inefficient; however, the moment efficiency is attained, the valuations of these investors become ineffective. Besides, if no one believed markets were efficient, then no one would use prices as signals, and the allocation of monetary resources would no longer be optimal.

This tension, it is supposed, will be resolved over time: first, investors believe markets are not efficient, but that they will eventually approach efficiency, getting closer to the individual valuation with which investors attempt to beat them; then, once the markets become efficient, investors must follow the price as a signal. This tension however develops into an outright contradiction when these various moments are simultaneously presupposed in formulas and reasoning. Thus, in order to evaluate share prices by discounting future cash flows, it is necessary to calculate the discount rate, which depends on the respective weights of debt and shares in the expected profit rate. Most manuals will therefore recommend calculating these weights using share and bonds prices, i.e. using the market price, considered to be representative, in order to find another price, considered truer than the market one. In the same way, the most widespread investment method consists of seeking to obtain an investment performance slightly superior to that of an asset index, which is replicated by over- or under-weighting certain assets. Yet, the replication of an index is a method established through 'Modern Portfolio Theory' and its mathematical formalisation of the notion that, when markets are efficient, it is useless to turn-over a portfolio, investment should instead consist simply of buying up the entire market, to diversify the risks, and then maintaining hold of it; a method appropriately labelled '*buy and hold*'. In this case, however, you cannot 'beat' the market using individual valuations like those the over- or under-weightings are supposedly based on. These weightings only make sense if the markets are inefficient, in which case there is no justification for replicating an index. In these cases, like in many others, the formulas and reasoning are thus established using the figure of the maximising investor, who would presume that the markets in which he operates are at the same time efficient and inefficient.

In most formulas, the notion of 'risk' indicates 'volatility', i.e. the standard deviation of revenues established from statistical series. This implies that the prices, considered representative of the value in accordance with the notion of efficiency, are also considered likely to correspond to statistical laws; a presupposition established at the end of the nineteenth century and on which contemporary financial theory is based. Furthermore, valuation and investment are generally based on the idea of a so-called 'risk-free' rate, which is usually established on the basis of the rates paid by states assumed to be insusceptible to defaulting. By eliminating 'risk', this rate would therefore be absolute, falling outside of the universe of that which is probable. This rate has several roles. On one hand, it establishes the standard of value for all other assets. Indeed, all financial assets considered to have higher 'risk' and paying a lower profit will systematically be excluded from investment. Thus, only financial assets paying a rate superior to the 'risk-free' rate are worthy of the gaze of the figure of the investor. Thereby, this rate constitutes the independence of the figure of the investor since, in principle, the investor can always back out of his investment and find 'refuge' in 'risk-free' assets. So-called *flight to quality* movements are supposedly based on this reasoning. The notion of the 'risk-free' rate is a variation on the notion of 'risk', which is itself often vague and can range from elements produced using mathematical concepts or intuitive feelings about the danger of defaulting payments, missed income opportunities or other more or less significant losses (Pradier, 2006).

In all their diversity, formulas and reasoning thus return to the figure of the investor as a departure point for financial activity, granting him a position of power in relation to the rest of the economic, social and political activity. Thus, all the variables within an investment object are considered to be sources of either expense or profit for this figure, whether they be the salaries of employees working for a company listed on the stock market or the expenditures and receipts of a state that issues debt. As part of the liberal economic logic of these concepts, only the efficiency of the markets is meant to impose 'discipline', the discipline of the truth represented in the price, which must therefore serve as a signal for the allocation of social resources. The state plays an ambiguous role as, contrary to liberal theory, it is expected to guarantee a minimum of revenue to owners of loaned capital, as the notion of 'risk-free' implies a state that is powerful enough to extract taxes in order to honour its debts and one that considers its creditors as taking priority over the rest of society. Thus, we can see that financial methods and reasoning, conceived of as technical tools that were meant to be both morally and politically neutral, nevertheless do mobilise – when deciding upon the variables and the use of calculation results – the political and moral imaginaries of liberal philosophies, out of which contemporary financial theory was created.

The practising of these techniques thus presupposes social truth in value and justice in distribution via market efficiency. It is therefore necessary to understand to what extent logics such as these make sense in the everyday lives of those who apply them, in order to understand the financial industry's capacity to be considered legitimate beyond the professional spaces that compose it. Research based on participant observation allows us to view the complexity of this practice, along with the distance between it and the descriptive and normative formalisation of finance in financial theory itself.

Legitimacy and meaning in professional financial practice

Although the figure of the investor is omnipresent in the procedures and reasoning of standard financial methodology, it is not on the other hand embodied as a subject of exchange, as liberal utopia conceives it. What differentiates 'qualified' investors from others is also what establishes the financial industry as the site wherein the application of financial methodology is supposed to enable market efficiency and therefore the optimal allocation of monetary resources. However, within this social space, the people making the calculations and giving orders to buy or sell assets are only investors because they represent the interests of clients who have assigned their money over to them, for example individuals who have signed up to a pension plan or purchasers of mutual fund shares. These actual rightful money holders, in turn, are only investors in that they delegate their money to experts authorised by regulation to handle it. As such, the investor responsible for most of the trade and volumes distributed throughout the world is not one specific person, but rather a figure formed from a representation of interests that are defined by the financial methodology formalised in standard financial theory. The markets that these investors are meant to establish are thus not arenas open to all individuals, but quite the contrary are commercial networks formed by financial industry employees, who must follow standardised methods and reasoning not applied for the purpose of acting with their own money, but with someone else's money in order to be remunerated, and as part of their career trajectory (Ortiz, 2011).

The figure of the investor as implemented in everyday procedures is often found to be contradictory within a single calculation or reasoning, as we have seen with indexed investments or the valuation of shares. Furthermore, several figures of the investor can be called upon by one same person, or by different people and professions within the same company. The so-called fundamental valuation model considers that the price of assets must reflect the discounted value of the future profits they will procure for their holder. On the other hand, the relative valuation model considers the price of each asset in relation to that of other assets, like for example in indexed investing employing the effect of weighting. Speculative valuation understands prices as reflecting the constantly changing opinions of those participating in the trade. Consistent with their divergent logics, these approaches to and definitions of value and investment are indeed opposed to one another. Nevertheless, in calculations and reasoning, they are usually used together and are interdependent. Their tensions and contradictions are used by professionals to position themselves amidst their competitive and complementary relations. Traders will often be associated with speculation and financial analysts with fundamental valuation, which presumes market efficiency over the long term, and on which indexed investing is also supposedly based. The multiplicity of approaches, in themselves partly contradictory, constitutes as a result the range of technical references – with their own tensions, fragmentations and oppositions – which employees use to make sense of their position and their trajectory in their professional space (Ortiz, 2013b).

Despite this contradictory multiplicity, each and every procedure is understood as resulting from the activity of the investor, whose maximising gaze and intent constitute the starting point for calculations and reasoning. Moreover, they are positioned in one way or another in relation to the notion of efficient markets, thought of as realised within the financial industry. The 'investor' and 'efficient markets' concepts therefore constitute the way in which the notion of 'crisis' is itself conceived in this space, and the way in which regulation takes on financial theory. Within this framework, as the disparate events described by the term 'crisis' over the last thirty years remind us, an 'erroneous' valuation by 'investors' would be what enables a 'bubble' (over-evaluation) or a 'crash' (under-evaluation), followed by 'corrections' demonstrating evidence of a trial-and-error movement, at times excessive, but – in free and perfect markets – which would inevitably return to an equilibrium in which prices reflect all the available information on traded assets. What is left out in this conception of the crisis, is the relation of power established by the hierarchical distribution of credit. Thus, although trillions of US dollars were created to contribute towards bailing out the 'subprime crisis', entire spans of the world's population remained cut off from the flows managed by the financial industry. These flows were consequently never invested into education, health or other public services. The "end" of the subprime crisis would therefore signal that the drastic nature of these inequalities and hierarchies represents the optimal allocation of monetary resources, in other words the morally and politically desirable result of market efficiency (Ortiz, 2012 and 2014b).

In the routine application of standardised procedures, each employee's validation of these practices comes from their tacit acceptance of their colleagues and the hierarchy, experienced as part of the obvious nature of everyday life and career progression, which is partially marked by remuneration. In this context, employees use the expression 'to create value' to indicate their participation in generating profits for their company's clients and their company, and therefore also for themselves in the form of wages, bonuses and career advances. However, this expression also communicates with liberal political and moral philosophies, according to which the creation of value (or of 'wealth' as Adam Smith has stated) comes from the optimal allocation of resources for the entire society, which the organisation of trade via so-called free markets should enable.

When moments arise that call for justifications, for example during professional conflicts between people, teams, companies, or even during what is labelled a 'crisis', employees consequently mobilise the following diverse references. They may on one hand justify their actions by arguing that the application of procedures was done in accordance with norms, which would clear them of any wrongdoing regarding the results of their actions. Or they may justify their position by referring to their participation in market efficiency, for example because speculation would eliminate inefficiency, or on the contrary, because a long-term investment would avoid the volatility caused by speculation.

Depending on the individuals and their professions, these discourses will be evoked in different ways, mobilising moral and political references in a tactical and often fragmented or contradictory manner, in order to resolve specific situations connected to professional trajectories. Emotional attachments to work and justifications for actions can vary from person to person, ranging from adhesion to rejection, with various modes of indifference or ambivalence. But in all cases, the references that can be mobilised to give a legitimising account of the work carried out and its social consequences, will be limited to bureaucratic procedural logic and to liberal discourses about the benefits of a distribution of monetary resources that would result from the activity of investors in efficient markets and from their use of the methods formalised in standard financial theory (Ortiz, 2014a and 2014b).

Conclusion: everyday practices in a global space

Participant observation research enables the contradictions, ambiguities and the often-fragmented nature of reasoning and justifications of everyday practices to be brought to light. This method also helps show that within the professional space of the financial industry practices can have multiple meanings, which are nevertheless limited to a certain number of references, to those financial imaginaries that are also political and moral imaginaries. However, if this type of study remains confined to the physical space that it helps to understand, it risks remaining silent about the wider social space, within which certain logics are at work in observed practices (Montagne and Ortiz, 2013). The formalisation of methods in standardised financial theory, must not lead us to forget that these methods have been and continue to be primarily produced to some degree in professional settings, through the circulation of concepts and people between vast social spaces such as academic, professional, regulatory, journalistic, political and associative spaces (Whitley, 1986). The meaning and the legitimacy of professional practices in the financial industry do not function in isolation, but rather operate within this circulation, which must be understood in terms of its history and the global space it contributes towards producing (Hart and Ortiz, 2014).

The standardisation of practices, as the conflicts and constant official controversies in these spaces remind us, also means providing a certain amount of leeway through which new methods and justifications can be produced. Nevertheless, currently, the limits of the official financial imagination are located in the procedural logic and liberal-inspired reasoning formalised in the financial theory taken on by regulation. This takes place in a professional space that today expands across the entire world, and which is accompanied by financial regulation that is fragmented by the legal borders of states, but that often mobilises the same logic, and even the same words. The global expansion of professional financial practices, with their financial, political and moral imaginaries, occurs together with more or less organised or developed contestations. The participation of state-owned Chinese financial institutions, or of sovereign investment funds, which have gained increasing importance over the last few years, mobilises justifications that do not fully correspond with the imaginaries described here. These imaginaries have been developed and instituted throughout a recent history, notably owing to changes in legislation, in macro-economic regulation, and in university settings since the end of the Second World War. They continue to be transformed, carried along by changes in global power relations.

Notes

1 This category also describes, in a marginal way, people who possess a significant amount of property.
2 The analyses that follow are based on several studies conducted via participatory observations in the financial industry, which lasted several months. They involved brokers in New York in 2002, investment fund managers in Paris in 2003 and 2004, merger and acquisitions consultants in Shanghai since 2014, and in financial education settings within business schools in Paris and Shanghai between 2008 and 2014. In all these cases I participated in a professional capacity, first as an assistant of financial analysts and, in following, as a teacher and a consultant. This research included more than a hundred interviews, as well as questionnaires (used in the teaching settings) and document analysis. Conjointly, numerous conclusions proposed in this chapter are based on results produced by other researchers, who cannot all be cited due to space limitations in the text.

3 I use the notion of 'imaginary' to designate the meaning that actors give to practice. This notion allows us to emphasise the changing and labile character of meaning, as well as the fact that it is not a matter of the representations of a reality that would be exterior to them, but rather of a constitutive element of the practice itself.

References

De Goede, M. (2005). *Virtue, fortune and faith: A genealogy of finance.* Minneapolis: University of Minnesota Press.

Foucault, M. (2004). *Naissance de la biopolitique. Cours au Collège de France, 1978–1979.* Paris: Gallimard and Seuil.

Guyer, J. I. (2004). *Marginal gains. Monetary transactions in Atlantic Africa.* Chicago: University Press, Chicago.

Hart, K. (1986). Heads or tails? The two sides of the coin. *Man,* 21, 637–656.

Hart, K. and Ortiz, H. (2014). The anthropology of money and finance: Between ethnography and world history. *Annual Review of Anthropology,* 43, 465–482.

MacKenzie, D. (2006). *An engine, not a camera. How financial models shape markets.* Cambridge: MIT Press.

Montagne, S. and Ortiz, H. (2013). Sociologie de l'agence financière: enjeux et perspectives. Introduction. *Sociétés contemporaines,* 92, 7–33.

Ortiz, H. (2011). Marchés efficients, investisseurs libres et Etats garants: trames du politique dans les pratiques financières professionnelles. *Politix,* 95, 155–180.

Ortiz, H. (2012). Anthropology – of the financial crisis. In J. Carrier (Ed.), *Handbook of economic anthropology* (pp. 585–596). Cheltenham: Edward Elgar Publishing.

Ortiz, H. (2013a). La "valeur" dans l'industrie financière : le prix des actions cotées comme "vérité" technique et politique. *L'Année sociologique,* 63(1), 107–136.

Ortiz, H. (2013b). Investir : une décision disséminée. Enquête de terrain sur les dérivés de credit. *Sociétés contemporaines,* 92, 35–57.

Ortiz, H. (2014a). *Valeur financière et vérité: enquête d'anthropologie politique sur l'évaluation des entreprises cotées en bourse.* Paris: Presses de Sciences Po.

Ortiz, H. (2014b). The limits of financial imagination: Free investors, efficient markets and crisis. *American Anthropologist,* 116(1), 38–50.

Pradier, P.-C. (2006). *La notion de risque en économie.* Paris: La Découverte.

Whitley, R. (1986). The transformation of business finance into financial economics: The roles of academic expansion and changes in U.S. capital markets. *Accounting, Organization and Society,* 11(2), 171–192.

Zelizer, V. (2005). *The purchase of intimacy.* Princeton: Princeton University Press.

4

THE ROLE OF FINANCIAL ANALYSTS IN THE SOCIAL CONSTRUCTION OF FINANCIAL VALUE

Isabelle Chambost

'The financial markets believe that....' Such an assertion as this signifies a concept reified by the financial markets, implicitly conveying an image of homogeneity, which for some is the result of the natural convergence of expectations, while for others it arises from social construct. Effectively understanding this intangible cognitive structure helps to reveal what has for a long time been obscured: in short, the importance of structures of financial intermediation for complex functioning (Adler and Adler, 1984). Within their ranks, financial analysts have at their disposal a remarkable visibility, offering coherency to the intensity of stock market upheavals. Being the privileged interlocutors of company management teams, they have at their availability numerous information sources who entrust a particular interest in their work on the valuation of companies on behalf of portfolio managers and, more broadly, the entire economic and financial community.

Analysts also represent a particular cog in the declension of concepts and precepts of neoclassical financial economics and finance, in terms of the informational efficiency of financial markets, transparency and shareholder governance. A direct link is thus established between the price of a stock on the financial markets and a so-called fundamental value, the purpose of which is to synthesise information originating from the real economy. This fundamental value remains forever unknown, with the current price on the stock market being its best possible estimation, when taking into account the information available to all investors. If we associate the general equilibrium theory with agency theory and the theory of property rights, the question of information becomes essential, both as a guarantee of the socio-economic efficiency of financial markets and as a means for company managers to orchestrate control.

The way in which financial analysts formulate judgements represents, for researchers in financial economics and finance, one of the many fields in which decision-making under 'uncertainty' is implemented, with this method being understood in a purely intrapsychic way, as an example of the application of Bayesian theories.[1] As referents for the neoclassical approach to financial markets, analysts thus also give form to the interests of accounting researchers, who wish to prove the contribution of this approach to orthodox financial theories. Although researchers in behavioural finance introduce the question of social interactions, these interactions are analysed as factors of bias, errors or even faults, emphasising the phenomena of mimetic behaviours or conflicts of interest. Only the field of conventions economics has incorporated interactions as constitutive of the development of a fundamental value, which did not exist before the exchange but rather resulted from it (Orléan, 2005). This particular analysis does not however truly integrate the issue of institutions.

By enlisting the contributions of institutional sociology, economic sociology and professional sociology, this chapter therefore proposes to analyse the social measures – relational structuring, symbolic and cognitive systems – implemented within financial intermediation that seek to institute the financial analyst as a professional guarantor for the informational efficiency of markets, and to control the development of his/her judgements.

Some empirical precisions

This research is based on 41 semi-structured interviews conducted with financial analysts working within brokerage firms (*sell-side*) or asset management firms (*buy-side*). These interviews took place over three periods – from September 2004 to March 2005, from July 2006 to January 2007 and in September 2007. These periods corresponded with different phases of theoretical sampling and encoding. Around ten interviews were conducted with asset managers, brokerage firm salespeople and investor relations managers. These interviews occurred during a period that included the end of the 2001 stock market crisis and covered the bull cycle, which preceded the 2007 crisis.

Instituted financial analysts as guarantors for the informational efficiency of markets

Through studying the construction of the French stock market and, in following, that of the European monetary unification, light may be cast on the foundations of the gradual professionalisation of financial analysts.

Professionalisation enlisted in the composition of the European monetary zone

While financial analyses have been practised in France since the nineteenth century by '*ingénieurs conseil*' (consulting engineers), economists or accountants, the profession of the financial analyst is much more recent. Until the end of the 1980s, analysts were essentially employed in banks, where the organisational divide between various analytical activities – credit or securities analysis versus primary or secondary market analysis – only rarely came into effect. During this period, the profession was widely considered to be of secondary importance (Kirchhof-Masseron, 2007). Among stockbrokers, very few analysts were therefore present.

The demise of the monopoly of stockbrokers (*agents de change*), their transformation into brokerage firms and the founding of asset management firms as autonomous corporate entities – a development initiated at the end of the 1980s and, with the prospect of the Euro zone, made mandatory by the European Directive of 10 May 1993 related to investment firms – have led to the current structuring (Kleiner, 2003). For financial management firms, the pre-eminence of the financial market and the fact – to use the term employed by *financiers* – 'that the market is always right', translated into the spread of *benchmarking* principles, a form of financial management based on referring to a stock market index, meant to represent a miniature image of the market. A division of work was introduced into asset management firms, and was isomorphically mirrored (DiMaggio and Powell, 1983) in brokerage firms, separating economists (analysing the evolutions of macro-economic parameters), strategists (defining the relative weight to be accorded to each sector), analysts (put in charge of rankings related to the stocks of a given sector) and sellers (responsible for contacting clients). This division of work is a declension of the theoretical division advocated by Modern Portfolio Theory, developed by Markowitz (1959) and further enriched by Sharpe (1964), which is founded on three phases: a) determining the profitability of a security, b) the analysis of asset combinations enabling 'efficient' portfolios to be discovered that optimally combine risk and return, and c) the choice of portfolio best suited to the client.

New systems for structuring relations were being carried out. Within brokerage firms, *sell-side* analysts had to thus coordinate with sellers and link together their own 'fundamental' view and 'the market vision'. They also became the primary contacts of *buy-side* analysts, who validate the financial coherence of their reasoning and use it to carry out a customised synthesis for the asset managers.

The analyst profession progressively moved towards obtaining legal recognition. The SFAF – *Société française des analystes financiers* (French Society for Financial Analysts) – was at the origin of ethical referents recorded in their code of ethics in 1992, and updated in 2002. The recent updates of the regulatory texts have strongly reinforced the ethical obligations in order to confront the likelihood of the legitimacy of financial analysts being challenged. These rulings were adopted as part of the rules and regulations of the 2002 *Conseil des Marchés Financiers* (Financial Markets Council), for the Code of Conduct of the French Association of Investment Firms and the French Banking Federation (AFEI-FBF), as well as within the rules and regulations of the Financial Markets Authority (*Autorité des Marchés Financiers*), which as of 2005, clearly outlined the conditions for exercising this profession.

Expertise built on orthodox financial theories

This professionalisation took root in a legitimacy founded, principally, upon the expertise handed down to financial analysts by economic and social authorities, in view of the role assigned to them as guarantors, responsible for the quality of information on the stock markets. This expertise is dispersed through the linking of academic and abstract knowledge, issued from financial theory, with practical *and professional* knowledge (Abbott, 1988). By 'overseeing' an important *corpus* of information and transforming it into recommendations, the analyst proceeds to transform an 'intellectual capital' into an 'economic capital'. He 'spans the boundary' and, more broadly, gives credibility to the relationship established 'between those who need capital and those who hold it', by 'absorbing uncertainty' (Fogarty and Rogers, 2005, pp. 338–341).

This expertise provides analysts with a highly symbolic basis and allows them to distinguish themselves from other professions, such as that of the financial journalist. However, the main breakaway would be the one introduced between 'fundamental' financial analysis and 'chartist' financial analysis. From a theoretical point of view, the former wholly denies the legitimacy of the latter, believing that the random walk of stock prices hypothesis dooms to failure any attempt to make predictions on the basis of past prices. From an operational perspective, this break is based on the nature of information intended to be utilised, with the former considering this information to be 'exogenous to the market' while for the latter it is 'endogenous to the market'. In addition, it is based on the distinction of temporal horizons of reference, considered over the long term by the fundamental analysis (more precisely from a few days to a few months) and over the short term by the chartist analysis (again more precisely from a few hours to a few days).

However, while financial theory is supposed to lay the foundations for the fundamental research carried out by the analyst, it does not for that matter bring with it any solutions for operational implementation.

As Abbott has analysed it (1988, p. 40), the core of professional practices is based on three activities – the diagnosis, the inference and the treatment – and most particularly the inference phase. The 'diagnostic' phase carried out by the analyst is often presented as the phase during which the collection and analysis of information occurs. It consists of transforming the problem presented into a problem that can be analysed in line with the knowledge system developed by the profession, in this case, financial theory. The 'treatment' phase can be summed up, for the financial analyst, as the act of formulating predictions and of setting out a recommendation to buy or sell. The core of the expertise is therefore located in the phase of inference, where the company being evaluated is categorised and modelled. Through the connection of formal knowledge and practical efficiency, abstract knowledge and concrete procedures, legitimate rankings and professional actions, this intermediary phase 'has qualities that make a professional work more or less accessible to competitors' (Abbott, 1988, p. 49).

In the following developments, we have subsequently focused on analysing those social and economic devices implemented in order to build, for the financial analysts, a former valuation interval to facilitate adjustment of their own valuation to the evolution of stock market prices.

The construction of value, institutionally circumscribed

The relational structuring of the financial analyst presented above is combined with the installation of symbolic reference systems. By providing analysts with structures for comparing and interpreting in order to choose and analyse retained information, these systems equally enable the immediate and public comparison of analysts' work with that of other analysts.

Analysts – guardians of financial valuation

Various financial measures guide the analyst's work by building likenesses, through gathering, polarising and thus excluding, and then comparing (Douglas, 1986). Throughout the analyst's work, these measures allow for equivalences to be constructed, which assure a common measure and the construction of 'commensurability' (Espeland and Stevens, 1998). They therefore intervene in particular when deciding whether to cover – or not – a given firm, during the firm's categorisation process, by structuring how the firm will be analysed and the valuation carried out, by integrating only information likely to have 'a financial translation' and by knowing if information has already been taken into account by the market.

The stock market indexes serve as a reference when choosing to cover this or that firm, a choice which is based on commercial concerns and more 'cognitive' ones. The commercial concerns are centred around the capitalisation of listed companies, which represents their importance on the market, and on the liquidity of their securities, representing the ease with which they can be resold. The cognitive concerns are wrapped up in sectorial belonging, on the basis of which analysts develop the analytical grids they implement, which in major brokerage firms leads to analysts becoming specialised according to sectors.

The construction of share indexes leads to giving prominence to those companies that belong to various indexes and relegating those that do not belong at all (Douglas, 1986). This exclusion potentially results from an overly weak market capitalisation and/or from difficulties arising in order to fit into a given sector, due to activities that are too diversified or too different. The challenge, for those companies wishing to be covered by analysts, consists of establishing a 'process of isomorphism', which leads to them becoming recognised within a category and, at the same time as trying, within that same category, to stand out from others. Moreover, this categorisation based on sectorial belonging enables financial analysts to carry out a relatively basic modelling. It allows them to centre their analysis on one or two key performance indicators, with these considered to be representative of the sector in question (for example, the actual evolution of company returns with regard to what was expected), in addition to focusing their analysis on warning indicators (or *drivers*), thought to enable the identification and anticipation of those events that will have a direct financial impact on the company.

Faced with the plethora of information, financial analysts have to choose the good one, and base their decisions on two main distinctions founded on market criteria: is the information 'potentially integrated' or 'already integrated or not' – by the market. For example, analysing how socially responsible information has been taken into account thus highlights the way in which a process of selection is carried out, based on the existence of a potential 'financial translation'. Consequently, the information integrated by the market is that for which – thanks to a socially constructed process – there is a clear link generally acknowledged, between this information and the evolution of a performance indicator (Chambost and Benchemam, 2010). The way the change of accounting standards (from French GAAPS to IFRS) has been taken into account by analysts, alongside the shift to international accounting standards intended for investors, equally highlights this necessity for the construction of referents. Indeed, the switch to IFRS was not viewed by French financial analysts as being the opportunity for improving the information communicated. Their concerns were instead focused on when listed companies were going to explain these 'new rules of the game' (Biondi and Chambost, 2009).

As 'guardians' of the financial markets' social and cognitive structures, the question could thus be raised as to whether the analysts contribute towards maintaining the 'system' (Zuckerman, 1999) and/or, in a more proactive sense, building it (Beunza and Garud, 2007). The following analysis of the role granted to the consensus of financial analysts will enable us to assess the centralised strength of this measure and the structuring of the power struggles at the core of this profession.

Guardians under surveillance

Much like stock market prices, the opinion of diverse financial analysts concerning a given stock is publicly and almost immediately broadcast under the label of the 'analysts' consensus'. This measure is constructed by financial information firms from information floated upstream by brokerage companies, who then have access to the 'consensus' in return. According to Euronext, the consensus helps by giving a 'common sense or feeling with regard to an expectation' and by 'not relying on the opinion of one individual analyst'. It does indeed prove to be an extraordinary tool for the homogenisation and convergence of practices. Through the representation developed, this device directs attention towards recommendations and specific data figures. By rendering this data commensurable, it structures practices, thus equally rendering the analysts commensurable.

As an information and expectation tool for the 'market', this consensus provides benchmarks. Depending on the degree of information held by the analyst, any future use of the consensus may vary, from research of a global reference to the reconstitution of assumptions used by one's colleagues. It appears however that while the contribution of this consensus may be stipulated as a source of information, it is above all the question concerning the interpretation of this information by other analysts that emerges, along with an anticipation of their behaviours. The consensus is equally proven to be a reference point in the sense that the analyst must know how to position himself in relation to the consensus. Both the salesperson from the brokerage firm and the director of the management corporation will ask the analyst to position his predictions and recommendations in comparison to how his colleagues have positioned themselves and to identify the underlying explanations for any potential differences.

However, the true disciplinary dimension of the consensus becomes apparent through the actions triggered in the behaviour of the analyst. The analyst's normative character is reflected in the fact that being part of the consensus can have a reassuring effect, while falling outside of it must be shouldered by the analyst. The existence of the consensus generates tendencies related to behavioural strategy, which can be expressed in static terms as knowing how to adapt oneself to the consensus or knowing how to make oneself stand out without for that matter becoming isolated from the rest of the group (Galanti, 2006). Given the public nature of this device, everyone can see if an analyst made a mistake alone or not. If the analyst, who was outside the consensus, makes an erroneous anticipation, he is solely responsible for his errors. If he was in the consensus, he is just wrong like the others. However, the true challenge is pronounced in a more dynamic sense as the ability to be 'ahead of' the consensus. As such, it is a matter of acquiring visibility and a higher degree of conviction; it is not enough to have anticipated events but rather more importantly, to have been followed by investors.

Indeed, if the consensus presents un-weighted predictions from various analysts, some of them will have bigger economic and social weight than others. A hierarchy is thus produced in accordance with the size of the brokerage firm to which the analyst belongs, the relations the analyst has succeeded in forging with the management of various listed societies and the importance of clients in terms of the portfolios being managed. These clients, by carrying out the recommended purchasing operations, are as such likely to bear out these recommendations. Behind the public exposition of the financial analyst, practices are established related to encounters that occur during private presentations (*road shows*) between portfolio managers and listed companies (Chambost, 2017). These companies delegate the organisation of this type of event to a financial analyst of their choosing. This analyst, now logistician, will thus be able to absorb the conveyed experiences and test his own hypothesis from behind the scenes.

Conclusion

Judgements made by financial analysts take place at the very centre of the market, in direct contact with other actors. Far from the mathematical modelling advocated by financial theory, the process enacted for this evaluation, with its strong social character, equally challenges the dichotomy traditionally borne out by economic theory, which opposes information that is endogenous to the market against information that would be considered exogenous in nature. In doing so, it highlights the socially constructed nature of their interpretation.

Note

1 Normative model according to which, when faced with new information, individuals form and revise their conditional probabilities, thus implementing a learning mechanism.

References

Abbott, A. (1988). *The system of professions. An essay on the division of expert labor.* Chicago: University of Chicago Press.

Adler, P. A. and Adler, P. (Eds.) (1984). *The social dynamics of financial markets.* Greenwich: JAI Press.

Beunza, D and Garud, R. (2007). Calculators, lemmings, or frame-makers? The intermediary role of securities analysts. *Sociological Review*, 55(2), 13–39.

Biondi, Y. and Chambost, I. (2009). Gouvernance, transparence et encastrement cognitif des marchés financiers: le cas des analystes financiers. *Revue française de gouvernance d'entreprise*, 5, 105–135.

Chambost, I. (2017). Analyser les dispositifs d'évaluation des analystes financiers: une clé d'entrée dans les coulisses des marchés financiers. In O. Cléach and G. Tiffon (Eds.), *Invisibilisation au travail: des salariés en mal de reconnaissance* (pp. 141–154). Paris: Octarès.

Chambost, I. and Benchemam, F. (2010). Quand l'analyse ISR devient financière: une analyse des dispositifs cognitifs et organisationnels de legitimation. *Économies & sociétés*, 44(11), 1799–1825.

DiMaggio, P. J. and Powell, W. (1983). The iron cage revisited: Institutional isomorphism and collective rationality in organizational fields. *American Sociological Review*, 48(2), 147–160.

Douglas, M. (1986). *How institutions think.* London: Routledge & Kegan Paul.

Espeland, W. and Stevens, M. (1998). Commensuration as a social process. *Annual Review of Sociology*, 24, 313–343.

Fogarty, T. J. and Rogers, R. K. (2005). Financial analysts' reports: An extended institutional theory evaluation. *Accounting, Organizations and Society*, 30(4), 331–356.

Galanti, S. (2006). Which side are you on? How institutional position affect financial analysts' incentives. *Journal of Economic Issues*, 40(2), 387–394.

Kirchhof-Masseron, M. G. (2007). Le métier d'analyste financier dans les banques, 1960–1980. Actes du colloque *Le salariat bancaire: enjeux sociaux et pratiques de gestion*, IDHE, Université Paris X – Nanterre, 2 February.

Kleiner, T. (2003). La consécration des gestionnaires d'actifs sur la place de Paris. *Actes de la recherche en sciences sociales*, 146–147, 42–50.

Markowitz, H. (1959). *Portfolio selection: Efficient diversification of investment.* New York: John Wiley & Sons.

Orléan, A. (2005). Réflexions sur l'hypothèse d'objectivité de la valeur fondamentale. In D. Bourghelle, O. Brandouy, R. Gillet and A. Orléan (Eds.), *Croyances, représentations collectives et finance* (pp. 21–39). Paris: Economica.

Sharpe W. (1964). Capital asset prices: A theory of market equilibrium under conditions of risks. *Journal of Finance*, 19(3), 425–442.

Zuckerman, E. (1999). The categorical imperative: Securities analysts and the illegitimacy discount. *American Journal of Sociology*, 104(5), 1398–1438.

5

PUBLIC–PRIVATE PARTNERSHIPS (PPP) BETWEEN FINANCING REQUIREMENTS AND MICRO-ECONOMIC GOVERNANCE

Complementary scientific and real-world justifications

Géry Deffontaines

During the first decade of the twenty-first century, the debate about the public procurement of large-scale facilities, buildings and infrastructure providing public services was undeniably dominated in France by the introduction of public–private partnerships. Several milestones left a mark on those years:

- The first legislations passed in 2002–2003, using existing legal tools to increase and speed up a major procurement plan of buildings and facilities connected to the justice department, interior security, defence, and the hospital sector;
- The enactment in 2004 of the order creating the *Contrats de Partenariat* (Partnership Contracts), for a widespread and legally secure use of the PPP procurement route for all government and local bodies and all sectors;
- The setup of the *Mission d'Appui aux Partenariats Public-Privé* [MAPPP], a dedicated task-force and monitoring authority within the Treasury, in 2005;
- The intense promotional campaign advocating PPPs (2004–2008);
- The modifications made to the legislation, targeted at lessening the legal risks and the psychological barriers for potential users, all reasons that had pent up 'market' take-off (2008);
- The opportunistic use of PPPs in the context of the 2009–2010 stimulus package – and finally the introduction of state-level guarantees to support private pre-financing, in order to counter the effects of the financial crisis. Such measures ended up making France, by 2011, the number one market in the EU for the private financing of public assets.

The 'PPP momentum' now seems as if it were behind us. Very few projects are initiated and 'closed' with regard to the bullish period between 2008–2010. However, from an economic sociology perspective concerned with examining financial activities, and more precisely analysing how new markets are shaped for the financial sector, it is still interesting to revisit the arguments that, for more than ten years, made the case for a public policy aimed at the creation of a PPP market, thus legitimising the private financing of buildings, facilities and public infrastructure.

The mere idea of a public–private partnership (PPP) 'market' may seem *a priori* contradictory to encapsulate a very segmented reality:

- Heterogeneous public procuring authorities, with various conditions for resorting to PPPs;
- Very diverse underlying technical infrastructure (hospitals, high-speed train lines, schools and university buildings, swimming pools, stadiums, local broadband networks, prisons, energy-efficient refurbishment of existing buildings, public lighting, to name only a few);
- Investment amounts figuring between a million and several billion euros;
- Suppliers stemming from a range of industries (not just building contractors);
- Institutions and regulations structuring PPPs far from unified or uniform.

Yet, this observation contrasts with the matter-of-fact observation that the MAPPP had a unified approach of PPPs, and so did the participating financial sector (banks, specialised investment funds, consulting firms, and financial and legal experts). All these actors quite naturally conveyed the idea of PPP *market*.

Although the introduction of PPPs in France clearly cannot be confined to this dimension (Campagnac, 2009), the review of the situation proposed in this chapter, reflecting the views and discourse conveyed by these actors, is that public policy, related to the creation and use of innovative public procurement tools, legalising the private financing of public facilities ('public assets' in the British glossary), can also be interpreted as the opening up of a new market for the financial sector. The development of a dedicated industry on the supply-side is both the condition and the outcome of this successful introduction.

The analytical framework pertaining to the social construction of markets (Bourdieu, 2005; Garcia-Parpet, 2007; Muniesa, 2003), therefore suits the study of PPPs well. The creation of this 'market' (where 'products' are a technical infrastructure and the pertaining service, pre-financed by the private sector, and embedded in comprehensive contracts that define them), of its institutions, and its technical devices, could only be achieved by disrupting nodes of institutional resistance. Conveyed by actors who themselves had an interest in the development of PPPs, or who for ideological reasons supported the project of 're-embedding' public procurement within an economic rationality defined *in theory* and *ex ante*, this demanded that the serious lack of legitimacy suffered *a priori* by PPPs be overcome. This opposition notably figured in certain objections conveyed politically by a section of the administration, or socio-professional categories (including architects, SMEs in the contracting industry, and by some members of the civil service, either from procuring units or attached to the central control for public spending and tax measures), who had a say against the creation of this public policy. The introduction of PPPs was also expected to wage critics of an economic nature: a financing cost allegedly higher than via direct public finance.

The promotion of PPPs combined numerous argumentative categories, specific to diverse interest groups and social bodies. The financial register represented just one dimension of this rationale. Nevertheless, the introduction of PPPs and the creation of a market of 'project finance' for public infrastructure are intrinsically and inextricably linked, as are similarly the justification (or the criticism) of PPPs for their unique logic and the justification for using private finance. Revisiting the historical period when PPPs had to be legitimised (2005–2008) thus allows us to emphasise a scientific and rhetorical outline that appears to be repeatedly used when the need arises to justify the *raison d'être* of numerous sections of the financial market.

Following an overview of the characteristics of PPPs, the economic theory supporting them and their proper functioning – which affiliates them with project financing and produces a form of public 'assets' securitisation – we will turn our attention towards the two main categories of arguments, which were (and still are) deployed to justify the use of PPPs as a means of private pre-financing. The first is noticeably macroeconomic and focused on the correct management of assets (*patrimoine*) and public finances. The second is more microeconomic, focused on supervision and governance by financial players. Both those arguments include a popularised rationale for the general public, and its more elaborated, scientific twin.

PPP fundamentals: project financing for public assets

PPPs: an ideal-type, not a definition...

Whereas PPPs cover such a broad variety of situations in the international context that they have become a buzzword, a precise piece of legislation is commonly referred to in order to provide a definition for them in the French context (the June 2004 ruling which created the *Contrats de Partenariat* – Partnership Contracts). However even in France it fails to cover the totality of PPPs, it therefore seems logical to substitute an ideal-type (Deffontaines, 2013), which would enable to *qualify* as PPPs, in all institutional contexts, any public procurement contract incorporating the following three features:

- Organisational: a comprehensive contract, entrusting to a single private service-provider every functional stage of the command – design, construction, servicing and maintenance of the facility and, potentially related commercial services;
- Economic: annuities will be paid by the procuring authority after the building, infrastructure, or facilities, have been commissioned and the attached service declared fully operational;
- Financial: the setting up of the private funding necessary to pre-finance (mostly through debt) and complete the infrastructure, including some equity for the 'special purpose vehicle' bearing the project. This financial scheme is supposed to be tailor-made to fit the characteristics of the project. But it is also rendered *possible* by a contract that the procuring authority is committed to respect, which guarantees any payment and loans.

This ideal-type allows PPPs to be viewed as an alternative (not mandatory or systematic) to the conventional procurement route (a fragmented and sequenced command under the aegis of the public procuring authority, with the funding of the public authority treated separately from the project) and as an extension of the economic functioning of concessions to non-commercial services sold to the public sector It is an answer to the classic failures of public procurement, which have long been identified by the economic theory.

...organises an optimum of efficiency theorised by micro-economics

Strictly speaking, no unified economic theory exists on the topic of PPPs, yet there are bodies of research (Marty et al., 2006) treating specific one-off problems on the basis of classical microeconomic models. Using theoretical frameworks anchored particularly in the new microeconomic theories (notably which the concepts of agency, transaction costs, incomplete contracts and incentives), this field of research deals with the optimisation of the structuring of public procurement. Pointing out the failures of the public administration and the very weak incentivising framework the latter is able to create, the aim of those economists is to improve the economic efficiency of public authorities as service providers, and therefore to assess the optimal scope of public intervention in the procuring phase, either direct or delegated.

In the case of 'assets' ideally concerned by PPPs, these arrangements create a form of economic optimum enabling, theoretically, an answer to be provided to problems traditionally observed in public procurement (cost overruns, missed deadlines, neglected long-term management, no provisions for repairs and maintenance, etc.). These problems are linked to the specific nature of the conventional procurement route, which is sequenced in time and directly coordinated by the public procuring authority. Moreover, in the case of social or sovereign services provided by the public sector, the absence or lack of revenues prevents the resort to delegated management. Using the PPP procurement route instead consequently aims at improving economic efficiency by combining contractual self-regulation and market-based measures, for example:

- The long-term comprehensive contract (Hart, 2003) is supposed to limit problems of coordination by making the interests of construction and servicing-maintenance roles consistent (for those actors the timeframes and income-expenses profiles differ across the life-cycle of a project);
- Competitive clout, reduced by such long-term comprehensive contracts (fewer suppliers and less transparency in the cost structure), is partly reactivated as it becomes internalised within the payment-based incentive structure. This payment framework is essential for transferring any consequences related to their planning or operational failures onto service providers themselves. Consequently, fixed payments staggered along the duration of the contract are subject to penalties in the event that quality objectives are not met (such quality targets pertaining to the facilities as well as to the services provided, measured by performance indicators). The payment schemes (starting with the successful commissioning of facilities complying with the contractual agreements, with no time extensions added to the end of the contract, nor any payment increase in the event of delays or cost overruns) strongly incentivises the contractor to deliver on time and budget. These obligations (and therefore these assumed risks) shouldered by the private service-provider with regards to the public procurer, are transferred onto to the members of the consortium, usually subcontractors of the *special purpose vehicle* (SPV) project company. The subcontractors are responsible for the design-build, servicing-maintenance, etc., as defined by the comprehensive contract;
- Combined with this payment structure, contracts drawn up as comprehensively as possible (dividing up risks, anticipating penalties and termination procedures) must avoid the classic problems of *moral hazard* and *hold-ups* observed in the execution and the *ex post* renegotiation of concession contracts (long-term, incomplete contracts). However, reducing these informational asymmetries, which can lead to issues of anti-selection and opportunistic behaviours, requires complex contractual engineering with high transaction and coordination costs, balancing virtuous effects which are *hoped for* by *certain* costs;

- From this architecture ensues a problem clearly anticipated by theory (Hart and Moore, 1988): the necessarily oligopolistic structure of the offer impedes the economic optimum according to which competition is the best way to reveal costs and force organisations to keep their prices at a level deemed reasonable. The solution though was theorised a long time ago: it is 'competition *for* the market' (Demsetz, 1968). In the case of PPPs, this takes form as a progressive market process, called 'competitive dialogue'. This competitive formula, adapted to the complexity of the product and contract and to the evolutionary potential of its definition, aims to obtain the best solutions at the best price (total cost across the duration of the project's life), by organising competition between the technical, organisational and contractual solutions (the latter defining the incentives framework). The technical and commercial offers of the pre-selected consortia, expected to answer to the functional requirements, are reviewed separately, and evolve thanks to the instruction of the procuring authority and under competitive pressure.

PPPs therefore aim to implement an efficiency optimum by turning the service-provider into an agent. This is obtained through the payment-based incentive structure. This structure contributes towards setting up a sort of self-regulating framework within the consortiums – set-up in advance, during the negotiating phase – and under the pressure of market procedure, which is controlled through the instructions given by the public procurer.

To sum-up, this economic corpus makes up a theoretical framework, which enables key issues traditionally identified in the management of long-term public contracts to be worked out. It seems relevant to note that it originates from the same fundamental elements (and at times the same authors) as the literature in financial theory, which itself seeks to define an ideal of *corporate governance*. However, while the function of risk management, or the pre-financing that makes it possible to wait for deferred payments, intrinsic to PPPs, naturally calls for finance, it is clear that finance is barely present in the most fundamental economic theories involving PPPs. The theory is not about finance. However, the concrete business is.

A project financing operation

Just as they are outlined in a more operational literature (Lyonnet du Moutier, 2006), the majority of PPP contracts implement a project financing structure:

- Based on a tailored financing structure (duration, amount, repayment and settlement profiles) for the contract;
- Organising debt repayments and remuneration for the SPV shareholders who pre-financed the infrastructure, on the basis of rents paid – once the ongoing obligations of servicing and maintaining the facilities and large-scale refurbishment and renovation (planned but displaying an irregular profile) have been covered;
- Potentially affected by a number of risks (some transferred onto technical partners, others, either specific or residual, being shouldered by banks and more importantly equity capital);
- Accumulating the project obligations and revenues into an *ad hoc* legal entity; and,
- Organising risks sharing and transfer between those stakeholders best placed to take charge of them at the lowest possible cost, and putting procedures into place for the long-term control and governance of contracts.

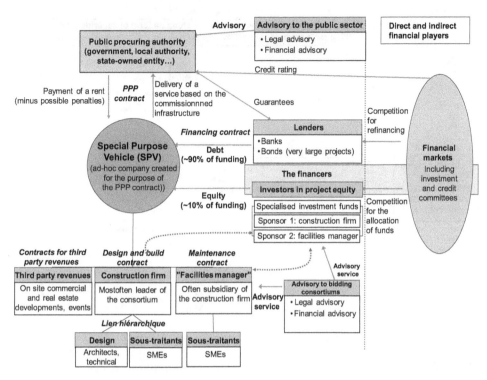

FIGURE 5.1 Framework of players and contracts in a PPP

The equity capital of the SPV is brought by financial investors and the leading firm in the consortium (most often stemming from the building sector in the French case). However, the SPV, established as the contracting partner of the public procuring authority (PPA), is mostly financed by banks, whose reimbursements will be based on the economics of the project and guaranteed by the PPA. The revenue stream of the project is supposedly very predictable: PPPs constitute a particular type of project financing, with the risks clearly limited once the infrastructure is delivered, as there are nearly no commercial contingencies (at the very most penalty threats in the event of insufficient availability). The limited risks allow for the structuring of high-geared financing structure, comparable in principle to that of leveraged buyouts (LBOs) but with lower risks and return, adjusting the overall cost of financing between the cost of liquidity and the risk premium attributed to the project. The goal of this arrangement is to reduce the cost of financing as much as possible.

The financial structuring of PPPs likewise enables them to be affiliated with a form of securitisation: the unique repayment stream available is tailored to correspond with the repayment of shareholder equity and the 'tranching' of various debt portions, with diverse risk-return pairings. A second, less obvious process takes place: the operations are 'repackaged' in order to become liquid resources on a secondary market. Demanded by investment funds, these practices are also carried out by lending banks (IGD, 2006). This process, consubstantial with structured financing, suggests that PPPs are equivalent to a form of securitisation.

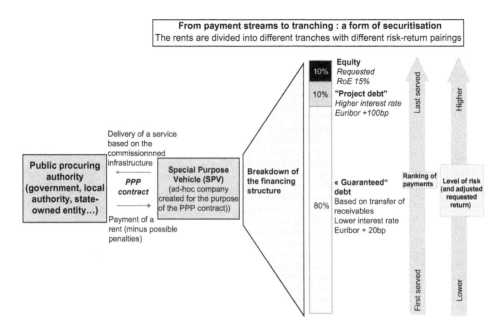

FIGURE 5.2 From payment streams to tranching: a form of securitisation

Disrupting economic positions and symbolic hierarchies, PPP schemes – generating substantial transaction costs and financing costs higher than those required had the public procuring authority collected debt directly by itself – can therefore also be accused of creating a new market for the financial sector, now capable of imposing its standards and requirements more directly upon the public procuring side, and of contributing to a securitisation henceforth considered suspicious. It is therefore interesting to recall the scientific case for PPPs – which legitimises using these forms of private financing and, out of necessity, the financial sector – and its variant targeted at the public and private decision-makers but also the political world and the greater public. Such academic and more common arguments have been enlisted by practitioners and promoters of PPPs, in official discourses, technical documents, colloquiums, professional publications or non-specialised media, or in discourses on legitimisation upheld by professionals stemming from involved sectors, during one-to-one interviews.

The need for financing, a popular political pitch for the use of PPPs

In practice, economic theory focusing on public contracting neglects this shameless aspect: as it is recalled in the white paper written by the members of the financial section of the *Institut pour la Gestion Déléguée* (IGD, 2006), the French lobby group for PPPs and delegated public services, 'the first function of private financing is to make cash available for projects' at an optimised cost – and thus to pipe resources from financial markets to public projects. This popular pitch for private financing is divided up into various different forms by PPP promoters, in particular political ones. For example, during budgetary restriction times, PPP are a welcome contribution to public services and infrastructure. This type of argument, which is not the most favoured by economists, echoes the case for an increased role of financial markets, and mirrors macroeconomic analyses of financialisation.

Between enthusiasm and resignation: using PPPs to fulfil requirements

This argument was particularly meaningful in the years 2005 to 2008, at the time when PPPs were being promoted and financial euphoria appeared to be the usual state of the world – the brutal end of was not in the slightest bit anticipated. In private, politicians, senior public servants and bankers acknowledged, with a more or less sincere state of distress, that 'the public sector no longer has the resources', but 'must still continue to invest': for growth, for the future, for sustainable development, to fulfil the 'social demand' emphasised by politicians... but also to justify its own *raison d'être*. In public – through written media, colloquiums, and promotional publications devoted to PPPs, in reviews targeted at senior civil servants and people working in public procurement, either national (*Revue du Trésor*, 2007) or local (*Pouvoirs Locaux*, 2007) – without finance ever explicitly being mentioned, PPP promoters emphasised the opportunity for PPPs, and more importantly their crucial trait in the context of budgetary pressure, in order to pursue and enhance public investment. PPP promoters? A vast category amassing together a number of political and economic groups with various interests and identities: high-level public servants, 'missionary' members of parliament, local and national political decision-makers, often coming from the *pro-business* fringe of the UMP right-wing ruling party in the second half of the 2000s, but at times also coming from the ranks of the socialist opposition (in that case self-labelled 'pragmatists'), the construction industry (mostly 'BTP majors') but also facility maintenance firms, banks and financial professionals, representatives of local authorities and major operators of public infrastructure, etc.

It is nonetheless necessary, though, to acknowledge that the argument concerning the need for private financing for infrastructure (thus in favour of PPPs) is found worldwide. 'The needs are huge' is heard everywhere: sustainable development, knowledge-based economy, territorial competitiveness, 'social demand', public transport and modal shift, employment, economic activity... the list goes on. Long before the financial, economic and budgetary crisis, resorting to PPPs was already necessary to bolster growth.

Fashionable media-friendly economists, sometimes appointed as experts, have highlighted the interests of the large-scale use of PPPs, 'a key for public investment', enlisting them as 'drivers for investment, activity and employment'. It is naturally all about 'good' or healthy public investment, with PPPs being seen as the way to efficiently link smart public spending with growth through the acceleration of investments in competitiveness factors, rather than considering them as a commonly accepted 'Keynesian stimulus' via public spending. While perspectives of 'endogenous growth', cherished by economists, justify PPPs, the case studies called upon focus mostly on investments that primarily concern the construction sector (bridges, parking lots, high-speed train lines, motorways, water sanitation services, etc.). It is only as of 2009 that PPPs became a paradoxical tool for the (attempted) re-boost of a failing economy.

Among the numerous contributions from management scientists or practitioners describing the mechanisms of PPP financing, only the white paper from the members of the IGD part of the financial sector (2006), pointed out the challenges for asset/liability management, emphasising the securitisation dimension – an emblematic measure from the financial boom years which allowed for maximising the effects of low rates and abundant cash on the markets, through financial engineering. It is only in the most recent retrospective assessments that economists clearly admitted that the development of PPPs in the years 2000s was linked to a very favourable financial environment (Marty and Spindler, 2013).

According to economists, financing via PPPs optimises budget management

Politically tempting, the argument for using PPPs as an easy financial resource to satisfy social and economic needs is not well regarded by economists writing about PPPs. For them, the question of the type and sector of public investments is of low interest, selectivity being mostly thought in terms of how to choose the best procurement route – the conventional one under the aegis of a public contracting authority *versus* PPPs. In the years 2005–2008, the long-term budgetary sustainability of investments was less worrying than the drawbacks of private financing. Such fears included the extra cost of financing (identified as the 'Achilles tendon' of PPPs), the fear that PPPs would be used as a creative accounting scam allowing off-balance sheet debt to be concealed (Marty, 2007), and finally fear of budgetary stiffening linked to PPPs – through the creation of non-reversible public spending.

However, these potential inconveniences, linked to poor public management, are not enough to erase the virtuous budgetary effects of PPPs as they are identified by economists – an optimisation connected to the intertemporal arbitrage naturally enabled by finance. As a result of the PPPs' capability to provide massive funding on projects, *a fortiori* at a time when constraints are burdening public finances, and also their ability to smooth out spending profile over time, ensues consequently the possibility of simultaneously launching more public projects, at a faster pace. This comes in stark contrast to the risk of arbitrage between projects, and the budgetary staggering and/or slicing which can result in the delayed implementation of infrastructure, when public finance is used. Thus, while providing a solution to the structural crowding out of investment spending, PPPs also have the virtue of better preserving the value of public assets. The staggered payment plan, in exchange for private financing, scheduling future operating and maintenance-renewal expenses, is praised for its capacity to counter the frequently observed damage done to infrastructure by wear and tear – whereas the public procuring authority's budgetary arbitrage is denounced to trade-off at the expense of quality when making investment decisions. At a later stage maintenance and renewal expenses normally fall victim to budgetary adjustments (Marty and Voisin, 2007).

Similar arguments for those in favour of financing firms via the market

A convincing argument targeting a wide and varied public, the possibility of mass cash injections on projects to fulfil social and economic needs or, and, on a more sophisticated note, that of better budget management, this implicit call for the financing of public projects by financial markets belongs to a category of economic discourse and reasoning that favours the extension of finance. From a macroeconomic interpretation, they take their place in the regulationist analysis of financial liberalisation seen as a tool intended to stimulate growth (Boyer, 2009), both through the simple impacts related to supporting business, and through the greater efficiency of financial innovations when compared with traditional intermediated financing (among which figures the creation of credit tools based on securitisation – a measure enabling the growth of readily available, inexpensive liquidity and risk dispersal and reassurance). Empirically, one can also observe an argument targeting the wider public that is quite similar to the *leitmotiv* announcing the need for capital so as to 'finance the economy and companies growth', a popular form of legitimisation for the stock market or LBOs.

Microeconomic justifications for using finance: the argument of control

Less showcased than the desired effect of PPPs generating economic and social surplus and that of a more rational management of public finances, a second type of argument is deployed with more or less force depending on the circles and contributors promoting PPPs. This argument consists in a higher level of economic efficiency for public procurement, creating more 'value for money' through better risks sharing. Attached explicitly, or not, to the *New Public Management* (NPM) movement, it reveals a more or less assured faith in the greater efficiency of the private sector. The scientific reasoning behind it lies in the virtuous organisation of competitive and contractual mechanisms, setting up the internal governance of projects and establishing the coordination of risks. Nevertheless, while the outlines of these self-regulating devices are taken up in the popularly promoted argument, the delicate mechanisms of financial governance remain outside its scope.

Reluctant to address PPPs as a source of financing for public projects, the 'applied' microeconomic analysis grants to the financial supports of a project an important role: acting as the supervisors responsible for assessing the feasibility and monitoring the proper execution of contracts. While the connection between the microeconomic theory of PPPs and the microeconomic analysis of the role of financers in the arrangement is slightly forced, it is nonetheless worthwhile highlighting the points shared with microeconomic literature on company governance.

The role of financers as agents of the public procurer – from 'due diligence' to surveillance

The role of financers as supervisors ensues naturally from the contractual and incentives architecture. The construction works are pre-financed by investors and bank loans, through a highly leveraged structure (often 90 per cent of *senior* debt), and then reimbursed by the *public procuring authority* through rents. As a result, the consortium's financers are strongly incentivised to supervise very strictly the obligations of the SPV in relation to the public procurer (to make sure the SPV will be capable of fulfilling the contractual objectives) and the SPV subcontractors (and beforehand the arrangements that define their responsibilities within the SPV). As the main feature of PPPs, project financing is therefore presented as a financial and contractual framework in which financers act as representatives (*agents*) of the public procuring authority's (PPA) interests. As the interests of financers – and most prominently banks – are practically in closer proximity to the PPA than to the project's main industrial sponsor, this should make it possible for the PPA to externalise the supervision costs to the financers of the project, so to speak.

Financers are esteemed to have aligned interests with those of the *PPA* in the governance of SPV. This makes the agency relationship at the foundation of PPPs more complex: rather it can introduce a third relation. Besides the main principal–agent relationship (between the PPA and the SPV that provides the service), a supervisory role is carried out *ex ante* and *ex post* by the investors and the banks. This essentially resolves the inadequacies of the traditional agency relationship, in which the buyer suffers from incapacity to perfectly define the obligations of the agent, and to perfectly observe the agent's behaviour.

This is the second argument: the work of financers, under the constraint of these incentives, is presented as an externalisation of the evaluation of public projects, and is as such useful as a way of reducing any risk of the SPV defaulting in its contractual obligations (either purposeful – moral hazard – or not), reducing the PPA's information gap, and achieving a contractual balance between the parties. Financers are encouraged to seek out information, in order to reassure themselves of the capacity of the SPV to honour the contractual obligations, as well as to reject financial arrangements that would expose them to too much risk. Marty and Voisin (2007) emphasise such *due diligence* work conducted by money lenders, pointed out as 'the the most experienced and equipped party' for this task of identifying the risks potentially affecting payment streams, risks that would result from the shortfalls of the service provider. Lenders and investors insist on strict rules of governance in order for the project to pay back debt. This preliminary structuring produces indicators like debt service coverage *ratios* and gearing ratios depending on the financial structure. For microeconomic theory, the financers' task of monitoring does not end with the signature of the contract: they continue to supervise over decisions related to project management and conserve the right to replace (*step-in rights*) any defaulting subcontractor.

Finally, financial theory even imagines (Dewatripont and Legros, 2005) the ideal division of the roles between lenders and investors: debt from banks is considered to trigger more efficient control. The specificities of the French 'market' have contributed towards hardening this role even more, as devices such as the 'Dailly' transfer of receivables and the strong pressure from the *Caisse des Dépôts et Consignations* (CDC – Deposits and Consignments Fund) whose saving funds are available to finance projects with very low interest rates, have pressed down bank margins and amplified the lenders' risk aversion, at times causing projects that were already well under way to nevertheless become blocked.

An argumentative corpus similar to that for corporate governance

Fundamental economic research is not focused *per se* on how PPPs work, but rather on the agency transfer, incentive devices and the issue of information asymmetry: the academic works on which this chapter is based are those of management scientists who themselves quote canonical economic literature. It therefore does not appear to us to be anecdotal that the theoretical construction of this regulatory architecture is very similar to that of *corporate governance*, the explicit objective of which is not to promote the development of the stock market and LBO arrangements (which would nonetheless be the logical result), but instead to theorise about a form of monitoring over firms which would align the interests of managers with those of shareholders.

Conclusion: moving from the need to resort to finance, towards financial requirements

It could almost seem tautological to consider that PPPs contribute towards increasing the influence and power of finance. Within this chapter, we have sought to consider the heuristic dimension of the connection between the promotional discourse and economic theorising of this 'necessity'. Beyond the case of PPPs, expanding the market for finance brings together popular justifications (normally conveyed politically) – the contribution of liquid resources to develop the economy or, here, public infrastructure – and the microeconomic theorising of higher efficiency based upon incentive mechanisms controlled by financers. The core hypothesis is therefore that the 'need for financing' is indissociable from the architecture of regulation theorised by microeconomics, which offers the financer a central role. This crucial element of market construction applied to finance greatly exceeds the situation of PPPs and we believe provides a very wide framework for interpreting financialisation. Notably, it seems to us to be homothetic to the case for increasing the role of the stock market or LBOs.

It is often via preliminary theoretical effort that finance is legitimised, via the connection between micro and macroeconomic levels, equally conveyed in a popularised way by interest groups or those charged with the design of public policies. Financial governance appears as it were to be a compulsory step for obtaining capital from the financial markets and enhanced microeconomic efficiency. That so much power is given in return to the financial sector falls outside the field of observation of economic science, whereas sociological or heterodox approaches are called out. Economic sociology however, gains much more influence when it acknowledges the space that previous economic theorising has made for finance and the way in which such theorising has been recycled in the public debate. As such, analyses concerning the social conditions of finance's rise in power (Aglietta and Rebérioux, 2005; Boyer, 2009) provide a fairly enlightening interpretive framework for identifying, behind the arguments provided by PPP actors and promoters aimed at improving market efficiency, the return to the basic requirements of finance – the implementation of which leads to heightened financialisation. Such financialisation obviously means a larger presence of financial players, which view PPPs as a potential for business and profit. These institutions and professionals will then use tools and methods imported from the technicalities of project finance to assess and structure the public infrastructure projects they help to finance. Later in the project life cycle, they will monitor the behaviour of this asset whereas it is circulated in the financial sector, during the decades-long contract's lifetime.

As a result, the very justifications which established the need for the involvement of finance in a new market, give way to expressing the need to adapt this market to the basic requirements of the financial sector (liquidity of assets, adapted tax measures, robust project pipe, etc.), in order to enable the financial supply-side to develop sustainably. For senior civil servants or politicians who promote PPPs, as for investors in shareholder equity, bankers, financial advisers, all specialists in PPPs and project financing, the opportunities to present arguments in favour of PPPs and project financing are also occasions for presenting and justifying the 'natural' requirements of finance. The crisis initiated in 2008 obviously pushed the argumentative register to evolve, and while it was initially a case of justifying the expectations of finance, from 2009 to 2010, the challenge later became to save finance... so that it may in turn save PPPs.

References

Aglietta, M. and Rebérioux, A. (2005). *Corporate governance adrift: A critique of shareholder value.* Cheltenham: Edward Elgar Publishing Limited.

Bourdieu, P. (2005). *The social structures of the economy.* London: Polity Press.

Boyer, R. (2009). Feu le régime d'accumulation tiré par la finance? La crise des *subprimes* en perspective historique. *Revue de la régulation*, 5, Retrieved from http://regulation.revues.org/index7367.html (first accessed 2010).

Campagnac, E. (Ed.) (2009). *Evaluer les partenariats public-privé en Europe: quelles conséquences sur la commande et le projet? Quels impacts sur la qualité des bâtiments et des services? Quelles méthodes d'évaluation?* Paris: Presses de l'ENPC.

Deffontaines, G. (2013). *Extension du domaine de la finance? Partenariats public-privé et 'financiarisation' de la commande publique. Une proposition d'analyse par la sociologie économique.* Unpublished PhD thesis. Paris: Ecole Nationale des Ponts et Chaussées – Université Paris-Est.

Demsetz, H. (1968). Why regulate utilities? *Journal of Law and Economics*, 11(1), 55–66.

Dewatripont, M. and Legros, P. (2005). Public–private partnerships: Contract design and risk transfer. *EIB Papers*, 10(3), 120–145.

Garcia-Parpet, M.-F. (2007). The social construction of a perfect market: The strawberry auction at Fontaines-en-Sologne. In D. MacKenzie, F. Muniesa and L. Siu (Eds.), *Do economists make markets? On the performativity of economics* (pp. 20–53). Princeton: Princeton University Press.

Hart, O. (2003). Incomplete contracts and public ownership: Remarks and an application to public-private partnerships. *The Economic Journal*, 113(486), 69–76.

Hart, O. and Moore, J. (1988). Incomplete contracts and renegotiation. *Econometrica*, 56, 509–540.

IGD [Institut de la Gestion Déléguée] (2006). *Le financement des partenariats public-privé en France. Rapport du groupe des banques et organismes financiers membres de l'IGD.* Paris.

La Revue du Trésor (2007). Special issue on PPP, 3–4.

Lyonnet du Moutier, M. (2006). *Financement sur projets et partenariats public privé.* Colombelles: Editions Management et Sociétés.

Marty, F. (2007). *Partenariats public-privé, règles de discipline budgétaire, comptabilité patrimoniale et stratégies de hors bilan.* OFCE *working paper* n°2007–29.

Marty, F. and Spindler, J. (2013). Bilans et perspectives des contrats de PFI britanniques (1992–2012). *Gestion et Finances Publiques*, 6, 43–62.

Marty, F. and Voisin, A. (2007). Finances publiques et investissements privés: quel nouvel équilibre pour les investissements des Etats? *Politiques et Management Public*, 25(3), 19–37.

Marty, F., Trosa, S. and Voisin, A. (2006). *Les partenariats public-privé.* Paris: La Découverte.

Muniesa, F. (2003). *Les marchés comme algorithmes: sociologie de la cotation électronique à la Bourse de Paris.* Unpublished PhD thesis. Paris: Ecole Nationale Supérieure des Mines de Paris.

Pouvoirs Locaux (2007). *Ni privatisation, ni panacée: du bon usage du partenariat public-privé*, 74, 46–118.

6

THE RISK FLUCTUATION

The consequences of avoiding interest rate risk

Anne EA van der Graaf

Introduction

This is a local account, one of a big bank that became small. The perspective is the risk managers', those working on the inside of the organisation to avoid trouble. In the process of becoming smaller, Bank F found more and more problems on its path. Even though the story is local, it resembles our contemporary problems. Financial market participants continuously show their capability to control their risks through specific rationales. At the same time, they are incapable of avoiding negative consequences for themselves but also those around them. The rationale of control actually causes problems afterwards. Within Bank F, risk managers fought a running battle, avoiding extreme financial losses. At the same time, the rationale of control that had caused these problems was relatively uncontested.

Risks are one of the cornerstones of modern day capitalism and some would even say modernity (Beck, 1992; Fressoz, 2012). Risk taking can also be seen at the genesis of our modern financial markets (De Goede, 2005). By accepting that technology can control natural risks, we also accept technologies' consequences (Mythen, 2004; Zinn, 2008). Take the example of a nuclear disaster but also of an oil spill. They cause significant natural damage and come from modern technologies. The complex systems that supposedly control these technologies are not able to control all negative events. Normal accidents are a great example of such a lack of control. A small mistake in a complex chain of production can lead to disastrous effects (Perrow, 1981). Technological risks carry a form of uncontrollability that can lead to extreme consequences.

Financial risks are no exception. Economic catastrophe can come from them, as we have seen with the financial crisis of 2007/2008 (Mishkin, 2011). However, financial risks have been mainly studied from the idea of controllability. Their calculations and reporting would theoretically allow for a, more or less, rational trade-off between profit and risks (Beckert, 1996; Knight, 1921; Power, 2004). Losses could thus be controlled with the right assessments. How can one deal with this contradiction between the control of financial risks and the lack of control of technological risks?

The social studies of finance have focused on investments rather than risks. One of the main strands of research is the diffusion of knowledge practices. The latter are standards of how one interprets financial information. Different types of knowledge practices exist across the financial markets, setting the standard for trades and evaluations (Arjaliès et al., 2017;

MacKenzie and Spears, 2014). These interpretations, in the case of asset management, can be both quantitative and qualitative (Larminat, 2013; Svetlova, 2008). Not only do these multiple assessments of financial information exist, their usages also have effects. Profits can go up when traders with different knowledge practices mix (Stark and Beunza, 2009). On the other hand, the diffusion of specific types of knowledge can also lead to the exact opposite of profits, such as the cases of LTCM and the subprime market have shown us (MacKenzie, 2003 and 2011).

Knowledge practices could also help us understand risk control and a lack of it. One of the causes of 2008's financial crisis can be found in the financial risk indications, ratings, that were given to subprime structured products. Where investors thought they bought relatively safe investments, they actually did not (Mishkin, 2011). Yet the reason they were made and sold was because investors wanted something that had a specific rating. The risk ratings of the structured products were calculated such that the best ratings were maximised (MacKenzie, 2011). However, these ideas also led to an increased exposure and once the subprime products started to default, the whole financial market fell with it. What had seemed like a safe investment was not safe any more (Longstaff, 2010; MacKenzie, 2012). The control of risks had seemed right but the financiers had created their own disaster.

But what happens afterwards, when the rationale causes problems? People might still prefer this specific knowledge practice over another. However, it is questionable that they continue their actions based on this rationale. So how do those that are responsible for the control of risks, the risk managers, deal with knowledge practices that turn into negative events? This chapter brings together the uncontrollability of risks with work on knowledge practices in finance. It is based on a four-month participatory observation I carried out in 2014 and 2015. It took place at the risk management department of Bank F, a European bank that had defaulted during the crisis. I show that even though a dominant rationality on risks existed, actions tried to prevent problems. Rather than following the knowledge practice, the risk managers acted to avoid negative consequences. The visible possibility of losses had priority over the ideas on how to assess those future losses as risks.

This chapter shows how the perception of risk control can lead to financial losses and how risk managers have different rationalities of the related risks. In order to do this, one specific risk is disentangled. Different risk definitions existed amongst one another. One definition dominated the others, that interest rate risk equalled the fixed, long-term, interest rates. Bank F had based its investment strategy on this idea, thinking that it could control interest rates. However, actions based on this singular definition had led to the exact opposite. Financial problems appeared that could default Bank F again. Risk managers tried to avoid further negative problems based on that interest rate. Some risk managers adapted their rationality of interest rate risks, others stuck to the dominant one. All tried to avoid the consequences the rationale of control had caused.

Controlling interest rate risk

Bank F had been in trouble ever since Lehman Brothers had defaulted in 2008. The problems just piled up afterwards. Bank F did not have the capacity to spread out the losses because the diversification of risks was not possible any more. The default of Lehman in 2008 had caused liquidity problems and after that, the risks that turned into problems had not stopped. They had been nationalised after a couple of years of muddling through. The difficulties continued afterwards. The risk managers had the responsibility to ensure that Bank F avoided financial problems.

One of the problems that hit them later on was created by interest rate exposure. However, some of the risk managers were convinced that there was no interest rate risk. There were multiple definitions of interest rate risk among the risk managers. This heterogeneity did not necessarily change the approach in risk management. It mainly reflected their past experiences.

Dominant rationale

At Bank F, different risk managers had different definitions of interest rate risks. However, in conversations, they would not distinguish between the different definitions. They all called it 'interest rate risk'. Some had a very clear-cut definition of a calculation, others dealt with the consequences of that definition. This heterogeneity did not necessarily change the approach in risk management but reflected past events and previous management. One clear-cut definition was known across the bank. Fixed interest rates had risks and floating or variable rates did not. This was the dominant rationale that had also led to specific investment strategies.

With the dominant rationale of fixed rates as risky, some risk managers were convinced that there was no interest rate risk. At the same time, Bank F had financial problems because of the interest rate. The problem was not one of measurement or asset quality, it was one of definition. Before the crisis, the interest rate risk had been determined to be one type of interest rates, the fixed interest rate. Since roughly a third of Bank F's assets before the crisis were susceptible to the fixed rates, management at the time had decided to get rid of it. They did so by buying derivatives that sold on the fixed interest rate in exchange for a floating rate. The organisation, in theory, limited this interest rate exposure.

The first person to explain the rationale to me was Albert. He worked on interest rate's impact on the balance sheet. He told me that the interest rate risk was the fixed rate. He explained it with the help of opportunity costs. If Bank F had a bond with a fixed interest rate, its future value would decrease. Namely, one had invested money in something that could not be invested in something else. However, if the interest rate was variable, that part of the investment could always be invested in something else. So there was no risk related to the interest rate. One always had the opportunity to invest that specific part of the investment somewhere else.

Albert's definition of interest rate risk was shared by others. The explanation, on the other hand, could differ. Even the dominant rationale had a multitude of underlying reasoning dependent on the person one talked to. Oswald, who worked on calculations of the bond values, repeated Albert's definition. The fixed rate was the interest rate risk at Bank F. However, he did not see it through the opportunity costs. Oswald saw the interest rate risk in the changes in cash flows one would receive. The coupon, periodical payment, of a bond was namely the interest rate plus the credit risk of that bond issuer (see Figure 6.1). The interest rate was fixed but in order to finance the purchase of the bond, Bank F would take a loan through the inter-banking market with floating interest rates. This meant that the costs of the cash flows changed on the short term and with the interest rates.

The dominant rationale of the fixed interest rates as risky led to a specific business strategy at Bank F. Almost all bonds in the portfolio had a one-on-one coverage with a swap to exchange interest rates. Each bond thus had an opposite interest rate payment attached to it. The swap was a contract of a periodical two-way transaction with another financial service provider. Bank F would receive the floating rate of that moment and pay the fixed rate determined in the contract. Theoretically, the bond's fixed rates converged into a floating rate, mitigating the interest rate risk as defined by both Oswald and Arthur (see Figures 6.1 and 6.2). In practice there were now two interest rate transactions.

The collateral problem

By including a swap to the bond transaction, Bank F had also added another financial product to its book that required maintenance. The swap was not just an exchange of interest rates. First of all, there were extra payments above the interest rate, the transaction cost. Second, and most importantly, most of the swaps had collateral agreements attached to them. The latter supposedly avoided negative consequences caused by a possible default of the swap counterparty. This meant that (part of the) value of the swap was paid to the other. In case one of the two counterparties was likely to receive more interest payments than the other, the other had to put in (a part of) that amount in cash. That way, in case one of the two would default, the value of the swap would not be lost. It supposedly eliminated the counterparty risk. In theory, the transaction that included the collateral was risk neutral.[1]

The policy seemed safe on paper. Bank F did not have interest rate risk or a counterparty who might give trouble. The opportunity costs were neutral and the cash flows would not change. They thought they had avoided the interest rates' negative effects. Reality turned out to be less easily defined.

By buying interest rate swaps Bank F had changed fixed interest rate income into a variable one, based on the floating interest rate. That way the risk was hedged and the bond only had a credit risk attached to it. However, financial market transactions are not this simple in reality. By buying most of the interest rate swaps into one direction, Bank F had no diversified income. Worst of all, the collateral exchange was not diversified. Bank F either received or put forward cash collateral.

The first years of the crisis, the cash collateral had not been a problem. But then the interest rates started to go down in the Euro area, from 2010 on. The situation changed. Suddenly, the balance sheet started to increase. The liquidity demand increased at the same time. The bank was not doing any new business. The balance sheet increase was exactly the opposite of what the people at Bank F expected to happen. Then they started looking at the specificities of their swaps.

When the gap between the floating and fixed rates, also called the different legs of a swap, increases, the value of a swap increases or decreases, depending on which rate one receives. For one of the parties the value becomes much higher, for the other, much lower. Bank F had mainly taken swaps where they would receive a floating rate. So the lower interest rate meant a decrease in their value. At the same time, it led to a higher demand of collateral. The counterparty would loose more and more money in case Bank F would default on its swap payments. This collateral thus became problematic. Bank F had to put forward an increasing amount of money into the collateral exchange. Liquidity was scarce for Bank F, which meant that the search for cash was very difficult. During my time at Bank F, the interest rates had even further decreased, with the ECB, the European Central Bank, heading for the zero point and negative rates part of the picture.

The head of the market risk team, Valery, passed by my office late one evening to discuss her day and mine. She explained the whole collateral situation. One of her meetings that day had been about the difficult cash collateral situation. She explained to me why the collateral was in cash and why bonds or credits were not accepted as a safeguard. She put it simply. What is the safest thing to make sure you are paid out in case you are not paid when required? You ask for cash in the background. Swaps and their cash collateral were thus similar to a landlord asking for a deposit or the judicial system asking for bail.

$$Income_{bond}\, t = Interest\ Rate_{Bond} - Interest\ Rate_{Funding} =$$
$$(Credit\ Spread + Fixed\ Interest\ Rate) - Floating\ Interest\ Rate$$

FIGURE 6.1 Expected income of bond at point t

$$Income_{bond\ hedged}\, t$$
$$= Interest\ Rate_{Bond} - Interest\ Rate_{Funding} + (Cash\ Flow\ Swap)$$
$$= (Credit\ Spread + Fixed\ Interest\ Rate) -$$
$$Floating\ Interest\ Rate + (Floating\ Interest\ Rate -$$
$$Fixed\ Interest\ Rate)$$
$$= Credit\ Spread$$

FIGURE 6.2 Expected income of bond at point t with swap

All of this could have been irrelevant. Bank F remained a bank. One thing that distinguishes banks from other firms is their access to (almost) unlimited amounts of money. Namely, a bank has access to the cash provisions of central banks and the inter-banking money market. However, the fall of Lehman Brothers had caused the inter-banking market to dry up. The latter had never fully re-established itself. Since Bank F could not carry out any new business, it could not attract savings. Besides that, what there was of an inter-banking market was not extremely willing to lend to Bank F. The last option was the liquidity arrangement at the Central Bank. However, the owners had spoken out against that. Bank F thus tried to scrape the money together on the inter banking market.

The cash collateral that had to be posed was not just a neutraliser of risk. It had effects and became a constraint. While the flexible rate had been seen as non-risky, it ended up having negative consequences in itself. As Oswald told me, the back-to-back swaps were the reason of a very troublesome liquidity situation. Bank F needed more and more money just to pay the swap guarantees.

Handling the interest rate risks

Not everybody saw the floating interest rate as risk free. It was an easy formula, as Robert said (see Figure 6.2). Maybe a bit too easy. He had seen people with a short formula, thereby able to cross out the interest rate when it was a floating one. He was not convinced though that that was the risk. There were other aspects that were part of the interest rates that were risky. However, this might have been a bit too simple for him. His opinion of the interest rate risk definition resembled the risks created by the collateral situation. He saw the risk as the overall impact of the interest rates on the balance sheet.

In a similar vein, Jacob, who like Robert worked on the risks of the balance sheet, described a multitude of risks of the interest rates. He saw three things. First of all, there was an overall question if a high interest rate or low interest rate was good for the profitability of the company. Second, there were the value changes that an interest rate change could bring. Valuations need discounting to account for the opportunity costs related to a long-term investment (see Figure 6.3). Then, there was a third aspect. The future cash flows one expected to receive could change based on the interest rates. With these three types of interest rate risks, Jacob focused on the overall balance sheet, not the bonds specifically.

$$Net\ Present\ Value = \sum_{n=1}^{t} \frac{E(CashFlow)}{(1+r)^n}$$

FIGURE 6.3 Discounted value of asset

The two went beyond the dominant rationale and looked at the overall consequences of the interest rates. Jacob and Robert's vision reflected the work that the risk managers carried out. At the same time as Albert and Oswald explain the interest rate risks through the dominant rationale, they worked on the consequences of the interest rate risks. Albert spent his days calculating the cash collateral position and the interest rate impact on them. Oswald had the daily task to calculate the bond values the swaps supposedly covered. They were not the only ones who spent their working days on controlling the collateral situation. Janice worked full-time on the swap valuations. Besides that, at least four other persons worked on it part-time. In a department of 20 people, one-fifth of the people looked at the interest rate risks, swaps and cash collateral.

A year after the end of the fieldwork, I met up with Valery, the head of the market risk management department. She recounted how she had been very nervous a couple of months after I had left. The interest rate changes had created an even worse cash collateral situation. The liquidity needs had been so high that default had been a clear possibility. The interest rate risk existed thus in certain practices outside of the fixed rate definition.

For something that was not supposed to be a risk, the risk managers did a lot of work on it. In daily activities, the interest rate situation was a problem. The lower the interest rate, the higher the collateral, leading to even more difficulties for Bank F's liquidity situation. The collateral that had to be put in had effects. It created constraints and problems. The floating interest rate of the swaps caused that. Thus a risk could actually be seen from the low interest rates. They calculated the effects and tried to find solutions to solve the cash collateral problem. They worked on it for months. The interest rate was part of the work on the bank's problems, part of the risk managers' practices. The daily activities of the risk managers thereby opposed the dominant rationale on the interest rate risk.

By choosing to have back-to-back bonds and swaps to avoid interest rate risks, Bank F had created a risk trap for itself. It had not expected that the interest rates would change the way they would, as well as a change in the once very secure liquidity situation. At the same time, the risks were still seen through the calculative lens of the floating versus fixed rates. Even though the dominant rationale became contested, it was still held. People worked on the consequences that came from this strict definition. They handled the collateral situation as best as they could, attributing it directly to the decision to have back-to-back swaps. The upcoming problems mattered more than the dominant rationale of the risk definition.

Conclusion

The interest rate risk control with the help of floating rates had thus created a problem on its own. Even though the consequences did not lead to a new financial crisis, they were out of control. Different rationalities work alongside each other to avoid risks, whilst at the same time a decision based on one of them can lead to unexpected consequences. However, not everybody worked alongside their knowledge practice of interest rate risk. What they did do was avoid their consequences, independent of the definition they gave the risk.

Similar to the studies of trading rooms and asset management, different rationalities existed alongside each other in risk management. This could even be the case within the same person, with a practice that seems to contradict a definition. One rationale was more used than others, namely that fixed rates were risky. However, when time went on, problems also came from the products that gave the floating rates. Everyone in risk management saw this as a problem, which endangering Bank F's existence. They did their best to avoid this risk becoming a reality. Independent of people's definition of interest rate risks, they identified the possible financial losses. They worked on those possible financial losses rather than following the dominant rationale.

To understand risks, we thus need to go beyond the knowledge practice. We need to look at the actions of the risk managers. The possible negative consequences of interest rates and the financial objects it could be linked to were more important to the risk managers' practices than the definition. It was the local that mattered in this moment of trouble, not the theoretical standards the risk managers had. The dominant rationale had been followed when things went well. However, when the control itself became a problem, the risk managers adapted their strategies. The knowledge practices had effects. However, their usage depended on the situation at hand.

Note

1 This is not necessarily the case. See for example the work of Riles (2011) on the different types of rules that are attached to these collateral agreements.

References

Arjaliès, D.-L., Grant, P., Hardie, I., MacKenzie, D. and Svetlova, E. (2017). *Chains of finance: How investment management is shaped.* Oxford: Oxford University Press.

Beck, U. (1992). *Risk society: Towards a new modernity.* London: Sage.

Beckert, J. (1996). What is sociological about economic sociology? Uncertainty and the embeddedness of economic action. *Theory and society*, 25(6), 803–840.

De Goede, M. (2005). *Virtue, fortune, and faith: A genealogy of finance.* Minneapolis: University of Minnesota Press.

Fressoz, J.-B. (2012). *L'apocalypse joyeuse. Une histoire du risque technologique.* Paris: Seuil.

Knight, F. H. (1921). *Risk, uncertainty and profit.* New York: Hart, Schaffner and Marx.

Larminat (de), P. (2013). Entre 'quantitatif' et 'qualitatif'. Comment les investisseurs professionnels évaluent les gérants d'actifs financiers. *L'Année sociologique*, 63(1), 77–105.

Longstaff, F. A. (2010). The subprime credit crisis and contagion in financial markets. *Journal of financial economics*, 97(3), 436–450.

MacKenzie, D. (2003). Long-term capital management and the sociology of arbitrage. *Economy and society*, 32(3), 349–380.

MacKenzie, D. (2011). The credit crisis as a problem in the sociology of knowledge. *American Journal of Sociology*, 116(6), 1778–1841.

MacKenzie, D. (2012). Knowledge production in financial markets: credit default swaps, the ABX and the subprime crisis. *Economy and Society*, 41(3), 335–359.

MacKenzie, D. and Spears, T. (2014). The formula that killed wall street: The Gaussian copula and modelling practices in investment banking. *Social Studies of Science*, 44(3), 393–417.

Mishkin, F. S. (2011). Over the cliff: From the subprime to the global financial crisis. *The Journal of Economic Perspectives*, 25(1), 49–70.

Mythen, G. (2004). *Ulrich beck: A critical introduction to the risk society.* London: Pluto Press.

Perrow, C. (1981). Normal accident at three mile island. *Society*, 18(5), 17–26.

Power, M. (2004). *The risk management of everything: Rethinking the politics of uncertainty.* London: Demos.

Riles, A. (2011). *Collateral knowledge: legal reasoning in the global financial markets.* Chicago: University of Chicago Press.

Stark, D. and Beunza, D. (2009). The cognitive ecology of an arbitrage trading room. In D. Stark (Ed.), *The sense of dissonance: Accounts of worth in economic life* (pp. 111–147). Princeton; Princeton University Press.

Svetlova, E. (2008). Framing complexity in financial markets. *Science, Technology & Innovation Studies*, 4(2), 115–130.

Zinn, J. (2008). *Social theories of risk and uncertainty: An introduction.* Malden: Blackwell Publishing.

7

WHAT MAKES A PRICE A PRICE? COMMENSURATION WORK ON FINANCIAL MARKETS

Hélène Rainelli-Weiss and Isabelle Huault

Introduction

In modern societies, the 'overwhelming appeal to quantification' (Porter, 1996) is relentless and plays a major role in the conduct of institutions as well as in the management of organisations. Espeland (1998) and Espeland and Stevens (1998) use the notion of commensuration to define the specific process of standardisation that occurs through numbers, whereby qualitative differences come to be measured with a single quantitative metric.

Markets seem to be the realm of commensuration and commensurative practices, where prices are such deeply institutionalised instances of commensuration that they sometimes constitute what they intend to measure (Cronon, 1991; Porter, 1996). The risk is therefore to envision commensuration processes on markets as taken for granted (Huault and Rainelli, 2011), thus overlooking what it takes to make a market price a legitimate instance of commensuration.

In this chapter, we study a situation where a regulator proposes a change in the commensuration system traditionally used to set prices on a market and meets resistance from market actors. More precisely, our research is based on a qualitative study of the proposed changes to over-the-counter (OTC) financial markets[1] resulting from the regulatory reform currently in progress in Europe. In rendering explicit the forms of commensuration that were on the market before reform, we contend that this empirical setting provides a unique opportunity to gain insight into the commensuration processes implemented in markets. We consider three main research questions: What does resistance to change in the form of commensuration reveal about the commensurative practices required to set prices? What dimensions of market actors' representations make a market price a legitimate instance of commensuration? What levers do market actors have at their disposal to influence the trajectory of change in a commensuration system?

Our evidence concerns a change that might appear minor compared to more daring commensuration issues, since the 'only' thing at stake is a change in the pricing mechanism of OTC financial markets involved in recent financial reforms. Our research however shows the enormous amount of work necessary to make this apparently 'simple' change a success. Denaturalising prices, we demonstrate that the absence of conflicts of moral values or individual identities found in other commensuration contests (Espeland, 1998; Lohmann,

2009) does not prevent actors from putting up resistance that makes the evolution of a particular market form a complex and labour-intensive social process.

Commensuration and resistance to commensuration in markets

The specific process by which different things, objects or organisations become standardised through numbers seems typical of modern societies. The ranking of business schools, universities (Espeland and Sauder, 2007) and increasingly hospitals and schools, the pricing of carbon markets (MacKenzie, 2009) or the emergence of so-called environmental accounting (Lohmann, 2009) are new instances that illustrate the growing importance of quantification and calculability in the modern world. Espeland and Stevens (1998) use the notion of commensuration to define this form of standardisation whereby different qualities are measured using a single quantitative standard or unit, constituting a common metric that transforms differences into quantity.

There are numerous reasons to attempt commensuration, but it is most often seen as a way to reform institutional systems based on personal relations and local knowledge (Samiolo, 2012), to introduce rationality and what Porter (1996) calls 'mechanical objectivity'. Consequently, for those who benefit from an existing system of authority and see the intrusion of commensuration as threatening the *status quo* (Espeland and Stevens, 1998), there is no shortage of reasons for resisting it. Those whose authority depends on expert judgement, character or informal knowledge are unlikely to welcome rigorous, quantitative and remote methods. These methods replace trust in individuals with trust in numbers (Porter, 1996), constrain discretion and are sometimes perceived as threatening a cherished identity (Espeland, 1998; Lohmann, 2009). All this explains why some actors might implement a variety of strategies in resisting commensuration attempts.

Among these, the creation of what Espeland and Stevens (1998, 2008) describe as *incommensurables* has been widely documented. Incommensurables are things that are defined as so unique that they cannot be expressed in terms of a standardised measure. Espeland (1998) gives the example of the refusal of the Native American Yavapai people to sell their land at any price to government authorities wanting to construct a dam; as the Yavapai perceived it, they were being asked to sell something priceless, namely their own identity. Like commensuration attempts, the creation of incommensurables requires effort. Drawing and defending boundaries, rallying others (experts or public opinion) around an innovative framing and contesting the relevance of commensuration in the name of higher-order values involve complex social processes.

Financial markets seem to be the realm of commensurative practices, where prices are the intensely institutionalised result of commensuration and contribute to constituting what they aim to measure. Cronon (1991, pp. 97–147) and Porter (1996, pp. 45–48) have emphasised how much the grading systems put in place in Chicago's nineteenth-century commodity markets created explicit categories of relative quality, thus making it possible to trade in products that did not yet exist. Futures and derivatives markets (Bryan and Rafferty, 2006) surprise by their capacity both to measure the relative value of various financial instruments and continuously to create new ones based on these relative valuations (Beunza and Stark, 2004) using price mechanisms that have seldom been studied in detail. Recognising that 'commensurative practices are fundamental for making markets' (Levin and Espeland, 2002), especially financial markets, we study the EU's Markets in Financial Instruments Directive (MiFID) project to reform OTC financial markets in Europe and change their commensuration system, focusing on the resistance efforts of the more powerful actors in these markets.

Several authors have emphasised that commensuration is often perceived as transgressing entrenched moral boundaries, leading to uneasy encounters between irreconcilable moral worldviews (Espeland and Stevens, 1998; Quinn, 2008; Zelizer, 1979). In this chapter, we hope to contribute to the understanding of commensuration contests where there are no obvious moral or existential identity conflicts.

Research context

The setting of our study is OTC financial markets, examined in the light of proposed regulatory change. OTC markets cover all transactions in financial instruments that occur off-exchange and involve direct agreement between two parties – generally banks – that do not usually make the price of the transaction public. OTC trading allows for considerable freedom in the design of contracts and is of special interest to parties looking for customised instruments to hedge or invest. OTC markets have high concentration and are dominated by large investment banks.

The proposed regulatory change

Among the most obvious issues revealed by the last financial crisis was the lack of knowledge of basic OTC market features, such as their size, the exact number and nature of players, the number of transactions involved, their prices and the liquidity of the products traded. This may explain why, in a collective move, regulators on both sides of the Atlantic have adopted an approach favouring displacement of as many OTC transactions as possible to organised markets. The September 2009 G20 summit explicitly stated: 'All standardised OTC derivative contracts should be traded on exchanges or electronic trading platforms, *where appropriate*, [our italics] and cleared through central counterparties by end-2012 at the latest.' Seen as a means 'to tackle less regulated or more opaque parts of the financial system and to improve the organisation, transparency and oversight of all market segments', the philosophy of the new regulations will be implemented through the Dodd Frank Act in the US. In Europe, the project has been developed mostly through MiFID 2.

The regulators plan to create specific platforms called Organised Trading Facilities (OTFs) in the European Commission Proposal and the transparency requirements applicable to these facilities are central to the debate between regulators and the industry. While post-trade transparency at first entailed limited debate, pre-trade transparency soon became the 'hot topic'. The MiFID proposal is that each venue 'would be required to make its quote both in terms of price and volume available to the public'. Opponents of over-stringent regulation, meanwhile, plead for as much flexibility as possible in the transparency regime that will be applied to the imminent electronic trading facilities.

Financial reform as a change in the commensuration system

The transformation proposed by the regulators is revolutionary. It amounts to converting bilateral, concentrated and non-transparent financial markets into a modern electronic form of Walrasian market where transactions are organised on a multilateral and transparent basis – numerous potential sellers facing numerous potential buyers in an auction where prices are public information. Before reform, regulators had no real-time information whatsoever on transaction prices and a buyer had to ask a series of brokers about potential prices, ignorant of the context in which his/her request would be treated. In post-reform markets, prices will be common knowledge, readily available to regulators as well as potential buyers, allowing free competition between buyers and sellers to play its part fully in price-setting. This intention builds implicitly on the financial theory of market efficiency, also known as the efficient market hypothesis (EMH). Transparency enjoys the positive status of a virtue in this paradigm, as it is *the* prerequisite for market efficiency. The large scale of the proposed change is due to the huge size of these OTC markets. The total *notional amounts outstanding*[2] of OTC derivatives stood at \$632 trillion at the end of December 2012. Experts from the TABB Group[3] suggest that 'as much as \$40 billion of annual revenues (excluding credit derivatives) [are] at stake in global OTC derivatives for the 20 largest broker dealers', mostly large investment banks. They point out that the proposed reform is likely to entail compressed margins and reduced profitability for major players. Unsurprisingly, the industry's reaction has been to resist these regulatory projects.

In sum, in proposing a new kind of price mechanism inspired by EMH, the regulators intend to make a radical change in the form of OTC financial markets. The new price mechanism now proposed will allow more surveillance by regulators, who seem willing to assume a disciplinary role in the aftermath of the recent financial crisis. It will constrain the discretion of large brokers in pricing deals and promote increased impersonality in transactions. This regulatory initiative can thus be interpreted as an attempt to change the core (prices) of the commensuration system governing OTC markets.

Methods

Our research is based on a qualitative case study.

We used several sources of empirical evidence, mainly textual, which can be divided into three main categories: archive material, press articles and MiFID consultation (Appendix). We analysed contributions to the public consultation organised by the European Commission (8 December 2010–2 February 2011). The purpose of the consultation was 'to consult market participants, regulators and other stakeholders on possible changes to the regulatory framework established by MiFID in the field of investment services and activities as well as markets in financial instruments'. Informal discussions with an International Swap and Derivatives Association (ISDA) member and an MEP's assistant also helped us understand their respective views of progress in the MiFID legislative process.

Our analysis was conducted in several stages. Starting with the press articles, we first arranged the data in order to identify the main actors and events in OTC markets between 2008 and 2011. We then focused on an initial set of narratives from the MiFID consultation, subsequent ISDA comments on MiFID and articles published on TabbFORUM.[4] We coded each text independently for words, phrases, terms or descriptions offered by narratives. These elements constituted first-order codes.

The next step of our analysis involved looking for links between first-order codes so that we could collapse these into theoretically distinct clusters, or second-order themes (Dacin et al., 2010, p. 1401). The final step involved organising the second-order themes into the overarching dimensions that underpinned our theorising. Two dimensions emerged. The first was 'Defining market nature' (in terms of market structure specificity and theory of the market); the second focused on 'Betting on the naturalisation of practices'.

Findings

When we first began analysing the contributions to the December 2010 MiFID consultation, we saw no apparent dissent among the actors; banks, bank associations, hedge funds, financial services providers or corporates all seemed to subscribe to general criticism of the proposed regulation, describing it as useless, ill-suited, difficult to enforce and potentially detrimental to the functioning of financial markets. The more developed and articulate answers, however, came from banks and bankers' associations, which is no surprise, given their concentration in OTC markets and the vested interest at stake (Huault and Rainelli, 2009). We concentrated our analysis on the responses of these powerful actors and observed that they anticipated the likely outcomes of the proposed reform to be lack of innovation, drying-up of liquidity in a period of market stress, increased costs for market participants and risk mismatches or increased exposure of retail investors to market risks. Further analysis soon revealed one major feature of interest. The issue of price mechanism seemed to play a major role in the debate. Incumbent banks contested the reforming of this mechanism along two main dimensions, defining market nature and betting on the naturalisation of practices.

Invoking market 'nature' in order to create incommensurables

Our analysis of the answers to the MiFID consultation suggests that market actors often refer to the market 'nature' of OTC markets, in terms of the structure of the market and how it should work.

Describing the specificity of market structure. Incumbent banks describe OTC markets as a specific species of market, the nature of which is insufficiently understood and not taken into account by the regulators. One of the strongest attacks on the spirit of the reform is the ISDA's defence, that a price on OTC trading markets is not the same as a price on organised markets. Contesting the term 'quote' used in the proposed legislation, the ISDA proposes that the price of OTC derivatives should be seen as a price for a 'solution' that can 'take weeks, if not months to finalise' and is therefore impossible to make public immediately. There will be 'by definition no benchmark price' for highly bespoke products and apparently identical products will differ in price according to the 'perceived creditworthiness of the counterparty'. The ISDA and major banks contend that a price on OTC markets 'will always reflect the situation at the time it is made and therefore will not necessarily be comparable'. This amounts to rejecting the very premise of the proposed price mechanism. Maintaining that prices are not comparable represents clear resistance to commensuration, which presupposes that idiosyncratic values can be expressed in standardised ways.

Envisioning a theory of the market: how the market should work. While the systematic resistance of major investment banks to any change in the *status quo* is not surprising, a close analysis of responses to the MiFID 2 consultation reveals an unexpected argument additional to those already mentioned. In blatant contradiction of the traditional EMH, in which financial markets ideally and unequivocally belong to the typical Walrasian auction model, opponents of the new price mechanism develop a particular theory of the market and how it should function. First, they have no hesitation in denying the virtues of transparency by highlighting how it plays against efficiency. Second, they query the motives and incentives for trading on specific OTC markets.

One commentator, while acknowledging the traditional EMH vision of the benefits of transparency, somewhat daringly challenges the universality of the theory to suggest that there are products and markets where it does not apply:

> In general terms, transparency in markets can help to build confidence, by ensuring that participants have access to information. However, there are products and markets, which are so illiquid, that revealing trade information could actually be detrimental to buyers and sellers. We have to balance the benefits of transparency versus the potential downsides.
>
> *(Citi – MiFID consultation)*

Many respondents to the consultation develop further unorthodox theories, building on the same idea. Mandatory transparency imposed on OTC markets is likely to entail a reduction of liquidity, which in turn will impair the 'sought-after price transparency'. This runs contrary to the EMH notion that transparency, especially pre-trade price transparency, is a condition for market liquidity, which in turn conditions market efficiency.

Market actors repeatedly express concern that there could be 'a disincentive for liquidity providers to publish prices'. This amounts to saying that a certain degree of opacity is necessary on OTC markets if some participants, such as 'liquidity providers', are to have incentives to trade. The clients' interests are also invoked to emphasise the specific nature of OTC markets. On such markets, transparency could prevent clients from keeping their market position secret and possibly 'breach client confidentiality'. Only a certain degree of opacity seems to provide participants with incentives to trade, thus producing some liquidity (although apparently not much, according to the argument above) and insuring a kind of market efficiency.

In sum, our first finding is that, in their attempts to resist the price mechanism proposed by regulatory bodies, markets actors reveal a certain definition and meaning of the market, whereby they highlight their representation of the market structure and their own theory of the market. OTC markets, they assert, must be understood differently from more traditional financial markets. They have their own irreducible 'nature', with a specific market structure: an individual price discovery mechanism and a liquidity that is distinct from the liquidity on standard markets. Overall, the strategy of large international banks can be interpreted as the defence of the idiosyncrasy of OTC markets and their incommensurability with other markets.

Betting on the naturalisation of practices

In this section, we elaborate on actors' strategy of betting on the naturalisation of practices in their struggle against the evolution of the commensuration system.

Invoking a Darwinian argument. The issue of the market form is developed in responses to the consultation that resort to a kind of Darwinian argument, according to which the current market form has emerged naturally and survived because it fits best the interest of 'clients' or 'customers':

> There have not been, to the best of our knowledge, any serious academic studies demonstrating that the transposition of the equity model to OTC derivative products will be economically more efficient and adapted to clients' needs than the current trading model.
>
> *(BNP-Paribas – MiFID consultation)*

Regulation is rejected as detrimental to the harmonious development of means of meeting investors' demands: transforming OTC markets into organised markets will 'reduc[e] consumer choice'. According to this line of argument, clients badly want the confidentiality provided by bilateral trading or customisability. The reform is criticised for not respecting the 'natural' emergence of the kind of market that fits these demands:

> OTC markets provide for bespoke risk management. As long as regulators are provided with the transparency they need [...] and removal of systemic risk then there would appear to be no reason to change the OTC nature of the product, or the trading venues where deals are executed.
>
> *(Deutsche Bank – MiFID consultation)*

Disputing the feasibility of the practices involved in the reform. This involves challenging the criteria defining which financial instruments will be eligible for moving from trading OTC to electronic venues. The principle of the MiFID 2 proposal is that once it is adopted, all 'eligible' OTC derivatives should move to organised platforms and be cleared through a clearing-house. This should take place, 'where appropriate', 'when a market in a market derivative is suitably developed' and it should concern all 'standardised OTC derivatives'. As all these expressions require further definition, the major industry players devote significant amounts of space in their consultation responses to contesting the definitions and categories proposed by the regulators. Most of their effort goes into presenting the practices needed to implement the reform as not operational, impossible to apply and unachievable. For example, the ISDA discusses at some length the difficulty of defining which OTC products would be 'suitable' or 'eligible' for specific items of regulation. It insists that suitability for trading on an electronic venue should be defined independently from the suitability for central clearing. This supports the theme that it will be very difficult if not impossible to implement the commensurative practice of technically defining which financial products will remain traded on pure OTC markets and which will move to a platform. The regulator proposes that standardisation is a suitable criterion for deciding whether a product should move from OTC to electronic trading. Opponents of the reform insist that standardisation is 'not always appropriate' and in practice very difficult to define. Liquidity is not considered any better a criterion, because it 'would be difficult to administer in practice'. The ISDA repeatedly warns regulators that including a liquidity threshold in the assessment of whether a product should be traded on a venue will be fraught with difficulties.

The argument that complexity is an equally irrelevant criterion is emphasised several times in responses from the ISDA, BBA and other investment banks:

> A false link is sometimes made between product complexity and product risk, which leads to the illusion that complex instruments are automatically high-risk instruments.

The same example, described at length in many banks' responses, is intended to demonstrate how product complexity in OTC derivatives markets often results from products being designed to reduce risks for the customer. This means that it is not possible to identify in advance products that warrant regulatory treatment because of their supposed complexity.

Overall, these arguments set out to undermine the feasibility of the commensurative practices required to implement the proposed legislation. Opponents attempt to convey that the commensuration system proposed by regulators does not fit OTC products. If standard-isation, liquidity or complexity cannot be adequately measured on OTC markets, if they do not exist in OTC markets in ways that are comparable to organised markets, then the trans-formation intended by the regulator is not only potentially detrimental – it also becomes unachievable. The struggle over the change in the pricing mechanism that we observe in responses to the consultation thus goes well beyond the technical debate it appears to be. At stake is nothing less than the preservation of the discretion of elite financial institutions and by extension the entire possibility of reform and regulation.

Our results highlight the challenges the regulator faces in attempting to change a price mechanism and the potential effort required to enable the commensuration system to evolve. Our findings show that the regulator runs up against a network of interests, with their specific definition of the market 'nature' and a commitment to reified practices. Changing the commensuration system would involve changing not only the representation of the market and the norm of an efficient market, but also undermining taken-for-granted practices, which might depend on how the market economy is reified in practice.

Discussion

In this chapter we have focused on the change in the pricing mechanism involved in a regulation project concerning financial OTC markets in Europe. We envisage the pricing mechanism that existed in these markets before reform as a specific commensuration system and represent the proposed change as a change in commensuration form. This allows us to examine the resistance to the reform exhibited by elite financial institutions as an instance of resistance to a commensuration attempt. Our empirical setting allowed us to gain insight into the commensuration processes implemented in markets, which have previously received much less attention than contexts involving more spectacular identity and moral conflicts.

Crafting market institutions and degrees of commensuration

We observe that resistance to the reform takes the form of resistance to a commensuration change that will reduce the discretion of elite financial institutions in structuring and pric-ing financial deals. We identify two channels of resistance. First, large international banks try to oppose the reform by constructing and defending the idiosyncrasy of OTC markets, a strategy Espeland (1998) and Espeland and Stevens (1998) describe as the creation of incom-mensurables. To convince the regulator, institutions opposing the regulation define what they perceive to be the market nature and sketch a theory, almost a model of how OTC markets should work. In doing so, they reveal the part played by what we call 'market craft-ing' in legitimising market infrastructures, functioning and, ultimately, prices as reliable measures of value. Second, market actors engage in resistance activities, trying to influence market practices in various ways. They naturalise the commensuration practices existing on the markets before the reform by contending that these practices result from a demand from end-users. This strategy can be understood as a way of institutionalising the functioning of the pre-reform OTC markets by reifying the market economy through practices.

Two main results emerge from this evidence. First, market crafting plays a pivotal, though usually invisible, role in making a price a legitimate instance of valuation in markets. According to our evidence, this crafting of market institutions relies on the theorisation of the market on the one hand, and naturalising practices on the other (see also, Rainelli-Weiss and Huault, 2016). Second, our work innovatively emphasises the existence of degrees of commensuration in markets. Before the proposed reform, there was a commensuration system that allowed market actors to recognise market prices as legitimate and to trade according to them. The proposed reform reveals that this original form of commensuration relies on the high degree of discretion of elite financial institutions; allows idiosyncrasies; and does not achieve the degree of impersonality we take for granted, especially in financial markets.

The creation of incommensurables and the naturalisation of practices

The literature has previously emphasised the role played by identity issues in commensuration contests. Lohmann (2009) shows how contingent valuation targets seem unwilling to be framed as 'quasi-consumers', instead demanding to be treated as 'citizens'. Samiolo (2012), examining the long-debated scheme for flood protection in Venice, evidences the importance of Venice's perception of its own identity in its rejection of commensuration forms involving impersonal, 'hypothetical' modelling. These are just two instances of the process masterfully depicted by Espeland (1998) in her account of the Yavapais' refusals to sell their land. It is, however, something of a surprise to find an echo of this process in financial markets. Although no historical, widely acknowledged or pre-existing existential, if not sacred, identity is at stake, we observe some tentative 'identity building' (our markets versus other market forms) in our context. This result supports the generalisability of the strategy of creating incommensurables to resist commensuration attempts.

However, we find no trace of moral contest in our evidence. The type of commensuration attempt we deal with does not seem to transgress deeply moral boundaries (Espeland and Stevens, 1998), a feature it shares with the situations described, for example, in Samiolo (2012) or Espeland and Sauder (2007). Acknowledging the fact that commensuration attempts often result in the encounter of irreconcilable moral worldviews (see, for example, Espeland, 1998; Fourcade, 2011; Lohmann, 2009; Quinn, 2008; Zelizer, 1979), we interpret the fact that this is not always the case as a sign that the instrumentation of identity forms is probably more universal than that of moral issues in the construction of incommensurables.

The existing literature has shown how crucial practice adoption is in explaining the success or failure of commensuration attempts. Commensurating housework with paid labour failed to become incorporated in practices and so failed altogether, despite repeated attempts (Espeland and Stevens, 1998). Efforts to build reporting mechanisms for greenhouse gases and, specifically, carbon disclosure have run into the difficulty of measuring variables of interests with precision, resulting in the relative failure of carbon disclosure as a project of commensuration (Kolk et al., 2008). Conversely, the ranking of law schools was highly appreciated, leading to the rapid adoption of a commensurative practice that deans, who had strongly resented the ranking, referring to it as 'Mickey Mouse' or 'idiot polls', soon had to take seriously (Espeland and Sauder, 2007). Practice adoption contributes so strongly to commensuration processes that the opposition efforts of the large investment banks trying to avoid reform – naturalising existing practices while attempting to make the proposed practices look impractical – seem well placed. The strength of the resistance process probably has much to do with the pace and extent of the adoption of the practices proposed by the regulator.

To conclude, we show that commensuration requires enormous work even on markets, where it would seem more taken for granted than anywhere else. Denaturalising prices, we demonstrate that the absence of obvious conflicts of moral values or individual identities found in other commensuration contests (Espeland, 1998; Lohmann, 2009) does not prevent actors from resisting some forms of commensuration while supporting others. This makes the creation of a particular market form a complex and labour-intensive social process. We believe this result is important, as disregarding this process may be detrimental to market stakeholders, e.g. states or regulators, that are not direct market participants. It may prevent them from addressing efficiently the issues they are accountable for to constituencies that might differ from the ones market participants are accountable to. The assumption that 'mechanical objectivity' is a given of any market risks ignoring where the discretion in organising the market and eventually setting market prices lies. In regulation processes, it also risks overlooking the likelihood of resistance to changes in the market form and the potential channels markets to which actors might resort in organising resistance.

Finally, we believe our findings provide some insights into the potential trajectory of commensuration contests in general. Namely, a factor that we do not document but that is repeatedly emphasised as crucial in the commensuration literature is the need for large bureaucracies and well-trained labour forces to engage in commensuration for it to succeed. Bourguet's (1988) investigation of the failed census conducted by the French Bureau de Statistique in 1800 shows the consequences of being unable to rely on such a strength in the process (see also Desrosières, 2002; Levin and Espeland, 2002). This allows us to consider the financial reform we studied with some scepticism, as the political muscle and labour resources of European regulators are notoriously weak.

Appendix

TABLE 7.1 Details of data collection

Source of data	Type of data	Use in the analysis
Archive materials	Official documents published by national and transnational organisations: • Bank for International Settlements, statistics 2011 • Studies by the International Organisation of Securities Commissions (IOSCO), e.g. Report on trading of OTC derivatives, February 2011 Information, texts, industry publications and discourses from: • International Swaps and Derivatives Association (ISDA) website (e.g. ISDA paper, MIFID/MIFIR and transparency for OTC derivatives, February 15, 2012) • Tabbgroup and Tabbgroup's TabbFORUM	Understand the context of the OTC market context Confirm the main events Provide first textual accounts of debates and discussions

Source of data	Type of data	Use in the analysis
MiFID consultation 8 December 2001–2 February 2011	Text of MiFID 2	Understand the motives of the proposed regulation
	279 publicly available responses were analysed	Analyse the justifications and the arguments of the industry opposing the new regulation
Completed by interviews	Interviews with an ISDA member and an MEP's assistant	Triangulate facts and analysis, enhance validity of insights and understand respective views of progress in the MiFID legislative process
Press articles	Factiva (2008–11): 150 articles analysed for key words: 'OTC markets' and 'regulation'	Retrace main events (see Appendix 3)
		Contextualise the analysis in terms of the evolution of the financial industry

Notes

1 Over-the-counter (OTC) markets are financial markets organised around OTC trading. OTC trading is sometimes called off-exchange trading as it occurs directly between two parties, without any intervention of an exchange. OTC trading is significant in some asset classes, such as interest rate, foreign exchange, equities and commodities, but can occur with any financial instruments. OTC trading allows for considerable freedom in the design of financial contracts and the main characteristics of OTC transactions are to be bespoke and bilateral. In OTC markets, prices are normally not made public information.
2 Bank for International Settlements Statistics, 2011.
3 Founded in 2003, TABB Group is a financial market research and strategic advisory firm focused on capital markets. Its goal is to help 'financial actors to gain an understanding of financial markets issues and trends'. Its services are offered through research, consulting and TabbFORUM. It frequently publishes commentaries on current events in the industry.
4 TabbFORUM is a discussion forum for the financial industry, where major financial actors publish their ideas about what is happening in the marketplace and their opinions about the impact of new events, such as regulation, on the industry. It is a relevant source of data for this study, since it reflects major financial actors' main discourses and justifications.

References

Beunza, D. and Stark, D. (2004). Tools of the trade: The socio-technology of arbitrage in a Wall Street trading room. *Industrial and Corporate Change*, 13(2), 369–400.

Bourguet, M. N. (1988). *Déchiffrer la France: la statistique départementale à l'époque napoléonienne*. Paris: Editions des Archives Contemporaines.

Bryan, D. and Rafferty, M. (2006). *Capitalism with derivatives. A political economy of financial derivatives*. Basingstoke: Palgrave McMillan.

Cronon, W. (1991). *Nature's metropolis*. New York: W.W. Norton.

Dacin, M.T., Munir, K. and Tracey, P. (2010). Formal dining at Cambridge colleges: Linking ritual performance and institutional maintenance. *Academy of Management Journal*, 53(6), 1393–1418.

Desrosières, A. (2002). *The politics of large numbers: A study of statistical thinking*, Cambridge: Harvard University Press.

Espeland, W. (1998). *The struggle for water*. Chicago: University of Chicago Press.

Espeland, W. and Sauder, M. (2007). Rankings and reactivity: How public measures recreate social worlds. *American journal of sociology*, 113(1), 1–40.

Espeland, W. and Stevens, M. (1998). Commensuration as a social process. *Annual Review of Sociology*, 24, 312–343.

Espeland, W. and Stevens, M. (2008). A sociology of quantification. *European Journal of Sociology*, 49(3), 401–436.

Fourcade, M. (2011). Cents and sensibility: Economic valuation and the nature of 'nature'. *American Journal of Sociology*, 116(6), 1721–1777.

Huault, I. and Rainelli, H. (2009). Market shaping as an answer to ambiguities. The case of credit derivatives. *Organisation Studies*, 30(5), 549–575.

Huault, I. and Rainelli, H. (2011). A market for weather risk. Conflicting metrics, attempts at compromise and limits to commensuration. *Organisation Studies*, 32(10), 1395–1419.

Kolk, A., Levy, D. and Pinkse, J. (2008). Corporate responses in an emerging climate regime: the institutionalisation and commensuration of carbon disclosure. *European Accounting Review*, 17(4), 719–745.

Levin, P. and Espeland, W. (2002). Commensuration, commodification and the market for air. In A. Hoffman and M. Ventresca (Eds.), *Organisations, Policy and the Natural Environment* (pp. 119–147). Palo Alto: Stanford University Press.

Lohmann, L. (2009). Toward a different debate in environmental accounting: The cases of carbon and cost-benefit. *Accounting, Organisations and Society*, 34(3/4), 499–534.

MacKenzie, D. (2009). Making things the same: Gases, emission rights and the politics of carbon markets. *Accounting, Organisations and Society*, 34(3/4), 440–455.

Porter, T. M. (1996). *Trust in numbers: The pursuit of objectivity in science and public life.* Princeton: Princeton University Press.

Quinn, S. (2008). The transformation of morals in markets: Death, benefits, and the exchange of life insurance policies. *American Journal of Sociology*, 114(3), 738–780.

Rainelli-Weiss, H. and Huault, I. (2016). Business as usual in financial markets? The creation of incommensurables as institutional maintenance work. *Organization Studies*, 37(7), 991–1015.

Samiolo, R. (2012). Commensuration and styles of reasoning: Venice, cost–benefit, and the defence of place. *Accounting, Organisations and Society*, 37(6), 382–402.

Zelizer, V. (1979). *Morals and markets. The development of life insurance in the US.* New York: Columbia University Press.

8

THE LEPTOKURTIC CRISIS AND THE DISCONTINUOUS TURN IN FINANCIAL MODELLING

Christian Walter

Introduction

Heterodox economics has, since its inception, stressed the extreme importance of financial crises to understand the nature of finance.[1] Both the French school of regulation and the economics of conventions sought to leave the framework of analysis imposed by the dominant paradigm of neoclassical finance, that of the all-powerful exchange in a financial world without crises.

In a completely different way, Benoît Mandelbrot emphasised the fundamental role of financial crises in his work on the mathematical modelling of stock market dynamics with fractals, a new approach which characterised heterodox modelling in financial economics. Initially, heterodox economics and fractals were unaware of each other, while each in its own discipline sought to propose another paradigm for finance. Heterodox economics and heterodox modelling seemed to await a new mathematical tool for rebuilding finance on new foundations. The first works that aimed to bridge the gap between these two attempts at rebuilding finance on alternative bases date back to the early 1990s. These works tried to establish a link between the approach of heterodox economics and the Mandelbrot approach, showing how fractals could both adequately describe the phenomenon of crises and allow the search for building an alternative finance. The beginnings of econophysics, for example the winter session of Les Houches School of physics in 1998, established the fertility of the fractal approach in this perspective.

Following Mandelbrot's intuitions, the alternative way of modelling risks (the 'fractal modelling') used other processes than the Brownian motion of the dominant paradigm of neoclassical finance, in particular with non-Brownian stochastic processes. These works challenged the mainstream view of finance by using an internalist approach, whereas other works challenged the mainstream view by using an externalist approach. Heterodox modelling and heterodox economics were in line with their objective: a critical posture of the neoclassical finance arising from orthodox financial theory. The heterodox modelling challenged a very particular and counter-intuitive representation of the dominant paradigm of neoclassical finance: the continuity of stock market fluctuations. With this continuity assumption, whose mathematical financial translation is the Brownian representation of market dynamics, finance refrained from thinking about crises. This finance 'empty of crisis' has produced the illusion of a taming of the risks: one understands now how this illusion was associated with the continuity assumption.

In this chapter, I focus on one aspect of these debates that seems crucial to me: the 'leptokurtic crisis' and its consequences in challenging the dominant paradigm of neoclassical finance. The observed behaviour of markets exhibits a specific feature: empirical distributions of returns are *leptokurtic*. The word *leptokurtic* comes from the Greek words *leptos*, peaked, and *kurtosis*, curvature. That means that the empirical distributions are more peaked than the Gaussian bell, the theoretical distribution expected in the Brownian representation. Instead of that, the empirical distributions exhibit fat tails and values clustered around the mean, with the result that extreme events like financial crises are more likely than under a Gaussian distribution. 'Leptokurtic crisis' is the name I give (Walter, 2002a) to the crisis opened by Benoît Mandelbrot in a series of contributions (Mandelbrot, 1962, 1963, 1967)[2] which introduce the Lévy stable processes to solve the leptokurtic puzzle. The term 'crisis' is chosen in reference to Kuhn's *The Structure of Scientific Revolutions* (1962). In Kuhn's words, 'confronted with anomaly or with crisis, scientists take a different attitude towards existing paradigms' (Kuhn, 1962, p. 91). In fact, the Mandelbrot papers exploded the field of financial modelling and launched violent controversies dividing the community of finance academics into two opposite camps: pros and cons of the discontinuity. The crisis started the quest for refinements of the Brownian representation: that is, for new models that could solve the leptokurtic problem with saving the 'mild randomness' assumption of Brownian motion.

Two distinct research programmes were currently established in financial modelling to tackle the leptokurtic issue: the first Mandelbrot programme based on stable Lévy processes and the alternative non-stable Lévy processes approach based on Merton's view. I named (Walter, 2017) these two programmes: the radical programme (RP) and the pragmatic programme (PP). During more than thirty years, these two programmes were incompatible in the sense that Mandelbrot and its opponents speak from 'incommensurable' viewpoints in Kuhn's words. There was no 'neutral statistical test' for model-choice. The RP initiated huge controversies in the financial academic field because of the infinite variance of the stable hypothesis. The PP began in the 1970s with explicitly renouncing the stable hypothesis. But the Lévy processes with finite activity and finite variation appeared too restrictive to solve the leptokurtic crisis. In the 1990s a new competitor appeared, called the econophysics programme (EP). To untangle these threads and to enlighten the issues, I use the Sato classification to describe the competitive programmes. Although the PP and the EP can be traced through separate lines in the academic fields, they shared the use of tempered stable processes and derive from their reliance on Mandelbrot's view. To conclude with a perspective on the history of financial thought, I argue that, for solving the leptokurtic problem, Mandelbrot introduced what I name the 'discontinuous turn' in financial modelling.

Two competitive representations of financial uncertainty

I have argued elsewhere that some of the key differences between the competitive representations of financial uncertainty can be illuminated by reference to a familiar debate in philosophy over the principle of continuity. Although this philosophical debate may seem to be a scholastic preoccupation within a tight circle of specialists in the philosophy of science, far from the financial stakes of modelling and with no impact on concrete financial practices, I have argued on the contrary that the divergent positions about the mind-set behind the price changes implicate entirely different views of what is important to capture and how to model it. Let us emphasise this point.

There are two fundamentally different ways of viewing price changes in finance. One assumes the principle of continuity, the other doesn't. According to the first view, price movements are modelled by continuous diffusion processes, whose canonical form is the famous Brownian motion. According to the other view, price movements are modelled by discontinuous processes, as for instance Lévy processes.

In physics, the principle of continuity states that change is continuous rather than discrete. Leibniz and Newton, the inventors of differential calculus, said '*Natura non facit saltus*' (nature does not make leaps). This same principle underpinned the thoughts of Linné on the classification of species and later Charles Darwin's theory of evolution (1859). In 1890, Alfred Marshall's *Principles of Economics* assumed the principle of continuity, allowing the use of infinitesimal calculus in economics and the subsequent development of neoclassical economic theory. As noticed by Norbert Wiener, 'just as primitive peoples adopt the Western modes of denationationalized clothing and of parliamentarism out of a vague feeling that these magic rites and vestments will at once put them abreast of modern culture and technique, so the economists have developed the habit of dressing up their rather imprecise ideas *in the language of the infinitesimal calculus*' (Wiener, 1966, p. 90, our italics).

Modern financial theory grew out of neoclassical economics and naturally assumes the same principle of continuity. One of the great success stories of neoclassical finance was the valuation of derivatives with the replicating portfolio technique and the risk-neutral approach. Examples include the 1973 formulas of Fisher Black, Myron Scholes, and Robert Merton for valuing options and the subsequent fundamental theorem of asset pricing that emerged from the work of Michael Harrison, Daniel Kreps, and Stanley Pliska between 1979 and 1981. As MacKenzie and Spears (2014, p. 401) put it: 'it is the strategy of Black-Scholes modelling writ large: find a perfect hedge, a *continuously-adjusted portfolio* of more basic securities that will have the same payoff as the derivative, whatever happens to the price of the underlying asset' (our italics); which means that the continuity principle is at the core of the 'market-consistent convention'. This specific convention is the 'quantification convention' of the dominant paradigm of neoclassical finance, which defines the neoclassical financiers' metrology (Chiapello and Walter, 2016). In fact, the twin pillars of neoclassical finance are efficient markets and the theory of asset pricing with no arbitrage. The way probability theory and economics were linked together to create these twin pillars exhibits the strong role of continuity (Walter, 1996). In fact, these twin pillars rest on the principle of continuity.

Following the mathematical breakthrough of Black, Scholes, Merton, Ross, Harrison, Kreps and Pliska, and despite the repeated financial crises following the 1987 stock market crash, neoclassical finance reaffirmed the principle of continuity. This principle was still predominant in the 1990s despite the emerging evidence of extreme values in the tails of empirical distributions. At the end of the century, many financial techniques such as portfolio insurance or the calculation of capital requirements in the insurance industry still assumed that (financial) nature does not make jumps and therefore promoted continuity. Despite many empirical difficulties arising with attempts to use it practically, and despite academic warnings coming from outside neoclassical finance, the principle of continuity remained vastly more popular than its discontinuous competitors.

One of the cognitive consequences of the continuity principle is a negative spill over about the extreme value issue: the truncation of financial time series into two market regimes. On the one hand, the 'normal' periods, corresponding to the supposed continuous market; on the other hand, the periods of 'insanity' where markets are deemed 'irrational' and 'greedy', corresponding to extreme value behaviours. This cleavage (explained continuity + unexplained jumps) leaves financiers unable to explain the transition from one period to another. For example, in an editorial in the *Financial Times* (16 March 2008), Alan Greenspan commented on the financial crisis of 2007–2008 with these words: 'We can never anticipate all discontinuities in financial markets.' For Greenspan, (financial) nature does not make jumps and extreme values are unpredictable outliers. This cognitive bias demonstrates the limits of a continuity-based framework completed with an extreme value approach, and advocates for the need for a global discontinuous framework (Le Courtois and Walter, 2017).

In the twentieth century, both physics and genetics abrogated the principle of continuity. Quantum mechanics postulated discrete energy levels while genetics took discontinuities into account. But economics – including modern financial theory – stood back from this intellectual revolution. As early as 1966, Wiener pointed that 'here *some recent work of Mandelbrot is much to the point*. He has shown the intimate way in which the commodity market is both theoretically and practically subject to random fluctuations arriving from the very contemplation of its own irregularities is something *much wilder and much deeper than has been supposed*, and that the usual approximations to the dynamics of the market must be applied with much caution than has usually been the case, or not at all' (p. 92, our italics).

The leptokurtic phenomenon: the case against neoclassical finance

The concept of 'leptokurtic phenomenon' (Walter, 2002a) has been introduced to suggest that a financial phenomenon has to be explained referred to as an *"explanandum phenomenon"* in Carl Hempel's sense: 'an event occurring at a particular place and time [...] some regularity found' in the markets (Hempel, 1966, p. 50).

The longstanding leptokurtic problem

The leptokurtic problem is not new. What is new is its institutional acknowledgement: it is common knowledge today that non-Gaussian empirical distributions are a 'fact' of the real markets. Yet it took almost forty years for this observable 'fact' to become an observed 'fact', as non-normality entered the field of scientific research. The leptokurtic bell of empirical distributions has long been known in the academic community. As early as the 1950s, empirical studies pointed out the problems of the Brownian representation of market dynamics. But, if statisticians highlighted the leptokurtic phenomenon many times, financial academics did not want to consider it. In 1962, the attempt by Mandelbrot to take explicit account of discontinuities on all scales in stock market prices by building a discontinuous global framework for taking account of financial crises led to the leptokurtic crisis.

Statistical evidence: 'it's full of extreme values!'

Let us pick up four examples of the pervasiveness of the leptokurtic phenomenon in the long term. In a 1953 landmark paper published in the respected *Journal of the Royal Statistical Society*, Maurice Kendall observed of price data between 1883 and 1934 that 'the distributions are accordingly *rather leptokurtic*' (our italics). In 1960, in *Food Research Institute*, Arnold Larson noted that 'examination of the pattern of occurrence of all price changes in excess of three standard deviations from zero [...] indicated [...] presence in the data of an *excessive number of extreme values*' (our italics). In a very important article published in 1961 in the

American Economic Review, Houthakker wrote that 'the distribution of day-to-day changes in the logarithms of prices does not conform to the normal curve. It is [...] *highly leptokurtic*'. The same year in *Industrial Management Review*, Sydney Alexander emphasised pithily that 'a rigorous test [...] would lead to dismiss the hypothesis of normality; this sort of situation (*leptokurtic*) is frequently encountered in economic statistics' (our italics). Many other examples exist in the early literature of market research.

Financial academics denials: 'don't tell me about extreme values!'

Although it has been observed for a long time in the statistical community, the leptokurtic phenomenon was long considered negligible or non-significant in the financial academic community: the 1960s worldview did not include tails in analysis of stock fluctuations. Extreme values were not considered a significant 'fact' for proper understanding of price variations. Some academics even indicated that the tails of distribution should be cut off to remove the extreme values. Financial academics were confronted with anomalies (extreme values) but dismissed the 'facts'; hence the 'facts' quite simply disappeared from the 'data'. For mainstream financial academics, extreme values were considered as '*outliers*', that is, not relevant for modelling. De Bruin and Walter (2017) present and discuss this intriguing episode of history of financial modelling and argue that specific research habits of mainstream had violated epistemic virtues.

Mandelbrot's challenge: 'extreme values are essential!'

The word 'outlier' has a precise technical meaning in statistics: it is an observation that is so very different from the other observations that it may be due to variability of the measurement or it may indicate experimental error like accidental foreign contamination. In his memoirs, Mandelbrot (2013) gives the example of 'astronomical cats': 'A classic example concerns astronomical observations that are contaminated by cats residing in the observatory. Yes, cats walking across the observatory floor shook the telescope a bit, causing some orbits to be miscalculated. For two centuries, economists and statisticians have looked for good ways of preserving real data while eliminating *would-be cats*' (Mandelbrot, 2013, p. 229). According to Mandelbrot, in finance, 'outliers' are not cats but are crucial to enter the puzzle of financial crises: 'the so-called outliers are *essential* in finance. In fact, a common thread of my work is that values far from the norm are the *key* to the underlying phenomenon' (*ibid.*, our italics). In Mandelbrot's view, the distribution (fat) tails are not a refuge for 'outliers' but on the contrary contained important information for correct understanding of the market's dynamics leading to financial crises.

Mandelbrot's intellectual stance thus constituted a radical change in the way of looking at market dynamics. In the dominant paradigm of neoclassical finance based on continuity, only the fluctuations of the means were considered as interesting: on the contrary, Mandelbrot suggested that attention should be paid to fluctuations in extreme values. It represented a huge challenge to the foundations of the dominant paradigm of neoclassical finance. Unlike the continuous representation of this paradigm, Mandelbrot argued that close attention should be paid to the discontinuities. Hence, the profoundness of the leptokurtic crisis came from the angle of Mandelbrot's attack: not only did he emphasise an *empirical inadequacy* of the continuous representation, but also he argued for an *inadequate grounding* of this representation. It was a frontal attack against the dominant paradigm of neoclassical finance.

The leptokurtic crisis: looking for alternative finance

Mandelbrot tackled the leptokurtic phenomenon by driving attention to the cognitive importance of extreme values. He emphasised the necessity of not ignoring the extreme values of the distribution tails by incorporating global discontinuity in the core of the probabilistic model. This challenge to the foundations of the dominant paradigm of neoclassical finance launched the leptokurtic crisis and the heterodox view of finance.

The hinges of the debates

Let us present the terms of the debates resulting from the leptokurtic crisis. First, Brownian motion increments have the important property of being independent and identically distributed (hereafter IID). The processes with IID increments are called Lévy processes after the French mathematician Paul Lévy. Brownian motion is a specific Lévy process: it assumes continuity. Other Lévy processes do not. Hence, a first epistemic choice is the alternative: to retain or not the IID framework.

Second, Brownian motion entails time scaling of distributions in the sense that a given horizon of return distribution is scaled to another with the *square-root-of-time rule* of scaling. This is the *scaling property* of Brownian motion. This scaling property supports the widely used practice to compute the annual volatility from the weekly one: the annual volatility is equal to the weekly volatility multiplied by square root of 52. This scaling property had been called the 'square-root-of-time law' in Jules Regnault's 1863 *Calcul des chances et philosophie de la bourse*. This square-root-or-time rule of scaling is a special case of scaling property of stable distributions. Gaussian distribution is a specific stable distribution: it uses a scaling parameter (characteristic exponent) with a value of 2. Other stable distributions do not. Hence, a second epistemic choice amounts to retaining the stable framework or not.

Third, Brownian motion supports a Gaussian distribution for the marginal distribution of returns. Hence, a third epistemic choice is to retain (or not) the Gaussian framework. The controversies following the leptokurtic crisis became entangled in the intrication of the marginal distribution view (Gaussian or non-Gaussian), the dynamic processual view (IID or non-IID) and the scaling rule view (stable or non-stable). It is worth noting that this intrication was sometimes a source of confusion in the academic literature, some analyses being based on approaches which didn't distinguish between Lévy distributions and Lévy processes. Here the semantics is misleading.

With or without IID

To solve the leptokurtic problem, the first two possible routes are either to remain in the IID framework or to leave the IID framework. If IID is retained, this epistemic choice leads to change the kind of Lévy process. This epistemic choice thus continues to use the Lévy representation of stock market fluctuations, although without the Brownian characteristic that ensures continuity.

Alternatively, if the Gaussian distribution assumption is retained and the IID assumption is dropped, it introduces a form of temporal dependence on successive stock market fluctuations. This epistemic choice is equivalent to focusing on the conditional distributions of stock market fluctuations, i.e. the market memory. Table 8.1 summarises the scaling rules.

TABLE 8.1 Scaling rules as epistemic choices

Increments	Stochastic process	Years	Scaling rule	
Non-I and non-ID			Joint distribution	
I and non-ID	Sato processes	2000s	Convolution product	
IID non-stable	Lévy processes	1990s	Convolution product	
IID alpha-stable	Lévy motion	1962	Fractal invariance	
IID 2-stable	Brownian motion	1900	Fractal invariance	'Square-root-of-time rule' (Regnault, 1863)

Source: Walter (2013)

With or without wild randomness

At this stage, the question arises whether the scaling property assumption should be kept or not. If the scaling property is maintained, stable Lévy processes have to be chosen. Let us consider now the second epistemic choice inside the IID representation.

Moving into the Fourier space, the explicit form of the characteristic exponent of a Lévy process is the Lévy-Khintchine formula which fully defines the process by the following specification:

Characteristic exponent = diffusive component + diffusion coefficient + Lévy measure

In financial words:

Market dynamics = trend of returns + scale of risk + morphology of risk

The scale of risk is the 'volatility' of markets. The role of the Lévy measure is decisive here. It contains all the information needed to characterise the path of the process, apart from its trend and its 'volatility'. It shapes the morphology of uncertainty, its 'roughness'. This morphology can be drawn with the notion of 'states of randomness', a notion introduced by Mandelbrot to describe the level of roughness of the price charts. He introduced a pivotal distinction between two types of randomness named 'mild randomness' and 'wild randomness':

> The traditional Gaussian way of looking at the world begins by focusing on the ordinary and only later deals with exceptions or so-called outliers as ancillaries. But there is also a second way which takes the so-called exceptional as a starting point and deals with the ordinary in a subordinate manner simply because that 'ordinary' is less consequential. These two models correspond to two mutually exclusive types of randomness: mild or Gaussian on the one hand, and wild, fractal or 'scalable power laws' on the other. Measurements that exhibit mild randomness are suitable for treatment by the bell curve or Gaussian models, whereas those that are susceptible to wild randomness can only be expressed accurately using a fractal scale.
>
> *(Mandelbrot and Taleb, 2006)*

In the 1960s two alternatives represented a kind of cardinal choice, in the literal sense of the revolving movement of thought (the word 'cardinal' comes from the Latin *cardo*, meaning the hinge of a door) that is required in response to the leptokurtic phenomenon. This was the hinge of financial modelling, summarised in Table 8.2.

TABLE 8.2 The hinge of epistemic choices in the 1960s, the 1970s and the 1980s

Hinge: choice between	Route 1	WILD randomness	IID with non–Gaussian distributions	Heterodox finance way
	Route 2	MILD randomness	Non-IID with Gaussian distributions	Neoclassical finance way

Source: Walter (2005)

At the end of the 1960s, in the 1970s and the 1980s, the situation resembled that described in Kuhn's analysis: with this pivotal choice, finance academics have 'before [them] a number of competing and incommensurable solutions to these problems, solutions that [they] must ultimately evaluate for [themselves]' (Kuhn, 1962).

The misfortunes of the stable model

Despite the promising results opened up with this new way of making finance, the adventure of fractal modelling in finance did not display a smooth (continuous) history. It was more of an eventful (discontinuous) progression of Mandelbrot's assumptions against the evolution of neoclassical finance over forty years, from 1960 until 2000. The Mandelbrot proposal for making finance with wild randomness was qualified as a 'monster'. The most violent debates were related to the 'scaling' property of stochastic processes and the Paretian tails of the empirical distributions of returns.

Infinite variance: a probability monster

The first and principal problem was that of the moments of distributions. With a Lévy motion, moments can be infinite. The infinity of the second moment (the variance) horrified the American academics of neoclassical finance. The rejection was massive, violent and total. So strong was the opposition to Mandelbrot's hypothesis that any kind of alternative model was preferred to the idea of infinite variance. At this time, Mandelbrot was working at IBM and 'ABM' ('anything but Mandelbrot') became the watchword of the neoclassical finance camp. As Mirowski (1995) observed, 'the economics profession dropped the Mandelbrot hypothesis largely for reasons other than empirical adequacy and concise simplicity. [...] The only purpose of the negative studies was to refute Mandelbrot.'

MacKenzie (2006, p. 105) stressed this point by saying that the financial academic community viewed Mandelbrot's model as a probability 'monster'. According to the old definition of Aristotle, a monster is what deviates from the norm. The norm of the dominant paradigm of neoclassical finance is variance. To imagine that the variance could be infinite was thus to attack frontally one of the pillars of the paradigm of neoclassical finance.

Scalable randomness: scaling anomalies

Underpinned by the desire to reject the infinite variance, the debates shifted to tests of the scaling property of the stable model. The objective was to reject the hypothesis of the infinite variance and since this hypothesis was confused with that of scaling, it was necessary to highlight anomalies in the scaling laws.

A story of this quest was produced with a review of over forty years of research for scaling laws in distributional properties of price variations (Walter, 2002b). This review exhibits a turbulent story with fierce controversies which stirred up the academic community with regard to the scaling/non-scaling debate. It ended with the empirical rejection of the stable model because the scale invariance principle was found too strong for adequately modelling observed price variations. The stable Lévy processes were abandoned. But the question remains of a partial scale invariance over a given frequency range, the breakdown of scaling. This leads us to consider the tails of distribution.

Power laws: a tale of fat tails

The scaling character of price variations was first established through the study of distribution tails, which brought out the connection between the scaling laws and the appropriate treatment of financial crises. The tails appear to be Paretian, which means the distribution of extreme values followed a power law the origin of which dates back to Pareto. When one rewrites the 1962 stable model with the Lévy-Khintchine representation, the Lévy measure exhibits Paretian tails (see details in Walter, 2015, pp. 467–468). This Paretian characteristic is precisely the origin of the non-existence of the variance when the Paretian exponent is less than 2.

To remedy the inconvenience of not having any moments for the stable models of the Mandelbrot programme for rebuilding finance, other models were developed with a truncation principle. In fact, a way of avoiding the problem of infinite variance is to weight the Lévy measure by an exponential quantity in order to reduce large fluctuations and therefore recover the moments. This idea corresponds to a class of Lévy processes whose marginal distributions are truncated stable distributions, so-called 'tempered stable' models. The stable distributions are truncated by exponential functions. The tails of these distributions, tempered by the truncation, are semi-light.

After the leptokurtic crisis: the discontinuous turn

The leptokurtic crisis exploded the field of financial modelling. We conclude this chapter by giving an overview of the posterity of the crisis in the renewal of financial modelling it produced.

The research programmes resulting from the leptokurtic crisis

On the one hand, after the leptokurtic crisis, two competitive programmes for solving the leptokurtic puzzle were launched in financial modelling: the Mandelbrot programme (heterodox) and the financial academics programme (mainstream). Both programmes investigated the ability of Lévy processes to capture the extreme values of price changes. On the other hand, physicists entered the race in the 1990s by tackling the question of scaling laws. Hence, in the 1990s, research in financial modelling split into two separate communities: that of financial academics and that of physicists.

The pragmatic programme of financial academics: what to do with jumps?

In the 1970s, the mainstream view of price changes made specific assumptions to defend the mathematical tractability of financial modelling based on continuous diffusion models, by using a compound ad hoc approach, which gained high recognition in the 1980s: I term this mainstream strand of research the 'pragmatic programme', to contrast the Mandelbrot program that I call the 'radical programme' (Walter, 2017). The pragmatic programme opened a period of model tinkering in neoclassical finance: a situation in which researchers, confronted with descriptive inadequacy, decide to 'repair' existing models with a new data-driven approach.

This story is characterised by two major stages. First, with the rediscovery of Poisson's law in the late 1960s, a jump component was added to the diffusion process (Brownian motion): this superposition of jump and diffusion processes opened the period of hybrid models known as jump diffusion processes (1970–1990), which state that prices undergo large jumps followed by small continuous movements. These models were initiated by Press in 1967. It is a simple case of Lévy process with finite activity and finite variation in the jump component. This is the first stage of the pragmatic programme. Then, in the second period, the diffusive component was removed leaving only the jump component, moving to Lévy processes keeping finite variation in the jump component but with infinite activity. This is the second stage of the pragmatic programme. The third stage of the pragmatic programme corresponds to the infiniteness of the variation.

The success of the pragmatic programme in the 1990s results from a reorientation of mathematical financial research due to European academics who put forward the fruitfulness of infinite activity of the Lévy processes in case of pure jumps models. At the time mathematical financial academics moved to the development of Lévy processes, physicists launched their new strand of research, addressing the scaling properties of tails.

The econophysics programme of physicists: what to do with scales?

In the 1990s, physicists began to propose models combining truncated stable distributions with exponential tails Bouchaud and Potters, 2003; Koponen, 1995; Mantegna and Stanley, 2000) and physicist research activity enters the financial modelling field. As Mantegna and Stanley (2000) noticed, 'since 1990, a research community has begun to emerge'. This new community baptised itself with the name 'econophysics'. Physicists continued along the way paved by Mandelbrot's model, working in particular with the scaling concept: as Mantegna and Stanley (2000) pointed out, financial academics were 'trying to determine a characteristic scale for a problem that has no characteristic scale'. This is the 'econophysics programme'.

Sato's classification

Now one turns to the disentanglement of the multiple research programmes resulting from the leptokurtic crisis. A convenient way to navigate the paths of financial modelling after the crisis is to return to Sato's classification. For shaping a Lévy process, either the activity is finite or infinite, or the variation is finite or infinite. The Sato (1999) classification defines a process by its pair (activity, variation) according to the double criterion finite or infinite. The models of the late 1990s and early 2000s used processes with infinite activity and infinite variation but with finite variance. In contrast to these pragmatic programmes, the radical programme proposed by Mandelbrot in 1962 had both infinite activity, infinite variation in the jump component and infinite variance. It was – for this reason – a complete heterodox view.

Table 8.3 exhibits the Lévy processes in financial modelling following this double criterion, the variation being that of the jump part of the stochastic process. The variance criterion was added in the table because the infinite activity case is itself divided into two subgroups, that of the pragmatic approach in which the variance is finite, and the radical approach (Mandelbrot's view) in which the variance is infinite. It appears that there are four types of stochastic processes depending on whether their activity and their variation are finite or infinite, and whether variance is finite or infinite.

Mandelbrot's legacy: the discontinuous turn in financial modelling

The Mandelbrot programme contributed to a better understanding of the radical discontinuous nature of price change, but the community of financial academics did not accept the first Mandelbrot models initially based on stable motions. The pragmatic programme succeeded in filling the gaps in the continuous representation of the dominant paradigm without losing the variance that was important for this paradigm. In the 1990s, pure jumps processes became the new way of modelling the discontinuities in mathematical finance.

But the Variance Gamma model of Madan, Carr and Chang and the CGMY model of Carr, Geman, Madan and Yor are special cases of the Koponen model.[3] Here there is

TABLE 8.3 Sato's classification and the research programmes after the leptokurtic crisis

Sato's pair			Examples of models in financial modelling	Research programmes
Activity	Variation	Variance		
Finite	Finite	Finite	Press (1967), Merton (1976), Cox and Ross (1976)	Pragmatic stage 1
Infinite	Finite	Finite	Madan and Seneta (1990), Madan and Milne (1991)	Pragmatic stage 2
Infinite	Infinite	Finite	Eberlein and Keller (1995), Barndorff-Nielsen (1997), Eberlein, Keller and Prause (1998), Madan, Carr and Chang (1998), Prause (1999), Carr, Geman, Madan and Yor★ (2002, 2003)	Pragmatic stage 3
Infinite	Infinite	Infinite	Mandelbrot (1962)	Radical

Source: Walter (2017)
★depends on exponent

TABLE 8.4 Several generations of Lévy processes in financial modelling

	Stochastic models	Type of Lévy process
1900	Bachelier	Brownian motion
1962	Mandelbrot	Stable motion
1976	Merton	Brownian motion and Poisson component
1995	Eberlein and Keller	Hyperbolic motion
1997	Barndorff-Nielsen	Generalized Hyperbolic motion
1998	Madan et al.	Variance Gamma process
2002	Carr et al.	Generalized Variance Gamma process
2001	Kotz et al.	Laplace process
2010	Le Courtois and Walter	Generalized Laplace process

an overlap with the physicist's approach: the academic territory of financial modelling is overlapping. The pragmatic programme and the econophysics programme develop similar readings of the Mandelbrot view they shared with the tempered stable family. Hence the financial field of modelling extreme values is not simply divided into two camps: mainstream finance (moving to pragmatic programme) and econophysics. Despite their separate lines in the academic fields, the econophysics programme and the pragmatic programme derive from their reliance on Mandelbrot's view: two offshoots of what I suggest calling the 'discontinuous turn' in financial modelling, introduced by Mandelbrot in 1962.

Notes

1 This chapter builds on my previous works. To avoid overloading with too many references, I will refer back to these works which contain the complete list of references used, mentioning here only the main ones.
2 Mandelbrot's second challenge on independence with long-run correlations is not discussed here.
3 The Lévy measure of the Koponen model includes the Lévy measures of the Variance Gamma model and CGMY model as special cases. For mathematical details see Le Courtois and Walter (2014), p. 102.

References

Bouchaud, J.-P. and Potters, M. (2003). *Theory of financial risk and derivative pricing: From statistical physics to risk management.* Cambridge: Cambridge University Press.

Chiapello, E. and Walter, C. (2016). The three ages of financial quantification: a conventionalist approach to the financier's metrology. *Historical Social Research*, 41(2), 155–177.

De Bruin, B. and Walter, C. (2017). Research habits in financial modelling: The case of non-normality of market returns in the 1970s and the 1980s. In E. Ippoliti and P. Chen (Eds.), *Methods and finance. A unifying view on finance, mathematics and philosophy* (pp. 79–93). Cham: Springer.

Hempel, C. (1966). *Philosophy of natural science.* Upper Saddle River: Prentice Hall.

Koponen, I. (1995). Analytic approach to the problem of convergence of truncated Lévy flights toward the Gaussian stochastic process. *Physical Review E*, 52(1), 1197–1199.

Kuhn, T. S. (1962). *The structure of scientific revolutions.* Chicago: University of Chicago Press.

Le Courtois, O. and Walter, C. (2014). *Extreme financial risks and asset allocation.* Singapore: Imperial College Press, Series in Quantitative Finance, vol. 5.

Le Courtois, O. and Walter, C. (2017). Lévy processes and extreme value theory. In F. Longin (Ed.), *Extreme events in finance: A handbook of extreme value theory and its applications* (pp. 171–193). Hoboken: Wiley.

MacKenzie, D. (2006). *An engine, not a camera. How financial models shape markets.* Cambridge: MIT Press.

MacKenzie, D. and Spears, T. (2014). 'The formula that Killed Wall Street': The Gaussian copula and modelling practices in investment banking. *Social Studies of Science*, 44(3), 393–417.

Mandelbrot, B. (1962). Sur certains prix spéculatifs: faits empiriques et modèle basé sur les processus stables additifs non gaussiens de Paul Lévy. *Comptes rendus de l'Académie des sciences* (Paris), 254, 3968–3970. Reprint in (1997). *Fractales, hasard et finance.* Paris: Flammarion.

Mandelbrot, B. (1963). The variation of certain speculative prices. *The Journal of Business*, 36, 394–419. Reprint: Chapter E14 of Mandelbrot (1997).

Mandelbrot, B. (1967). The variation of some other speculative prices. *The Journal of Business*, 40, 393–413. Reprint: Chapter E15 of Mandelbrot (1997).

Mandelbrot, B. (1997). *Fractals and scaling in Finance. Discontinuity, concentration, risk.* New York: Springer.

Mandelbrot, B. (2013). *The fractalist. Memoir of a scientific maverick.* New York: Vintage Books.

Mandelbrot, B. and Taleb, N. (2006, 23 March). A focus on the exceptions that prove the rule. *Financial Times.*

Mantegna, R. and Stanley, E. (2000). *An introduction to econophysics: Correlations and complexity in finance*. Cambridge: Cambridge University Press.

Mirowski, P. (1995). Mandelbrot's economics after a quarter century. *Fractals*, 3(3), 581–600.

Sato, K. (1999). *Lévy processes and infinitely divisible distributions*. Cambridge: Cambridge University Press.

Walter, C. (1996). Une histoire du concept d'efficience sur les marchés financiers. *Annales. Histoire Sciences Sociales*, 51(4), 873–905.

Walter, C. (2002a). Le phénomène leptokurtique sur les marchés financiers. *Finance*, 23(2), 15–68. Reprint: Chapter 7 of Walter (2013).

Walter, C. (2002b). La recherche de lois d'échelles sur les variations boursières. In P. Abry, P. Gonçalvés and J. Lévy Véhel (dir.), *Lois d'échelle, fractales et ondelettes* (pp. 243–272) Paris: Hermès. Reprint: Chapter 7 of Walter (2013).

Walter, C. (2005). 1900–2000 : un siècle de processus de Lévy en finance. In G. Bensimon (dir.), *Histoire des représentations du marché* (pp. 553–588). Paris: Michel Houdiard. Reprint: Chapter 8 of Walter (2013).

Walter, C. (2013). *Le modèle de marche au hasard en finance*. Paris: Economica.

Walter C. (2015). Benoît Mandelbrot in finance. In M. Frame and N. Cohen (Eds.), *Benoît Mandelbrot. A life in many dimensions* (pp. 459–469). Singapore: World Scientific.

Walter, C. (2017). The extreme value problem in finance: comparing the pragmatic programme with the Mandelbrot programme. In F. Longin (Ed.), *Extreme events in finance: A handbook of extreme value theory and its applications* (pp. 25–51). Hoboken: Wiley.

Wiener, N. (1966). *God and Golem, Inc.* Cambridge: MIT Press.

9

BEYOND PERFORMATIVITY, HOW AND WHY AMERICAN COURTS SHOULD NOT HAVE USED EFFICIENT MARKET HYPOTHESIS

Franck Jovanovic

This chapter provides a critical perspective on the performativity of the Efficient Market Hypothesis (EMH) by studying its use by practitioners, particularly courts and judges in the United States; then it analyses the dialogue of deaf this use has created. EMH was formulated in the period from 1959 to 1976 to give a theoretical explanation to the random character of stock market prices. The EMH was proposed on the intuition that a pure random-walk model would verify two properties of competitive economic equilibrium: the absence of marginal profit and the equalisation of a stock's price and value. Thus, its initial formulation suggested that stock prices fully reflect all available information, and that, consequently, the actual price of a security is equal to its intrinsic value. In addition, because new information is supposed to arrive randomly, stock prices fluctuate randomly. EMH laid down one of the cornerstones of financial economics and the importance of the pure random-walk model and the Gaussian distribution (Poitras, 2006; Poitras and Jovanovic, 2007, 2010; Rubinstein, 1975; Sewell, 2011): validating the random nature of stock-market variations would, in effect, establish that prices on competitive financial markets are in permanent equilibrium as a result of the effects of competition (Jovanovic, 2008). This is what the EMH should be: the random character of stock market variations would demonstrate that the prices reflect the competitive equilibrium by incorporating the available information.

In 1996, two economists, Houthakker and Williamson, tested the random character of stock prices during three periods: January 1969 to June 1975; July 1975 to June 1982; July 1982 to June 1992. They concluded that 'the stock market, as measured by the S&P500, did not follow a random walk during the first two periods but did so in the third period. In other words, the market became more efficient over years' (Houthakker and Williamson, 1996, p. 136). They added, 'it is somewhat ironic that in the 1970s, when the EMH gained widespread acceptance, there were significant departures from a random walk. Fortunately for financial theory – and for the functioning of our capital markets – the market now conforms closely to a random walk. Reality has caught up with theory.' In a certain way, which will be clarified thereafter, these authors provide a telling example of how financial economics, and particularly EMH, has not merely described or explained but also actively shaped financial markets and practices. This is precisely the way performativity is most commonly understood (Boldyrev and Svetlova, 2016).

The performativity of financial economics has been well analysed and documented (Boldyrev and Svetlova, 2016; MacKenzie 2006; MacKenzie and Millo, 2003; MacKenzie et al., 2007; Mason et al., 2015). Following the perspective opened by this literature, this chapter argues that EMH leads to the creation of a fiction, and by trying to shape the real financial markets from this fiction, practitioners and academics have generated a gap between the observation of real financial markets and the reality they observe from this fiction. This gap has increased, creating and fuelling several misunderstandings between on the one hand financial economists and on the other hand academics and practitioners trained in other fields, like lawyers.[1] Moreover, from Le Gall (2008), Gordon (2013) and Schinckus (2018), this article sheds some light on these misunderstandings by discussing the 'financial reality' created by financial economists from EMH, suggesting that beyond the possible performativity of EMH, these misunderstandings can reflect the coexistence of several realities or a hyper-reality which is 'the generation by models of a real without origin or reality' (Baudrillard, 1994, p. 1).

The creation of performative fiction

Efficient market is a very well-known term in finance, widely used by academics and practitioners. EMH constitutes one of the major theoretical foundations of the financial economics' framework (Fama, 1991; Jovanovic, 2010; Jovanovic and Schinckus, 2017; Malkiel, 1992; Poitras, 2009; Zuckerman, 2013). In 2013, the 'Nobel Prize in economics' was awarded to Eugene Fama, mainly for his work related to this hypothesis:

> In the 1960s, Eugene Fama demonstrated that stock price movements are impossible to predict in the short-term and that new information affects prices almost immediately, which means that the market is efficient. The impact of Eugene Fama's results has extended beyond the field of research. For example, his results influenced the development of index funds.
>
> *(http://www.nobelprize.org/nobel_prizes/economic-sciences/laureates/2013/fama-facts.html)*

Despite this claim, we must clarify Fama's contribution. Given that several authors demonstrated the unpredictability of stock price movements before the 1960s (Jovanovic and Le Gall, 2001; Jovanovic, 2009, 2010; Poitras and Jovanovic, 2007; Sewell, 2011), Fama's major contribution concerns the introduction of the term of 'efficient market' and the affirmation according to which 'new information affects prices almost immediately' (Jovanovic, 2010, 2008). EMH has largely shaped financial markets and practices. Among the telling examples, we can mention its use for implementing the computerisation of financial markets (Schinckus, 2008), the international standardisation of accounting conventions (Chane-Alune, 2006; Miburn, 2008), the legal policies in U.S. (Fischel, 1989a; Hammer and Groeber, 2007; Langevoort, 2009) or the financial regulation policies (Muniesa, 2003; Pardo-Guerra, 2015); EMH has also changed trading practices (MacKenzie, 2006; Schinckus, 2018), particularly the equities managed by institutional investors like exchange-traded funds.[2] Given the influence of this hypothesis on real financial markets and practices, we could view this hypothesis as a telling example of performativity (Brisset, 2016; MacKenzie, 2006).

While the performativity of this hypothesis seems obvious, it is, in a certain way, highly paradoxical. Indeed, the EMH is hardly testable because any empirical test of this hypothesis refers to what is called in the literature a 'joint-test'. A joint-test refers to the fact that, on a given market, any test of the efficiency (i.e. the fact prices fully reflect available information) tests at the same time the notion of efficiency and the asset-pricing model used to price securities on this market. In other words, any empirical refutation (or validation) can be due either to the fact that the market is not efficient (or efficient) or that the model used is not appropriate (or appropriate) for the test. In other words, such a joint-test implies that market efficiency per se is not testable (Campbell et al., 1997; Cuthbertson, 2004; Fama, 1976; Jovanovic, 2010; LeRoy, 1976, 1989; Lo, 2000). Consequently, the random character of stock price or return variations (i.e. they cannot be predicted) does not guaranty that the EMH is validated (Cornell, 2013; Cutler et al., 1989; De Meyer and Saley, 2003; Longin, 1996).[3] This result is supported by another major drawback of this hypothesis: the demonstration between the EMH and the main stochastic process (martingale), provided by Fama (1970) is tautological and questionable (LeRoy, 1976, 1989).

Despite this paradoxical situation, EMH has kept a strong influence among financial economists, and the whole financial economics mainstream is based on this hypothesis (CAPM, Black and Scholes option pricing model, Harrison-Kreps-Pliska theoretical framework, etc.). This scientific survival is certainly not estranged from the methodological foundations of this hypothesis. The latter is based on Milton Friedman's positivism according to which the realism of the hypotheses has no relevance in judging the validity of a model because its predictions are all that really matters (Crotty, 2013; Frankfurter and McGoun, 1996, 1999; Friedman, 1953; Findlay and Williams, 2001). In the case of EMH, the predictions are the consequence of a competitive market, such as the no-arbitrage opportunity or the no-profit opportunity. Consequently, EMH does not pretend to provide a description of real markets. However, focusing on the predictions and the empirical tests, the lack of realism of this hypothesis has created the proliferation of definitions leading to the lack of a consensual meaning of this hypothesis. For instance, according to Fama (1970, 383) 'a market in which prices always "fully reflect" available information is called "efficient"'; on the other hand, Fama et al. (1969) defined an efficient market as 'a market that adjusts rapidly to new information'; Jensen (1978) considered that 'a market is efficient with respect to information set θ_t if it is impossible to make economic profit by trading on the basis of information set θ_t'; according to Malkiel (1992) 'the market is said to be efficient with respect to some information set […] if security prices would be unaffected by revealing that information to all participants. Moreover, efficiency with respect to an information set […] implies that it is impossible to make economic profits by trading on the basis of [that information set]'; Malkiel (2003) stated that efficient financial markets 'do not allow investors to earn above-average returns without accepting above-average risks'. Harrison and Kreps (1979) and Harrison and Pliska (1981) associated the efficiency with the arbitrage-free. These definitions are clearly different. Given the lack of consensual definition of what efficient financial markets are, nobody knows what an efficient market should be! Only a consensus can be found on its possible consequences, such as the no-profit, no-arbitrage opportunity, or the no-predictability.

To sum up, EMH is a fiction and not a description of real financial markets. This fiction was built from what a financial competitive market should be in order to mimic the idealistic framework of economics. This fiction performs financial markets thanks to the implementation of some of its logical consequences in regulations, conventions, computerisation and practices. However, because this hypothesis cannot be tested per se, we cannot provide a quantitative measure of the efficiency of a financial market, as Houthakker and Williamson (1996) suggested.[4] Consequently, this performativity seems to be evaluated only through the way new regulations, computerisation rules, or laws are implemented. Fraud on the Market Doctrine (FoMD), also called Fraud on the Market Theory, is one telling example of such performativity due to the fact that U.S. courts have used EMH for creating a new jurisprudence about this doctrine. The next part details and discusses this point.

Some consequences of the use of EMH fiction by U.S. courts

EMH has played a key role in the Fraud on the Market U.S. Doctrine by changing its interpretation and its scope. The legal roots of this doctrine can be traced back to the first attempts to safeguard financial markets as well as the interests of investors from fraud and manipulation after the 1929 stock market crash. Initially, this doctrine required plaintiffs (i.e. investors) to provide evidence of an intentional misstatement or omission of a material fact on which they had relied and which had been the proximate cause of their injury. Since 1980 U.S. courts have used the EMH for changing the FoMD in order to open the door to class action lawsuits (Gordon, 2013; Jovanovic et al., 2016). A securities fraud case will therefore typically involve a debate around whether or not the market in which the securities were traded, was efficient, with the plaintiffs (investors) trying to demonstrate this efficiency and the defendants (generally officers of the company) trying to disprove it. U.S. courts referred directly to the EMH to justify the introduction of this presumption in the court system in order to strengthen the case for class actions in securities fraud litigation. In this perspective, the EMH is used for demonstrating that every fraudulent misrepresentation was necessarily reflected in stock prices, and that every investor could rely solely on those prices for transacting. Courts were therefore justified in relinquishing the requirement of direct reliance on the alleged misrepresentation whenever public information could have an automatic influence on prices.

In their demonstration, U.S. courts radically changed the interpretation of the FoMD thanks to the EMH definition introduced by Fama (1970). However, by using Fama's definition, they seemed to (voluntarily) ignore or underestimate the fact that market efficiency per se is not testable, has a polymorphous definition, is a fiction, and doesn't designate real financial markets. As Gordon (2013, 10) explained 'when the law is using a hypothesis to settle a fact, that may be one indication that we are in the presence of a fiction'. 'The fiction here is that its version of the fraud-on-the-market theory pivots on the Court's belief that the efficient-market hypothesis not only reflects reality but that there was general agreement at the time that this was so' (Gordon, 2013, p. 513). It is worth mentioning that, according to this author, some judges and courts were aware that market efficiency is a fiction. However, they probably underestimated all of the consequences of such a performativity based on a fiction when they had to analyse a real fraud. However, it is worth mentioning that there is a sole interpretation among courts and judges. As Jovanovic et al. (2016) explained, considering the impossible validation of the EMH, several courts used a less literal definition of efficiency stipulating that prices must reflect 'most' (and not 'fully' reflect 'all') public information as Fama (1970) claimed. For instance, in *PolyMedica* (2004 and 2005), the court considered that an efficient market 'is simply one in which "most publicly announced material statements about companies" affect stock market prices'. In response to this definition of market efficiency, the defendant appealed, alleging an error of law arising from the use of 'most' in the definition of efficiency, instead of 'all' and 'fully' (Jovanovic et al., 2015, p. 185). The practical difficulties inherited from market efficiency definition led the Supreme Court of U.S. to take a position for the second time about the FoMD in June 2014. Indeed, while this definition using 'most' is easier to satisfy, it opened the door to criticisms according to which lawyers were said to have initiated class action suits as soon as they saw a significant drop in the stock price of a company, and it is only afterwards that they are looking for evidence of fraud (Erdlen, 2011, p. 897). In 1995, the Congress responded to these criticisms by adopting a major reform of securities law that was expressly aimed at holding back class action suits (Oldham, 2003). This reform did not stop the controversy, and harsh debates still continued between the district courts, the Court of Appeal and the Supreme Court about the definition of market efficiency. The last judgement of the Supreme Court of U.S. shows that 'Securities class actions are here to stay' (insidecounsel.com – September 2014, 11), recognising the legal reality created by the use of the EMH inherited from Fama (1970) (Jovanovic et al., 2016).

It is worth analysing the controversy between 'most' and 'all/fully'. This controversy reveals that U.S. courts refer to two realities although they did not mention it: the use of the term 'most' directly refers to the real financial markets while the use of terms 'all' and 'fully' are directly related to the EMH fiction.[5] Indeed, the definition using the term 'most' is crafted for the practical legal purpose guarantying the applicability of the FoMD (Jovanovic et al., 2016). In this case, courts interpret real financial markets. By opposition, by using the terms 'full' and 'all', courts interpret a fiction. Indeed, as explained, the observation of a full reflection of all available information does not exist in real financial markets. This non-existence is at least the logical consequence of the lack of demonstration between EMH definition stated by Fama (1970) and the hypotheses that are really tested (no-profit, arbitrage free, etc.). In other terms, the paradoxical situation pointed out in the first part has led to a deaf dialogue between the U.S. courts because they based their demonstrations and interpretations on two incompatible realities.

This result calls for a new look on the performativity of EMH.[6] Remember that the performativity supposes to have access to the real financial markets, because performativity implies that EMH actively shapes the real markets. Discussing the computerisation of financial markets, Schinckus (2018) suggests that while the relation between EMH and real financial market does not exist, a relation exists between the EMH and a hyper-reality created from this hypothesis:

> Computerization of the financial sphere is based on an a priori representation (the efficient-market hypothesis) that does not exist outside our textbooks […]. This hyper-reality enhanced by the computerization of financial markets does not result from potential reality (efficient markets do not exist), but paradoxically shapes reality.
>
> *(Schinckus, 2018, p. 58)*

Following this point, the EMH hyper-reality has replaced the real financial markets, which are not accessible anymore. In this perspective, this hyper-reality is not plainly compatible with the idea of performativity because it is not the real financial markets that are shaped. Considering our previous discussion, by using 'fully/all' to define the efficiency, efficient market becomes a hyper-reality for courts (i.e. an imaginary projection of what is a market) from which they extended the FoMD. Judging the 'real' markets from this 'imaginary construction of financial markets' (Schinckus, 2018, p. 61) could appear paradoxical, but it is not! Given that efficient market hypothesis is used in order to open a class action lawsuit, showing statistical data proving that stock prices or returns are stochastic, is supposed to validate the EMH,[7] and to prove the market efficiency for the tenants of the

EMH hyper-reality. Doing this is generally enough to find a deal between the two parts and then to stop the lawsuit without making a real demonstration that markets are efficient. Therefore, a real confrontation with real financial markets never occurs. In other terms, the FoMD extended with EMH has allowed the existence of two realities and the maintenance of the deaf dialogue previously pointed out.

Conclusion

This chapter showed that EMH is a fiction that created a hyper-reality rather than performed financial markets. The fact that some courts interpret a fiction and other courts interpret the real markets has some practical implications. According to the definition of EMH and then the reality (i.e. real markets or hyper-reality) in which the courts will base their inter-pretations, we can have more or less class action lawsuits: if we interpret the reality ('most') we will increase the number of class action lawsuits; by opposition if we interpret the hyper-reality ('full/all') we will decrease number of class action lawsuits.

Notes

1 We could also mention econophysicists for instance (Schinckus, 2016, p. 7).
2 An exchange-traded fund is an investment fund traded on financial markets and that tracks an index.
3 It is also true for the other methods used for testing EMH.
4 We could argue that if we define the efficiency as the no-arbitrage opportunity, as Harrison and Kreps (1979) and Harrison and Pliska (1981), we could estimate the efficiency on foreign exchange markets for instance. Such exceptions are rare and supposed to use a definition of EMH different from that of Fama's and that does not refer to the information.
5 The controversy between 'most' and 'all/fully' is not the only one created by the use of EMH. Jurists introduced for instance a dual definition of market efficiency depending on the impor-tance given to the notion of fundamental value, leading to distinguish between a 'trading-rule efficiency' and a 'value efficiency' (Fischel, 1989, pp. 912–913).
6 See also the position defended by Zuckerman (2013) about the performativity of EMH.
7 We have the same result if we use any other statistical tests that validate one of the three forms of the EMH.

References

Baudrillard, J. (1994). *Simulacra and simulation*. Ann Arbor: University of Michigan Press.
Boldyrev, I. and Svetlova, E. (Eds.) (2016). *Enacting dismal science. New perspectives on the performativity of economics*. New York: Palgrave Macmillan.
Brisset, N. (2016). Economics is not always performative: Some limits for performativity. *Journal of Economic Methodology*, 23(2), 160–184.
Campbell, J. Y., Lo, A. W. and MacKinlay, A. C. (1997). *The econometrics of financial markets*. Princeton: Princeton University Press.
Chane-Alune, E. (2006). Accounting standardization and governance structures. *Working paper n° 0609, University of Liège*.
Cornell, B. (2013). What moves stock prices: Another look. *Journal of Portfolio Management*, 39(3), 32–38.
Crotty, J. R. (2013). The realism of assumptions does matter: Why Keynes-Minsky theory must replace efficient market theory as the guide to financial regulation policy. In M. H. Wolfson and G. A. Epstein (Eds.) *The handbook of the political economy of financial crises* (pp. 133–158). New York: Oxford University Press.

Cuthbertson, K. (2004). *Quantitative financial economics: Stocks, bonds, and foreign exchange*. Chichester: John Wiley.

Cutler, D. M., Poterba, J. M. and Summers, L. H. (1989). What moves stock prices? *Journal of Portfolio Management*, 1(5), 4–12.

De Meyer, B. and Saley, H. M. (2003). On the strategic origin of Brownian motion in finance. *International Journal of Game Theory*, 31, 285–319.

Erdlen, A. M. (2011). Timing is everything: Markets, loss, and proof of causation in fraud on the market actions. *Fordham Law Review*, 80, 877–922.

Fama, E. F. (1970). Efficient capital markets: A review of theory and empirical work. *Journal of Finance*, 25(2), 383–417.

Fama, E. F. (1976). Efficient capital markets: Reply. *Journal of Finance*, 31(1), 143–145.

Fama, E. F. (1991). Efficient capital markets: II. *Journal of Finance*, 46(5), 1575–1617.

Fama, E. F., Fisher, L., Jensen, M. C. and Roll, R. (1969). The adjustment of stock prices to new information. *International Economic Review*, 10(1), 1–21.

Findlay, M. C. and Williams, E. E. (2001). A fresh look at the efficient market hypothesis: How the intellectual history of finance encouraged a real "Fraud-on-the-Market". *Journal of Post Keynesian Economics*, 23(2), 181–199.

Fischel, Daniel R. (1989). Efficient capital markets, the crash, and the fraud on the market theory. *Cornell Law Review*, 74(5), 907–922.

Frankfurter, G. M. and McGoun, E. G. (1996). *Toward finance with meaning. The methodology of finance: What it is and what it can be*. Greenwich: Jai Press.

Frankfurter, G. M. and McGoun, E. G. (1999). Ideology and the theory of financial economics. *Journal of Economic Behavior & Organization*, 39, 159–177.

Friedman, M. (1953). *Essays in positive economics*. Chicago: The University of Chicago Press.

Gordon, R. D. (2013). Fictitious fraud: Economics and the presumption of reliance. *International Journal of Law in Context*, 9(4), 506–519.

Hammer, H. M. and Groeber, R. X. (2007). Efficient market hypothesis and class action securities regulation. *International Journal of Business Research*, 1, 1–14.

Harrison, J. M. and Kreps, D. M. (1979). Martingales and arbitrage in multiperiod securities markets. *Journal of Economic Theory*, 20(3), 381–408.

Harrison, J. M. and Pliska, S. R. (1981). Martingales and stochastic integrals in the theory of continuous trading. *Stochastic Processes and their Applications*, 11(3), 215–260.

Houthakker, H. S. and Williamson, P. J. (1996). *The economics of financial markets*. New York: Oxford University Press.

Jensen, M. C. (1978). Some anomalous evidence regarding market efficiency. *Journal of Financial Economics*, 6(2–3), 95–101.

Jovanovic, F. (2008). The construction of the canonical history of financial economics. *History of Political Economy*, 40(2), 213–242.

Jovanovic, F. (2009). Le modèle de marche aléatoire dans l'économie financière de 1863 à 1976. *Revue d'Histoire des Sciences Humaines*, 20, 81–108.

Jovanovic, F. (2010). Efficient markets theory: Historical perspectives. In R. Cont (Ed.) *Encyclopedia of Quantitative Finance*. Chichester: John Wiley & Sons.

Jovanovic, F. and Le Gall, P. (2001). Does God practice a random walk? The 'financial physics' of a 19th century forerunner, Jules Regnault. *European Journal for the History of Economic Thought*, 8(3), 323–362.

Jovanovic, F. and Schinckus, C. (2017). *Econophysics and financial economics: An emerging dialogue*. New York: Oxford University Press.

Jovanovic, F., Andreadakis, S. and Schinckus, C. (2016). Efficient market hypothesis and fraud on the market theory: A new perspective for class actions. *Research in International Business and Finance*, 38, 177–190.

Langevoort, D. C. (2009). Basic at twenty: Rethinking fraud on the market. *Wisconsin Law Review*, 2009, 151–198.

Le Gall, P. (2008). *L'économie est-elle une science fiction? Récit et fiction en modélisation économique et en art*. Working paper.

LeRoy, S. F. (1976). Efficient capital markets: Comment. *Journal of Finance*, 31(1), 139–141.

LeRoy, S. F. (1989). Efficient capital markets and martingales. *Journal of Economic Literature* 27(4), 1583–1621.

Lo, A. W. (2000). Finance: A selective survey. *Journal of the American Statistical Association*, 95(450), 629–635.

Longin, F. M. (1996). The asymptotic distribution of extreme stock market returns. *The Journal of Business*, 69(3), 383–408.

MacKenzie, D. (2006). *An engine, not a camera: How financial models shape markets*. Cambridge: MIT Press.

MacKenzie, D., Muniesa, F. and Siu, L. (Eds.) (2007). *Do economists make markets? On the performativity of economics*. Princeton: Princeton University Press.

MacKenzie, D. and Millo, Y. (2003). Constructing a market, performing theory: The historical sociology of a financial derivatives exchange. *American Journal of Sociology*, 109(1), 107–145.

Malkiel, B. G. (1992). Efficient market hypothesis. In P. Newman, M. Milgate and J. Eatwell (Eds.) *The New Palgrave Dictionary of Money and Finance*. London: Macmillan.

Malkiel, B. G. (2003). The efficient market hypothesis and its critics. *Journal of Economic Perspectives*, 17(1), 59–82.

Mason, K., Kjellberg, H. and Hagberg, J. (2015). Exploring the performativity of marketing: Theories, practices and devices. *Journal of Marketing Management*, 31(1–2), 1–15.

Miburn, J. A. (2008). The relationship between fair value, market value, and efficient markets. *Acounting Perspectives*, 7(4), 293–316.

Muniesa, F. (2003). *Des marchés comme algorithmes : sociologie de la cotation électronique à la bourse de Paris*. Ph.D: Ecole Nationale Supérieures des Mines de Paris.

Oldham, J. L. (2003). Taking 'efficient markets' out of the fraud-on-the-market doctrine after the Private Securities Litigation Act. *Northern University Law Review*, 97(2), 995.

Pardo-Guerra, J. P. (2015). *Evaluation cultures, organizational logics, and the limits of financial regulation*. Working paper: University of Leicester.

Poitras, G. (Ed.). (2006). *Pioneers of financial economics: Contributions prior to Irving Fisher*. Vol. 1. Cheltenham: Edward Elgar.

Poitras, G. (2009). From Antwerp to Chicago: The history of exchange traded derivative security contracts. *Revue d'Histoire des Sciences Humaines*, 20: 11–50.

Poitras, G. and Jovanovic, F. (Eds.). (2007). *Pioneers of financial economics: Twentieth-Century Contributions*. Vol. 2. Cheltenham: Edward Elgar.

Poitras, G. and Jovanovic, F. (2010). Pioneers of financial economics: Das Adam Smith Irrelevanzproblem? *History of Economics Review*, 51, 43–64.

Rubinstein, M. (1975). Securities market efficiency in an Arrow-Debreu economy. *American Economic Review*, 65(5), 812–824.

Schinckus, C. (2008). The financial simulacrum. *Journal of Socio-Economics*, 73(3), 1076–1089.

Schinckus, C. (2018). Pataphysics of finance: An essay of visual epistemology. *Critical Perspectives on Accounting*, 52, 57–68.

Sewell, M. (2011). History of the efficient market hypothesis. *Research Note*, University College London.

Zuckerman, E. W. (2013). Market efficiency: A sociological perspective. In A. Preda and K. Knorr-Cetina (Eds.) *Handbook of the sociology of finance* (pp. 223–249). Oxford: Oxford University Press.

PART II

Structural dynamics in the financial industry

Introduction

Up until the early years of this millennium, banking and financial activities were by and large approached via the dominant paradigm of modern finance, which in turn served to reinforce the dominance of this paradigm. The financial intermediation industry has become institutionalised, shoring up its legitimacy by invoking portfolio theory and the supposed efficiency of the financial markets. The industry has even succeeded in avoiding scrutiny as a topic of research in its own right, instead promoting approaches which focus on the ways in which supply and demand are 'naturally' reconciled.

Given the overbearing normative weight of this paradigm, counter-analyses which seek to understand the specific mechanisms at work in financial intermediation are invaluable: what do financial enterprises do, where are they based, how do they manage their sales, their finances and their staff, and how do they assess their performance? What are the dynamics governing their relationships with one another, how does the division of labour work across the whole financial chain, how is value distributed? What are the different roles fulfilled by public-sector authorities? How and by whom are regulations enforced, and how is their effectiveness monitored? Studying the transformations at work in the financial industry, particularly in different socio-economic contexts, allows us to identify and describe the dynamics in play.

The contributions collected in this section analyse the shifting geographical base of the financial industry, looking at its business models and connections with other industries (Tadjeddine) as well as the processes of recruiting and training workers, highlighting the transition observed in French banks from a model based on internal mobility to a greater reliance on external recruitment (Dressen). The positions adopted by banks in relation to the dominant model are also analysed in terms of their fidelity (or lack thereof) to their specific identities, for example the way in which mutual savings banks regard their cooperative heritage (Moulévrier), or German banks and their specific attitudes to lending (Keller). These dynamics are also analysed with regard to the manner in which innovation challenges (or fails to challenge) existing positions and profit-sharing arrangements within the financial intermediation industry, including the impact of new markets such as socially responsible investing (Pénalva) or the Alternative Investment Market (Revest). Such innovations are also analysed in terms of the risks they involve, and the ways in which these risks are transferred within and beyond the financial sphere (Oubenal and Deville). While reading this section you may also find it useful to refer to the diagrams showing the organisations involved in placing investments (Figure 0.1), the organisations providing financing (Figure 0.2) and the infrastructure of the market (Figure 0.3).

Adopting an institutional approach, particularly via the question of how the industry should be regulated, allows us to analyse the very foundations of finance. Lenglet looks at the manner in which regulation of practices actually works within financial organisations, through the medium of compliance managers who are responsible for deciding how the rules should be respected and how they might apply – a question of specific context. Charron, meanwhile, examines the viewpoint tacitly enshrined in regulation: that of investors, of taxpayers, or of investees. What emerges from his analysis is the prioritisation of investors' interests over the other two groups and the accompanying failure, on the part of the financial markets, to take sufficient account of the broader societal consequences of the actions of individuals, employees, businesses and governments. The historical research conducted by Lagneau-Ymonet and Riva also chimes with this perspective, revealing the dynamics at play in the privatisation of market data, the fragmentation of liquidity and the near-impossible task of effectively monitoring all behaviour on the markets.

TABLE II.1 Structural dynamics in the financial industry – classification based on scale of observation

Techniques	*Organisations*	*Institutions*
(c.10) Oubenal & Deville *Economic sociology* (ETFs)	**(c.11) Revest** *Institutional economics* (Market design)	**(c.16) Keller** *Institutional economics* (Capitalisms)
	(c.12) Penalva-Icher *Economic sociology* (Asset management)	**(c.17) Lagneau-Ymonet & Riva** *Economic history* (Financial market regulation)
	(c.13) Tadjeddine *Geography of finance* (Asset management)	**(c.18) Lenglet** *Philosophy of norms* (Soft laws and regulations)
	(c.14) Dressen *Labour sociology* (Banking)	**(c.19) Charron** *Convention economics* (European laws and regulations)
	(c.15) Moulevrier *Economic sociology* (Banking)	

10

SOURCES OF RISKS IN FINANCIAL INNOVATIONS

Embedded and Additional Risks in Exchange Traded Funds (ETFs)

Mohamed Oubenal and Laurent Deville

Introduction

Although the importance of financial innovation is widely recognized, this recognition has long been focused on where it originates and how beneficial it is to the financial industry and the economy (Tufano, 2003; Lerner, 2006). Since the 2007 financial crisis, financial innovations have been under scrutiny for the risks they bear (Allen, 2012; Diaz-Rainey and Ibikunle, 2012). The case of Exchange Traded Funds (ETFs), which set a new standard for the trading of index funds, is typical of such a reversal. ETFs, open-ended index funds whose shares trade like ordinary stocks on exchanges, were created in the 1990s in the US and listed in Europe in 2000. They grew steadily and almost silently during the 2000s until the 2007–2008 crisis when growth in assets managed came to a halt for the first time. But this slowdown was short-lived and growth resumed as early as 2009. But by the turn of 2011, ETFs had become the center of the regulation agencies' attention. Within a few months, the IMF (IMF, 2011), the Financial Stability Board (FSB, 2011) and the Bank for International Settlements (Ramaswamy, 2011) stated that the development of ETF markets raised issues about whether these instruments could still be regarded as innocuous for market stability. The ESMA responded to these concerns by launching a public consultation with regard to the regulatory regime applicable to ETFs (ESMA, 2011). Once an innovative instrument extolled for its many virtues in the financial press, ETFs had come to be seen as complex, opaque and highly risky securities.

We study in this chapter the evolutions of the ETF market and the perception of its associated risks, from its inception in Europe in 2000 through to 2013. We explore the sources of the risks they present and the way they were revealed. We feel it is important to understand whether the risks involved in the ETF market are inherent to the trading of index funds or subsequently incorporated in the structure for reasons whose legitimacy may be discussed. Following Amenc et al. (2012), we think that the assessment of ETF risks should focus on the interests of investors. We pay specific attention to the marketing of these instruments in order to shed light on the agreements and disagreements at play in the industry.

To do so, we exploit a set of semi-structured interviews with actors involved in the creation, development and operation of the ETF market. Our dataset includes a total of

57 interviews conducted between March 2009 and May 2010. All the interviewees had devoted at least part of their principal activity to ETFs: they include members of the French financial regulator (AMF), the Euronext stock exchange, ETF issuers, brokers, market makers, index providers, journalists, conference organizers, academic experts and institutional investors. We also attended conferences where ETFs were promoted to either institutional or retail investors. During these events, we observed the relationships at play between some of our interviewees. We listened to the promotional discourse targeting institutional investors and talked with some of them about the way they perceive ETFs. As a secondary source of data, we analyzed articles on ETFs published in the financial press.

The major innovation of ETFs lies in the specific trading process that was set up, intended to allow continuous trading while avoiding the significant premiums and discounts that are generally observed in fund trading. The market for ETFs is based on two co-existing trading venues: a primary market open to Authorized Participants (APs) for the creation and redemption of ETF shares in blocks directly to/from the fund, and a secondary market, the stock exchange, where shares trade like ordinary stocks. The fund is open-ended: at any time, new shares can be created and existing shares redeemed directly from the fund against a portfolio underlying the benchmark index. In theory, this specific trading process fits the requirements of continuous trading of funds as it ensures a high level of efficiency and liquidity in the secondary market. When the ETF's share price departs too much from the value of the fund's holdings per share (Net Asset Value or NAV), arbitrages consisting in buying the ETF where it is undervalued and simultaneously selling it where it is overvalued can be easily implemented, closing the gap between the two values.

Financial innovation is a perpetually evolving process. Products are adapted to new markets, new actors, changing legal environments and, of course, to evolutions in technology. Early ETFs achieved index replication by simply holding a stock basket perfectly reflecting the composition of the benchmark index (physical replication). With the evolution of the market came new forms of fund management. ETF providers developed profit enhancing activities to remain competitive in the indexing industry. The use of statistical techniques allowing for an optimization of the portfolio held by the fund and stock lending activities is widespread. In Europe, the development of more exotic underlying indices together with a more liberal regulation soon called for a second generation of ETFs based on swaps (synthetic replication). In such swap-based ETFs, the fund does not hold the underlying securities of the benchmark index but a substitute basket. It enters into a total return swap, a derivative agreement under which the counterparty commits to delivering the exact index return in exchange for the effective performance of the ETF holdings and a fee. Both the use of OTC derivatives and the practice of securities lending lead ETFs to hold securities that are different from those constituting the replicated index and thus expose its holders to counterparty risk.

In its 2011 Global Financial Stability Report, the IMF expressed concerns about the complexity and lack of transparency of new types of ETFs, such as synthetic ETFs, leverage and inverse ETFs, and about the use of securities lending by ETF providers. Under stressed market conditions counterparty risk may become systemic, affecting the liquidity of underlying securities and overall market liquidity. Regarding physical replication, the IMF notes that "the disproportionately large size of some ETFs compared with the market capitalisation of the underlying reference indices poses a risk of disruption in some markets from heavy ETF trading" (IMF, 2011, p. 68).

Other concerns are raised by the dysfunctions that the ETF market experienced during the flash crash episode that occurred on May 6, 2010. This episode put the spotlight on the technological content of the ETF industry. If the emergence of ETFs finds its roots in Modern Portfolio Theory, its success would not have been possible without the technological progress the finance industry has witnessed in the last ten years. The ability to provide efficient intraday exposure to an index at low cost is one of the key advantages ETFs have over traditional index mutual funds. With ETFs, investors are offered immediacy in index fund trading. One measure of this immediacy is intraday liquidity. It is of particular importance to issuers and markets that compete for the order flow. The ability of market makers to display tight quotes depends on their capacity to incorporate technology. Speed and connectivity are essential to quote ETFs: any time the index value changes, quotes have to be updated right away or low-latency traders enter into arbitrage trades.

What is intriguing about the controversy on risks in ETFs is that these risks only came to light in 2011, at a period when the market had not experienced any significant change for some time. We show that the risks were kept hidden through a promotional discourse shared by all participants and through active social control. They were finally revealed thanks to the controversy on replication techniques that followed the credit crisis of 2007–2008. The controversy was initiated by issuers who were competing for asset growth in index funds, and was relayed by the financial press. It gave the regulators an opportunity to tackle the issue of risks in ETFs. Hence, it was not the crisis per se that led to the revelation of risks at play in the ETF markets but its use by issuers as an opportunity to aggressively promote their products. Faced with promoters that were no longer able to agree in this highly competitive industry, the regulators had a window of opportunity to tackle the issues of risk and transparency in ETFs.

The remainder of the chapter is organized as follows. We first describe the trading of index funds and ETFs and show the way they have evolved since their introduction in Europe. The next section separates risks in ETFs according to their source, inherent or additional. We then explain how the revelation of this risk was made possible, before concluding the chapter.

Trading index funds

The first generation of ETFs

During the 1980s and 1990s, the integration of computing and new information and communication technologies in finance resulted in a reduction in transaction time (Knorr-Cetina and Bruegger, 2002). Increasing connectivity in finance combined with the development of computing, illustrated by the introduction of Bloomberg terminals in 1980, fostered the virtual proximity of global places and traders. The beginning of electronic handling of orders in major exchanges and investment banks enabled the development of "program trading." It became possible to trade portfolios consisting of all stocks in an index such as the S&P 500 in one single order. This new era of instantaneity and technological improvements was to contribute to the emergence of innovations such as ETFs (Ruggins, 2018).

The main hurdle to the trading of index funds is the problem of premiums or discounts. The main trading venue for an ETF is the exchange, where ETF shares trade almost like simple stocks with no limitation on order size. It is also possible for some institutional investors to ask for the creation or redemption of ETF shares directly from the fund: they can deposit the stock basket underlying the index with the fund trustee and receive fund shares in return (and conversely). The shares thus created can then be traded on an exchange as simple stocks or later redeemed for the stock basket then making up the underlying index. In this dual structure, each market provides a distinctive price for the ETF. The ETF Net Asset Value (NAV) is displayed at the end of the day, on the basis of closing prices of the funds' holdings while the ETF market price varies continuously throughout the day depending on supply and demand. The NAV obeys an accounting logic, while the second price corresponds to a market logic.

The principal advantage over traditional funds lies in this specific trading process that aims to allow for continuous trading while avoiding these distortions in the market price. Actually, arbitrage links the two markets in such a way as to avoid price discrepancies. Arbitrage is a mechanism allowing traders to take advantage of differences between two different but related securities (Beunza et al., 2006). In the case of ETFs, what must be compared is the market price of the ETF and the value of the creation basket that can be delivered to the fund in exchange for ETF shares. When demand weakens for an ETF and its price falls compared to its benchmark index, traders can redeem ETF units, get back the underlying stocks and sell them on the exchange to benefit from the discrepancy. Conversely, when the ETF price increases, they can create units by delivering the underlying securities and sell the units on the ETF secondary market (Ben-David et al., 2014). The possibility of "in-kind" creation and redemption ensures that departures between the share price and the fund's Net Asset Value (NAV) are not too large.

The second generation of ETFs

The ETF operational structure can be viewed as an ideal for the trading of index funds. The fund is invested in the index underlying stock basket, perfectly reflecting the composition of the benchmark index. The performance earned by an investor creating new shares and redeeming them later should always equal the index return less fees. As efficient as it may be, this process does not ensure a perfect replication of the underlying index. In practice, ETFs tend to underperform their benchmark indices and their index mutual fund competitors (Elton et al., 2002; Blitz et al., 2010). Changes in the composition of the index, constraints on the use of dividends and management fees induce underperformance and tracking error. First, ETFs charge management fees as a percentage of the asset under management of the fund. Second, adjusting the portfolio when the index composition changes is costly, which explains the underperformance with respect to their benchmark of index funds in general. Moreover, Gastineau (2004) shows that the passivity of ETF managers when faced with such changes is likely to explain the poor performance of ETFs. While mutual fund managers typically anticipate upcoming events to reduce transaction costs embedded in the index modification process, ETF managers generally wait until the announcement. Third, the legal structure of some funds forces fund managers to hold received dividends in cash, causing a dividend drag in rising markets.

At inception, ETFs were marketed as a low-cost alternative to traditional mutual funds, focusing on their low management fees and expense ratios. As ETFs attracted more and more cash, fierce competition between ETFs and mutual funds led to the fees war described in Dellva (2001) and Bogle (2004). Expense ratio comparisons used as a competitive tool by issuers were obviously in favor of ETFs and traditional mutual fund providers had to progressively lower the fees on their top funds to reach a historical low of 10 basis points or even less a few years after the introduction of ETFs. Such aggressive cuts on fees from Fidelity and Vanguard, now offering ETFs, and responses from BlackRock were again in the news at the end of 2012. With expense ratios coming down to the 0.10 percent range, the profitability of this industry became problematic and ETF providers had to be creative to both enhance the performance of their funds and find alternative sources of revenue.

The first developments of the ETF operational structure were based on an optimization of the stock basket held by the fund. Although the US regulation requires index funds to principally hold stocks that constitute its benchmark index, it leaves room for modification of the weight that is assigned to each security. Such possibility is essential as funds have to comply with limits on their concentration. For ETFs, this served to reduce costs by investing only in the most liquid index constituents while achieving replication through statistical techniques such as stratified sampling. The next evolution consisted in improving the performance of the fund by lending the securities it held. In these operations, the fund lends some securities against a fee and receives collateral that serves as a guaranty. In the event that the counterparty fails to hand back the securities, the fund can liquidate this collateral. On top of the fee received, stock lending can be a way of reducing the fund's dividend tax liabilities.

In Europe, the development of more exotic underlying indices together with a more liberal regulation soon called for synthetic replication based on total return swaps. In such swap-based or synthetic ETFs, the fund no longer holds the underlying securities of the benchmark index. The ETF uses cash from investors to buy a substitute basket of securities. It then enters into a total return swap whereby the counterparty commits to delivering the exact index return in exchange for the effective performance of the ETF holdings and a fee. The funded swap model is a subsequent evolution of this so-called un-funded swap model where the collateral is not directly owned by the fund but posted on a segregated account. One advantage of these structures is to produce very low tracking errors even for indexes composed of securities that are difficult to trade, such as emerging market indices.

Sources of risks in ETFs

In 2011, red flags seemed to rise from everywhere for ETFs. The increasing complexity and the opacity of the synthetic structure raised doubts about what was really behind ETFs in terms of risks. However, the debate on counterparty risk in synthetic replication soon extended to the risks involved in ETFs in general. In assessing the different risks associated with ETFs, we distinguish in this section between the risks that are inherent to the trading of index funds and those that appeared with subsequent evolutions of the model.

Inherent risks of ETFs

Practitioners created ETFs as an improved version of index mutual funds, allowing investors to trade the "market portfolio" instantly on the exchange. ETFs show common positive attributes with traditional index funds, such as low management fees, but they have also inherited their risks. ETFs may trade at a discount or a premium but have been shown to do so less than conventional index funds thanks to their creation/redemption process. Still, even with no tracking errors, an ETF exposes investors to no more or less than the returns of its benchmark index. As such, ETF holders are exposed to the risks an index brings with it.

Like index funds, any ETF may incur losses that could threaten its existence. A sudden drop in the underlying index or significant volatility may dangerously reduce the fund's value. Liquidity risk exists at the fund level as well as at the underlying basket level. Liquidity may become scarce in the secondary market, as the flash crash illustrated. Investors could in theory still redeem their shares against the underlying basket. When liquidating it, investors may suffer additional losses related to the illiquidity of the associated stocks.

In terms of performance, ETFs present the same limits as the index it replicates. The S&P 500 index consists of 500 large stocks listed on the NYSE or NASDAQ. It is broad enough to cover several sectors of the US economy, but asset classes such as bonds or private equity are not included. The S&P 500, like any other stock index, thus fails to represent *the* optimal portfolio incorporating all risky assets as defined by the CAPM. Moreover, the performance of ETFs can significantly deviate from the benchmark (Shina and Soydemirb, 2010; Petajisto, 2017).

Tracking errors may depend on the manager's skills but may also be inherent to the benchmark index. The inability of managers to anticipate changes in the composition of the index leads to underperformance and tracking errors (Gastineau, 2004). But a large tracking error can also be the result of intended actions in the form of "hidden active management." ETF managers using statistical methods to select a subsample of the underlying securities to replicate the index face the risk that estimated correlations change over time. On the other side, some constraints cannot be avoided. For instance, creating and redeeming units on emerging market ETFs generates buy-and-sale operations on securities with different currencies. These operations, especially on hard-to-trade currency pairs, create currency risk. Stamp duties applied in some countries and the local taxation of the dividends delivered by the underlying securities can increase the ETF tracking error.

Other risks lie in the selection of the benchmark itself. Indices that are used as benchmarks are not neutral. They broadly contribute to the future performance of the funds. With the success of ETFs, index providers start tailoring benchmark indices for ETF issuers. In some cases there is a kind of conflict of interest between two subsidiaries of the same group, one issuing indices while the second manages ETFs that replicate those indices. In other situations index providers depend on a limited number of ETF issuers that constitute a large percentage of their turnover. As in the Libor scandal (Rauterberg and Verstein, 2013), there could be changes in the index to the benefit of the issuer that will impact the ETF value.

At the macro level, an extreme situation where a large number of funds held by an issuer default can lead to the issuer's bankruptcy. In a context of market concentration with three issuers controlling more than two-thirds of ETF assets, either in the United States or in Europe, the bankruptcy of one of the leading issuers could transfer risks to other sectors of finance. This contagion effect is an unintended consequence of this financial innovation (Diaz-Rainey and Ibikunle, 2012). Additionally, the growth of the ETF market on broad indices combined with the generalization of devices that integrate the constraint of the benchmark, even for active managers, may lead to the standardization of investors' behavior. In addition to the significant correlation between stock prices of the largest companies in the United States (Sullivan and Xiong, 2012), the development of ETFs could jeopardize the principle of diversification on which index management and modern portfolio theory are based (Da and Shive, 2016). If the liquidity of exotic ETFs increases, investors may choose these index products rather than a direct investment in their less liquid underlying securities (Bradley and Litan, 2010). So an unintended consequence of ETF development (Diaz-Rainey and Ibikunle, 2012) could be a reduction in investments in companies displaying low liquidity, even if they have a high growth potential.

ETFs, being traded on exchanges, bring new risks in addition to those inherited from index management. Traditional passive investment consists in a broad diversification with a low fee vehicle sustained over a long time horizon regardless of market fluctuations. Exchange Traded Funds bring a fluidity and an instantaneity of transactions unavailable in the traditional index fund industry. These innovative products radically transform index management by offering the possibility to actively manage portfolios of ETFs without paying any entry/exit fees. But immediacy has a cost. Investors have to pay commissions on transactions whenever they buy or sell ETFs. In volatile markets, these operations are common for investors using ETFs to implement active trading strategies. This should not concern long-term investors that are supposed to be the initial target of these funds, but turnover and short selling figures evidence the dynamic use of these supposedly passive instruments (Bogle, 2004).

The arbitrage technology is the core of the dual structure of ETFs but it involves the risks of failure or contagion. Failure of the arbitrage technology occurs during market stress when traders prefer to stay away from ETFs and their underlying securities rather than jumping on apparently profitable arbitrage opportunities. This amplifies the discrepancy between the market price of ETFs and their NAV. The arbitrage technology can also transfer liquidity shocks (Ben-David et al., 2014; Cespa and Foucault, 2012). Ben-David et al. (2014), who studied the impact of arbitrage on stocks with high ETF ownership, showed that traders' arbitrage operations can transfer exogenous liquidity shocks and/or volatility from ETFs to their underlying securities.

Additional complexity, additional risks

ETFs are presented as extremely transparent products. You can hardly find a brochure or a website dedicated to ETFs that does not mention the word "transparency." With respect to other non-traded funds, it is true that the information on their value as well as the number of outstanding shares has to be reported to the exchange and made public. The creation basket is also published every day, with the implicit message that, if you can create shares by delivering the basket, then the fund should hold these stocks. In fact, as has recently become clear to investors and journalists, funds need not hold the index constituting stocks and this topic became the centre of discussions with the failure of Lehman Brothers and the AIG bailout. Counterparty risk became the central issue in finance and regulators pointed their fingers at ETFs for this hidden risk.

Synthetic ETFs were initially blamed for the supposedly high counterparty risk involved in their structure. The controversy came back to physical ETFs like a boomerang when their stock lending activities were revealed. What the fund really holds is of importance in the event of a failure of the fund or its issuer. In this case, investors will be in possession of the assets that are effectively managed. For swap-based ETFs, by definition, the basket held by issuers does not match the index. It is the swap that provides the index return in exchange for the fund return and the model is beneficial only if the swap counterparty can optimize the stock basket deposited to the fund.

> What you should know is that when you buy an ETF, if it is a synthetic replicator, things that you bought are very different from what you really have in the fund. [...] So if you think you have the CAC 40 and DAX you can find yourself [in the event of the failure of the issuer or the fund] with something that has nothing to do with them.
>
> *(An asset manager)*

Still, the fund holds securities and the relevant question has to do with the quality of these securities. If the substitute basket is composed of liquid and highly rated securities, the investor can still recoup the index value by liquidating it. Problems arise when the substitute basket is composed of assets that are difficult to trade. It surprised investors to learn in 2010 that the collateral of some European equity ETFs was heavily composed of Japanese shares.[1] Ramaswamy (2011) argues that investment banks could be tempted to post illiquid securities they have on their books as collateral assets for a synthetic ETF, effectively funding them at zero cost. The effect of such operations would be an increase in the risks associated with the mismatch between the index underlying basket and the substitute basket effectively held by the fund.

For full replication ETFs, counterparty risk should not represent a real issue since the fund manager holds, if not all the stocks composing the index, then most of them and, in general, the most liquid. The practice of stock lending gave the lie to this theory, as the counterparty may not be able to hand the lent securities back. In that case, the collateral they get in return may strongly depart from the fund index composition. Once again, the quality of collateral is of prime importance. According to regulation, the risk exposure to counterparties cannot exceed 10 percent, meaning that, at any time the value of the collateral cannot be lower than 90 percent of the ETF's NAV.

New forms of ETFs such as leverage and inverse ETFs also raise new risks that could be classified as an abuse of financial innovation in the taxonomy developed in Diaz-Rainey and Ibikunle (2012). Although these ETFs seek to magnify the performance of the indexes they track for a single day, some investors used them like traditional ETFs, holding them for longer periods. Cheng and Madhavan (2009) show that their structure, among which their daily re-leveraging, creates unintended consequences. In particular, in times of volatile markets, the long-term performance of such products can be below that of the levered benchmark. The risk of abuse is particularly significant when these quite complex securities are sold to retail investors. In 2012, the Financial Industry Regulatory Authority fined brokers including Citigroup Global Markets, Morgan Stanley, UBS Financial Services and Wells Fargo Advisors for improperly selling these types of ETFs.

The control and revelation of risks

Information and social discipline

ETFs combine the passive nature of index funds with the active nature of exchange traded securities. Like any financial security, they involve risks. What is questionable is that these risks were revealed only years after their introduction despite wide press coverage. It seems as if these risks were kept hidden. The presence of ETFs in the press during the first few years resulted from the promotional efforts of issuers to ensure that people knew what ETFs were. Most of this promotional discourse was not about the true aspects of the product, but was rather a set of adapted and contextual arguments that were carefully selected to convince targets to invest in ETFs. This does not mean that it was a false discourse. It disseminated correct information but ignored or hid some relevant aspects. When a head of communications spoke to journalists, she said, "I am taking my colleagues' expertise and simplifying it to put it into normal language." For the sake of pedagogy, the technical side was filtered out. ETFs were simply described as financial products that offered almost all the possible benefits – practical, cheap, transparent, and liquid – while remaining extremely simple to use.

In order to relay the promotional discourse on ETFs efficiently, promoters managed their relationships with the press carefully, through implicit rules such as the exchange of information and trust. Journalists talked with promoters in order to obtain topics and data to fill their articles. ETFs were a hot topic, but were still new and not yet properly understood. This enabled promoters to pass on their views about the product. Journalists mainly relied on banks and their management companies as their source of information on ETFs, which led them to maintain permanent and mainly cordial relations with the managers of these companies.

Even in press companies known for their editorial independence, the pressure on journalists was great:

> The marketing team always wants to do a kind of push editorial part, it's not really the problem of [our journal], it's a general problem. With my previous employer part of the job was arguing with sales people.
>
> *(Journalist 1)*

It can also be considered that the sums of money that promoters invested in advertisements put them in a strong position to monitor the press and above all relay their own discourse on ETF:

> The space purchased by management companies [ETF issuers] for their advertisements makes them big contributors.
>
> *(Journalist 3)*

In return they asked journalists to participate in the effort to promote ETFs, as mentioned by another journalist:

> If an advertiser arrives and puts a large sum on the table, they can ask for pages of editorial comment to feature alongside the advertisements.
>
> *(Journalist 4)*

Likewise, when promoters found themselves face-to-face with a journalist who had not yet assimilated the commercial facet of their activity, they reacted like this manager:

> If there's a problem, we call their boss who knows that we're in a partnership type relation, meaning that we pay for their advertising banners.
>
> *(Head of communication – ETF issuer 1)*

The financial crisis as an opportunity

The equilibrium achieved by calling journalists to order whenever they deviated from the promotional discourse and by applying financial pressure through advertisements held until the 2007–2008 crisis. The synthetic replication technique was developed in a context of fierce competition between asset management firms that were leading the index fund industry in the US (iShares, State Street Global Advisors, Vanguard) and investment banks dominating the distribution of funds in Europe (Deutsche Bank, Société Générale, BNP Paribas). The marketing war between these two types of issuers was exacerbated by the financial crisis. ETF issuers started to criticize the replication technology of the opposing side. By pointing out the risks embedded in the competing structure, both sides mutually obliged each other to describe in detail the complexity of their own model.

The entry of Deutsche Bank into the ETF offering is emblematic of this war. Deutsche Bank's trading desk was acting as broker on ETFs for issuers such as iShares. They observed the growth of trading flows and the opportunity to benefit from ETFs not only as brokers but also as issuers. In 2007, they decided to launch their own ETFs with an aggressive strategy. Their model was based on the complementarity between the execution abilities of the trading desk of Deutsche Bank and the distribution capacities of their subsidiary db X-trackers. They made intensive sales efforts toward professional investors and won a significant market share in a short period. According to a manager from Deutsche Bank, these initiatives "shocked people a little bit."

The response from iShares, the market leader, was immediate. They launched a marketing strategy called *"Not all ETFs are created equal"* highlighting the existence of differences between operational structures. The promotional discourse of iShares focused on the idea that their rivals using derivatives to get a low tracking error may not have been as innocuous as presented. By suggesting the existence of an additional risk not mentioned by the investment banks issuing synthetic ETFs, they tried to impose the superiority of full replication in the process of building ETFs. When Lehman Brothers went bankrupt, iShares took this opportunity to point to the counterparty risk of swap-based ETFs. This marketing war led to a process of risk disclosure. iShares warned investors on the risks of default of the counterparty of the swap as well as on the kind of securities held by their funds. The collapse of a major investment bank and the distrust toward derivatives after the crisis magnified investors' worries about synthetic ETFs.

According to ETF issuers and brokers, this communication campaign "created confusion regarding the main message of the industry which was: ETFs are simple products regardless of the replication." Even Lee Kranefuss, who elaborated the aggressive strategy of iShares, explained years later that "this perception that synthetics are the enemy is an accident of history."[2] After 2008, investors started asking questions about the composition of their funds, the existence of derivatives and the counterparty of the swap. This undermined the image of transparency and simplicity of ETFs.

The criticisms brought by iShares offered an interesting opportunity for journalists to circumvent social control. As highlighted by a financial reporter, "sometimes the only way we get information about what some firms are really doing is when rival providers suddenly come out and advertise."[3] So journalists started relaying the arguments of the asset manager side and asked investment banks to answer. These banks shed light on the securities lending activity and its risks. The financial press thus became the battlefield of the marketing war between the two sides. This controversy offered the authorities an opportunity to intervene in order to regulate this growing market and to protect investors.

Financial journalists confronted issuers of swap-backed ETFs with the description given by iShares. Db-trackers and Lyxor[4] argued that their swap counterparties are not risky and that, under UCITS regulation, counterparty risk could never exceed 10 percent of the funds.

They claimed that the substitute baskets were made of high-rated securities and denounced the security lending operations used by asset managers such as iShares. Investment bankers unveiled the counterparty risk that existed in the case of physically backed ETFs:

> We met an institutional investor who wants to buy only physically-backed ETFs because of counterparty risk. We said: "Do you know that your issuer lends the underlying securities?" He told us: "I don't think so." Well, he finally asked his issuer, iShares, who confirmed it.
>
> *(Manager of an issuer using swap-backed ETFs)*

Building on the controversy, some financial reporters started challenging the "ETF-ization of nearly everything."[5] Others suggested that "ETFs are not really transparent" because portfolio disclosure was incomplete or delayed.[6] In other situations, the scandals were helpful for journalists to relay critical discourse on certain issuers or practices. The UBS scandal for instance shed light on "a widespread practice in Europe of failing to confirm immediately those ETF trades that are conducted on a bilateral basis."[7] Another journalist who was looking into the monitoring of the industry explained that he was released from the shackles thanks to the AIG crisis:

> ETF Securities arrived in France. Their name can be assimilated with traditional ETFs but they are ETCs. [...] I immediately noticed that and put it in my paper and I got phone calls. I met them and they argued that it was the same, that there was no difference. But the AIG crisis changed everything. I had written a good article and they understood that they had to behave differently.
>
> *(A French journalist)*

The industry failed to impose social discipline after this controversy. Although an effective response to these criticisms by international institutions would have required ETF promoters to move a step further in cooperation, they could not agree on any unified action. Lyxor and Deutsche Bank-x trackers proposed the creation of a European lobby involving all issuers to promote ETFs, but iShares finally refused. The asset management associations and issuers finally gave a piecemeal response to the ESMA consultation. While the head of the European Fund and Asset Management Association (EFAMA) suggested speaking with one voice, the chairman of the UK's Investment Management Association responded: "It's difficult to get a single, united voice for investment managers. Each firm has a different view of the world, for a start. Then some are independent, while others are owned by banks and insurance companies."[8]

Conclusion

ETFs are often presented as the most successful financial innovation of the last 20 years. They allow investors to trade index funds like ordinary stocks on exchanges. Starting from a very simple and passive structure, ETFs evolved into a more complex security necessitating more advanced management skills and subject to new risks, as already illustrated in Diaz-Rainey and Ibikunle (2012). Counterparty risks resulting either from the stock lending activity of physical ETFs or from the OTC swaps used by synthetic ETFs attracted the attention of the European regulators. We argue that, while such risks are of importance, it is also essential to identify all the other risks associated with ETFs and find their source.

The chief source of risks in ETFs, either physical or synthetic, remains the investment risk that is inherent to index funds. In that respect, it seems natural that the regulation applying to ETFs should find its roots in the regulation that applies to index funds in general. However, as listed securities, ETFs call for specifically adapted regulations. Arbitrage is central to the efficiency of the ETF market, but some claim that it brings with it systemic and liquidity risks. Further evolutions of the ETF operational structure and the new uses of ETFs led to new sources of risks that took the regulators almost 10 years to address.

We show in this chapter that most of the risks are inherent to the ETF structure per se. The industry managed to hide even those risks and the complexity of further evolutions of ETFs through the control of information and social discipline. It was only the marketing war between competing issuers offering ETFs built with different models that allowed journalists and regulators to circumvent social control and question the legitimacy of these subsequent innovations brought to the initial ETF structure. The regulator pointed to the need for greater transparency: in indices, in holdings, in replication technology, and more generally in data. It is only on the basis of fully disclosed information that investors can really decide whether the instrument is legitimate. As long as investors get rewarded for the risks they willingly take, risks may be legitimate.

Notes

1 See "Oh No, My ETF is Turning Japanese!" by Izabella Kaminska, April 19, 2010, http://ftalphaville.ft.com/2010/04/19/203796/oh-no-my-etf-is-turning-japanese/
2 In: "Kranefuss: Europe Needs a Real Competitor," by Rebecca Hampson, January 29, 2014, http://europe.etf.com/europe/news/9564-kranefuss-europe-needs-a-real-competitor.html?showall=&fullart=1&start=2
3 In: "Unappreciated Risks: The FT's Izabella Kaminska Plumbs What's Really on Offer in ETFs," welling@weeden, Vol. 13, No. 14, July 22, 2011, p. 6.
4 Db-x trackers is the ETF issuer of Deutsche Bank while Lyxor is the ETF issuer of Société Générale.
5 In: "The ETF Blowup Begins," by Izabella Kaminska, July 27, 2009, http://ftalphaville.ft.com/2009/07/27/63961/the-etf-blowup-begins/
6 In: "The ETFs Are Not Really Transparent," by Matt Hougan, March 02, 2010, http://www.indexuniverse.com/sections/blog/7342-etfs-are-not-really-transparent.html
7 In: "The ETF Loophole (Almost) Everyone Missed," by Paul Amery, September 21, 2011, http://www.etf.com/sections/blog/9909-the-etf-loophole-almost-everyone-missed.html
8 In: "Levelling the Playing Field," by Paul Amery, July 13, 2011, http://ftalphaville.ft.com/2009/07/27/63961/the-etf-blowup-begins/

References

Allen, F. (2012). Trends in financial innovation and their welfare impact: An overview. *European Financial Management*, 18(4), 493–514.
Amenc, N., Ducoulombier, F., Goltz, F. and Tan, L. (2012). *What are the risks of European ETFs?* EDHEC Risk Institute discussion paper.
Ben-David, I. Franzoni, F. and Moussawi, R. (2014). Do ETFs increase volatility? Working paper, Dice Center for Research in Financial Economics, Fisher College of Business: http://papers.ssrn.com/sol3/papers.cfm?abstract_id=1967599

Beunza, D., Hardie, I. and Mackenzie, D. (2006). A price is a social thing: Towards a material sociology of arbitrage. *Organization Studies*, 27(5), 751–745.

Blitz, D., Huij, J. and Swinkels, L. (2012). The performance of European index funds and Exchange-Traded Funds. *European Financial Management*, 18(4), 649–662.

Bogle, J. (1997). The first index mutual fund: A history of Vanguard Index Trust and the Vanguard Index Strategy. Source: http://johncbogle.com/speeches/JCB_first_index_mf.pdf

Bogle, J. (2004). Convergence: The great paradox? (Remarks before "The Art of Indexing" Conference). September 30 Washington DC.

Bradley, H. and Litan, M. (2010). *Choking the recovery: Why new growth companies aren't going public and unrecognized risks of future market disruptions*. Ewing Marion Kauffman Foundation.

Cespa, G. and Foucault, T. (2014). Illiquidity contagion and liquidity crashes. *Review of Financial Studies*, 27(6), 1615–1660.

Cheng, M. and Madhavan, A. (2009). The dynamics of leveraged and inverse exchange-traded funds. *Journal of Investment Management*, 7(4), 43–62.

Da, Z. and Shive, S. (2016). Exchange-traded funds and asset return correlations. Working paper: https://papers.ssrn.com/sol3/papers.cfm?abstract_id=2158361

Dellva, W. L. (2001). Exchange-traded funds Not for everyone. *Journal of Financial Planning*, 14(4), 110–124.

Diaz–Rainey, I. and Ibikunle, G. (2012). A taxonomy of the 'dark side' of financial innovation: The cases of high frequency trading and exchange traded funds. *International Journal of Entrepreneurship and Innovation Management*, 16(1), 51–72.

Elton, E. J., Gruber, M. J., Comer, G. and Li, K. (2002). Spiders: Where are the bugs? *Journal of Business*, 75(3) 453–472.

ESMA (2011). *ESMA's policy orientations on guidelines for UCITS Exchange-Traded Funds and Structured UCITS*, Discussion paper, European Securities and Markets Authority, N° 220.

FSB (2011). *Potential financial stability issues arising from recent trends in exchange-traded funds (ETFs)*. Financial Stability Board publications.

Gastineau, G. (2004). The benchmark index ETF performance problem. *Journal of Portfolio Management*, 30(2), 96–103.

IMF (2011). Annex 1.7. Exchange-traded funds: Mechanics and risks. In: *Global financial stability report* (pp. 69–73). New York: International Monetary Fund publications.

Knorr-Cetina, K. and Bruegger, U. (2002). Global microstructures: The virtual societies of financial markets. *American Journal of Sociology*, 107(4), 905–950.

Lerner, J. (2006). The new new financial thing: The origins of financial innovations. *Journal of Financial Economics*, 79(2), 223–255.

Petajisto, A. (2017). Inefficiencies in the pricing of exchange-traded funds. *Financial Analysts Journal*, 73(1), 24–54.

Ramaswamy, S. (2011). Market structures and systemic risks of exchange-traded funds. Bank for International Settlements Working Papers, N° 343.

Rauterberg, G. and Verstein, A. (2013). Index theory, the law, promise, and failure of financial indices. *Yale Journal on Regulation*, 30(1), 101–162.

Ruggins, S. M. E. (2018). *Building blocks: A historical sociology of the innovation and regulation of exchange-traded funds in the United States, 1970–2000*. Doctoral dissertation. University of Edinburgh.

Shina, S. and Soydemirb, G. (2010). Exchange-traded funds, persistence in tracking errors and information dissemination. *Journal of Multinational Financial Management*, 20(4/5), 214–234.

Sullivan, R. N. and Xiong, J. X. (2012). How index trading increases market vulnerability. *Financial Analysts Journal*, 68, 70–84.

Tufano, P. (2003). Financial innovation. In G. Constantinides, M. Harris and R. Stulz (Eds.), *Handbook of the Economics of Finance (Volume 1a: Corporate Finance)* (pp. 307–336). New York: Elsevier.

11

JUNIOR STOCK MARKETS AND SMEs: AN IDEAL RELATION?

The case of the *Alternative Investment Market*

Valérie Revest

Financing for SMEs (small and medium-sized enterprises) and support for innovation have for several decades figured as large-scale political issues for European governments. Numerous economic studies tackle the difficulties affecting SMEs' access to financing, including the effect of credit rationing. The lack of security, the presence of information asymmetries and the financial fragility of some companies represent many of the arguments expressed when defining the obstacles confronting these organisations. Added to this is the behaviour of discouraged executive managers who, anticipating the refusal of their application files, choose not to turn to funding organisations and instead favour internal sources of financing. The innovation dimension furthermore increases these above-mentioned difficulties and plunges both the companies concerned and their financers into the depths of radical uncertainty during the decision-making processes.

The construction of markets dedicated to SMEs illustrates one of the initiatives taken by stock exchanges in order to facilitate the access to financing for these businesses. The main global financial centres have for a long time consecrated certain sections to small and medium market capitalisations. This was certainly the case in Europe during the 1980s with the *Second Marché* in France, the Unlisted Securities Market in the United Kingdom and the *Geregelter Markt* in Germany. A major turning point was observed in the mid-1990s, under the impetus of the European Community, with the creation of the 'New Markets' of Continental Europe, created for small and medium companies with promising growth prospects (Posner, 2009). The collapse of these New Markets following the burst of the Dot-com bubble in 2001 contributed to the *Alternative Investment Market* (AIM), created in 1995 by the London Stock Exchange (LSE), taking centre stage. In the beginning, the AIM was created as a *feeder* market for the Main Market listing, i.e. a temporary market capable of propelling the top businesses towards a main listing on the London stock exchange. Today, for many political and economic actors, the AIM has become the leading reference model for *junior stock markets*, that is, new markets dedicated to small and medium market capitalisations.

The aim of this chapter is to investigate the connections between SMEs and junior stock markets. Do SMEs access market-based financing more easily, thanks to the AIM? What types of support does this market offer to listed companies? Analysing how the AIM operates and the characteristics of those companies admitted to this market sheds light on the advantages and limitations of this market model for those businesses concerned, as well as for investors, stock market authorities and policy-makers. Moreover, it reveals two significant transformations that affect the very nature of stock markets, with the first being the heightened reliance on private decentralised regulation and the second, the growing influence of practices originating from within private equity firms.

The Alternative Investment Market (AIM) model

The AIM is based on a unique market model, which stands apart from other configurations. Organised stock market operations, main or second tier listings, generally rely upon a form of regulation based on rules: the *rule-based approach*. In accordance with this approach, the system of regulation consists of general, universal and abstract rules, defined by an *ex ante* regulatory body. These rules affect all the stages required for listing a company, from the company's initial admission to the list through to it maintaining its place. The AIM follows another form of regulation: the *principle-based approach*. There are no pre-established rules, but instead basic principles that are meant to guide those involved in the decision-making process. Specialist independent intermediaries, the Nominated Advisors (Nomads), authorised by the LSE, hold the legitimate authority to accept or refuse a company's admission to the AIM list. Any company wishing to be listed on this market is therefore obliged to contact a Nomad and submit a request for admission. All the same, the Nomad's role is not limited to the admission process as they must also ensure those companies being admitted comply with the norms for maintaining a place and guide these companies towards implementing 'good practices' with respect to governance and ethics (Mallin and Ow-Yong, 2010).

According to the AIM's supporters, the main advantages of this market model lie in the low costs of admission and listing, and most importantly, in the flexibility of the regulation mechanism adapted to suit small and medium capitalisations. The Nomads possess discretionary powers and they examine requests for admission case-by-case, adapting the decision-making criteria to the context and the particular nature of the applicant companies. Replacing the collection of rigid conditions defined *ex ante* is a customised process of evaluation carried out by these intermediaries. The Nomads are therefore considered to be responsible for the integrity and the reputation of the AIM (Rousseau, 2007; Mendoza, 2008). All the same, the viability of a market model relying almost uniquely on a system of reputation as the means for the coordination of exchange is still open to questioning.

A few (relative) indicators of the AIM's success

The first indicator of the AIM's success appeared with its increase in size. The number of businesses listed on the AIM increased almost continuously between 1995 and 2014, with 1,104 businesses noted in December 2014, and the peak of 1,694 having been reached in 2007. While the AIM was slightly weakened by the 2008 financial crisis, it was not affected by the burst of the Dot-com bubble in March 2001, thanks to the co-occurrence of several factors such as the diversification of its listing, the presence of the Nomads and the reputation of the London Stock Exchange (Revest and Sapio, 2013). The disappearance of Europe's 'New Markets' (including the French *Nouveau Marché* and the German *Neuer Markt*) also generated a resurgence in admission requests to the AIM. Furthermore, a massive arrival of non-European companies was observed during the 2005–2007 period. Two interpretations have been put forward to explain this phenomenon. For some, the mounting demand by these companies coincided with the Sarbanes-Oxley legislation (2002) coming into force in the United States, which would have disadvantaged small and mid-caps due to the rise in listing costs. For others, it was linked to the presence of numerous companies which had their corporate headquarters located in off-shore territories, which would have been a rather negative warning sign regarding the quality of the foreign companies admitted to the AIM at this time.

Furthermore, although the evolution of market capitalisation was virtually continuous since the creation of the AIM, its overall level remained relatively low in comparison with other markets. For example, NASDAQ's capitalisation in 2012 was forty times higher than that of the AIM. A detailed analysis of the AIM's composition tends to show that it is made up of a few large caps and a multitude of very small ones (Lagneau-Ymonet et al., 2014). Another interesting effect to note is related to movements occurring between the AIM and the LSE. Although the AIM was initially created in order to 'feed' this list, the reverse effect was produced, as more companies demanded to be transferred from the Main listing to the AIM than vice versa: 210 versus 54 during the 1995–2009 period. The companies that moved from the AIM to the LSE's Main listing cited three key reasons: investors' interest, increased visibility and enhanced growth prospects. As for the movements in the opposite direction, from the LSE's Main list to the AIM, several reasons have been noted, such as the low cost of listing, the potential for carrying out mergers/acquisitions, shareholders' interests, increased flexibility and reduced regulation (Vismara et al., 2012).

In summary, painting a preliminary portrait of the AIM brings to light signs of a market that is attractive to companies with small market capitalisation, hoping to benefit from low admission and listing costs, as well as the flexibility of this market's regulation. However, in order to complete this basic outline, it is necessary to look closer at what the outcomes of a listing on the AIM are for those companies concerned.

An initial assessment of the AIM's impact on listed companies

In 2007, the AIM was at the centre of a controversy that opposed on one side managers of the American financial markets and on the other side those of the London Stock Exchange. Roel Campos, a commissioner for the SEC (Securities and Exchange Commission), publicly compared the AIM's operations to that of a casino: 'I am concerned that 30% of issuers that list on AIM are gone within a year. That feels a bit like a casino to me.' This comment provoked lively reactions in the United Kingdom, in particular from those in charge at the LSE. In following, empirical research attempted to verify Campos' assertion and, more generally, to evaluate the impact of an AIM listing for those companies concerned. A summary of existing research has illustrated both positive and negative outcomes (Revest and Sapio, 2014). Among the impacts judged negative, inferior financial returns were noted on the AIM in comparison to other stock markets (LSE's Main listing, NASDAQ, NYSE), for similar companies over three-to-five-year periods post-IPO. Moreover, the principal–agent problem has proven to be higher on the AIM. In the past, several scandals such as those associated with the companies Regal Petroleum and Langbar International were made public. In this latter example, the admitted company did not possess any of the declared assets (£375 million UK pounds). Lastly, the AIM's impact on the real economic performance of companies is not entirely convincing. For one, the AIM does not represent a springboard for young innovative companies; a point that was indirectly recognised by the LSE, when they launched a new market segment in 2013 specifically dedicated to these companies. And second, a comparative study examining companies listed on the AIM and private companies with similar profiles based in the UK appears to show that the productivity growth rate of listed companies was inferior to that of private companies (Revest and Sapio, 2013).

Despite this rather pessimistic assessment, the AIM continues to remain appealing for the following two reasons: First, companies in this market are relatively active in terms of secondary equity offerings; and, second, for certain companies an AIM listing corresponds to market opportunities for corporate control strategies such as buyouts, mergers or even reverse mergers (see the final section).

The role(s) of stock markets dedicated to SMEs

An assessment of the AIM brings to the surface ambiguous results that can only be interpreted in light of the motivations and expectations linked to the creation of this type of market. On the one hand, the growth in size of this market is evidence of a real interest in this type of model from small, medium and intermediary-sized companies. Stock exchange authorities in several countries have therefore seized upon this opportunity, taking inspiration from the AIM, and have created junior markets. The AIM model has thus influenced France, with the *Alternext*, and certain Nordic countries through the *First North* segment. Other versions of the AIM have recently emerged such as the AIM Italia (2009) or the AIM Tokyo (2009). On an international scale, the major global stock exchange centres look upon junior markets as showcases through which they can demonstrate their own dynamic nature, enabling them to increase their number of listed companies. Moreover, for a decade now, stock exchanges have been continuously decreasing the criteria required for admission to junior markets in order to attract an ever-increasing number of companies (Carpentier et al., 2010). From the governments' perspective, the creation of a market based on the AIM model can be considered favourable, as it opens the way to market-based financing for SMEs, allowing them to advance relatively easily towards increases in capital and towards carrying out diverse corporate control strategies following the example of major companies present on the stock markets. On the other hand, if the emphasis is placed on real company performance indicators (growth rate, productivity), then the AIM does not live up to expectations with respect to the production of innovative products/services, the creation of jobs or the stimulation of growth and exports (Mazzucato, 2011). As such, depending on the objectives being pursued, the 'quality' anticipated by those companies accessing the market can vary greatly. In one case, the growth perspectives of admitted companies do not really come into account, as emphasis is placed on the financial and non-financial opportunities provided to companies via the access to a stock market; in the other case, they are fundamental, as companies' expectations are centred around the effects on the real economy due to the existence and operation of this type of market. Those political and economic actors either directly or indirectly involved in the creation of junior markets must consider the ends being sought and the balance created between these ends and the proposed market model. Regardless of the objectives, it is nevertheless our opinion that there exist real dangers in leaving the private and decentralised regulation of junior stock markets to develop freely. Derivatives have already appeared on the markets which, following the lead of the AIM, authorise *back-door listings*, in other words alternative means of admission that are less restrictive for companies. In the following section, we demonstrate to what extent the dividing line between market-based financing and non-market-based financing is blurred, and we underline the potential threats inherent to these metamorphoses.

A reflection on the evolution of junior stock markets

For a long time, economies financed via the market have been distinguished from economies financed through debt due to elements such as the diversity of capitalisms, institutional contexts and the weight of history. Since the end of the 1980s, the expansion of stock markets in association with the transformation of banking professions has contributed towards blurring this distinction. A secondary disruption to company financing mechanisms is currently taking place through the junior markets, with it being a question of diminishing the dividing line between private equity financing (real capital) and public equity financing (market). Two examples illustrate this phenomenon. First, the evolution of these markets towards a continually decreasing regulation has allowed immature companies, i.e. achieving neither profit, nor revenue, to access stock markets. The most striking example is on the Toronto stock market, with the Toronto Stock Exchange Venture (TSXV). This market is intended for micro-capitalisations, in other words companies that are in the early stages of development and not yet gaining revenue. This market is considered by stock market authorities to be in direct competition with venture capital financing (Carpentier et al., 2010).

Second, on the global scale the rise in the number of admissions via alternative, less restrictive measures, notably through reverse mergers, also attests to a shift in the financing practices of private equity directed towards junior stock markets. A reverse merger is defined as a non-traditional method for gaining access to the status of a public company. A private company not wanting to complete an IPO sets out in search of a company already listed on the market, a type of 'cash shell', which displays no economic activity. The private company then merges with the listed company and, following this merger, the assets and liabilities of the private company are transferred to the public one, which then passes under the control of the private. This type of operation has been labelled 'private equity with listing' by the *Financial Times* (4 November 2007). This alternative way of admission is a choice motivated by several aims. For a private company, it is a question of going public relatively rapidly and at the lowest possible cost, while also securing the conditions for admission and an already established shareholder base. However, the few empirical studies dealing with reverse mergers reveal rather worrying results concerning the nature of the companies accessing the market via this strategy. Companies born from reverse takeovers are usually young, small in size and less profitable than similar companies. They are characterised by weak liquidity on their balance sheets, a consistent leveraging effect and more information asymmetries than those companies accessing the market via the traditional IPO path. Moreover, insiders have a tendency to quickly sell their shares, to the detriment of outside investors. Thus, building stock markets practically customised for SMEs and with increasingly alleviated requirements, leads to attracting companies whose objectives do not coincide with economic growth and development.

Conclusion

A dual trend sustains the recent evolution of stock markets committed to small and medium market capitalisations. On one side, the regulation model of these markets is increasingly based on private intermediaries (the Nomads and AIM), illustrating the market authorities' recognition of the efficiency of decentralised regulation. On the other side, the barriers between market-based financing and private equity financing appear to have lowered, showing evidence of a progressive erasure of the lines separating these modalities of financing, up till now deemed different in nature. In context, stock markets no longer appear at the end of the traditional financing process, where they signal the success of a company's evolution to a stage of maturity. Instead, they represent an alternative mode to other systems – such as bank financing, private equity, formal or informal (e.g. 'business angels') venture capital – with the company's stage of development being of little importance. According to this approach, how these markets operate is based largely on the participation of private structures, much like the model of private equity financing. Such transformations should not be ignored as they illustrate a change in the configuration of financial systems and the nature of stock markets (Michie, 2006). Most importantly, they urge us to consider the goals of junior stock markets and the role of public and private actors in their construction.

References

Carpentier, C., L'Her, J.-F. and Suret, J.-M. (2010). Stock exchange markets for new ventures. *Journal of Business Venturing*, 25(4), 403–422.

Lagneau-Ymonet, P., Rezaee, A. and Riva, A. (2014). *Is the proof of the pudding in the eating?* Comparaison entre l'*Alternative Investment Market* et Alternext. *Revue d'Economie Financière*, 114(2), 189–206.

Mallin, C. and Ow-Yong, K. (2010). The UK alternative investment market-ethical dimensions. *Journal of Business Ethics*, 95(2), 223–239.

Mazzucatto, M. (2011). *The entrepreneurial state*. Londres: Demos.

Mendoza, J. M. (2008). Securities regulation in low-tier listing venues: The rise of the Alternative Investment Market. *Fordham Journal of Corporate & Finance Law*, 13(2), 259–328.

Michie, R. (2006). *The global securities markets. A history*. Oxford: Oxford University Press.

Posner, E. (2009). *The origins of Europe's new stock markets*. Cambridge: Harvard University Press.

Revest, V. and Sapio, A. (2013). Does the Alternative Investment Market nurture firm growth? A comparison between listed and private firms. *Industrial and Corporate Change*, 22(4), 953–979.

Revest, V. and Sapio, A. (2014). L'*Alternative Investment Market*: un modèle pour le financement des petites et moyennes capitalisations? *Revue d'Economie Financière*, 114(2), 167–188.

Rousseau, S. (2007). London calling? The experience of the Alternative Investment Market and the competitiveness of Canadian stock exchanges. *Banking & Finance Law Review*, 23(1), 51–104.

Vismara, S., Paleari, S. and Ritter, J. (2012). Europe's second markets for small companies. *European Financial Management*, 18(3), 352–388.

12

STRUCTURES AND MEASURES FOR RESPONSIBLE FINANCE

Elise Penalva-Icher

Since its definition in 1992 at the Rio de Janeiro Earth Summit, sustainable development has become a notion introduced into numerous spheres of society. For example, household waste separation has become normalised in the domestic sphere; corporate social responsibility has become a widespread theme in companies; labels denoting low-energy buildings (*Bâtiment Basse Consommation* – BBC) and High Quality Environmental standards (*Haute Qualité Environnementale* – HQE) have appeared in the construction industry. The justification methods enlisted to initiate and perpetuate these practices have proven numerous: some refer to an essentialised nature, while other, more pragmatic, approaches attempt to measure the economic benefits. While the economic argument may initially seem ill-placed, we must recognise that ultimately it is quite often employed to legitimise and enforce environmental or social practices. Therefore, institutional research carried out in order to justify sustainable development and legitimise practices which result from it, should not be side-stepped.

Finance is one of the spheres of society that appears furthest removed from sustainable development and which could be believed to be impenetrable to any form of outside influence. Nevertheless, the notion of sustainable development does interact with the financial world. There exists for that matter a type of investment called 'socially responsible investment' (SRI) which proclaims its identity from this very notion. We can therefore, using the case of SRIs, examine the manner in which sustainable development and finance influence and/or clash with one another. Carrying out an analysis of the history of SRI, even though quite recent, offers us the opportunity to examine the notion of social responsibility in the financial world. The genesis of SRI shows how it is based on sustainable development, even though this type of investment does not really draw its origins from this domain. But how did this interaction between two initially differentiated worlds take place? This process was socially constructed thanks to a network of actors who in the midst of their interdependencies founded the SRI market.

The work of analysing the social construction of a market figures as part of the recent stream of new economic sociology. In fact, since the 1970s, the revival of economic sociology around the notion of *embeddedness*, inherited from Polanyi, has greatly illuminated the mechanisms that economic science had become so used to ignoring within economic activity. Whether we talk of historical, cultural, regulatory or relational embeddedness, research reveals how markets function as sites in which systems of judgement are established in order to define assets or, consequently, how social processes such as solidarity or learning can be implemented alongside competition, which is not the all-governing force that rules over market regulation (Smelser and Swedberg, 1994; Zelizer, 1985). Likewise, economic sociology and, in particular, the taking into account of the social relations between actors who were non-fragmented, but integrated into the various relational structures, enable a better understanding of the mechanisms studied at great length by the economic sciences, such as price setting or access to the labour market (Baker, 1984; Granovetter, 1995). Within this chapter, the contribution of this theoretical stream to the social study of finance is based around considering these market structures. The embeddedness of the SRI market presents heterogeneous actors in situations of interdependency as a way of constructing an evaluation measure for social and/or environmental policies within companies. This technical measure evolves throughout the various interdependencies into a measure for the 'captation' (Cochoy, 2004) of clients through the use of companies' social and environmental dimensions of finance.

In examining this issue, we first explore SRI practices throughout its history, since the birth of the first ethical foundations at the beginning of the twentieth century right up to the current day, and within various countries: USA, Great Britain, the Netherlands and France. Originating from ethical foundations first established in America, today French SRI is based on the formulation of grades called '*ratings*'. Accordingly, it is clearly a system of evaluation backed up by figures representing companies' social and environmental conduct. In the following pages, we go on to describe the actors of this market and the manner in which they interact within their relational networks, in order to formulate this evaluation. Finally, using the research of Alain Desrosières (2002) on public statistics and the political value of numbers, we ascertain that a numeric figure is a social construction and that in order to read it we have need of a collective agreement. It is therefore necessary to analyse the agreement, which underpins SRI evaluations. We conclude that this agreement is inscribed in the social structures of classical finance, which shifts the technical measure towards evolving into a measure of 'captation' (Cochoy, 2007). In accordance with the theoretical project of the social studies of finance, we thus propose to use the contribution from economic sociology and the analysis of social networks to understand the way in which a market is built, around which particular actors, and how during their interactions these actors define the quality of what becomes 'socially responsible' within the world of finance.

Which type of practices for SRI?

At the beginning of the twentieth century, SRIs in the United States were not 'responsible' but instead 'ethical'. As it were, ethical, and often religious, investment funds which did not wish to invest in economic activities that were counter to their principles (such as tobacco, gaming or alcohol) appeared during this era. These ethical funds were imitated in France during the 1980s by the parish community of *Notre Dame de la Sagesse* which was concerned about its members' retirement funds. Yet, these initial ethical funds do not correspond at all to the responsible investment practices of today, as they answered to a logic based on the *negative screening* of shares, while today the main responsible investment practice is built on filters that select (instead of excluding) the 'best' companies in each sector, also known as the '*best-in-class*'.

In truth, there exist several ways of practising SRI. Negative screening excludes a certain number of sectors or companies from the investment realm for religious or moral reasons. This way of implementing SRI is particularly practised in the United States where religion, or other forms of activism, underpin investment. Other forms of activism can also be political, which was the case for example during the 1980s, when a call to boycott was launched against investing in companies with activities in South Africa during the apartheid regime.

However, in France, negative screening is rarely practised. When it is, it is incidentally legitimised on the basis of economic and non-activist reasons. As such, tobacco may be excluded, not because it is a condemnable practice from a moral perspective, but because the fund manager considers that with increases in smoking bans in public places and advances in knowledge regarding the effects of tobacco in cancer development, it therefore represents more or less a bad long-term investment. Whether it is because they quit smoking or succumb to cancer, smokers will eventually become an extinct species!

SRI practices thus prove to be extremely varied in terms of contexts, especially national ones. While responsible investment in the US appears to be primarily ethical, Great Britain and the Netherlands experiment with investments in which shareholder activism is held to be responsible. In this case, it is no longer only the management of funds that is altered but the relationship between shareholders and companies. Shareholder activism advocates for the idea that the fund manager, in the name of the responsible shareholders' interests, must have a more prominent role in company policy, for example by adopting a *voice* attitude during the Shareholders' General Assembly, that is to say assuming asking unsettling questions to the company. These types of practices are still quite scarce in France where the legal modalities for filing motions or voting during a General Assembly continue to remain fairly technical and complicated.

Generally speaking, French fund managers prefer to build investment funds by activity sector, selecting the 'best' companies (in this case similar to *positive screening*) from each sector (representing the *best-in-class*). This may seem surprising, but it's for this very reason that we find oil companies for example in French SRI funds, with those chosen representing the companies with the best practices in terms of environmental conduct.

France equally possesses the particularity of having developed community and solidarity investment funds alongside SRI funds. In this specific case, the practice of investment is for the most part classic, however a share of the funds (from 5 to 10 per cent) is paid back to the associations or invested into public benefit projects (housing, fighting against unemployment, etc.). Solidarity investments are therefore not quite the same as SRIs: the portion invested 'solidarily' respects the principle of a donation and not an investment; nevertheless, solidarity investments and SRI still remain financial sectors that are closely linked. This connection can only be understood by considering the regulation of the SRI market. This type of investment has been largely boosted by the government. The State created frameworks for favouring the development of this market in the form of laws. For example, SRI was facilitated by the 2001 law related to *Nouvelles Régulations Economiques* (New Economic Regulations, also called NRE), which obliged major groups to provide information related to the socially responsible behaviour of companies, from which extra-financial analysts could construct their evaluations. Extra-financial analysis is a profession which appeared in conjunction with SRI as a way of producing social and/or environmental evaluations of company policies. It was notably developed through extra financial ratings agencies. This obligation was expanded to include smaller companies following the Grenelle 2 law. Alongside these laws, retirement reforms in 2003 introduced the possibility for certain employee savings plans to invest 5 per cent in solidarity investments.

However, these regulatory frameworks remained feeble and were invested in by market actors. The State proposed the SRI, quite irresolutely, though refrained from assigning a precise definition to it within the texts, leaving it instead in the hands of private actors to give meaning to what would become SRIs. For example, the decrees for applying the NRE law were long-awaited and the boundaries of application were in the end recognised as being less demanding than what might have been expected of the law. This form of joint regulation was decisive in the present case, as it rendered the various actors of SRI independent, yet connected through relational networks. These private actors, at times greatly heterogeneous and interested in defining the subject, would evidently need to interact in order to have a say in what SRI must be and could become.

So how did we move from religious funds to funds that advocate for investing in the best companies in each sector, in terms of their social and environmental behaviour? It was the result of legitimising efforts carried out by various SRI actors. While the public authorities supported these measures, it was well and truly those actors involved in this market who fixed the course for defining what would eventually become SRI. This brings to mind notably the essential role which the extra-financial ratings agencies played at the very beginning of the market, through imposing forms of evaluation such as *ratings*, which offered a quantified measurement system for social and environmental behaviours. The advantage of this measurement was that it offered an answer to the demands of finance, which sought to evaluate within the context of technical and mathematical procedures.

Interdependencies of heterogeneous SRI actors: bringing the market into existence and making it work

In order to understand how this socially and historically situated practice of French SRI emerged, we will now examine the structures of this market, that is to say the actors that comprise it as well as the relations which link them to one another.

We must begin by specifying for whom the SRI products are intended and how this offer is established, as it is above all a market aimed at institutional investors. Even though SRI attempts to develop its capacities in line with private individuals through the organisation of information weeks targeting the wider public, or thanks to training campaigns for professionals across banking networks, it still remains a market in which private investors are not majority shareholders. It is considered to be a product aimed at institutional investors and designed for them. According to the organisation Novethic, in 2014 the market accounted for €182 billion in stocks for institutional investors, in comparison to 40.9 billion for private investors.

The creation and promotion of SRI targeted institutional investors of a particular profile, those linked to long-term investment and willing to let themselves be persuaded by arguments related to social responsibility. This was better suited to the responsibility demanded than a short-term vision considered to be speculative. Consequently, the development of SRI was linked to that of employee savings funds – as in the previously cited example of the retirement reforms – which opened up the possibility of investing a share of the employee savings plan (PERCO – *Plan d'Epargne pour la Retraite Collectif*, Group Retirement Savings Plan) as a solidarity investment. But we can equally cite another example, that of the 2001 law introducing the *Fonds de Réserve pour les Retraites* (Retiree Reserve Fund), which obliged this national fund to partly invest in a responsible way.

Accordingly, this proximity between SRIs and institutional investors introduced elements of pension funds retirement products into the French system. The trade unions therefore seized hold of the subject and insisted on being present during discussions on the creation of these employee savings funds, notably through the *Comité Intersyndical de l'Epargne Salarial* (CIES – Inter-Trade Union Committee for Employee Savings Funds). This committee released a label to distinguish between the range of employee savings funds. The social responsibility of funds was one of the criteria attributed by this label.

The SRI market must therefore be defined as a concrete market (Courpasson, 1994), which is not a meeting place for buyers and sellers, but a social construction determined by the interests of heterogeneous actors, which is equally engaged in activities other than the simple act of buying or selling. For example, these actors may qualify what should be considered socially responsible through the bias of a label, such as that of the CIES. In addition to this example of certification, numerous SRI stakeholders participate in the activity of this market by providing extra-financial information or by taking part in debates concerning 'good practices'.

Qualifying the social and/or environmental behaviour of a company is not an easy thing to do. Indeed, added to the problem of defining what these behaviours should be, is the quest for relevant information and more importantly the translation of this information into indicators which can be applied to management routines. One of these stakeholders held this role of institutionalising the SRI market at the beginning of the century: a company then known as Arese, which has today become Vigeo, a leader in extra-financial ratings in France. This organisation's success was based on having immediately offered fund managers gradings and spreadsheet files, similar to those proposed by standard ratings agencies with their triple A rating (Callon and Muniesa, 2003; Déjean et al., 2004). This evaluation of companies' social and environmental behaviour thus took on the name of *rating*. The naming of this measure revealed a particular form of measurement implemented into the financial system, which would in the future have performative effects on SRI.

Here a long list of diverse actors who take part in all sorts of activities on this market become apparent: asset managers, extra-financial ratings agencies, consultants, NGOs, trade unions and other stakeholders. These actors interact during the course of numerous activities: defining what socially responsible means, searching for information, verifying this information, promoting the market, qualifying products, etc. Economic sociology, according to Harrison White (1981), reveals that markets are the product of interactions between competitors who rub shoulders, take measure of one another and consequently position themselves in relation to each other. Studying SRI exposes the fact that not only can competitors collaborate together in order to establish a business transaction, but more impressive is the fact that they do so with other stakeholders and while implementing extremely varied forms of relations. In the case of SRI, the informal relations within networks help financial actors to acquire positions as intermediaries (Penalva-Icher, 2010), positioned between historic actors such as ratings agencies and stakeholders who have more recently emerged on to the market. This position as intermediary offers financiers the advantage of a type of 'structural hole' (Burt, 2009) in the interest of acquiring a central role in defining SRI.

The SRI agreement 'towards the financialisation of responsibility': the social construction of a quality

Apart from the necessities of finding clients and calibrating the market via financial tools, the market must also be rendered durable by finding it a legitimate mode of operating.

The links that are woven within the relational networks of this market therefore go further than just facilitating the manufacturing of funds. They also participate in the institutionalisation of the market. In doing so, SRI actors established working relations among very heterogeneous actors. Thus, around the same table we see a fund manager and an extra-financial analyst, but also representatives of trade unions or NGOs supporting environmental protection, all of which is testament to quite an exceptional social situation.

This heterophily of the market originates from the interdependencies between actors: they have need of each other in order to accomplish the work of qualifying and managing SRI funds. Though further afield from this, we equally see informal relations being woven. In addition to their utility in work, these relations enable certain forms of status to be acquired. As such, while in the beginning SRI drew its roots from worlds external to finance, it is a 'mainstream' understanding which today renders it legitimate, positioning SRI not as a niche investment, but as a new way of doing finance. This understanding is shouldered by actors from the financial world, fund managers and brokers, who today have the technical and symbolic resources to establish themselves within the market's structures, and this is thanks to the earlier work of actors situated further out on the peripheries of finance, such as rating agencies or trade unions (Penalva-Icher, 2009).

We have therefore emerged into a paradoxical situation: initially born outside of finance, SRI is today completely integrated with it. Instead of importing other logics into finance, it exports financial logics based on subjects that are external to finance, such as society and the environment. Furthermore, SRI is in the process of shedding its qualifier 'socially' and is being transformed into simply 'responsible investment'. Responsibility has proven itself to be a measure for captivating companies' social and environmental aspects through finance (and not the other way round). From its origin as a technical tool, SRI has become an arrangement for evaluating in a financial way, not only the economic performance of a company, but also its impact on the society and the environment, which is what locates it at the confluence between financial market and public space.

References

Baker, W. (1984). The social structure of a national securities market. *American Journal of Sociology*, 89(4), 775–811.

Burt, R. S. (2009). *Structural holes: The social structure of competition*. Cambridge: Harvard University Press.

Callon, M. and Muniesa, F. (2003). Les marchés économiques comme dispositifs collectifs de calcul. *Réseaux*, 6, 189–233.

Cochoy, F. (2004). La captation des publics entre dispositifs et dispositions, ou le petit chaperon rouge revisité. In F. Cochoy (Ed.), *La captation des publics: 'c'est pour mieux te séduire, mon client'* (pp. 11–68). Toulouse: Presses universitaires du Mirail.

Cochoy, F. (2007). A brief theory of the 'captation' of publics: Understanding the market with Little Red Riding Hood. *Theory, Culture & Society*, 24(7–8), 203–223.

Courpasson, D. (1994). Marché concret et identité professionnelle locale. La construction de l'identité par rapport au marché. *Revue Française de Sociologie*, 35, 197–229.

Déjean, F., Gond, J.-P and Leca, B. (2004). Measuring the unmeasured: An institutional entrepreneur strategy in an emerging industry. *Human Relations*, 57(6), 741–764.

Desrosières, A. (2002). *The politics of large numbers: A history of statistical reasoning*. Cambridge: Harvard University Press.

Granovetter, M. (1995). *Getting a job: A study of contacts and careers*. Chicago: University of Chicago Press.

Penalva-Icher, E. (2009). Construire une qualité pour le 'socialement responsable'? *Revue Française de Socio-Economie*, 2, 59–81.

Penalva-Icher, E. (2010). Amitié et régulation par les normes. *Revue Française de Sociologie*, 51(3), 519–544.

Smelser, N. J. and Swedberg, R. (Eds.) (1994). *The handbook of economic sociology*. Princeton: Princeton University Press.

White, H. C. (1981). Where do markets come from? *American Journal of Sociology*, 87(3), 517–547.

Zelizer, V. (1985). *Pricing the priceless child: The changing social value of children*. Princeton: Princeton University Press.

13

TERRITORIES OF FINANCE

The Parisian case

Yamina Tadjeddine

The terms virtuality, mobility and globality are often heard in connection with the financial world. And increasingly, cash flows appear to be abstract numbers which circulate at the speed of light between digitalised worlds. Within this financial transformation, some geographers have identified the coming of a new era liberated from territorial and national anchoring. The internationalisation of trade and the digitalisation of financial securities have indeed allowed for the free circulation of capital and a growing interconnectedness between financial centres. For all this though, finance is not by any means a stateless abstract concept: the people, the organisations and the machines that shape finance are physically embedded in specific locations. Financialisation therefore brings with it the increased exposure of this industry within locations historically dedicated to its activity, such as Wall Street or the City, but also in newer zones, whether they be fiscal paradises or particular neighbourhoods. The global or urban territory thus becomes a reflection of this financial transformation.

The French geographer Labasse (1974) was without doubt the first to take note of the new territorial tensions produced by the financialisation process. Two decades later, it became possible to draw up an outline of this movement. The geographer Sassen (1991) highlighted the territorial hierarchy produced by financial transformation through the emergence of global interconnected cities dominating the world-wide economic circuit. Along with the collective works of Martin (1999) appeared an increased diversity in the focus, the scale (world-wide, national, urban) and the measurements (capital flows, payrolls, job market, number of companies, etc.) applied in order to study this event. It is presently possible to observe the financialisation process taking place in a chosen space by studying how these measurements evolve.

The quantification of the financialisation effect at a global level experienced sweeping success as of the late 1970s due to the measurement of global capital flows and the emphasis of their growing integration. The issue of financialisation at a national level is more recent. It concerns principally the influence of the financial sector on the national economy and pinpoints the resulting outcomes, whether they are in relation to capturing revenue or uncovering inequalities (see the contribution by Olivier Godechot in this collection). The local level remains the least favoured of the three, however the transformations here are just as interesting. Crevoisier and Theurillat (2012) enlighten the effects of internationalisation on pension funds in Switzerland through the study of the geographical allocation of their investment portfolio.

Since the eighteenth century, Paris has been reputed as an international banking and financial centre. There was even a time, in the second half of the nineteenth century, when Paris rivalled London for financial supremacy (Cassis, 2006). According to the Global Financial Centres Index, Paris has remained an international centre though it is positioned far behind global centres such as London, New York, Hong Kong, Singapore, Tokyo and henceforth the Chinese financial centres.[1] Moreover, the physical transformation of the Parisian centre was the result of urban, national and international influences. This chapter focuses on the effect of financialisation on the localisation of the financial industry in the Parisian territory.

The Ile-de-France region houses close to 40 per cent of the French financial and banking employment market (in 2012, INSEE counted 330,298 jobs in Ile-de-France, out of a total of 855,694 across the whole of France). This concentration is not new and communicates the need for finance to be in close proximity with individuals who wield power and those who possess economic and monetary capital. The first section of this chapter goes on to demonstrate the historical reasons behind this geographical concentration.

Financialisation here has led to the dispersal of jobs, first relocating them in the direction of La Défense (major business district of Paris) and second to inner suburban areas. A similar evolution can also be seen in the cities of both London and New York. This new dispersal within the financial sector represents the hierarchised fragmentation of professions, witnessed equally within the manufacturing industry and other services. However, finance's geographical location cannot be summarised uniquely through the location of employees. It is also necessary to consider the implantation of those manufacturing tools necessary for the production of financial services, for example the connecting to communication networks and storage areas. Today, *data centres* constitute the centrepiece for the operational functions of finance. These more recent transformations will be analysed in the second and third sections of this chapter.

Finance's ancestral concentration at the heart of the city

Parisian history contains a rather significant chapter on finance, which developed thanks to the centralisation of economic powers within the capital. The financial industry was established very early on in the economic and political heart of the city. From the twelfth century, exchange and trade activities were established on the *Pont au Change*, a bridge connecting the royal castle, located on the Île-de-la-Cité, with the economic quarters alongside the Seine river on the Right Bank. Following that, financial activity was set up along the Right Bank, at the Palais Royal and eventually in rue Quincampoix, where between 1716 and 1720 the infamously frenzied episode involving securities issued by the Banque Royale took place. Following this period, the Royal Order of 24 September 1724 was declared in order to regulate financial activities and impose a centralised trading area within the Hôtel de Nevers (Lagneau-Ymonet and Riva, 2012). Napoléon restructured the banking and financial system through a series of decrees from 1801 onwards and eventually decided to erect a new building dedicated to financial exchange. Palais Brongniart was thus inaugurated in 1826 and is today more commonly known as *la Bourse de Paris*.

La Bourse was located in close proximity to important sites of French power, namely the Louvre Palace, the Tuileries Palace and the Elysée Palace. It constituted the nerve centre around which all the banking and financial organisations set up shop throughout the nineteenth century – though they were not the only ones. It was also where the newspapers and head offices of major companies assembled. La Bourse also benefited from Haussmann's urban developments, with the construction of wide boulevards facilitating people's mobility, and later on from access to urban transport with the construction of a metro station in 1904. La Bourse was also the first establishment to have a telegraph office at its disposition, installed in complete secrecy in 1830. The redevelopment of the nearby Monceau plain by the Pereire brothers, extended the heart centre of Parisian business out towards the west. Numerous banking corporations invested in these new and attractive neighbourhoods between the Parc Monceau, Miromesnil and the Etoile districts, which were part of a huge real-estate plan, embarked upon by the banks.

The installation of the Parisian banking and finance sector was solidified at the end of the nineteenth century. Employment opportunities in finance were concentrated within the rich arrondissements of the Right Bank: around La Bourse (from the *Banque de France* all the way to the *grands boulevards*), Place Vendôme and Opéra, and also around Etoile (Champs Elysées, Parc Monceau, avenue Kleber). This situation continued right up until the mid-1990s. Consequently, in 1993, 62 per cent of financial sector employment in Ile-de-France was to be found in the 1st, 2nd, 8th, 9th, 16th and 17th arrondissements of Paris.

This concentration within the economic and political centre is a stylised fact of financial activity, which can be explained by its nature – being an immaterial service – though additionally by its link to both money and power. In the first instance, finance is an immaterial service in the same way as research or IT services. Production within these services is dependent upon the skills of human employees and their accumulated knowledge. Growth within such sectors is facilitated in one regard when companies are situated near educational facilities, connected service providers and knowledge producers; and in a second regard, when the people involved are concentrated together and are able to meet and take part in discussions, which enables knowledge to spread. Finance in Paris like IT in Silicon Valley needs universities to educate their employees with the top qualifications, as well as IT experts and legal representatives specially educated in the profession. It also needs transportation infrastructure to accommodate clients and employees, in addition to convivial places that enable encounters to take place.

However, finance is different to IT in that it needs to be close to people of power, as they are the possessors and bringers of capital and information, both of which are pivotal to finance's activity. It must therefore seduce them, be readily available and easily accessible for them. Being established in central neighbourhoods, with good connections to public transport and communication resources, guarantees the mobility and movement of employees, clients and any informers governing within public organisms or private companies. It enables informal encounters to take place within prestigious locations: discrete reception halls, luxurious hotels and private clubs. But above all, what this localisation offers to the building of this connection is trust between the client and the finance company which facilitates the business relationship (see our other contribution in this book). An address bears with it a reputation, a guarantee communicated via the symbolic nature globally associated with certain neighbourhoods. Pinçon and Pinçon-Charlot (2007) speak of the 'spatial signature'. The social and symbolic capital associated with a territory due to the history of its occupants is transferred to any entities domiciled within that location. This is clearly the case with neighbourhoods occupied by the aristocracy or the upper bourgeois classes. Finance has for a long time used this symbolic capital in order to persuade clients to place their trust in them when it comes to investing their assets (Pinçon and Pinçon-Charlot, 1998). Any expatriation into a neighbourhood not endowed with such a signature would be *a contrario* a negative message sent out to the community.

As such, until the 1990s, the Parisian finance scene was situated in neighbourhoods associated with the upper classes of the late nineteenth-century society. Bank cooperatives nevertheless set themselves apart by choosing more 'remote' set-ups, such as the Crédit Agricole which was situated in the Montparnasse quarter of Paris (on the left bank of the Seine) during this period.

Financialisation and invasion in the Parisian space

This concentric installation was shattered around the mid-1990s with the emblematic re-location and installation of the Société Générale banking group in La Défense. Private banks, major specialised financial institutions and insurance corporations followed in turn, investing in this neighbourhood by renovating historic towers and at the same time earning substantial real estate profits due to the real-estate bubble. In a few years, La Défense became the epicentre of market finance in France. It had taken thirty years before this location, envisaged by politicians during the 1950s as France's national business centre, had finally managed to attract the financial sector. In a document dated 28 October 1971, issued by the associate minister responsible for territorial planning and design, it is moreover underlined that financial institutions were able to obtain a detailed dispensation in order to remain and build within the centre of Paris. This dispensation was justified with regard to the specific characteristics of the financial services sector. The installation of the Société Générale thus constituted a spatial, cultural and symbolic rupture. At the end of the 1990s, it signalled the coming of a new type of finance, which presented itself as modern, innovative, defiant and which was in need of space so as to group together all of its many activities. La Défense at the time possessed all the qualities relative to image and infrastructure (transport, tele-communications, convivial spaces) that were required for the development of the financial industry. Yet despite this, the major players continued (even today) to maintain buildings in prestigious central locations, notably those companies involved in the activities of private banking. Accordingly, the Société Générale has for many years now maintained a property in place Vendôme, so as to accommodate and receive its wealthy clients.

A second and even more surprising movement took place at the turn of the twenty-first century, with the installation of financial and banking activities in historically working-class suburbs (Boulogne-Billancourt, Issy-les-Moulineaux, la Plaine Saint-Denis, Pantin, Ville-juif, Montreuil and more recently Montrouge). The disappearance of industry had liberated new territories at the gates of Paris. These industrial wastelands had the advantage of being less costly than Paris, of being linked to similar transportation and telecommunications infrastructure, and finally of having already undergone gentrification due to urban man-agement measures and renovations that saw the working classes moved off further afield.

The result was that although the financialisation of the economy manifested itself via an increase in financial jobs between 1993 and 2012 (from 303,927 to 330,298), the centre of Paris lost more than 40,000 jobs during this same period.

The biggest winners in this so-called suburbanisation movement were the French de-partments of Hauts-de-Seine (37,447 jobs gained, an annual growth rate of 273 per cent), Seine-Saint-Denis (14,170 additional jobs, a phenomenal growth rate of 434 per cent) and Val-de-Marne (13,744 jobs, with a similarly exceptional rate of 421 per cent).

The historical concentration was replaced by the out-spreading of banking and financial jobs. While some remained within finance's traditional locations, such as the private banks

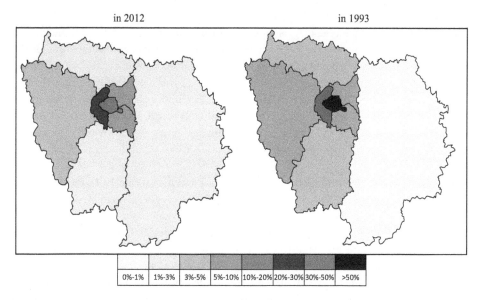

in 2012   in 1993

| 0%-1% | 1%-3% | 3%-5% | 5%-10% | 10%-20% | 20%-30% | 30%-50% | >50% |

FIGURE 13.1   Employment in Ile–de–France region, between 1993 and 2012

or hedge funds, others migrated to La Défense and the rest were consigned to the nearby suburbs. This movement was the result of financialisation and digitalisation which led to the segmentation and hierarchising of financial professions. This force which fragments sites of production has long been witnessed within the industrial sector.

The localisation of activities no longer depends on the sector in which the activity belongs, but on the specific characteristics of each task. According to Leamer and Storper (2001), there are two criteria which can help to explain these different developments. The first concerns the nature of the skills required for the task: are they common and standardised or specific and rare? And the second is linked to the degree of codification in the production process: is the process easy to replicate through objective-based routines or is it personalised and *ad hoc*? Tasks requiring commonly available skills and which are easily outlined using routines do not present significantly high added value and can be externalised. On the contrary, those professions demanding specialised knowledge and which propose a customised service for sophisticated clients are maintained within the group. Table 13.1 summarises this analytical grid, by categorising professions and providing examples of financial jobs.

The (1) category groups together jobs in which the tasks are explicit and do not require advanced knowledge in financial subjects. This is the case with *back office* roles involving

TABLE 13.1   Classification of financial activities based on Leamer and Storper (2001)

	Standardised skills	*Specific skills*
Routinised production	(1) Back office on regulated products	(3) Back and middle office on innovative, unregulated products
Personalised Production	(2) Financial analysts, sales	(4) Front office, engineers

regulated financial instruments, such as shares or bonds. In the (2) category figure jobs that do not require having an expert knowledge in financial subjects, yet in which the service provided is adapted to each client. A relation of trust which binds the client and the financial employee is essential for a successful exchange. Financial analysts and salespeople dealing with regulated financial products fall into this classification. The (3) category groups together tasks for which the work in itself is repetitive but the nature of the products being handled requires financial expertise. Here we find *back* and *middle office* activities involving complex products such as derivatives. Finally, the (4) category brings together roles in which expertise is required and in which the production process is intimately linked to the client and the producer. This is the case with trading activities and the creation of financial contracts.

Financial activities with high added value (roles 3 and 4 in Table 13.1) are always concentrated in the economic heart, except that here the latter was relocated from Paris to La Défense. In the *belle* neighbourhoods of the capital therefore remained those professions for which it is pivotal to seduce and gain the trust of clients (roles 2). Finally, any standardised financial professions were migrated to the working-class suburbs; with geographers qualifying this final movement as suburbanisation. London experienced the same phenomenon, with the congestion of the City being the reason for the construction of Canary Wharf. The hedge funds elected the heart of Mayfair as their domicile, being that it is the neighbourhood of the English aristocracy. While close to a quarter of finance jobs within the London basin are now presently located in the outer suburbs.

The localisation of non-human entities

Financial activity requires the prior existence of calculation instruments (Latour, 1987) which will enable data storage, programme development and the reception of information. Personal computers (microcomputers), screens and small servers are installed in financial establishments; making up the work space of *traders* (Beunza and Stark, 2004). Yet the non-human work space required for financial activities is these days externalised. Large servers are no longer found on-site but instead are stored in deliberately discreet warehouses that are hyper-secure and equipped with specific atmospheric qualities for stocking hundreds of machines. *Data centres* represent the hidden face of contemporaneous finance. The most emblematic figure known as high-frequency trading is just some algorithms which are in need of highly substantial calculation power. Understanding the territories of finance, therefore also means understanding the localisation of these non-human entities.

Data centres are warehouses in which a highly significant number of IT servers are installed for various businesses. As such, it is possible that one single location may house servers dedicated to finance, but also to other activities. For security reasons, it is difficult to find out where exactly servers are located. Photographs do circulate but are only ever taken from inside the warehouse and never allow for the actual location to be determined. The Atelier du Grand Paris has constructed a map featuring the data centres connected to companies located in La Défense.[2] We can see the sizeable presence of these centres around zones where financial enterprises are situated (La Défense, Montreuil, la Plaine Saint-Denis) and around scientific hubs (Saclay).

Criteria for the domiciliation of these machines varies when compared with the criteria for humans. The difficulty is no longer related to gaining clients' trust by being present in posh locations, but rather is concerned with installing machines in secure zones (protected from climatic events), where they remain discrete (protected from terrorist attacks), yet are not too far from the financial centres (to ensure the fast circulation of data). The centres traditionally used by financial workers on Wall Street and in the City are not capable of satisfying these criteria and prove, moreover, to be overly congested and unable to offer the aerated spaces required for storing increasingly large and more numerous servers. The move towards delocalising servers was initiated in the US (New York and Chicago) and London at the end of the 2000s. Laumonier (2014) has described the migration of Wall Street to New Jersey, and notably the setting-up of the New York Stock Exchange in Mahwah. He has also examined the chosen location for the Euronext (European stock market) server, which up until 2010 was located in the Parisian suburb of Aubervilliers, then was relocated in the same year to the town of Basildon, 20-odd kilometres outside of London. This relocation was motivated by the capacity to reduce latency by several milliseconds, and additionally it facilitated high frequency transactions, notably on the UK LIFFE market. The warehouse chosen was an old building previously used to store merchandise, which offered vast amounts of space for setting up the servers (the equivalent of six football stadiums) and was, in addition, discreet.

Conclusion

The urban scale makes it possible to reveal unique markers within both the human and non-human worlds which shape finance. The transformation of finance contributed towards reconfiguring the financial space. Financial activities are no longer exclusively localised in the centre of major metropolitan cities and the move towards suburbanisation is presently underway for activities with low added value, as well as for the servers and IT specialists who work with them. This transformation on the urban scale has also been accompanied by the more globally scaled *de-localisation* of these same services towards remote countries such as India, for tasks involving the handling and processing of data.

Notes

1 See the annual rankings for financial centres currently produced by the Qatar Financial Centre Authority (http://www.longfinance.net/Publications/GFCI23.pdf, accessed 2018/06/08).
2 See the interactive map of the Atelier du Grand Paris in relation to this subject, available at the following address: http://www.ateliergrandparis.fr/ateliersdebats/croaif/defense/# (accessed 2018/06/08).

References

Beunza, D. and Stark, D. (2004). Tools of the trade: The socio-technology of arbitrage in a Wall Street trading room. *Industrial and Corporate Change*, 13(2), 369–400.
Cassis, Y. (2006). *Capitals of capital. A history of international financial centres, 1780–2009.* Cambridge: Cambridge University Press.
Crevoisier, O. and Theurillat, T. (2012). Une approche territoriale de la financiarisation et des enjeux de la reconfiguration du système financier. Retrieved from http://www.sciencespo.fr/coesionet/sites/default/files/financeTerritoire_Crevoisier%20def.pdf. Accessed 06.07.2018.
Labasse, J. (1974). *L'espace financier, interprétation géographique*. Paris: Armand Colin.
Lagneau-Ymonet, P. and Riva, A. (2012). *Histoire de la Bourse*. Paris: La Découverte.

Latour, B. (1987). *Science in action. How to follow scientists and engineers through society.* Cambridge: Harvard University Press.

Laumonier, A. (2014). *6|5.* Bruxelles: Zones Sensibles.

Leamer, E. E. and Storper, M. (2001). The economic geography of the Internet age. *Journal of International Business Studies*, 32(4), 641–665.

Martin, R. (1999). The new economic geography of money. In R. Martin (Ed.), *Money and the space economy* (pp. 3–27). Chichester: John Wiley & Sons.

Pinçon, M. and Pinçon-Charlot, M. (1998). *Les Rothschild, une famille bien ordonnée.* Paris: La Dispute.

Pinçon, M. and Pinçon-Charlot, M. (2007). *Sociologie de la bourgeoisie.* Paris: La Découverte.

Sassen, S. (1991). *The global city.* Princeton: Princeton University Press.

14

THE WORKFORCE AND PROFESSIONAL TRAINING IN BANKS

Marnix Dressen

Introduction: an atypical system

For a long time, the banking (and commercial) sector has figured among those who have entertained the closest of relations with education, literacy and written culture. Although banks are neither the inheritors of the Babylonian banking system, nor of the systems of Classical Greece or Ancient Rome, instead being descendants of medieval Lombardi exchange tables, it should be well noted that since Antiquity financial activities have nonetheless required the upkeep of written accounts (Andreau, 2001). And this is not without good reason. Generally speaking, as 'economic associations of a monopolistic or plutocratic character' (Weber, 1978, p. 44) and being 'profit-making "trading" enterprise which make a specialised function of administering or procuring money' (*ibid.*, p. 159), banks obey first and foremost a logic based on 'legal rationality' and 'instrumental rationality' (*ibid.*) which involves writing and requires a specific logic. It is precisely because banks target 'the profitable economy' (Weber, 2003), and to best administer the funds entrusted to them and which they invest, that they call upon categories of employees displaying particular skills. Throughout history, it has been possible to acquire these skills via specialised instruction, which before the Great War, was labelled as a 'professional capacity'.

The need for a body of rigorously trained collaborators comes down to the vital position held by the banks within the role of intermediation. They accumulate and generate a colossal sum of information. And in short, the collection, analysis and mobilisation of this symbolic data, not to mention the elaboration of evermore sophisticated financial products targeting a client base whose education level is ever-increasing, requires having employees who are armed with a high level of training. Even at the very bottom of the pyramid of banking qualifications, their employees, in the past selected for their calligraphy skills and ability to maintain registers with a Sergent Major quill, and later to fill out forms using a Remington, are today comfortable with all types of computer software and financial products, at times highly abstract.

These preliminary remarks perfectly illustrate that broaching the subject of finance via the bias of professional training is an excellent way of grasping the characteristics of the banking workforce. It is not without reason that out of all the professional fields, banks are historically one of those that have devoted the highest rate of spending on staff training. In France, since

1994, at the inter-professional level, employers have been required to devote 1.5 per cent of the payroll to staff training. However, within the banking sector, management committees invested much more, often a minimum of 6 per cent up until the 1990s. The only other companies to reach such levels were those specialising in computer engineering services.

A unique history

Banks also distinguished themselves on a level other than that of their expenditure on professional training. It is not very well known that the educational system employed by French banks has a unique history within the universe of professional training, in that like insurance firms, the industry obtained the right to award diplomas on its own authority (with the French *Education Nationale* only exercising its control – in the form of certifying such qualifications – *a posteriori* (Möbus and Verdier, 1993). The training system exclusive to this field of activity has long been closely linked to the cordoning off of its employment market, in other words the creation of a system in which *insiders* (recruited employees, often young and on the bottom rungs of the pay grade) are protected from any competition in the form of individuals seeking jobs on the open employment market. Moreover, for a long time banks have figured as a paradigmatic example of the interdependency between training systems and the cordoning off of the employment market (Freedman, 1969 in Guillon, 1970, p. 209), a problem which is of primary interest to us here. Employees were equally protected from competition stemming from their colleagues in the sense that, in a more or less formal way, the closed employment market (which economists call 'internal') operated on the basis of the hierarchical rules governing career development, i.e. the formation of a queue of *insiders* lined up for the best positions, which as such side-stepped the logic of every man for himself. Above all, and most importantly, this type of employment market was directly linked to an internal training system, which enabled supervisors and managers to be prepped in advance to take on their new roles. In summary, without the highly developed training system the employment market would not have been cordoned off to such an extensive degree, and in return no sophisticated internal training system would have existed if the nature of the employment market with its internal collective balance of power had not rendered this type of configuration indispensable.

In the language of the economies of conventional forms, one can speak of training as an 'investment in forms', in other words 'a set of constructed mediations alongside which the skills of workers attain a value' which must be 'located in the spaces that contribute to producing it' (Salais, 1986, p. 110 and p. 180). Historically, banks have as such developed an 'exceptional' system, which can be divided into four separate phases. These phases are not purely sequential but instead overlap in line with the fade-in/fade-out principle. And as we will see, establishing a socio-history of the bank training system represents a privileged entry point for understanding how finance is constructed across the long term by banking employees.

The first phase, known as pre-composition, preceded the setting up of training bodies created to attribute diplomas, more or less recognised within the profession, in accordance with the banks and perhaps more importantly in accordance with the period, with the obligation to recognise them also being the result of the balance of power between social actors.

Until 1918, the pre-composition phase

Right up until the end of the Great War, the banking sector underwent what can be called the pre-composition phase with regard to professional training (which involved individual initiatives and a relative disinterest on behalf of the government). In the two ideal types outlined by C. Durand, it can be said that banking education was as a result essentially integrative (education as social work or training aimed at reducing tensions between employees and their employers, see Durand, 1963, pp. 316–328). However, at the beginning of the interwar period, this traditional design was no longer sufficient enough when it came to dealing with the inflow of staff within larger establishments (Crédit Lyonnais, Société Générale, etc.). Due to the increase in Taylorist 'rationalisation', which relied on a labour force with a low-level of basic education, the concepts linked to pre-composition were revealed to be insufficient. There was also another factor that pushed employers in the industry towards abandoning the empirical-style, pre-1914 training: 'a large portion of the banking personnel had become nomadic; for example, in certain administrative areas, the career of the employee unfolded from city to city' (Simon, 1952, p. 42 and p. 46).

1919–1984, the composition phase: the Government get involved

From 1919 to around 1939, the modern conception of professional training emerged, not only due to the influential Astier Law of 25 July 1919 which put a halt to the differentiation established between girls and boys (even though a female *baccalauréat* was created in 1919), but essentially because the industry-wide education system became rationalised. Within the typology of C. Durand, the training concept that took over was thus integrated into the objectives of the technological and organisational changes of the company (Durand, 1963, pp. 316–328). This composition phase linked together private initiatives issued from the profession itself with government initiatives that ordered companies to take responsibility for the education of their apprentices. The legislator was concerned about the lack of qualified manpower within various fields of the economy.

In closed labour markets, four super-rules hinder the 'equity-matching' of *insider* employees with *outsiders*:

a access rules from below;
b strict training/employment relationship;
c legitimacy of careers in seniority;
d compensation rules (grid, weight of seniority)

During the interwar period, the major banks were concerned with training middle and upper management levels, which in turn would be responsible for organising and monitoring the work executed by operational agents. Under the *Front Populaire*, it was under pressure from Finance Minister V. Auriol, that on the 3 July 1936 the first nation-wide collective agreement was literally snatched up from the *Union Syndicale des Banquiers de Paris et de la Province* (Professional Union of Parisian and Provincial Bankers). This collective agreement reinforced the education of apprentices. It has been noted that the divide established by the law between those over or under eighteen years of age was met with general approval within the banking profession. For under eighteens, education was mandatory, while for over eighteens it was optional. Under the Vichy government (1940–1944), training did not disappear, instead it provoked a certain craze and, for the first time in the history of French banking, the government took upon itself to regulate lending establishments by way of a banking law (proceedings known as the Law of 14 June 1941). Through this law, they engaged in a purely neo-corporatist logic, which made it mandatory for all banking institutions to belong to a monopolistic body of representation.

From 1947 to 1982 the system was perfected and took root. The banking law of 2 December 1945, which tidied up more than it repealed of the 1941 law, restructured the system once again when it introduced the distinction between business banking and deposit banking, with only the latter being nationalised. The two collective agreements of 1947 and 1952 updated, defined and complemented the collective agreement fathered by the *Front Populaire*. They introduced salary clauses and the principle of a freely nego-tiated pay scale (Quévarec, 2000, p. 7), and they also acknowledged training as an essen-tial requirement. Professional training reached its golden era thanks to two measures: first, diplomas of various levels became formally qualifying, and second, training for them henceforth took place during work time (which had previously only been the case for those unique apprentices preparing to take a CAP – *certificate d'aptitude professionnelle* or vocational qualification).

'All these reforms are inspired by a central idea, writes two decades later the former Pres-ident of Indosuez and AGF, to locate at the heart of finance a vast money market as free and open as is possible, to open it to as many actors as possible... The government is promoting a banking and financial policy of a radically new type!' 'It's (...) the most icono-clastic (...) the most Anglo-Saxon in its inspiration!' (see Jeancourt-Galignani, 2002, p. 44).

On the inter-professional level, the law of 16 July 1971 breathed new life into training and helped to diversify it, opening up limitless training opportunities 'from the violin to cross-stitch', which was its way of incorporating France's revolutionary 'spirit of 1968'. In particular, in the area of professional relations, it provided the industry's collective nego-tiation with a boost and, as a result, contractual training agreements – rarely a conflictual domain – grew in abundance and have done so right up until the present day. From the 1980s to 1990s, these were supplemented by company agreements, which borrowed the principal measures while adding a few additional incentives to encourage employees to educate themselves.

While professional bank training was progressively amended, this was also largely a result of the transformation of the characteristics of the employment-seeking workforce. Increasingly, new recruits were holders of a BEPC (*Brevet d'études de premier cycle* – National diploma received at the end of middle school), or even a *baccalauréat* (even though, in com-parison to other industries, banks will continue employing managers not holding a *bacca-lauréat* for quite some time). However, the cordoning off of the employment market did not disappear along with this restructuring (Ferrary, 2002), and even during the 1990s the length of service of current staff members remained highly influential in banks such as BNP Paribas (Dressen and Nemiri, 2010). Though this cordoning off began to take on a new form.

A study of annual training reports between 1968 and 1992 gathered from one bank which was, at the time, as structurally influential on banking culture as the Crédit Lyonnais bank, shows that over the years, professional training had seldom been considered a means of quali-fication, but was instead increasingly thought of as a tool for human resources management – a notion that emerged in the 1980s – to favour 'employment developments and adaptations'. From the mid-1970s and further still the 1980s, there was clearly a decline in recruitment flows and, in correlation, a rationalisation of management. The nationalisation of almost the entire non-cooperative or *mutualiste* financial sector via the law of 11 February 1982 could potentially have reinforced the precedent logic by establishing a close relation between training/employment. However, the control held by the government was surprisingly short lived.

1984–1992: the decomposition phase

Following a volley of texts introduced during the 1980s, with the first in line being the banking law of 24 January 1894, defined by P. Bérégovoy, Minister of the Economy and Finances, the conditions were established for a major turning point. This banking law opposed many points in the preceding banking laws. Marketisation of the economy, intro-duced via the Debré decrees of 25 January and 23 December 1966 and that of 1 September 1967, was launched and, in the banking sector, the state and governmental teams (perhaps more successive than in any other area of activity) manifestly organised their retreat, thus entrusting finance to define its own rules within a renewed neo-corporatist approach.

In 1986 (law of 2 July), the parliamentary right's return to business opened the way for the progressive privatisation of the collection of 'commercial' banks (i.e. those belong-ing to the *Association Française des Banques* [AFB], the professional representative body of deposit banks). Through their subsidiaries, 73 banks left the public sector. In 1993–1994, the second privatisation phase resulted in 12 additional banks returning to the private sector, and in 2001 the return of the bank Hervet finally rounded out the applause. On 15 December 1993, the 'Law of Independence' of the *Banque de France* was adopted separat-ing it from the State. This law finalised the logic of the *Front Populaire* which had tightened its grip on the *Banque de France*'s Council of Regency and, more importantly, it clearly marked a rupture with the 1945 banking law which had nationalised it. As was expected, the intensification of inter-banking competition did not fail to have a direct impact on work (an impact that was felt three-fold in terms of the workforce, productive action and the creation of goods and services).

As anticipated by its architects, the third banking law threw the banks into a period of intense restructuration liable to help them emerge from impinging globalisation. This phase signalled the decomposition of banking education in the sense that its traditional role lost out in terms of its vitality. Budgets, programmes and pedagogy were massively reoriented. The objectives of professional training were redefined in view of retraining any adminis-trative personnel who chose to stay on board with companies when the opportunity arose to take a combination of redundancy plans and 'social contractual employment agreements' negotiated with trade union organisations (Dressen and Roux-Rossi, 1996).

The banks relinquished themselves with 'paid-reward training' for cooperative and deserving employees. Pedagogical innovations (in the form of games, for example) emerged which targeted instantaneous efficiency. While this process was more concerned with employees at the bottom of the qualifications pyramid, it nevertheless took place on work stations rather than in class. These innovative teachings targeted a new public, at times battered by years of working in administrative centres, domains in which tasks were meticulously broken down. All the major banks possessed, notably in western France (Bayeux, Nantes, Tours, etc.), one or more 'paper-pushing factories' which at times employed more than a thousand people organised according to Taylorian principles. In summary, training tried hard to target efficiency as part of achieving the new objectives. Whatever the target public, it was expected that the training incorporate the new vision of the social and commercial relations, in keeping with the turning point of the 1980s and 1990s. At the same time as the banks were streamlining their teaching methods, the training services sector was also expanding. For example, in 1984, 112 people were involved in organising and running staff training programmes at the Crédit Lyonnais bank. In this same bank, the annual 1989 training report consisted of more than 80 pages.

From this decade onwards, training set out on the path towards decentralisation. In 1992, this flagship of the national economy reaffirmed its position of wanting to 'break with global approaches' and 'make room for individualised pathways (through the bias of skills assessments, potentially with external organisations)'.

From 1993 onwards, the recomposition

We can symbolically date the recomposition phase back to the industry-wide agreement on training dated 12 February 1993. Reinforced to a certain extent by the *Convention collective des banques* (Collective banks agreement – signed in 2000, it replaced the National collective agreement of 1952, amended numerous times though maintained for almost half a century), training thus became part of the fashionable themes promoted throughout the 1990s, which also included the notion of the 'employability' of its beneficiaries ('employability' in the managerial sense) and the notion of skills which accompanied employability in a certain way.

> 'If we are to have responsibility', declared a training manager from BNP-Paribas, 'then it is in our interests to be trained. Otherwise, we become just another pawn in history that never served any purpose. [...] [One's] accumulated skills base, is one's capital.'
>
> *(Cox, 2003)*

This agreement was part of the inter-professional developments related to training. Nevertheless, the agreement was not entirely innovative. As was already the case with the 1988 agreement, the agreement of February 1993 reconfirmed the existence of a general banking education with its own specific diplomas (i.e. CAP, Brevet Professionnel) awarded by the *Institut Technique de la Banque* and the *Centre d'Etude Supérieur de la Banque*, most likely in order to fulfil a trade-union demand. The agreement equally noted those courses that drew their roots from the end of the institutionalisation phase and more importantly the transitional phase (1984–1992), i.e. the decomposition phase. And in this way, it concretised certain social practices.

The agreement, however, impacted more than just this. It insisted on the need to retrain staff and to confront the growing complexity of banking employees' tasks and the rise in the level of expectations maintained by the client, who was henceforth categorised according to the net banking product that he/she could generate. In other terms, this agreement was part of a logic based on transforming the characteristics of the labour force in view of developing another type of relation with clients and constructing a new service relationship.

It legitimised various types of work-study training programmes ('*alternance*' programmes), encouraged 'practical training actions within the workplace which could constitute a concrete and progressive training approach, particularly suitable for acquiring operational modes needed for maintaining a position or job', and it introduced a 'training indemnity' which illustrated the managerial desire to ensure training investments were ultimately profitable (i.e. a training programme would have to be reimbursed if the employee quit the company within the months following its completion).

From on-the-job training to business schools

'*Alternance*' becomes the cornerstone of the system

Let us look back and examine the approach of the *alternance* contract (a paid work-study internship), one of the major characteristics of the new system. Timidly making their way onto the scene in 1984, *alternance* programmes took form by way of *contrats d'adaptation*, degree qualification contracts or apprenticeship contracts, all of which came under the label of 'professional youth employment insertion' (Marry and Tanguy, 1986, p. 29). For banking employers:

> *alternance* programmes represented, for the companies, a clever and flexible way of recruiting young people with high potential, and of almost certainly making them operational by offering them the opportunity to acquire the knowledge and know-how that they specifically need.
>
> *(OPCA-banques)*

During the same period, the HR department of the Crédit Lyonnais bank also rather prosaically considered *alternance* to be the way 'to identify the best candidates on offer and keep them within the company' (*RH Pratique* n°2, February 1999). *Alternance* was, in a way, similar to a period of observation, which exceeds the length of the trial period mandated by the Collective agreement. It has also been noted that women represent the highest majority within the banking sector's *alternance* pathways and that young people make varied use of these devices (Mignot-Gérard et al., 2014).

This new pathway to training can be analysed as a result of the transformation in the characteristics of the young new arrivals on the job market, though just as equally as an illustration of the new social balance of power and the weakening of the previously held logic of the closed job market. Henceforth, employees would have to both prove their obedience (on which they are told the survival of the company hangs precariously) and take responsibility for their own development via training initiatives, all while demonstrating – which was no doubt essential – their willingness to accept and 'comprehend any new challenges'. Behind these, ultimately, very political objectives, one could believe it possible to discern a desire to weaken the collective organisations and numerous forms of traditional professional socialisations. The individual project involves a particularisation of training paths. And according to some, group courses became suspect insofar as they provided an opportunity for peer-to-peer interactions. This is due to training programmes also acting as scouting sites for resistant or, on the contrary, right-minded individuals. More than ever before, diplomas have become part of the necessary conditions, though are considered not quite enough to rise to an executive level.

During the recomposition phase, bank training became synonymous with the idea of a joint 'investment' by the employer and employee in the latter's 'human capital'. The bank structured its training according to three major divisive categories: job training (which took up the lion's share, due to the impact of sales teams), cross-sector training (management, communication, etc.) and professional teaching targeted predominantly towards investment banking. This situation merits some explanation.

Investment banks and training

Under the mandate of the 1984 banking law, banks in France were considered in principle to be 'universal' or in other words 'global', as the notion of the 'business bank' that had appeared in 1945, had by this time disappeared. The coordination of the labour force and its relevant training however remained highly divided. We can schematically observe two employee categories within major banking firms. Retail bank employees are distinguished from those who work for financing and investment banks or asset management banks, which have their own separate professional market. This market is numerically inferior (in 2012, close to 70 per cent of the jobs in 390 establishments represented by the *Fédération Bancaire Française* – French Banking Federation – were connected to retail banking), however investment banking has increasingly strengthened its influence on both a financial and symbolic level. Here we can bring to mind the existence of employees, at the heart of banking and notably on the trading floors, who receive such exceptional salaries that most banking employees would never even imagine such a thing possible (Godechot, 2001). The connection between training pathways and these employees, some of whom earn more than their employers (Godechot, 2017), is very specific. As one executive manager from BNP-Paribas has declared (in Cox, 2003),

> They want the most basic course outlines which leave them with the most autonomy. There is very little training in the *front office*. They arrive having already been trained or qualified and they learn the rest after. They buy books and train themselves on-the-job or by reading at home in the evening, but it isn't a traditional type of training.

We can also place in this category, those employees who carry out consulting missions with major companies, notably with regards to merger-acquisition operations. In short, we find ourselves here in the middle of those spaces in which the industry's job market is essentially split in two. To this horizontal divide are added the vertical divides that oppose 'skilled workers within the bank' (more 'senior' and 'highly promoted' employees) against executives of various levels.

This leads to the emergence of differentiating factors in training programmes designed for the diverse categories of executive staff (in 2012 in those banks affiliated with the AFB,[1] executives represented 55 per cent of employees with almost as many women as men). One of the most significant traits of the recomposition phase involves these famously trusted employees: '*top managers*' (not affiliated with the Collective agreement), '*middle managers*' and *local managers*, without forgetting to include sales managers (Contrat d'Étude Prospective, 1998). In 2012, 68 per cent of employees within banks affiliated with the *Association Française des Banques* held a 'sales role', while in 2000 this figure sat at 52% per cent This shift in employment's gravitational centre, from the administrative increasingly towards the commercial, is what has without doubt led to banking experts assigned to the *back offices* becoming less favoured, even neglected to an extent, when it comes to training. At the beginning of the 2000s, senior executive staff altogether totalled training sessions that were on average twice as long as those of bank clerks. This was the result of an inversion of the social balance of power and also due to the fact that these 'manipulators of symbols' (R. Reich) were passed off as genuine creators of added value; as they embodied skills ratified on the international markets. As regards executive staff at a senior level, 'corporate' training sessions became one of the key foundations for the new pathway of banking education within the recomposition phase. These training sessions were aimed at developing a company culture, a pugnacity that did not hesitate to borrow from the art of war in relation to the expectations of their management. And in this case, the training, which could last two weeks full-time, would logically not have been subcontracted.

Rationalisation in the assigning of training budgets

By 2012, from the perspective of the AFB banks, training costs had been reduced by almost two percentage points in a quarter-century, if correlated with the total payroll. Henceforth, they skimmed in at 4 per cent (i.e. €2,000 per employee), though the banking sector nevertheless remained at the head of the pack in terms of spending in this area. The reduction in their training efforts was the result of a combination of diverse factors which encapsulated the new faces of the training sector and separated the new incarnation of the workforce from its management. First, newly recruited employees held a high level of academic capital (the average entrance age in AFB-affiliated banks was, in 2012, more than 29 years old and for executives more than 32 years old). In 2012 the AFB banks recruited 50 per cent of their staff at graduate level (*Bac*+2/3) and 40 per cent at post-graduate level (*Bac*+4/5) (with close to 60 per cent being women). These were graduates of vocational degree courses (*licences professionnelles*), Masters programmes or private-run business schools, institutions which had placed great importance on their technical skills and their 'immediate' entry into the workforce, with this outcome rendered even easier as major banking representatives were often present on the orientation committees of such schools. It is today even possible to track down on the web 'university-grade' vocational degrees dedicated to a specific corporate company. Moreover, these young recruits have very often worked as interns for several months or as part of *alternance* (work/study) programmes, in other words they have already acquired the necessary and complementary professional training 'on-the-job at the lowest cost' in view of their minimal remuneration at the beginning of their career (Sarfati, 2014).

Several new pedagogical techniques are also showcased as less expensive for educational establishments than the traditional 'classroom' training sessions. 'Virtual classes', 'e-learning' and 'open and distant learning' typically outsource onto the employee (most often a woman) all or part of the expense required for the training which they (or she) agreed to carry out. This occurs to an even greater extent in that they often take part in training during breaks (lunch breaks or other) or personal leisure/rest time. HR departments strongly encourage self-study and the co-investor is of the same mind: if the training is implemented at the employee's request, a portion of the time they devote is subtracted from their free time (for example time-off in lieu). One HR department in particular talked about it as 'skills just-in-time and at the best price'.

Conclusion: the recomposition

One most important change is that the payroll percentage which banks previously devoted towards training their various personnel categories has declined in comparison with what it represented during the 1980s. The importance of sector training has now declined and each bank has internalised the training of its own staff. Without doubt, this is the result of the rising intensity of inter-banking competition induced by neo-liberal logic, of which financial establishments are the incontestable heralds. Once training no longer represented the simple adaptation to a job, it henceforth became increasingly targeted towards certain personnel categories (e.g. sales representatives and *managers* at various hierarchical levels), which were responsible for acclimatising banking establishments in accordance with the new direction of the world economy, which banks greatly contributed towards defining. Logically, these training sessions were aimed explicitly at indoctrinating a vision of the world presented to individuals as the only way to survive in the competitive environment. Employees are required to embrace a corporate culture that HR departments dream of shaping at their convenience.

For some years now, the banks have no longer hired *agents* (a term which belonged to the para-administrative culture) and certainly not *employees* (a term illustrating the subordinate relation that they sought to conceal). Today, banks maintain that they only work with *collaborators* (i.e. skilled clerks or executives). As specified by M. Maurice, it has indeed been a case of 'changing the employees before changing the work'. Employees have been moreover continuously encouraged to exceed beyond their limits and take initiatives in the form of training by signing up for the latest up-and-coming courses, in order to develop their 'skills portfolio' and their employability, even if it sometimes means, due to a lack of time, never being able to step away and take a break from their job. Any dead weights who hinder others from thinking straight, any rebels or simply any lack-lustre or fed-up employees are pushed towards the exit. In banks as in many other companies, compliance with the mono-coloured values of the organisation is expected and sought out, even mandatory (Linhart, 1994), which does not mean that it became or even could become mandatory.

While almost clear of the grand anti-establishment armies of the *baby boomer* generation (they only represented 18 per cent of active employees in 2012), financial establishments appear herein to be hiring younger generations – quite often former interns adept at following orders – of which a certain number aspire to be counted among the victors of globalisation. This claim merits however some refinement, as banks equally employ call-centre staff or other lesser known staff concealed from their clients and assigned to *back offices* to handle glamourless tasks which have not (as yet) been outsourced.

Note

1 Association Française des Banques.

References

Andreau, J. (2001). *Banque et affaires dans le monde romain, IVe siècle av. J-C.- IIIe siècle après J.-C.* Paris: Seuil.

Cox, J.-C. (2003). *La formation professionnelle continue dans le secteur bancaire: de la formation qualifiante au management sélectif des identités? Tendances récentes de la formation professionnelle dans les banques, le cas d'une banque en processus de fusion.* Unpublished Master thesis. Paris: CNAM.

Dressen, M. and Nemiri, F. (2010). Banking sector the dominance of internal (closed) labour market in France and Algeria (at the beginning of XXIth c.), presented at CRESC conference *Finance in question, finance in crisis*, University of Manchester 12–14 April.

Dressen, M. and Roux-Rossi, D. (1996). La reconversion des employés de banque faiblement classes. *Travail et Emploi*, 68, 3–22.

Durand, C. (1963). La signification des politiques de formation et de promotion. *Sociologie du travail*, 4, 316–328.

Ferrary, M. (2002). Mécanismes de régulation de la structure des qualifications et spécificité du capital humain. Une analyse du capital social des conseillers bancaires. *Sociologie du Travail*, 44(1), 119–130.

Godechot, O. (2001). *Les traders. Essai de sociologie des marchés financiers*. Paris: La Découverte.

Godechot, O. (2017). *Wages, bonuses and appropriation of profit in the financial industry. The working rich*. London: Routledge.

Guillon, R. (1970). Les marchés internes de l'emploi. *Sociologie du travail*, 2(70), 208–213.

Jeancourt-Galignani, A. (2002). *La finance déboussolée*. Paris: Odile Jacob.

Linhart, D. (1994). *La modernisation des entreprises*. Paris: La Découverte.

Marry, C. and Tanguy, L. (1986). La constitution d'un champ de recherche, tableau économique et social. In L. Tanguy (Ed.) *L'introuvable relation formation : emploi, un état des recherches en France* (pp. 13–34). Paris: La Documentation Française.

Mignot-Gérard, S., Perrin-Joly, C., Sarfati, F. and Vezinat, N. (2014). *Entrer dans la banque par la voie de l'alternance. Une enquête auprès d'étudiants en Master 2 Banque-Finance dans un IAE*. Noisy-le-Grand: Centre d'Etudes de l'Emploi, #87.

Möbus, M. and Verdier, E. (1993). La gestion de la formation continue au niveau des branches. Le cas des banques et des assurances. In A. Jobert, J.-D. Reynaud, J. Saglio and M. Tallard (Eds.), *Les conventions collectives de branche : déclin ou renouveau* (pp. 247–261). Marseille: Cereq, La Documentation Française.

Quévarec, C. (2000). *Genèse et crise de la convention collective des personnels de banques*. Unpublished PhD. Paris : Université Paris-X.

Salais, R. (1986). Les formes de la négociation. In R. Salais and L. Thévenot (Eds.), *Le travail. Marchés, règles, conventions* (pp. 17–28). Paris: Economica/Insee.

Sarfati, F. (2014). L'alternance au risque de la sur-sélectivité. *Revue Française de Sociologie Economique*, 14, 71–92.

Simon, P. (1952). *La formation professionnelle dans les banques*. Paris: Foucher.

Weber, M. (2003). *General economic history*. Mineola: Dover publications.

Weber, M. (1978). *Economy and Society*. Berkeley: University of California Press.

15

COOPERATIVE BANKING

Finding a place for the social in finance?

Pascale Moulévrier

Understanding the positions of cooperative banking in the French banking market leads the sociologist to not only revisit logics related to the placement of banking institutions within this competitive finance space, but more importantly towards contemplating them with regard to the modalities of exercising the profession of *banker*, with this figure similarly considered in relation to his social background and the economic dispositions that it imparts upon him. Moreover, these professional realities appear to be an integral part of the distribution process for clients in various banks. The banking relationship between a client and a 'banker' can certainly be understood as a commercial exchange bringing into play the creditworthiness of the borrower and the risk ratio established by the banks, as they too are bound within a space regulated by the calculation of interests. Like every economic relation or activity, this relationship is also socially constructed and, in this sense, it likewise structures this 'money market'[1] in return. As such, what we are able to grasp through this sociology of the banking world are the social logics in practice that position banking establishments and perpetuate their activities on a market, evidently competitive and legally restricted, but created to say the least by the encountering of banks, bankers and suitable clients.[2]

Some empirical guidelines

Interviews were carried out from January 2002 with client account managers and agency directors – the latter being systematically responsible for a portfolio of clients – (80 in total) connected to *banques mutualistes* (mutual savings banks), namely the *Caisses d'Epargne*, the *Banques Populaires*, the *Crédit Mutuel*, and the *Crédit Agricole*, commercial banks such as *Société Générale*, the BNP, the CIC, the LCL, and finally the national postal bank (*La Poste*), which during the interview period was renamed the *Banque Postale*, all of them primarily located in the Pays de la Loire region of France. This measure rounds out on one hand the surveys previously conducted with agents from the *Crédit Mutuel* (1995–2000) (112 in total), and on the other hand a study examining six student year-groups enrolled in Bachelor degrees in banking-insurance (with a professional orientation – *license professionnelle*) between 2005 and 2010, in addition to interviews carried out with young graduates previously enrolled in a Masters of Banking-Finance or from the *Grandes*

Ecoles with this same specialisation (25 in total). In examining the daily professional routine, the ways of carrying out the profession and dealing with client requests, the interviews and observations revealed disparities concerning points of view and positions, which were dependent upon the individuals and the professional spaces in which their exercised their profession. These observations progressively reinforce the hypothesis of heterogeneity within the banking field.[3]

Cooperative banks thus form, as a counterpoint to their commercial counterparts but equally contrary to consumer credit organisations and micro-credit institutions, a unique space marked by the dual necessity for financial profitability and socio-educative ambition. Moreover, this space is also diversified when one considers the various means used by each banking establishment to exercise and maintain their activities within it.

Cooperative banking in the banking market

As such, far from the intentions proclaimed by the cooperative movement since their very beginnings (late nineteenth century), of having practised the type of finance widely known today as 'socially responsible', and beyond the local categorisation that separates commercial banks from cooperative ones, the social reality of banking cooperatives is less homogeneous than it might seem and alone it constitutes a sub-market, a subspace for diversified practices. It would appear that even though these banking establishments have a cooperative status in common and the obligation to develop signs that their activities are affiliated with a social dimension, they take up and maintain a place on the market through their capacity to draw from it either a maximum profit, or at the very minimum the resources for competitive profitability.

The same status for two models

There exist in France two types of cooperative banks. The first – *Crédit Agricole*, *Crédit Mutuel*, *Banques Populaires* and *Crédit Coopératif*, to only cite the most influential national networks – embody the traditional form of the legal model on the subject, namely a group of regional bodies, themselves originating from a local network of agencies which were the historical foundations of the enterprise, and which are today amalgamated into one national group. Each has its own organisational grades, with the organism being co-directed by a director – paid – and an elected representative – volunteer.[4] What is particularly unique about these banks is that in the beginning they were prompted by the commitment of individuals who, on their local territorial scales of existence, championed for the need to expand access to credit and savings accounts to those social categories who were at the time excluded from them. For these individuals, it was essentially their social positions and their beliefs – religious, class-based, professional, political – that led them to believe in the benefits of such an enterprise.

The *Caisses d'Epargne* today in France constitutes the exclusive figure of the second form of cooperative banking. Since the law of 20 January 2000, the *Caisses d'épargne* has become a *banque mutualiste* (mutual savings bank), shifting from its status as a public establishment to that of a cooperative establishment, and as such has acquired the status of a private company nonetheless conserving a special link with the State, notably through the public interest mission assigned to it.[5] Here, instead of privatisation, we could speak of a form of specifically

French *mutualisation*, during a time in which European cooperative banking networks were instead opting for de-mutualisation. While still having to amass the resources for its market competitiveness, the bank is in a position to invent forms of *mutualism* from top-down, which greatly differs from the 'first generation' local cooperatives, the inheritors of which are today the previously cited *Crédit Mutuel* or *Crédit Agricole* agencies.

The historical division of clients

Revisiting the history of these banks allows us to rapidly distinguish the former processes used to attract a specific client-base, leading each of these cooperative banking establishments to take up a place on the market of domestic money management. Indeed, at the end of the nineteenth century, the urban and commercial banks oriented their activities towards the financing industry and the *bourgeoisie* (upper classes), while holding at a distance the mass of industrial labourers, agricultural workers, small business owners and artisan craftsmen, both in the cities and the countryside. For all that, changes to agricultural activity by way of a more entrepreneurial logic and the increasing salaries paid to labourers and employees nevertheless contributed towards producing a demand for banking services (savings and credit) around which local 'leaders' built their offering. Consequently, backed by relationships established on the basis of professional corporatism with farming communities, those in charge of the agricultural trade unions took part in setting up the very first agricultural credit funds, for which the client base was thus comprised exclusively of agricultural workers. In the same way, the goal of the *Banques populaires* was to answer the cash-flow needs of small businesses and artisan craftsmen, counting on the professional networks already in place to develop their banking activities. It was similarly a network – this time association-based – which would contribute towards developing the *Crédit coopératif*. In point of fact, the bank is historically linked to labouring associations and their members, and its aim was to finance the cooperatives and their members. Alongside this, relying on the parish networks and the system of social relations built on the trust that existed between priests and their parishioners, the secular and ecclesiastic managers of religious institutions saw to organising savings and credit funds for catholic populations of modest means. They liked to consider their 'enterprise' as a 'general calling', in contrast to the professional calling which they attached to the initiatives of the agricultural funds.

All proud of having responded to a need identified by their long-term involvement in – activist, professional, religious – networks, the initiators of these cooperative banks organised a banking subspace that was not exclusively profit motivated, which they collectively defended each time the unique dimension of their activity – and the economic and symbolic advantages which they derived from it – were menaced.[6] They equally hollowed out their place within a competitive market using their historically founded connections with *their* clients as the basis for their ongoing involvement and their development.

Making a virtue out of necessity

The socio-historical background of cooperative banks also reflects that of their integration into the banking field, conveyed by the willingness of their agents to be recognised as 'genuine bankers', all while conserving the financial and symbolic benefits of belonging to an economy which was more 'social' than speculative. The entire first half of the twentieth century is marked by the setting up of local funds across the entire national territory and the creation of central control bodies; development being nonetheless slowed by the 1930s financial crisis and the Second World War.[7] The 1950s and 1960s represented, in broad terms, the period in which the State recognised their existence as financial organisations at the service of public interest missions. As an example, during the 1960s the *Crédit Agricole* was favourably granted the exclusivity of government subsidised loans for agricultural workers and was thus legitimately recognised as an institution both autonomous from (1966) and as a medium for agricultural policy,[8] while the *Crédit Mutuel* obtained in 1958 a special legal status through which it notably acquired financial advantages linked to the *livret bleu* (exclusive savings account with special conditions) and the financing of social housing granted by the State. The 1984 banking law aimed to better organise the banking field and the competition between the various establishments – commercial and cooperative, national and regional. This law intervened following a strong development period for cooperative banks, which over the space of thirty years had opened banking agencies that progressively replaced the premises – either parish-based, municipal, associative or union-affiliated – on which their savings and credit fund activities previously took place, in addition to them recruiting a staff of paid banking professionals. It was the high point of their assimilation as banking establishments, yet through embarking on a process to remove certain financial privileges (subsidised loans for the *Crédit Agricole* and *livret bleu* for the *Crédit Mutuel*, for example), the law consequently immersed them more resoundingly into the problems of maintaining market shares against their commercial sales counterparts who had been condemning this imbalance for several years.

As such their respective clientele, primarily made up of modestly resourced yet numerous clients, geographically situated further away from the banking agencies of profit-making groups and thus attracted by the cooperative networks spread across the national territory and faithful to the family or corporatist bank, became the best way for these banks to hold onto their dual position as a profitable and 'social' bank. The liability that a client base with 'small portfolios' may have represented in terms of financial profitability was converted into development capital realigned to the social, economic and human resources of these cooperative banks, who were consequently conveyed to permanently but effectively play the role of the integrated outsider, within a banking space in which each player fought to maintain their place.

'Cooperative' bankers

The realignment between a social ambition in finance and its practice, and the perpetuation of a shared belief in its possible existence, goes beyond the sole incantatory desire of cooperative banking directors and finds its structural principle not only in the genesis of institutions, but also in the process of structuring the market of banking employment. In truth, the permanence of client bases in each of the networks also alludes to the reality of structural homologies between bankers and clients, brought together through a shared ambition and economic language that is more domestic than speculative.

Cooperative banks in the banking employment market

By tracing back along the educative pathways of bankers or more precisely client advisers, also known as client coordinators – with these positions corresponding to functions involved in the commercial interaction with clients in agencies – it is possible to pinpoint what characterises and distinguishes present-day recruitment in cooperative banks. Like their commercial competition, they have developed partnerships with training centres combining formal education with *in situ* work experience, which allows them to co-educate their employees. However, contrary to the BNP or the *Société Générale*, both of which very often establish employment contracts at Masters level, the partner institutions of cooperative banks are primarily schools offering a BTS (*Brevet de technicien supérieur* – two-year French higher education qualification) in 'Sales' or Bachelors' degrees with a professional orientation in 'banking and insurance'. Taken on as part of an internship lasting several years, the students are (at least 70 per cent of the 250 students followed since 2005) recruited within their training network. It should be specified that these short-term pathways are composed of applicants issued primarily from working- and middle-class backgrounds (unlike once again the long-term pathways which take on and educate students more often from higher social classes, who will go on to fill out the ranks of commercial banks[9]) and that cooperative banks constitute for such individuals a potential career space within a serious profession, which is nonetheless practised in line with their beliefs and preferences for 'reasonable' finance.

Small-time careers in small-time banks

As such, while up to the 1980s cooperative banks largely recruited their first-generation employees from those networks which brought about their own existence (with volunteers becoming the initial funds directors, and *sociétaires'* sons and daughters with secondary school diplomas fulfilling positions as inspectors, administrative employees, then sales-personnel), today they can no longer count on this social proximity with the company and its client base which protected them from the overly strong autonomy of financial logic.

For all that, the cooperative banks position on the banking market today attracts young graduates whose predominately modest origins, titles and ambitions prepare them for the reproduction and practice of a finance embedded in the domestic sphere. Furthermore, young employees often educated in their family region are attached to geographically localised careers that can provide them with cooperative networks organised into regional federations. These unique organisational characteristics, themselves linked to the company's (cooperative) status, are understood to be the conditions which structure an encounter between a type of bank and a type of banker. As it happens, being employed within a commune close to their home town or family home is an argument that systematically pre-empts career ambitions. Concretely, those surveyed prefer to accept a less prestigious position (in terms of title, responsibilities, salary) that is close to their home, over a more professionally promising position that is further away, especially if taking on that role will not guarantee them a rapid return to their home region.

Conclusion

The efforts made by sociology to understand the socially and historically constructed positioning of cooperative banks in the banking market, should not be viewed as reducing this positioning to the idea that agents put forth their own interests disguised as if identical to those of their commercial counterparts. On the contrary, this positioning is embodied within a history initially constructed by actors with specific characteristics and, today, within a collection of beliefs and certainties which distinguish them from others.

Notes

1 See Moulévrier (2012).
2 In this sense, our approach 'seeks to reconnect actors' backgrounds to current, diverse and competitive institutions, and to the existence of power relations that characterise capitalism and distinguish it from an economic market ideal and fantasy' (Postel, 2009, p. 11).
3 This hypothesis is not at odds with analyses in terms of the generalised rationalisation of activities. Indeed, the banking relationship is also a normative relationship in which 'interchangeable' client account managers progressively become sales-personnel for banking services. The large majority of banking sales personnel, restricted by profitability objectives, link their clients – thanks to *scoring* software – to the profiles of investors, lenders and savers that are more or less risky or profitable. In this sense, our analyses (Moulévrier, 2002) agree notably with the research of Jeanne Lazarus where she has specified that 'as an institution guaranteeing solid monetary order, it [the bank] has become a commercial enterprise' (Lazarus, 2012, pp. 145–146). Without calling into question this obvious process of rationalisation and change in the relations between clients and bankers, the observed realities only partially reflect this standardisation. Indeed, depending on the situation, the clients, but also the agencies, the so-called sales-personnel do not translate the sales recommendations using the same terms, with the same ease or the same conviction, when faced with clients who follow more or less obediently their propositions and who are more or less aware of the bank's expectations.
4 Alongside the employees and volunteers, clients often referred to as '*sociétaires*' have at their disposition a legal right to vote within the General Assemblies, during which the balance sheets and future prospects, both in terms of accounting and ethics, are validated. As such, they possess a 'dual quality' as owner and client, an expression of the principle claimed by cooperative banking of 'one man, one voice'. On the subject of the 'dual quality' of clients, see notably Gianfaldoni and Richez-Battesti (2006).
5 Since 2008, this public interest mission was replaced by an obligation to finance public interest projects as a percentage of their profits.
6 As evidence of this, for example, the recent movement (see *Le Monde*, 5 May 2014 issue) of banks and insurers, both cooperative and mutualist, against the project for an *Autorité de contrôle prudentiel et de résolution* (ACPR - French Prudential Supervision and Resolution Authority). In the section dealing with banking supervisors, presidents of banks and insurance companies are less and less regarded as effective administrators. Assembled together around the *Crédit Agricole*, the mutualist organisations were mobilised for the withdrawal of this decision which is contrary to their principle of governance.
7 The first half of the twentieth century was equally a time for negotiations between cooperative banks and the public authorities with regard to the privileges accorded by the State to these financial institutions of 'public interest' and to the limitations of their autonomy. The Second World War interrupted this process not only due to prolonging the financial crisis, but also because the Vichy regime attempted to heighten its administrative supervision.
8 See research by Gueslin (1985) on the history of the *Crédit agricole*.
9 Students from these long-term pathways only very rarely contemplate cooperative banks as an area for professional insertion, favouring the 'real banks', in other words French or, better yet, international commercial banks.

References

Gianfaldoni, P. and Richez-Battesti, N. (Eds.) (2006). *Les banques coopératives en France. Le défi de la performance et de la solidarité*. Paris: L'Harmattan.
Gueslin, A. (1985). *Le Crédit Agricole*. Paris: La Découverte.
Lazarus, J. (2012). *L'épreuve de l'argent. Banques, banquiers, clients*. Paris: Calmann-Lévy.
Moulévrier, P. (2002). *Le mutualisme bancaire. Le Crédit Mutuel de l'Eglise au marché*. Rennes: PUR.
Moulévrier, P. (2012). Les structures sociales du marché bancaire en France. *Revue Française de Socio-Economie*, 9, 23–41.
Postel, N. (2009). Sur les relations entre l'éthique et le capitalisme. *Revue Française de Socio-Economie*, 4, 9–13.

16

RELATIONSHIP BANKING – AN "ENDANGERED SPECIES"?

Evidence from Germany

Eileen Keller

Introduction

Banks are an integral part of modern financial systems as they fulfil important economic functions. Contrary to other financial intermediaries, such as investment societies or insurance companies, they have access to central bank refinancing and they play an important role in the transmission of monetary politics. In addition, banks are central to the provision of a payments system, that is, the infrastructure through which cashless transfers of money can be realised. Finally, banks collect deposits and they grant credit to businesses and households. By transforming liquid assets, such as deposits, into long-term credit, they play an important role in the funding of the economy and they bear considerable economic risks.

While it is hard to imagine a modern financial system without banks, they neither have had the same importance everywhere, nor have they exercised their role in the same way. Financial intermediation by banks plays a prominent role in many continental European countries; in the Anglo-Saxon world, in contrast, disintermediated, market-based forms of funding, such as shares and bonds, are a more important external source of funding for businesses. The difference between intermediated and more disintermediated economies is, however, not only a matter of the relative quantities of different sources of funding. Rather, the two are associated with different funding cultures – a distinction which goes beyond the banks versus markets divide. While so-called market-based financial systems tend to rely on publicly available information when lending and investment decisions are made, private, proprietary information that is only known to insiders and accumulated thanks to stable relations over time has played an important role in so-called bank-based financial systems. With the financial services revolution, financial globalisation and the financialisation of even larger fractions of the economy, relationship banking is generally seen to be declining.

This chapter presents the institutional foundations of intermediated economies and discusses the extent to which they have been questioned with the emphasis given to market-mechanisms, stochastic approaches to risk management and the rise of the shareholder value. The chapter thereby draws on the German experience, where the interactions between the financial sector and the real economy have been particularly relationship-intense.

From financial intermediation to relationship banking

One important function of financial sectors is to provide financial resources to the real economy. Households, businesses and corporations often need more liquidity than they have to meet different sorts of payment obligations and required investments. In this case, *external* sources of funding from entities with a surplus of liquidity can be an option. A significant share of surplus liquidity is, however, not transferred directly to fund investments. This is not surprising since providing equity or debt capital is a time-consuming and risky exercise: it is only when an enterprise is prospering and in a financially sound situation that an equity investment is likely to pay off and a credit paid back. In order to make sure that this is the case, an investor/lender needs to have good knowledge of the specific situation of the enterprise, the market it is operating in, the macroeconomic context, etc. and s/he has to monitor the situation of the enterprise closely.

Not every individual with surplus liquidity (e.g. savings) is able to do this, especially when the amount of surplus liquidity is small. In order to overcome this problem, *financial intermediaries* have emerged from the thirteenth century on. Financial intermediaries intervene, as their name indicates, between those who have a liquidity surplus and those who have a liquidity deficit (or need). Since they specialise in the collection of information about borrowers and the management of associated risks, they can exert the monitoring function more efficiently than individual investors or lenders could do (Diamond, 1984). This is generally considered as the main reason why financial intermediaries, such as banks, exist.

While the accumulation of information and the centralisation of the monitoring function is true for all financial intermediaries, the extent to which private information is accumulated and the extent to which client relations are seen in a long-term perspective varies among banks and countries. The term 'relationship banking' is therefore used to describe the relation-intense end of bank–client relationships. The term emphasises the *privileged* relations between one or a few banks and their clients over time. These relations are ultimately conditioned by the *mutual commitment* of both parties to maintain their special relations. The specificity of relationship banking as opposed to more transaction-oriented forms of banking is that the interaction between the debtor and the borrower is not exclusively considered on the moment of the interaction (or the transaction) itself, but is embedded in a longer term, relational perspective with repeated interactions and transactions. Thanks to stable relations over time, lending and investment decisions can be more strongly based on client-specific information.

Relationship banks usually have a preponderant role in the provision of financial services to a business both in terms of depth, that is mutual exposure, and breadth, that is the different services provided by the bank including long- and short-term credit, credit lines, a payment system, asset management services and investment banking, depending on the needs of the company (Boot, 2000). In the German context, when a business maintains close, privileged relations with one (or several) of its banks, the latter is termed as being the *Hausbank*. In some cases, these relations have persisted for generations and German businesses usually put the name of their Hausbank in their official letterhead (Braouet, 2017).

The effects of relationship lending may, however, go beyond the mere aggregation of information that results from the repeated interactions according to standard economic theory. If these privileged relations work well, mutual trust may emerge and the bank–firm relationship can develop into a form of partnership. Bank relations are not merely financial relations; they are social relations between agents and it is this social dimension based on trust and mutual understanding that can ease economic exchanges. A business owner may, for instance, be inclined to share information with its bank that it would not share otherwise; because, in principle, sharing information can also be disadvantageous for a business owner. Inversely, an enterprise may profit from better financial advice and a stronger commitment in terms of risk sharing that may go beyond the pure financial interests of the bank. The different forms of relationship banking in Germany, their evolution over time and their implications will be discussed in the following pages.

The changing role of the big universal banks

One specificity of financial intermediation in Germany up to the 1990s was the close integration of the large German universal banks and the productive sector. Due to universal banking, which allows a bank to engage in different activities within one subsidiary, notably commercial and investment banking, the German banks did not only grant credit to large corporations, but also intervened as investors, holding significant equity participations in a given firm. Thanks to these blockholdings, banks were often seated on the supervisory boards of their customers. This gave them privileged access to proprietary information about the corporation and at least some influence on a corporation's strategic decisions. Stakeholder-friendly corporate governance dispositions and blockholder-friendly tax incentives underpinned the close relations between the productive sector institutionally.

This form of close integration of the banks and the productive sector emerged from the late nineteenth century on and is generally seen to having played a considerable role in the German industrialisation process by providing patient long-term capital (Gerschenkron, 1962). From the onset on, the large German corporations and the banks had been embedded in an interwoven net of shareholdings and interlocking directorates. The two large German commercial banks, Deutsche Bank and Dresdner Bank (integrated into Commerzbank in 2009), and the insurance company Allianz were at the very centre of the network, holding significant equity participations in all major firms (Höpner and Krempel, 2003). At the beginning of the twentieth century, each of the then eight largest German commercial banks sat on the supervisory boards of dozens of German corporations. Deutsche Bank alone was on the board of more than one hundred firms and endowed with the position of the chairman or vice-chairman in more than one-third of them (documented in Riesser, 1911, p. 897 ff.).

This dense network remained surprisingly stable until the 1990s but then things began to change rather rapidly. With the abolition of various restrictions to the cross-border flow of money, stock exchange reforms and the introduction of new financial instruments and financial market segments in many western countries from the 1970s on, the German insider-system that privileged private information to insiders over publicly available information for all market participants was increasingly called into question. The German corporate governance and financial sector regime appeared increasingly outdated at that time and both were strongly criticised for their non-transparent character.

In this context, the German system of close bank–industry relations came under pressure. From the 1970s on, with increased competition and new business opportunities in financial markets, the German banks began to shed away from equity holdings, a trend that was fuelled by various reforms of corporate governance, disclosure requirements and the taxation of capital gains. Deutsche Bank and Allianz reoriented their business strategy away from industry participations and many German banks began to build up expertise in investment banking, mainly by acquiring foreign investment banks. In parallel, the corporate culture within the largest non-financial German corporations began to move towards a shareholder-oriented strategy (Beyer and Höppner, 2003). Due to this process, the dense network of equity holdings dissolved rather rapidly during the late 1990s and early 2000s. Equity holdings by banks decreased from 4.1 per cent in 1994 to 0.4 per cent in 2005, the share of board seats held by bankers fell from 9.6 per cent to 5.6 per cent and the number of corporations on whose boards bankers were represented decreased from 51 per cent to 33 per cent over the same period (Dittmann et al., 2010, pp. 36–37).

Relationship banking and SMEs

While the specificities of the close integration of the large German universal banks and the productive sector seem to be 'a closed episode of German economic history' (Höpner and Krempel, 2003), a relationship-intense form of banking has persisted between many German banks and (parts of) the *Mittelstand*, the landscape of small and middle-sized German enterprises. Many of these enterprises are family-owned and they have maintained a preference for bank over market-based forms of funding, even though a certain percentage of them could, in principle, raise capital on the markets rather easily.[1] When it comes to managing their bank relations, survey data indicates that relational criteria, such as reliability, commitment and risk taking play, even for the large German businesses, a more prominent role than transaction-oriented criteria, like pricing and product quality (Farruggio, 2014). Relationship-intense forms of banking do, of course, not mean that German businesses all only have one bank, that all businesses have long-standing bank relations and that bank–firm relations are always easy. Nevertheless, there is a trend towards long-standing bank relations with one (or few) main banks even if the use of internal funding has considerably increased over the last years.

Relationship banking in Germany is associated with measurable economic effects. When one compares the characteristics of bank lending in Germany to those of other countries, comparatively (although not unparalleled) low interest rate levels can be found. In addition, long-term bank credit has played a more prominent role in financing a business' investment than in many other countries (Vitols, 1998). German banks also tended to tolerate relatively high levels of indebtedness for a long time, a feature that was attributed to the close Hausbank-relations and a debtor-friendly bankruptcy code (Deutsche Bundesbank, 1999, p. 35 ff.). It has also been shown that relationship banking can provide a liquidity insurance in the case of a rating downgrading, a higher commitment to workout activities to financially distressed firms, better credit availability, lower collateral requirements and lower interest rates (Elsas and Krahnen, 2004; Harhoff and Körting, 1998).

Relationship banking is strongly associated with the dense network of the relatively small and regionally anchored savings and the cooperative banks, which play a primary role in bank lending to SMEs. Since the financial crisis of 2008, the savings and the cooperative banks with their focus on retail and SME banking have accounted for 82 per cent (!) of the pre-tax profits of the German banking sector (Fitch Ratings, 2015, p. 3). The Sparkassen-Finanzgruppe comprises 580 firms, employs almost 342.000 people and has a balance sheet volume of almost 2900 billion EUR. The cooperative financial group has 18 million members, 191.000 employees and a balance sheet volume of 1136 billion EUR.

The cooperative and the savings banks are appreciated for the ways in which they manage their client relations. According to a survey among 961 German businesses, customers of the savings and cooperative banks are more satisfied with their banks with respect to advisory skills, customer orientation, and financing conditions than the clients of the private banks (Die Familienunternehmer, 2010). In a similar vein, a survey among 300 business owners and financial officers, all clients of one of the largest four banks of at least one of the three banking groups, confirms the high satisfaction with the cooperative (ranks 1–4), and, to a minor extent, with the savings banks (ranks 6, 7, 8, and 10); while the private banks tended to be in the bottom half of the list (ranks 9, 11 and 12 with the exception of Commerzbank ranked 5th) (Deutsches Institut für Service-Qualität, 2016). This illustrates the special relations between German businesses and the savings and cooperative banks, while it is obviously not restricted to them.

In order to understand the special role played by the savings and cooperative banks, it is decisive to see the ways in which they are organised and how they exercise activities. A first specificity lies in their ownership structure. Neither the savings nor the cooperative banks are joint stock companies. The German savings banks have – contrary to the developments in many other European countries – remained in public ownership. Most of them are owned by the municipalities or the Landkreise (roughly counties). The savings banks are endowed with a public interest mission, which implies promoting popular savings and supporting regional economic development. The cooperative banks are owned by their members whose interests they serve. Neither of the two are thus profit-maximising entities and neither of the two has to conform to the return expectations of international investors.

A second specificity relates to their size: On the local level, the savings and the cooperative banks form dense nets of independent banks, many of which are relatively small. Among the almost 1900 banks that operated in Germany in 2016, 976 belonged to the cooperative and 412 to the savings bank sector (Bundesbank statistics), although a continuing trend towards consolidation has reduced their number considerably over the past decades. Each of these banks takes its every-day business decisions autonomously. The limited size of the banks matters to relationship banking, since it levels the playing field with the clients. As the business and the bank can be of equal order of size, they may face similar challenges when it comes to managing staff, the client base, etc. In addition, for a small bank, a larger SME is an important client that matters to the overall well-being of the bank and is thus of strategic importance. Consequently, the bank will treat this client carefully. This is much less the case for a large bank concerning a client that makes up for a tiny fraction of its own balance sheet. The bar for what is an important client that requires special treatment is thus much lower and mutual understanding is often easier.[2]

A third specificity relates to their regional anchorage: Both the savings banks amongst each other and the cooperative banks among each other do not usually compete for clients because each bank operates according to the regional principle, i.e. on markets that are segmented along territorial lines. Consequently, the customer base needs to be handled carefully since it cannot be broadened endlessly and the well-being of the bank is closely tied to the well-being of the local economy. In addition, since the market is territorially defined, these banks tend to know the local economy rather well. One of the reproaches often made by businesses is that many bank advisors do not understand the functioning of their respective economic sectors sufficiently. The specific institutional setup of the cooperative and the savings banks can thus help overcome this problem.

Finally, the high degree of group-integration matters. Both the savings and the cooperative banks form closely integrated banking and liability groups. An important number of functions and services is pooled in special entities that belong to the group. The central associations of both sectors (Deutscher Sparkassen- und Giroverband, DSGV and the Bundesverband der Deutschen Volks- und Raiffeisenbanken, BVR) provide, for instance, risk management solutions, professional training and they help with the application of regulatory stipulations. In addition, specialised financial institutions that belong to the group provide financial services and standardised products to all banks, including wealth management, leasing or investment banking. Thanks to these features, the savings and cooperative banks are much more competitive than banks of their size would be on a stand-alone basis. Group integration allows them to compete with the much larger commercial banks as they are able to offer a large array of services.

Relationship banking in the free market era[3]

Even though the savings and cooperative banks have, in general, maintained close relations with the productive sector, the above-mentioned developments in financial sectors and of financial regulation have not left banking in Germany unchallenged. With increased competition in the banking sector, cost pressure and the continuous process of harmonising banking regulation at the European level, many specificities of the institutional set up of the German banking sector have been questioned over the past decades. Despite these challenges, some features have been surprisingly stable due to the strong commitment by different parties to defend the outstanding features of the banking model. It is precisely for this reason that developments that are commonly seen as a threat to relationship banking, namely asset securitisation and new approaches to risk management, have not led to its abandonment but to its adaptation.

Coming to the impact of the securitisation of bank credit first. With the propagation of securitisation techniques from the late 1980s on, bank debt has lost its character of being illiquid and held on balance until maturity, that is until the credit is paid back. Thanks to securitisation, bank debt (as other liabilities) and associated cash flows (or default risks) can be transformed into tradable financial products and handed over to investors. It is often assumed that is has an immediate impact on relationship lending, since the evaluation of the underlying credit portfolio relies on standardised methods, and banks may be less inclined to invest in the costly search of private information if a credit is not held on balance.

In Germany, interest in securitisation techniques increased significantly in the late 1990s and early 2000s. The securitisation of bank loans was considered by some as a promising means to modernise the German financial system, while the bank–firm relationships could be maintained. The hope was that the securitisation of bank credit would alleviate profitability problems from which many German banks were suffering, and grant German businesses an indirect access to financial markets (e.g. Ranné, 2005, p. 57). A framework for asset securitisation under German law was therefore developed from the late 1990s on. The issue was promoted considerably by the large commercial banks and some of the publicly owned Landesbanken and it was supported actively by the German federal promotional bank Kfw.

So far, the effect of asset securitisation on relationship banking in the savings and the cooperative sector bank sector has, however, been rather limited. The banks of both groups do not sell their credit on to investors outside the banking group, also because this was heavily refused by many of their clients. Many credit contracts specify that the credit may not be sold on to external investors. All the savings and cooperative banks therefore do is lowering their geographic risk exposure and achieving some risk diversification by pooling credit within the banking group. Just as market-based forms of funding are refused by parts of the

German economy, so is the principle of selling credit on. Together with the reappraisal of its respective risk and benefits that asset securitisation has seen since the crisis, and the need to secure the quality of the underlying credit portfolio, securitisation may have less an impact on relationship lending than commonly expected.

Another challenge for relationship banking stems from risk management. Bank internal procedures to evaluate the risks associated with different banking activities have undergone tremendous modifications since the 1980s. With the emergence of presumably more sophisticated risk management techniques, the process of credit attribution has become increasingly formalised. The basic rationale, which underlies the decision of a bank to lend money nowadays, is the bank-internal rating, which classifies an enterprise in a standardised way, depending on its financial situation. Any borrower is characterised as an instance of a group of cases with similar default probabilities. This approach to risk management makes it more difficult to value the specific added value of relationship banking, which precisely lies in the accumulation of client-specific information that cannot be standardised and integrated in the rating easily. Even though the ratings include qualitative, 'soft' criteria, such as the quality of the management, corporate strategy, controlling, etc., besides the 'hard' financial data, the assessment is relatively standardised and often made by the risk management department, which is not in charge of the client on an every-day basis.

In Germany, the use of internal ratings increased significantly from the 1990s on and was supported by all German banking groups even before Basel II became effective. The period back then was characterised by increased financial distress in the German banking sector and many banks, especially the smaller savings and cooperative banks came under significant pressure. At least part of the problem was attributed to a lack of risk management techniques (BAKred, 2000, p. 48). In this context, many banks concluded that they had to improve their approach to risk management and the banks of all three banking groups intended to implement tools that were more sensitive to the individual creditworthiness of the borrower. Surveys among non-financial enterprises from that time confirm that banks often asked for more transparency, higher equity ratios and additional guarantees (Plattner, 2002).

Thanks to the close relations many banks have maintained with their customers, however, the banks were rather successful in communicating the new requirements to their customers. The new rules were clearly perceived as a threat to many businesses but since the banks communicated clearly and in advance, many SMEs were able to respond to these developments by a professionalisation of accounting, a proactive transparency strategy and the build-up of a higher equity capital ratio (Bluhm and Martens, 2008). In addition, the business federations of the craft sector and the industrial sector prepared and trained the businesses with respect to the new requirements and the banks' expectations. This helped to make the adjustment to the new rules smoother than this was the case in other countries (developed further in Keller, 2014).

Despite these adjustments, the banks have continued valuing their close customer relations when lending decisions are made as they do not rely on the output of the rating procedure only. Banks have used the qualitative aspects of the rating in the past to improve the final rating. In addition, and more importantly, it is not uncommon that a bank consultant argues against the rating when it is unfavourable for a client to whom the bank has a long-standing relation. In these cases, the consultant argues why s/he thinks that the bank should diverge from the conditions (or the decision to lend at all) that the rating would suggest, a suggestion that is subsequently evaluated by further steps in the hierarchy of the bank, depending on the financial risk at stake. Hence, in cases where the bank maintains long-standing and close relations with one of their costumers, the coupling between the rating and the lending decision may be rather lose. The available evidence therefore suggests that a case- besides a class-based, stochastic approach to bank lending has persisted in Germany.

Conclusion

Evaluating the extent to which banking in Germany is 'special' and has remained relation-intense is a difficult endeavour. Since the issue touches upon sensitive bank-internal information on risk management and customer relations, the evidence at hand is rather limited and more in-depth research is desirable. It is undisputable that banking in Germany – as elsewhere – has undergone tremendous modifications over the past decades. Some features of the traditional Hausbank-model, such as direct shareholdings and board representation have lost the importance and the implications that they once had. In the areas of banking and corporate governance that were the strongest exposed to international competition, a strategic reorientation away from the traditional set-up has taken place and many of the formal institutional dispositions that have once contributed to the emergence and the consolidation of this form of banking have been abolished or modified.

Another form of relation-intense banking has, however, persisted so far. The close relations between the banks and their clients are also much less protected by institutional dispositions than in the past. If this sector persists against odds, this is because relationship banking has been a viable business model for the smaller German banks and satisfied the needs of many businesses. It has therefore also profited from considerable political support. The mutual understanding that relationship banking fosters and the capacity to communicate and understand each other help smoothening financing relationships. Relationship-intense forms of banking can be a useful corrective to statistical approaches when it comes to appraising changing risks that come along with innovations and changes in the market environment.

The main challenge for the banks of both groups nowadays relates to the decreasing interest rate spread, i.e. the difference between what banks have to pay to their depositors and the money they earn when they lend to investors. Yet, here again, relationship banking with the purpose of becoming an encompassing partner for their business clients is for many banks the only way forward. In the current low-interest environment, it is only thanks to provision-based income that the banks can survive economically in the mid-term. Sustainable relationship banking therefore means nowadays more than ever to go beyond bank lending, professionalise consultancy activities and be a competent and reliable partner for the productive sector.

Notes

1 This is the reason why Germany is generally considered to be the country with the highest number of firms that could raise money on the capital markets if they wanted to.
2 The empirical evidence on the development of banking in Germany is taken from a larger research project (Keller, 2014). Besides an encompassing document analysis, it draws on 16 mainly face-to-face interviews with bankers and representatives of the banking federations and the employer federations, conducted between 2013 and 2017.
3 This section is based on Keller (2014).

References

BAKred (2000). Jahresbericht 1999. Retrieved on 28 December 2012, from: http://www.bafin.de/SharedDocs/Downloads/DE/Jahresbericht/dl_jb_1999_bakred.html?nn=2818588.

Beyer, J. and Höppner, M. (2003). The disintegration of organised capitalism: German corporate governance in the 1990s. *Western European Politics*, 26(4), 179–198.

Bluhm, K. and Martens, B. (2008). Change within traditional channels: German SMEs, the restructuring of the banking sector, and the growing shareholder-value orientation. In K. Bluhm and R. Schmidt (Eds.) *Change in SMEs. Towards a new European capitalism?* (pp. 39–57). Houndmills: Palgrave Macmillan.

Boot, A. (2000). Relationship banking: What do we know? *Journal of Financial Intermediation*, 9(1), 7–25.

Braouet, C. (2017). Ungleiche "Genossen" in Deutschland und Frankreich. In Deutsch-Französisches Institut (Ed.) *Frankreich Jahrbuch 2016. Sozial- und Solidarwirtschaft in Frankreich und Europa*. Wiesbaden: Springer VS.

Deutsche Bundesbank (1999). *Monatsbericht Oktober 1999*. 51. Jahrgang Nr. 10. Retrieved on 28 March 2013 from: http://www.bundesbank.de/Redaktion/DE/Downloads/Veroeffentlichungen/Monatsberichte/1999/1999_10_monatsbericht.pdf?__blob=publicationFile.

Deutsches Institut für Service-Qualität (2016). *B2B-Kundenbefragung Mittelstandsbanken*. Retrieved on 26 June 2017 from http://disq.de/2016/20160201-Mittelstandsbanken.html.

Diamond, D. (1984). Financial intermediation and delegated monitoring. *Review of Economic Studies*, 51(3), 393–414.

Die Familienunternehmer (2010). *Bankenrating 2010*. Retrieved from https://www.familienunternehmer.eu/uploads/tx_wfmedienpr/10_04_21_Bankenrating_2010.pdf.

Dittmann, I., Maug, E. and Schneider, C. (2010). Bankers on the boards of German firms: What they do, what they are worth, and why they are (still) there. *Review of Finance*, 14(1), 35–71.

Elsas, R. and Krahnen, J. (2004). Universal banks and relationships with firms. In J. P. Krahnen and R. H. Schmidt (Eds.) *The German Financial System* (pp. 197–232). Oxford: Oxford University Press.

Farruggio, C. (2014). Ausgestaltung und Steuerung des Netzes von Bankbeziehungen – Update nach 25 Jahren mithilfe einer explorativen Unternehmensbefragung. *Schmalenbachs Zeitschrift für betriebswirtschaftliche Forschung*, 66, 694–723.

Fitch Ratings (2015). *Genossenschaftliche FinanzGruppe. Full Rating Report*. Retrieved on 18 December 2015 from http://www.bvr.de/p.nsf/0/ACEC8E2F44E41B0BC1257F080049D321/$file/GFGreport25.11.2015.pdf

Gerschenkron, A. (1962). *Economic backwardness in historical perspective. A book of essays*. Cambridge: Belknap Press of Harvard University Press.

Harhoff, D. and Körting, T. (1998). Lending relationships in Germany – Empirical evidence from survey data. *Journal of Banking & Finance*, 22(10–11), 1317–1353.

Höpner, M. and Krempel, L. (2003). *The politics of the German company network* (MPIfG Working Paper, 03/9). Retrieved on 2 August 2014 from http://www.mpi-fg-koeln.mpg.de/pu/workpap/wp03-9/wp03-9.html.

Keller, E. (2014). *Negotiating the future of banking. The coalitional dynamics of collective preference formation in France and Germany after the crisis*. Dissertation. Humboldt-Universität, Berlin.

Plattner, D. (2002). *Unternehmensfinanzierung in schwierigem Fahrwasser. Wachsende Finanzierungsprobleme im Mittelstand. Auswertung der Unternehmensbefragung 2002. KfW*. Retrieved on 10 May 2013 from https://www.kfw.de/Download-Center/Konzernthemen/Research/PDF-Dokumente-Unternehmensbefragung/Unternehmensbefragung-2002-lang.pdf

Ranné, O. (2005). Kreditverbriefung und Mittelstandsfinanzierung. *Mittelstands- und Strukturpolitik*, 33, 43–66.

Riesser, J. (1911). *The German great banks and their concentration in connection with the economic development of Germany*. Washington: Government Printing Office.

Vitols, S. (1998). Are German banks different? *Small Business Economics*, 10(2), 79–91.

17

THE FUTURE OF STOCK EXCHANGES HAS A LONG PAST

What can we learn from financial history?

Paul Lagneau-Ymonet and Angelo Riva

Introduction

In the late 1970s, the financial markets played a marginal role in the European economy; today, however, they occupy a key position, because their reaction determines the success of many economic policies and management decisions. Focusing on the French context, this article will show how Europe has moved so quickly from having an economy characterised by the marginalisation of the financial markets to having an economy influenced, if not dominated, by them. It will therefore analyse the transformations that have taken place within the French economy itself and those that have accompanied its integration onto the international stage, particularly in Europe. For this is a general trend: even though the resurgence of financial activities occurred a bit later in France than in the United States or the United Kingdom, the same basic movement pretty much affected all the developed economies, including the most resistant such as that of Germany. After giving an account of the rebirth of financial activities in France, since the late 1970s, we shall discuss their long-term development. By comparing the development of the financial markets before 1914 and today, we shall show that their contemporary evolution does not replicate that of the nineteenth century. The privatisation of exchanges, the ascendency of institutional finance and the trans-nationalisation of the banks and markets are specific to the contemporary period. While 'the world of yesterday' was largely internationalised and open for capital, the *organisation of financial transactions* through exchanges and their official intermediaries remained national, at least in powerful countries such as the United Kingdom, and France. Considering this comparison, we will eventually analyse the risks that the current organisation of financial transactions poses to the economy.

From the administered economy to the return of the financial markets: the post-war financial system challenged by international openness

Economists inspired by Keynesian theory (e.g. Jean Denizet, Vivien Lévy-Garboua) put forward the concept of an 'overdraft economy' to characterise the French financial system of the 1960s. They maintained that the overdraft economy allowed abundant credit to be compatible with the lack of high inflation thanks to competition and decentralisation of credit by banking networks and their control by the State and its central bank. In hindsight, however, the financial system of that era was not so coherent or stable, only a stage in the gradual but consequential alteration of the post-war administered financial system.

As early as the 1950s, politicians and neo-liberal civil servants (Denord, 2016) tried in vain to give financial markets a greater role in the financing of the economy (through IPOs, seasoned equity offering, and debt issuing). Promoting them was intended to help non-inflationary financing of companies and allow monetary policy to focus on bringing inflation under control. The transformation of the financial system was also seen as the way to circumvent two limitations of the administered financial system inherited from the post-war period: the growing imperfection in the allocation of savings (which, incidentally, contributed to inflation) and the control of exchange control. While these hindrances were relatively easy to control in a stable technological and international environment, after 1970 they became obstacles that strangled growth as the European integration and the rise of the Euromarkets in London reopened the boundaries of the national financial system. As the share of profits in value added slumped, companies were investing only at the expense of growing indebtedness, which the State selectively maintained. This administered allocation of savings was, however, affected by political and social goals, so that the credit framework contributed less to industrial restructuring than to the acceleration of inflation, which upset the fragile performances of French companies subject to intensifying competition (Feiertag, 2006; Hautcoeur, 1996; Quennouëlle-Corre, 2000).

The opening-up of the French economy also posed a challenge to the movement of capital. Moreover, when the international environment became unstable following the end of the Bretton Woods system, exchange control was maintained only by tightening the regulations governing national actors, whereas multinationals avoided this through book-entry systems and used the international capital markets, a situation that was unsustainable in the long term but which persisted until the 1980s, when exchange control was abandoned.

Finally, the slowdown of growth followed by the restrictive monetary policies introduced in the United Kingdom and the United States in 1979 highlighted the unsustainable nature of the debt accumulated by major companies during the previous decade, which led to their liquidation or recapitalisation and restructuring through nationalisation in 1982. The State bore some of the cost, thereby rapidly increasing its debt, which could then only be financed in a renewed and internationalised financial market.

1980s reforms

The reforms made after 1984 aimed to establish this type of financial market and unified money market in order to effectively implement an anti-inflationary monetary policy. The dismantling of exchange controls from 1986 made it possible for the French financial market to re-enter the world stage. New derivatives markets emerged in France in 1986 and 1987, and in 1988 the law paved the way for the gradual phasing-out of stockbrokers' monopoly on stock market brokerage (Feiertag, 2001; Lagneau-Ymonet and Riva, 2010).

These reforms quickly brought results: the financial markets developed rapidly; prices and issuance of shares and bonds skyrocketed; stock trading volumes soared. As was the case abroad, the opening of markets and the 1984 banking law, which promoted the universal-bank model, caused the banking sector, its regulators, the Treasury and the governments to focus on 'national champions' capable of competing with the Anglo-Saxon banking giants. The

1987 economic crash did not have any lasting impact, and the markets continued to develop during the 1990s, when European and global financial integration increased.

By freeing up the flow of capital transfers and risk transfers via the derivatives markets, the expansive monetary policy – which had, since 1987, been the central banks' primary response to crises (particularly the US Federal Reserve) – also perpetuated the 'global imbalances' of the globalised economy (especially the American balance of payments deficit, and Japanese and, more recently, Chinese surpluses). Imports of goods from emerging countries no doubt limited inflation in Western countries, but the 1990s and 2000s were marked by the formation and bursting of bubbles that were the consequences of the uncontrolled growth of financial markets and of overtrading. However, at least until the major financial crisis started in 2007, the dominant paradigm among financiers and their regulators remained that of 'efficient' and therefore 'self-regulating' financial activities. The central argument was the same: through the liquidity they provided to investors, these markets were better capable of allocating risk while providing the means of easily passing it on.

Stock market deregulation in the 1990s and 2000s

Financial deregulation, supported by the main financial institutions that are the primary beneficiaries, also affect the organisation of the markets themselves. Long organised according to the mutual model, the stock markets operated like local monopolies that were tightly regulated. During the 1990s, they transformed into profit-driven joint stock companies, and at the beginning of the 2000s, they were listed on the very same markets they managed. Having been institutions that organised competition between intermediaries and publicly advertised their exchanges, the stock markets entered into competition with private trading devices and international banks in order to make a profit from financial brokerage.

This competition was institutionalised in Europe by the Markets in Financial Instruments Directive (MiFID) which came into force in 2007. This directive ended stock market monopoly in countries where it still existed, such as France, thus authorising the creation of alternative, opaque platforms without, however, tackling the exponential growth of over-the-counter markets. In the minds of legislators, won over to mainstream financial theory, competition reduced transaction costs and thus increased market liquidity, which would ultimately lower the cost of capital for issuers. Moreover, it was supposed to promote the integration of the European financial market, which was fragmented by divisions inherited from the particular financial contexts of EU member states (Posner, 2009). The MiFID directive has actually reinforced fragmentation and hence entrenched the dominant position of the largest financial institutions: only they have the financial and human resources to get the IT infrastructure necessary to operate on multiple trading devices, to consolidate the information, and develop the algorithms to treat them (Lagneau-Ymonet and Riva, 2012; Lenglet and Riva, 2013). The MiFID II, which enters into force in January 2018, promotes the creation of new and more transparent additional markets and puts some constraints on the trading in opaque markets. Nevertheless, the core philosophy of MiFID I based on fragmentation and privatisation of the financial transactions did not change. If it is too early to assess its consequences, some market participants express concerns about the complexity of the new rules that could worsen the trading environment, particularly for smaller institutions.

The Paris stock exchange also played a key role in this drive: demutualised in 1988, it contributed to the establishment of the Euronext group in 2000 along with the Brussels and Amsterdam stock exchanges, joined two years later by Lisbon and the London International

Financial Futures and Options Exchange market (LIFFE). In 2006, Euronext merged with the New York Stock Exchange (NYSE). In 2011, however, the American board of the new group agreed to merge with Deutsche Börse, the continental rival of the Paris stock exchange, which had refused its offer to merge in 2006. For the Paris financial market, this snub was a foreshadowing of its marginalisation on the international stage (Hautcoeur et al., 2010). By 2015, the owner of the transatlantic operator sold its continental-European activities and Euronext recovered operational autonomy, despite its domination by its arch-rivals, the London Stock Exchange and Deutsche Börse.

A return to 'yesterday's world'?

It was not until the 1990s that the financial markets regained a level of development comparable to that of the *Belle Époque*, following the major decline that had begun in 1914 and reduced them to the bare minimum (Lagneau-Ymonet and Riva, 2018). According to the traditional interpretation, the 1929 crash, the Second World War and their socio-political consequences were indeed the final blow for markets already weakened by First World War inflation levels, monetary tensions, and risky speculation during the Roaring Twenties. Government hostility towards finance, blamed for the Great Depression, led to an ineffectual attempt at so-called 'financial repression' which was intended to prevent the markets from expanding between the 1930s and the 1960s or 1970s. On a deeper level, no doubt the development of large corporations led them to become independent from their shareholders and self-finance their investments and innovation.

The growth of the stock exchange in the nineteenth century

In hindsight, it appears that the specificity of the long nineteenth century lies in the emergence of a centralised market, the stock exchange, for issuing and trading public and private securities. Certainly, a decentralised financial market organised by notaries under the *Ancien Régime* had already enabled the financing of private agents whereas the stock exchange had been limited to government securities (Hoffman et al., 2000). The first private beneficiaries of these new markets were the rail companies, whose issuance absorbed 1 per cent of annual GDP for several decades, well beyond the financing capacities of any financial institution. The banking system, which evolved in the latter half of the century with the establishment of deposit banks (Société Générale, Crédit Lyonnais) and merchant banks (Crédit Mobilier, Banque de Paris et de Pays-Bas), also relied on the stock exchange to finance itself and to meet its clients' long-term financing needs throughout issues of shares and bonds. After the railways, corporations for the distribution of gas, water, electricity, urban transport as well as the steel, metallurgical, chemical and electrical industries relied on the Exchange. The liberalisation of public limited companies, reforms of bankruptcy law and the legalisation of derivatives transactions that took place between 1860 and 1890 went hand in hand with the transformation of French capitalism and the growth of its financial markets (Hautcoeur, 2007; Levratto and Stanziani, 2010).

Before the First World War, the Paris financial market was the second largest in the world after London. The market value of securities listed on the Paris stock exchange was roughly four times French GDP and securities represented around half of the national wealth

(Lagneau-Ymonet and Riva, 2018). The power of savings, fuelled by a favourable trade balance, as well as the attractiveness of its market structures made France the second largest exporter of capital: foreign securities made up half of capitalisation on the Paris markets. Because of its relative stability, the stock market thus played a pivotal role, not just in France but in Europe, the undisputed centre of gravity for global finance characterised at the time by its greater freedom of international movements of capital and the stability of the gold standard (Flandreau and Zumer, 2004; Hautcoeur, 2007; Michie, 2006).

The organisation of the Paris markets

This central position owes a great deal to the particular organisation of the Paris markets, which ensured that they were dynamic and safe. Paris was home to a regulated market (the *Parquet*) and an unofficial market (the *Coulisse*) which provided complementary guarantees of transactions and liquidity in combination, and therefore was able to attract different categories of issuers and investors.

The *Parquet* was the regulated market organised by the Compagnie des agents de change (CAC), a body of 60 official brokers (70 after 1898) with a legal monopoly on transactions on listed securities and operating under the authority of the Ministry of Finance. These brokers were responsible, with no limitations and jointly, for the transactions they concluded at auction (therefore in public) on behalf of their clients, offering significant guarantees to investors. In order to limit the risks inherent in financial transaction (a client defaulting or one or several colleagues failing), the brokers established a relatively transparent and safe institutional market. Through strict listing and trading conditions, as well as tight control over its members' activity, the CAC helped not only to stabilise the market by reducing the likelihood that its brokers would default and by reducing price volatility, but also to frame stock market transactions including the most speculative. From the turn of the century, the CAC developed a safe delivery system in close collaboration with the Bank of France, which came to its rescue when it ran out of liquidity.

In contrast, the *Coulisse* was a loosely organised market, illegal for a long time but de facto tolerated and even protected by the government, which took advantage of its activity to sell government bonds. Its members were often well connected in international networks of European finance, acting as both brokers and dealers. There was no fixed number of them, and the listing requirements were loose. It was an opaque market: transactions were bilateral, transaction prices were not registered and were published with no guarantee for investors. There were no criteria for listing securities before the start of the twentieth century, and so the *Coulisse* traded a high volume of securities, mostly foreign, that did not satisfy the listing requirements of the Parquet. The only guarantee for investors was Coulisse brokers' low level of capital. On the other hand, they were given free rein to trade as they wished.

These radical differences between the two markets explain their specialisation, with stiff competition developing only in the more profitable niches. The *Parquet* had a virtual monopoly on spot transactions and the more established French firms, whereas the *coulissiers* dealt mostly with derivatives transactions on foreign firms for whom they could trade for their own account by taking advantage of the fact that they were better informed than ordinary savers. Competition between the two markets was focused on the most liquid securities, the French and foreign government bonds. As was to be expected, individual investors sent the bulk of their orders to the *Parquet*, while informed investors and professionals split their orders between the two markets (Hautcoeur and Riva, 2012).

The financial crisis of 2007–2010 in the context of the history of the French financial markets

The specificities of contemporary finance in relation to that of the nineteenth century

At the beginning of the twenty-first century, the financial markets play a key role in the economy, as they did during the Belle Époque. However, their contemporary development does not reflect that of the nineteenth century. In particular, the financial sector of recent years is characterised by three specific traits: the rise of institutional finance, the transnationalisation of institutional investors, and the privatisation of trading.

The rise of institutional investors

Whereas 90 per cent of American shares were owned directly by households in 1950, in the early twenty-first century, this proportion fell to less than 30 per cent; in addition, today, shares are primarily owned by directors and managers who owned shares in the firms they ran. Nowadays it is institutional investors (pension funds, investment firms, insurance companies, banks and foundations) who own shares (Zingales, 2009). The same is true for France. Before the First World War, 3 million people held French public bonds and 1 million held railway bonds. After 1929, these figures plummeted. However, after a rapid resurgence in the late 1980s (due in particular to privatisations), the number of direct shareholders quickly declined in favour of indirect ownership through institutions (investment funds, employee savings, life insurance). Even though France is, along with Italy, the OECD country with the lowest rate of share ownership by banks and insurance companies, by the end of the 1990s their asset-management subsidiaries or spin-offs and stand-alone mutual funds were already the primary holders of stocks in large-cap French listed companies. From then onward, the predominance of institutional investors constantly increased. This predominance of institutional investors has radically altered the nature of the financial markets by promoting a more active management that significantly increases the volumes exchanged and their sensitivity to price variations.

The transnationalisation of investors

This change has been reinforced by a broad shift towards the transnationalisation of financial operators (James and Kobrak, 2009). At the beginning of the nineteenth century, international flows of capital comparable to those we see today were organised by private banking institutions that guided them towards their destination through a network of independent correspondents (Flandreau and Zumer, 2004; Michie, 2006). With regard to the secondary market, while the main stock exchanges listed large quantities of foreign securities, the operators were primarily national, with arbitrage carried out through networks of corre-spondents on the other markets. Today, the multinationals of finance establish subsidiaries in all the financial centres of the world: using increasingly high-speed computer networks, they have internalised a growing share of transactions that previously took place between separate entities. Multinationals have thus replaced networks and markets. This development has made internalised transactions opaque.

The privatisation of trading

The opaque nature of the financial system intensified in the twenty-first century due to the privatisation of trading and the measures that made it possible. Fernand Braudel skilfully demonstrated that the tension that existed between transparent and opaque trade mecha-nisms was inherent to capitalism (Braudel, 1979). While the public authorities did not place any constraints on them, the largest professional operators always had an interest in trading in an opaque market because they took advantage of information that they might not dis-close to other financial players. They therefore had a structural interest in institutionalising the opacity of trading, which they promoted by lauding the self-regulation and natural order of the markets. The nineteenth century, on the other hand, was a reflection of what the organised development of financial activities owed to the complementary duality, guar-anteed by the authorities, between regulated stock markets and over-the-counter markets.

Since the 1990s, deregulation policies have disrupted that division of financial interme-diation. Rather than lowering the cost of capital for issuers and providing all stakeholders with the liquidity they need, market liberalisation has created a market structure that is all the more opaque because the reconsolidation of stock market information – dispersed among a growing number of exchange systems, whereas in the past it focused solely on of-ficial stock exchanges – is *de facto* the privilege of a small number of transnational operators who can control all the profits that finance generates: as originators organising issuance, own-account operators, order collectors, shareholders of stock exchanges and alternative platforms, and as curators.

The dangers linked to the opacity of market structures

The financial globalisation of the twenty-first century therefore developed within market structures so opaque that it became impossible to control the overabundant liquidity that was being injected by the central banks and then multiplied by the behemoths of trans-national finance. In the nineteenth century, the Paris stock exchange was not the temple of private capitalism but rather a hybrid extension of the public authorities, and therefore a potential mechanism for organising capital trading and effectively intervening in times of financial crisis, sometimes even against the immediate interests of the biggest financial intermediaries. By privatising them in the name of competition and the theory of market efficiency, the government, in line with the policies promoted throughout the European Union and in the United States opened a Pandora's Box. They rescued the large banks when the system almost collapsed. 10 years after the beginning of the financial crisis, there still is an urgent need for governments to contain liquidity and reverse the trend towards private transactions on privatised trading venues.

References

Braudel, F. (1979). *Civilisation matérielle, économie et capitalisme, XVe-XVIIIe siècles.* Paris: Armand Colin.

Denord F. (2016). *Le néo-libéralisme à la française. Histoire d'une idéologie politique.* Marseille: Agone.

Feiertag, O. (2001). Finances publiques, 'mur d'argent' et genèse de la libéralisation financière en France de 1981 à 1984. In S. Berstein, P. Milza and J.-L. Bianco (Eds.), *Les années Mitterrand, les années du changement, 1981–1984* (pp. 431–455). Paris: Perrin.

Feiertag, O. (2006). *Wilfried Baumgartner, Un grand commis des finances à la croisée des pouvoirs (1902–1978).* Paris: Comité pour l'histoire économique et financière de la France.

Flandreau, M. and Zumer, F. (2004). *The making of global finance, 1880–1914.* Paris: OECD.

Hautcoeur, P.-C. (1996). Le marché financier français de 1945 à nos jours. *Risques,* 25, January–March, 135–151.

Hautcoeur, P.-C. (Ed.) (2007). *Le marché financier français au XIXe siècle.* Vol. 1. Paris: Publications de la Sorbonne.

Hautcoeur, P.-C., Lagneau-Ymonet, P. and Riva, A. (2010). L'information boursière comme bien public. Enjeux et perspectives de la révision de la directive européenne 'Marchés d'instruments financiers'. *Revue d'économie financière,* 98–99, 297–315.

Hautcoeur, P.-C. and Riva, A. (2012). The Paris financial market in the 19th century: Complementarities and competition in microstructures. *Economic History Review,* 65(4), 1326–1353.

Hoffman, P., Postel-Vinay, G. and Rosenthal, J. L. (2000). *Priceless markets. The political economy of credit in Paris, 1660–1870.* Chicago: Chicago University Press.

James, H. and Kobrak, C. (2009). From international to transnational finance: The new face of global financial markets, presented at the World Economic History Congress, Utrecht.

Lagneau-Ymonet, P. and Riva, A. (2010). Entre marché public et marché privé : la fin de la Compagnie des agents de change de Paris. *Genèses,* 80(3), 49–69.

Lagneau-Ymonet P. and Riva A. (2012). Market as a Public Good. The Political Economy of the Revision of the Markets in Financial Instruments Directive (MiFID), in Huault I. and Richard C. (Eds.). *Finance: The Discret Regulator. How Financial Activities Shape and Transform the World,* Londres: Palgrave MacMillan, 134–163.

Lagneau-Ymonet, P. and Riva, A. (2018). Trading forward: The Paris Bourse in the nineteenth century. *Business History,* 60(2), 257–280.

Lenglet, M. and Riva, A. (2013). Les conséquences inattendues de la régulation financière : pourquoi les algorithmes génèrent-ils de nouveaux risques sur les marchés financiers? *Revue de la Régulation,* 14(2). Retrieved on 18 January 2018 from http://journals.openedition.org/regulation/10385

Michie, R. (2006). *The global securities market. A history.* Oxford: Oxford University Press.

Posner, E. (2009). *The origins of Europe's new stock markets.* Cambridge: Harvard University Press.

Quennouëlle-Corre L. (2000). *La Direction du Trésor, 1947–1967: l'État-banquier et la croissance.* Paris: Comité pour l'histoire économique et financière de la France.

Levratto N. and Stanziani A. (Eds.) (2010). *Le capitalisme au futur antérieur. Crédit et spéculation en France, fin XVIII e -début XX e siècle.* Bruxelles: Bruylant

Zingales, L. (2009). The future of securities regulation. *Journal of Accounting Research,* 47(2), 391–425.

18

COMPLIANCE AND THE REGULATION OF PRACTICES

A two-fold paradox

Marc Lenglet

Financial markets offer a fascinating place for studying rules and how normativity comes into play in the face of radical uncertainty. Indeed, trying to understand what 'complying with a rule' means in such an environment amounts to reemphasising the paradox of the rule as classically set out by Wittgenstein. Rules should always be considered incapable of producing anything whatsoever as long as we avoid putting them into practice; by way of explanation, as long as they are not deployed, spread, circulated, or inscribed in a consistently specific context. Or further still, as long as rules do not succeed at attaining their material form in movements, discussions, decisions, in short, any type of performance which may grant their embodiment at the constitutive moment of their expression.

But what exactly do these rules consist of, and how do they find themselves expressed in the specific case of financial activities? In contrast to what might be implied by a none too discerning ear listening in on the public discourse, financial universes consist of highly standardised spaces, in which the bank employee, the market operator, or even the investor-client often have trouble accurately determining whether the practice in which he or she intends to engage actually complies with (or not) the applicable body of rules. Banking and financial activities are indeed favourable to the deployment of highly diversified practices and products, the essential complexity of which makes them difficult to understand. Consequently, an understanding of their compliance – judged in the light of standardised frameworks at times disconnected, over-abundant or just as likely non-existent – is achieved through a hermeneutic work carried out *in situ*. This work, which is carried out by the compliance function, has carved out its place in the system of internal control (Lenglet and Taupin, 2017).

The paradox of the rule

Before putting into perspective the role held by this function, a few indications should be given concerning the rule, and what the act of following it signifies and entails. Among the philosophical thoughts devoted to the conceptual study of the rule, the remarks formulated by Wittgenstein in paragraphs [185] to [242] of his *Philosophical Investigations* offer an expression that is typical of the paradox of the rule, a paradox that would seem to be more of a *misunderstanding* (Laugier, 2009, p. 217). In truth, what the author of *Investigations* puts into perspective is essentially the belief that the act of acting by the rule is incapable of giving rise to any interpretive space, and that such an act would find its sole purpose in the mechanist application of norms. Contrary to this, *Investigations* demonstrates in numerous ways how illusory such an understanding of the relation between the context and its practice, or between the rule and its use, would be; as it is always through friction (the 'rough ground | *rauhen Boden*' of the empiric evoked by Wittgenstein in paragraph [107] of his book) that something akin to the meaning of the rule is able to emerge. It is as if within the resistance offered by the context, and within the difference separating what the latter allows in relation to the norm, that the rule is able to emerge in full.

Hence a 'regulist' approach in the sense proposed by Brandom (1994), that is formalist and idealist, would be incapable of meeting the challenges brought about by the rule embodied within the practice. That a rule is explicit takes nothing away from the fact that its meaning is only able to be expressed through its usage alone, therefore itself arousing the deployment of implicit normative forms. Respectively, it can be held that 'the norms implicit in regularities of conduct can be expressed explicitly in rules, but need not be so expressible by those in whose regular conduct they are implicit' (Brandom, 1994, p. 27). It is therefore in the margin between the explicit and implicit that the hermeneutic work intervenes, as if to fill the gap between on one side a rule expressed more or less clearly, more or less distinctly, and on the other side a material context often uncooperative when it comes to wholly and fully grasping the situation. It is in this sense that one must ascertain the remark made by Wittgenstein: 'That's why "following a rule" is a practice [...] And that's why it's not possible to follow a rule "privately" | '*Darum ist "der Regel folgen" eine Praxis* [...]. *Und darum kann man nicht der Regel "privatim" folgen*' (Wittgenstein, 1953, pp. 87–88).

Neither a mechanist application of the rule, nor contextual relativism, the hermeneutic work is deployed above all as an act of reading, interpreting and writing about the usage *in situ*. In summary, and it is the point that we will illustrate in the lines to come, it is because a rule manages to withstand the wear and tear of its repeated applications that it can be said to be relevant and legitimate. This is yet another way in which to follow Brandom (1994, p. 20) when he notes that: 'norms explicit as rules presuppose norms implicit in practice [...]. Rules do not apply themselves; they determine correctness of performance only in the context of practices of distinguishing correct from incorrect applications of the rules.'

The implicit contained in the practice therefore requires recognition in order to survive, regardless of whether this takes the form of acceptance or denunciation. Thus, it is here that the intersubjective relation takes place, which directly contributes to defining the acceptable frame of normativity and its objectivation. Beginning with the fundamental disconnection between the regulist understanding (ideal, formalist) of the norm and that which we might call its vital phenomenology, the Wittgensteinian notion thus brings into play the combined recognition of the practice and its imperfections, with regard to the objectivity (too often assumed essential) of the norm.

On the compliance of banking and financial practices

The rule, such as it is, only takes on meaning as a coordination complex (in the chemical sense of the term), and is significant because it is recognised as such by a community of actors. It plays a determining role, on various levels: as it were, it may be perfectly determinate which rule a given rule is, and still open for determination by occasions what following the rule in such-and-such case is to come to, or requires.

(Travis, 1989, p. 43)

Similar situations, in which the 'occasion' plays a determining role when it comes to deciding upon the compliance or non-compliance of a practice, maintain a vital position in certain financial spaces and contribute towards unfolding realities that are almost always dilemmatic, and at the very least which call for a reading, a questioning and a challenging of the predetermined interpretive solutions. It is via the intermediary action of sharing meaning within one community of actors that the norm finds itself objectified and maintained throughout time (Bloor, 1997, pp. 17–18).

In the banking and financial field, applicable rules are established by various institutions responsible for regulation. These rules are often discussed – and are therefore co-constructed within one epistemic community – in conjunction with the operators to whom they are applied (Huault and Richard, 2012). Once the rule is enacted, it falls to a specified group of functions to ensure that it has been properly followed, for example auditing and monitoring functions, for the most part specialised in the supervision of risks and intervening most often *a posteriori*, in other words, after the practice found its inscription in the real world. However, we have seen how much the implementation of the rule, i.e. its application within a given context, could not be reduced to a formal mechanist application. Hence there exists a function among the professions devoted to monitoring banking and financial activities, for which the role consists fittingly of handling the hermeneutic work of the rule *in situ*. This function is the *compliance function*: contributing at least partly towards implementing the rule, though not by being content to estimate *a posteriori* whether the rule has or has not been followed correctly, but rather having the ability to *implement* the rule or, more precisely, to contribute to its expression in the actual moment of its implementation by the operator.

In France, compliance officers were previously identified as '*déontologues*' between 1996 – the year in which the function was first institutionalised – and 2006, the year which saw their renaming: following modifications applied to the CRBF regulation no. 97-02, introducing into the law the notion of compliance risk ('*risque de non-conformité*'), in other words,

> the risk of judicial, administrative, or disciplinary sanction, significant financial loss or damage to the reputation, which results from non-compliance with measures specific to financial and banking activities, whether they are of a legislative or regulatory nature, or whether they are associated with professional or ethical norms, or instructions from the executive body notably issued pursuant to the guidelines of the deliberative body.
>
> *(CCLRF, 2005, art. 4., §.p)*

It is this specific risk that those compliance officers are in charge of mitigating. As such, they assume a dual function of: (a) monitoring and guaranteeing the efficiency of measures destined to detect any risk of non-compliance affecting professional obligations defined in the Monetary and Financial Code (AMF, 2014, art. 313-1), and resolving any shortcomings potentially observed; and (b) providing advice and assistance to operators, in such a way as to guarantee that they comply with the rules in force (*ibid.*, art. 313-3). This essential duality, located at the centre of the activity carried out by compliance officers, renders the workload complex: assuming the mantle of inspector – and if we read the texts correctly, it is seemingly the inspectors who rule over the rest, at least in the spirit of the regulator – at the same time as offering advice, i.e. writing and discussing the rules, demands taking on two activities that at times come into conflict with each other, and do not necessarily require the same set of skills (Lenglet and Taupin, 2017). Whatever the situation, those in charge of compliance nevertheless attempt, against a contextualised interpretation of the banking and financial rules, to apply their normative mark to the behaviours, practices and habits of people for whom they are also responsible for ensuring the supervision.

Qualifying the implicit

Unravelling the tangle of the implicit within the explicit – such an act could be considered a good characterisation of what those responsible for compliance do, as market events rarely resemble the descriptions written about them in regulatory texts, which preserve a naturally high level of generality. Measures concerned with preventing market abuse offer an excellent illustration of this. Accordingly, the General Regulations of the AMF stipulate that 'all persons must abstain from manipulating prices', i.e. carrying out operations that:

> a) give or are likely to give false or misleading signals as to the supply or, demand for, or price of financial instruments, or; b) secure, by a person, or persons acting in collaboration, the price of one or several financial instruments at an abnormal or artificial level, unless the person who entered into the transactions or issued the orders establishes that the reason for effecting such transactions or issuing such orders are legitimate and conform to accepted market practices on the regulated market concerned.
>
> *(AMF, 2014, art. 631-1)*

The regulatory text continues over several pages, and attempts to define the rule by providing several possible examples contributing to the identification of abusive practices. But, strictly speaking, what do these rules mean? And how does one apply them, *in situ*? How does one accurately estimate whether such an intervention is likely to mislead other market participants? Beyond the easily identifiable scenarios (those for which the implicit part is found to be replaced by the explicit character, in other words closely 'responding' to the text), there exists an entire range of possibilities in this area that one would undoubtedly struggle to exhaustively describe.

One clear example allows us to explain this point.[1] One 22 January 2009, one of the employees responsible for monitoring trading flows, who was working on the floor of Global Execution Services hastily approached the desks of compliance officers:

> On Arkema, [client name] is sending an order at third volume for 15,000 shares. It is clearly liquid, but it's a bit large... and it's currently shifting/moving... [turning to his desk and shouting to a colleague]... by how much?... [turning back to the compliance desk]... by 5% and it's not stopping... what should we do?

The order was issued via a *Direct Market Access* (or DMA) facility, a routing system that allows the client to directly issue orders without needing to discuss via the telephone with the broker, while at the same time using this broker's market connections. A filtering system anticipates any errors and unusual orders with regard to their size, their amount and the buying and selling quotes. However, the system is not capable of determining *a priori* what the impact of an order will be on the micro-structure of the order book, which would otherwise notably imply that the system is capable of qualifying the intentions of the investor, by taking into account the market context. While observing their trading stations, those monitoring the activity noted that the order, generated by an algorithm, was participating at 33 per cent of the volume traded on the market. At the moment it was placed, the order's high volume began to shift the prices, a sign of its impact on the normal course of the market (which consists, we should recall, of enabling the 'meeting' of supply and demand).

Those in charge of compliance thus come face to face with a situation in which market behaviour requires some sort of qualification. The client's intention is only apparent indirectly, through the consequences of the acts in which he finds himself engaged; yet, an interpretation of these consequences through the eyes of an outsider cannot determine with certainty whether the client seeks to explicitly influence prices, by taking part in fixing them artificially, or whether on the contrary, the client is acting without fully understanding the consequences of his acts on the reality of the market. Only a discussion with the client, at the very moment the act is taking place, will enable a decision to be made as to whether or not the order currently under way is indeed an evident breach. At the same time, it can be extremely difficult to ask a client to justify their strategy when it has not yet come to completion. Consequently, faced with a choice that must be made (calling the client, stopping his order or on the contrary allowing the market to absorb the shift in prices), both the perception of the context and past experience, and indeed discussion and debate with fellow peers, can help those responsible for compliance to decide on what action to take. In this instance, the individual in charge decided to ring the client to inform him of the situation and obtain more information so as to make his judgement call.

In his report written at the end of the day, once the order had been issued and the market was closed, the following indications were written:

> [...] The client possesses extensive liquid assets, initially invested in monetary open-end investment funds: instructions were issued internally at the beginning of January to use part of this treasury to carry out transactions on the share market.

- On 09/01, he requested the increase of his intervention authorisations, an authorisation granted with regards to his financial situation.
- The 15/01, the client issued a series of orders which were carried out between 4.38 pm and 4.41 pm, generating abnormal variations in the minimal prices (which did not trigger any alert in our systems).
- The 22/01, the client again issued an order for 15,000 Arkema securities at third volume and at the time impacted the prices by 6 to 7%. While the order was under way the compliance contacted the client.
- [...]

- Taking into account the company's current treasury, the operations carried out on the accounts of the company since the start of January, the client's profile (equally discussed with the DMA team) and the conditions via which the order was issued, we believe that he was not aware that the volume of shares bought could have generated such a fluctuation in the prices.
- The impact on stock-market prices was rapidly absorbed by the market.

Considering the information we have at our disposal at this time, we believe that the client did not issue this buy order with a view to carry out an operation that could be qualified as price manipulation, but rather was issued uniquely for speculative purposes in the context of a favourable market.

This example demonstrates the work of qualification based on which the compliance officer attempts to establish the legitimacy of the event, with this work possibly occurring *a posteriori* or, as is the case here, in the precise moment of action. This is what is necessary for the compliance officer to come to a successful conclusion: it is the formulation of a possible justification explaining the event and summarising it within the categories of financial regulation. The example illustrated here also allows us to see the role played by context in establishing meaning around an act performed *in situ*: the client's financial situation, his obvious intentions and the market context are all equally elements related to the 'coordinated complex' making markets. It is in this way that the rule is found to be worked, implemented, applied, in other words, utilised or used.

Within banking and financial activities, there exist many similar situations, based on which we could have mobilised the same reasoning (for further details, see Lenglet, 2009, 2011 and 2012 in particular). While a naive interpretation (functionalist, formalist, mechanist) of the regulatory texts might lead one to believe in the possibility of establishing an act's compliance to a rule, which cannot however by definition describe the surrounding conditions of the action, it is on the contrary necessary to reaffirm the prevalence of context and the modalities of its application when seeking to understand what 'following a rule' actually means. This certainly does not mean slipping into limitless relativism; quite the opposite in fact, as it is only through clearly grasping the vital connection linking together rules and usages, through this vocabulary of situated action, that the meaning (at times, if not often, lacking) of key financial acts can be produced.

Note

1 The empirical elements called upon in this chapter have been gathered as part of a long-lasting participant observation of the compliance function, which was notably conducted in the trading room of a Parisian brokerage firm (here named as Global Execution Services), between 2006 and 2009. For more details, see Lenglet and Taupin (2017).

References

AMF [Autorité des Marchés Financiers] (2014). *General Regulation*. Version dated June 16th.

Bloor, D. (1997). *Wittgenstein, rules and institutions*. London: Routledge.

Brandom, R. (1994). *Making it explicit. Reasoning, representing, and discursive commitment*. Cambridge: Harvard University Press.

CCLRF [Comité Consultatif de la Législation et de la Réglementation Financières] (2005). *Regulation 97-02 of 21 February 1997, relating to internal control in credit institutions and investment firms.*

Huault, I. and Richard, C. (Eds.) (2012). *Finance: The discreet regulator. How financial activities shape and transform the world.* Basingstoke: Palgrave MacMillan.

Laugier, S. (2009). *Wittgenstein. Les sens de l'usage.* Paris: Vrin.

Lenglet, M. (2009). Aux marges de la triche. Innovation normative et déontologie financière en salle de marché. *Management & Avenir, 22(2),* 263–284.

Lenglet, M. (2011). Melting the iceberg: Unveiling financial frames. In S. Long and B. Sievers, B. (Eds.), *Towards a socioanalysis of money, finance and capitalism. Beneath the surface of the financial industry* (pp. 249–261). London: Routledge.

Lenglet, M. (2012). Ambivalence and ambiguity. The interpretive role of compliance officers. In I. Huault and C. Richard (Eds.), *Finance: The discreet regulator. How financial activities shape and transform the world* (pp. 59–84). Basingstoke: Palgrave MacMillan.

Lenglet, M. and Taupin, B. (2017). The rise and fall of the compliance function: A perspective on internal control in banking and finance. *Comptabilité, Contrôle Audit, 23(1),* 11–40.

Travis, C. (1989). *The uses of sense. Wittgenstein's philosophy of language.* Oxford: Oxford University Press.

Wittgenstein, L. (1953). *Philosophische Untersuchungen–Philosophical Investigations.* Oxford: Basil Blackwell Ltd.

19

FINANCIAL REGULATION

A question of point of view

Jacques-Olivier Charron

When the subject of the regulation of finance and its necessity is raised in discussion, the first thought that comes to the wider public's mind is that of battling against behaviours characterised by various forms of excess or irrationality. This individualising and psychologising perception has a tendency to incite a call for ethical or behavioural norms and, in a more practical way, for judicial sanctions. Now if we seek to understand what is demanded of financial actors in terms of substance, we may be struck by the fate of one particular term: transparency. Well before the financial crisis, this term was one of those rare notions that had become the subject of near unanimous approval. The only notable criticisms with regard to such discourses are concerned with their supposed hypocrisy and not with the notion itself.

This nevertheless presents a problem. Debates on the gathering of personal data thus make appear a transparency from the weak (the individual) to the strong (the organisation: major companies, the State, etc.), recalling the reality of domination phenomena vs. a communication ideology seeing in the development of the circulation of information a vehicle for equality. This is what leads us to raise the question of the *point of view* of regulation, a point of view understood as the theoretical position of the social space from which the area being regulated is understood, grasped and questioned.

This approach will be carried out in three stages: we will first attempt to describe the *investor's point of view* in financial regulation, what it means, where it comes from and what it implies. We will then look at the development of a *taxpayer's point of view*, related to a particular acceptation of the notion of systemic risk. And finally, we will attempt to draw out what could be the *investee's point of view*.

The nest egg: is nothing else worth considering?

The regulators' message is clear on one point: their number one priority is the protection of investors. We could speak here of the 'protection of savers', but it is more accurately a case of always protecting those actors who invest some of their liquidities on financial markets. Additionally, the emphasis is placed on 'small' investors (which the word 'savers' also suggests), such as households – aside from the more fortunate ones. This prevalence can be traced all the way back to the Great Depression: at the heart of the mission of the SEC

(Securities and Exchanges Commission), the American regulatory authority created in 1934, was a concern for establishing norms, standardising the disclosure of information regarding issuers, and ensuring that no investor category would be favoured over another in this matter. This idea, still present today, features as part of a much larger project: to ensure that the relations between investors on one side, and the intermediaries and financial service providers on the other, would remain as balanced and 'symmetrical' as possible; with the objective being to ensure investor-savers are not defrauded, be it through false or biased information, excessive commissions, obscure and/or too binding contractual arrangements, and so on.

This objective assumes finance has to be considered as it is basically defined in economics handbooks, i.e. the set of market-based relationships which globally allow savings to fund investment. This aim being achieved through intermediaries, the project of regulation is to ensure they do not derive any unjustified benefit from their position as a 'compulsory gateway'. The debate surrounding financial regulation thus concerns a type of relationship between 'consumers' and 'producers'. In this context, the role of the regulator is to protect the savers-investors from excessive risk-taking by the intermediaries to whom they have entrusted their savings, and to ensure, via restrictive rules, that these savers only commit after having been correctly informed of the risks they incur; 'toxic' financial products must be identified and banned, much like expired foods, and basically for the same reason, i.e. they present too high a risk for those who buy them. The proximity with consumer protection logic is obvious. From this perspective, we could be tempted to liken the triggering of the 2008 financial crisis to a problem of 'subprime' horse meat present in 'triple A' lasagnes, hence a 'traceability' problem, for example.

The kind of actor the regulator adopts the point of view of, then, is an investor. A small and vulnerable one, preferably, for it vindicates its very existence, but an investor. This has many consequences regarding the questions raised, or not, by this regulator, and also on the way it considers the issue of conflicts of interest, for example.

On this last point, let's take as an example the way the regulation of financial analysts is conceived. These analysts produce notes and reports, which are converted into predictions and stock market recommendations. These forms of argued judgement remain confidential when they are produced by *buy-side* financial analysts, i.e. analysts working for management companies, because the user (the fund manager) and the judgement producer belong to the same structure. On the other hand, the production of *sell-side* analysts, that is those working for *brokers*, is presumed public. In practice it is primarily disclosed to brokers' clients, however part of it is also more widely spread.

The idea that the judgement of sell-side financial analysts might be biased due to conflicts of interest was at the heart of controversies before it sparked off the adoption of new regulations during the 2000s. The entire situation stemmed from the specific context of the US stock markets during the 1990s, characterised by two striking phenomena:

- a rise in stock prices, especially stand-out during the 1994–2000 period, which provoked a growing craze for buying shares among private individuals as part of the 'Internet bubble'; and,
- strong growth in investment banking activities, more specifically mergers and acquisitions and IPOs.

These two phenomena contributed toward placing certain sell-side analysts at front-and-centre: the demand for stock market advice from an increasingly wide public turned some of them into stock market 'stars', and merger-acquisition or IPO departments of investment banks wanted to take advantage of this growing visibility of sell-side analysts and their supposed ability to influence investors by seeking to enlist them into their services, a phenomenon facilitated by the integration of major *brokers* within banking groups practising this type of activity. The remuneration of some sell-side analysts thus began to be partially linked to their ability to 'boost' IPOs or merger-acquisitions by issuing optimistic predictions and recommendations on these operations in order to attract more investors. At the same time, the recurring question of the analysts' possible leniency toward the listed firms they were covering was revived.

This situation, again, related to a specific context, began to be uncovered and denounced in the press by the end of the 1990s. A typical narrative thus emerged: the analyst, who should be in the investors' service, is corrupted by other interests. And, *because this narrative is a criticism made from the investor's point of view*, it was echoed within the regulation (Fisch, 2006). In this area, everything stemmed from legal cases triggered in the United States within the context of the bursting of the Internet bubble in 2000 and 2001, cases which brought fame and recognition to the attorney general of New York State, Eliot Spitzer. His investigations ended in 2003 with what was called the 'Global settlement', an agreement reached between the American regulators and ten banking groups. The terms of this agreement stipulated that these latter were obliged to pay 1.435 billion dollars, of which 450 million would be devoted to the development of a financial analysis independent from these groups. Besides, various provisions were adopted between 2000 and 2003 in the US in order to specifically tackle analysts' conflicts of interest (stricter separation from the investment bank, mandatory disclaimers within analysts' reports, etc.). Later on, Great Britain in 2006 and France in 2008 made it compulsory for brokers to bill distinctively 'research', i.e. the production of sell-side analysts. Previously, this 'research' was freely offered to brokers' clients, as an add-on to execution services, duly billed for their part. The point was to ensure that in this way analysts' interests would be better aligned with those of the investors.

What we wish to highlight here is that this narrative of the analyst who disregards investors because of conflicts of interest continued to inspire research and regulation during periods and in countries in which the *real* situation of sell-side analysts no longer bore any relation to the American context of the 1990s. In France, Chambost's thesis (2007) on the formation of judgement by sell-side analysts showed, based on a sociological investigation, an 'institutional embeddedness' relationship between these actors on the one side, and buy-side analysts and fund managers on the other. Our own thesis (Charron, 2010) saw it emerge that non-public ratings of fund managers were playing a decisive role in the evaluation and the control of sell-side analysts, this institutionalised dependency being consistent with the finding of their 'trend-following' attitude on stock markets. We can see here that satisfying investors, which is what sell-side analysts are strongly encouraged to do via control devices, means first and foremost producing a discourse that responds to their expectations, which is not necessarily the same thing as estimating the fundamental value of firms, or even seeking to anticipate stock market trends. Their dependency on clients may therefore be thought as problematic with regard to what is supposed to, for that matter, found the legitimacy of analysts.

Yet the implicit or explicit adoption of an investor's point of view means that, by its very nature, not only can the analysts' dependency not be seen as a problem, it cannot even be recognised at all. It is indeed a dependency towards investors or those who represent them (fund managers), thus towards the perspective from which one examines, problematises, raises questions. We observed an example of the effects of imposing this point of view when, whilst encountering a *sell-side* analyst for the first time for an interview, he began – *although we had not yet begun to ask him any questions* – to explain that he did not know the people working at the investment bank within his group, that he did not have lunch with them, that he barely ever saw them, that, besides, they didn't even really work in the same place, etc. In short, he could not imagine one could ask him questions other than those seeking to verify that he was clearly aligned with the interests of investors and far removed from the kind of conflicts of interest which had been identified and thought about ten years before in the United States. It was by recommencing the interview on the basis of questions *a priori* disentangled from this point of view – for example seeking to find out how and on the basis of what criteria was his performance being tested and measured – that we were able to progressively bring to light what problems he was effectively coming up against. Here is something no database would have been able to tell us.

Too powerful to lose

Is this to say the investor's point of view still reigns supreme in financial regulation? Did the 2007–2008 crisis really not change anything? It may well be the case, even if the question of knowing what is substantially new, not in terms of quantity but in terms of normative framework, has to be raised.

In quantitative terms, there is no doubt that the regulators have not lain idle over these last years (Mayntz, 2012). The hundreds of pages of the Dodd–Frank law in the United States and the imposing reform program initiated in 2010 by the European Commissioner for Internal Market and Services Michel Barnier show that the still widely spread perception claiming that 'nothing has been done' does not match the reality. The institutional landscape itself has changed, with the creation of the FSB (Financial Stability Board) on the global stage and the three new watchdog authorities and the ESRB (European Systemic Risk Board) on the European stage.

It is true that part of these new texts and institutions have brought nothing new to the table in terms of normative framework. They still reason on the basis of the 'producer-consumer' polarity previously described, simply trying to give more weight to the 'consumer' side – therefore to the investor – and more specifically to non-professional investors, supposed to be the less protected. A significant part of this regulatory work, nevertheless, has been organised around the idea of fighting systemic risk, which is somewhat different.

The Lehman collapse, its catastrophic ripple-effects and the last-minute AIG bailout by the American government in September 2008 determined the way states, regulators and international institutions introduced and defined in practice this notion of systemic risk, equalled in official texts to the risk presented by 'too big to fail' financial institutions. Having noted that leaving a major investment bank to go bankrupt had much more severe consequences than expected, and that preventing the default of another major financial institution could only be done at the cost of a massive intervention from public authorities, governments thus became preoccupied with preventing the repetition of this scenario, to avoid the return of a situation in which the collapse of one single institution provokes such a profound destabilisation on the financial markets and the economy as a whole that the states have no other choice but to bail it out using public funds, thus at the expense of taxpayers. Since then, whenever concrete measures need to be taken, systemic risk is understood and presented by legislators only from this perspective, thus expressing what we may call a *'taxpayer's point of view'*.

The first step was the identification of those institutions likely to present such risks: the SIFIs (Systemically Important Financial Institutions). The FSB played a leading role in this area. The Basel Committee and the European and national regulators contributed by defining specific rules to be applied to these institutions: capital requirements, rules regarding the remuneration of 'risk takers', stress tests, etc. All this has been accomplished keeping as a priority protecting these institutions from bankruptcy, therefore limiting their capacity to take risks on financial markets on their own account.

Can we say this development truly moves us away from the investor's point of view? In our view, it does not seem to be the case, insofar as it is clearly a matter of protecting these famous SIFIs *as investors*. The size of these institutions and/or the importance and variety of their counterparts on financial markets imply their bankruptcy resulting from losses on these markets, hence their failure as investors, may have devastating ripple-effects. Consequently, for this special category of investors, transparency, in the sense of information on risks, is not enough: the very ability to take risks has to be curbed a priori, and this is what the measures targeting systemic risk intend to do.

The *investor's point of view*, then, is not really abandoned, for financial regulation still is about protecting investors. It's just that some of them are gifted with such strength and have such an impact on the markets, that they have to be protected from themselves, for their own good and the good of others, those who are *not* 'too big to fail'. At the same time, declaring that these institutions have a certain impact on the financial markets also says these markets are not a reality that is external to them, but a reality these actors partly *constitute*.

Putting the object back in the picture

Finance is not only a set of means to make savings feed investments, which is, as we have seen, the basic presupposition of the classical interpretation which confronts 'consumers' or saver-investors with 'producers' or intermediaries. It is also a valuation institution which gives financial assets a price.

If we consider the financial markets from this perspective, we then no longer see 'consumers' and 'producers' of financial services, but a different polarity: one which opposes *investors*, who, through a collection of procedures, value financial assets, and *investees*, who are evaluated and judged by this valuation. What should be understood by the term 'investees' is the collection of entities which are the objects of financial investments the investors are in last resort the subjects thereof: these are therefore firms and collective bodies (including the governments) which resort to markets to be financed.

It will surely be remarked on this point that we have merely found a particular way of naming entities the regulators usually call issuers. It nevertheless seems to us that this designation can be justified if it contributes to make finance more visible in its valuation function, to bring into existence a point of view symmetrical to that of the investor, and to renew theoretically and practically the discussion on finance and its regulation.

Legal and natural persons are not just last resort decision-makers on financial markets, which is the case when they are considered as consumers, as entities that make consumer choices that just have to be clearly informed, rationalised, protected from deception, etc. They also are entities which bear the consequences of judgements produced by these same markets.

Adopting an *investee's point of view* means interrogating the criteria and procedures of these judgements. The investees, whether they suffer from or profit from these decisions, not only have no say over these procedures or criteria, but they do not even have the capacity to impose the existence of criteria, or at least some minima of stable and accepted criteria. As their particularity, the financial markets, by their very nature, produce their judgement in a self-referential, one could almost say sovereign, way (Orléan, 1999 and 2005) and this judgement is intrinsically unstable (Minsky, 1986). In summary, if it is a matter of testing, in the sense of Boltanski and Thévenot (2006), then this is not a fair test, because it is not defined as the test of something that is clearly identifiable.

The objects, which are judged this way, are companies or governments, in any case organisations, therefore collective bodies of people. An object cannot criticise the price that it is given, a human collective can, if it is given the possibility and if it has the tools to do so. This is the challenge essentially assumed by the constitution of institutional devices enabling the investee's point of view to exist and to be expressed (Charron, 2013).

References

Boltanski, L. and Thévenot, L. (2006). *On justification. Economies of worth.* Princeton: Princeton University Press.

Chambost, I. (2007). *Contribution à l'analyse de la formation du jugement des analystes financiers sell-side.* Unpublished PhD thesis. Paris: CNAM.

Charron, J.-O. (2010). *La relation entre estimation publique de la valeur fondamentale des sociétés cotées et évolution de leur cours: une contribution basée sur des études de cas.* Unpublished PhD thesis. Paris: CNAM.

Charron, J.-O. (2013). Transacting without pricing, pricing without transacting. A case for disconnecting the valuation function from the exchange function of financial markets. *World Economic Review*, 2, 48–53.

Fisch, J. E. (2006). Regulatory responses to investor irrationality: the case of the research analyst. *Lewis & Clark Law Review*, 10(1), 57–83.

Mayntz, R. (Ed.) (2012). Crisis and control, institutional change in financial market regulation. Frankfurt am Main: Campus.

Minsky, H. (1986). *Stabilizing an unstable economy.* New Haven: Yale University Press.

Orléan, A. (1999). *Le pouvoir de la finance.* Paris: Odile Jacob.

Orléan, A. (2005). Réflexions sur l'hypothèse d'objectivité de la valeur fondamentale. In D. Bourghelle, O. Brandouy, R. Gillet and A. Orléan (Coord.), *Croyances, représentations collectives et finance* (pp. 21–39). Paris: Economica.

PART III

A new system of accumulation

Introduction

Championing the efficiency of the financial markets, mainstream financial theories are invoked to justify the role of these markets as the defining economic reference point for wealth transfer over time, for the management of associated risks and, as such, for the ownership of future wealth. The very structure of economic and social relations thus becomes a product of financial institutions, thereby rendering political, social and economic scrutiny of the financialisation process all the more important. Examining the phenomenon of financialisation means analysing the way in which financial institutions and organisations legitimise their regulatory role within the economic and social spheres, how they challenge existing systems of value creation and distribution, how they influence the decisions of businesses, governments and individuals in their day-to-day lives, and what the political, economic and social consequences of this influence might be.

In doing so we must examine the specific dynamics of capital accumulation and reproduction, fundamentally based on the circulation of money and a process of speculation and debt. We can then consider the ways in which risk is generated, transferred and handled, and how malfunctions in these processes ultimately lead to crises. This system has evident consequences for the behaviour of company directors, employees, students, consumers and citizens.

A process of denaturalisation aimed at financial techniques and the modes of thought they embody, particularly in terms of the colonisation of future wealth, allows us to get to the root of the phenomenon of financialisation. Martin employs just such a process of denaturalisation in his genealogical analysis of derivative assets, as does Chiapello in her study of the ways in which valuation methods have crept into different areas of the economy.

But this work can also be undertaken at organisational level. Studying the private equity industry allows us to get to the heart of financial power and understand the concrete consequences of the transformation of productive companies into financial assets, as well as the domination imposed upon employees and their collective organisations within companies acquired in this manner. The same themes emerge in Taupin's study of rating agencies and their continued prosperity despite regular criticism of their work. Ouroussoff, meanwhile, analyses the central role occupied by these agencies from an ethnographic perspective. On the other hand, taking client–banker relations as a starting point allows Moiso to analyse the manner in which Italian mutual banks have survived the profound transformation of the European banking industry induced by the implementation of the Basel reforms.

From a more institutional perspective, putting the legal framework governing the operations of mutual funds into historical perspective allows Granier to demonstrate the extent to which legal reforms have contributed to the international expansion of such funds and their development in Europe. It is also through legal analysis, with particular focus on the evolution of standards of diligence, that Montagne is able to illustrate the effects of financialisation on wage relations, via the changes observed in the management of social protection assets. No institutional analysis of this kind would be complete without examining, as Aglietta does, the role of money as a mode of coordination embodying both the inherent instability of finance and its constitutive unity. Thinking of money as debt also helps to elucidate some of the internal contradictions of the financial system. Analysing the way the markets handle the sale of an emblematic form of debt, government bonds, enables Lemoine to get to the heart of those social mechanisms by which wealth is distributed and inequalities reinforced. In conclusion, it is surely in the very fabric of our daily lives that the consequences of financialisation are most apparent. As Lazarus demonstrates, credit ratings are capable of playing a decisive role in our job prospects, our love lives and the other phenomena which define social inclusion and exclusion.

TABLE III.1 A new system of accumulation – classification based on scale of observation

Techniques	*Organisations*	*Institutions*
(c.20) Martin *Economic sociology* (Derivatives)	**(c.22) Moiso** *Economic sociology* (Cooperative banks)	**(c.26) Granier** *Institutional economics* (European law)
(c.21) Chiapello *Sociology of quantification* (Pricing models)	**(c.23) Taupin** *Pragmatic sociology* (Rating agencies)	**(c.27) Montagne** *French regulation theory* (Pension funds)
	(c.24) Ouroussoff *Antropology of finance* (Rating agencies)	**(c.28) Lemoine** *Political sociology* (Sovereign debt)
	(c.25) Chambost *Sociology of management* (Private equity)	**(c.29) Lazarus** *Economic sociology,* (Financial literacy)
		(c. 30) Aglietta *French regulation theory* (Capitalisms)

20

SOCIOLOGICAL DOMESTICATION OF A FINANCIAL PRODUCT

The case of derivatives

David Martin

Focus on the products to get finance back into sociological analysis

Since their very foundation, sociology and anthropology have taken an interest in institutional forms such as money and credit. However, products originating from the financial market have not been made the focus of a significant examination for many decades. Despite this, the reconquering of the field of finance currently taking place within the social sciences consequently requires the re-appropriation of its coveted objects, those products long abandoned to the fields of economics, financial mathematics, accounting or legal studies. More commonly called 'assets', 'securities', 'instruments', 'transactions', or more precisely delineated as shares, bonds, treasury bills, trackers, forward contracts on commodities, index options, currency swap, or even CDS, ABS or CDO, they are only occasionally referred to as 'products' by professionals or experts. They are however well and truly objects of exchange and involve a preliminary form of production, if considered in product terms from the perspective of disciplines such as marketing or the sociology of markets. Like all commodities, the financial product is subject to fetishism, as described by Karl Marx, in that its social conditions of production and its underlying social relations are commonly obscured in favour of economic and technical reductionism accompanied by a positive as well as negative fascination. Consigned to the status of instruments reserved for experts that does not concern lay people, they are held to be graspable only through the most sophisticated and specialised stochastic mathematical techniques, usually reserved for the natural sciences or physics. Typically, the Brownian motion became a referent model for financial asset prices behaviour, thus indicating that the dominant way of thinking considers it normal to process financial facts 'as things', to employ the Durkheimian expression.

The sociological domestication of the financial product consists in un-fetishising the commodity in order to 're-socialise' and 're-politicise' it (De Goede, 2005). This is a rather radical and frontal contribution of the *Social Studies of Finance* in that it stares at the very products of finance with the aim to make out their social, political and/or cultural texture and significance. This chapter is centred on products known as derivatives, a rich and dynamic family of financial products that have single-handedly fascinated, due to the sheer volume of transactions they give rise to, and equally because of their complexity or 'toxicity', as they were almost systematically involved to some extent in the numerous local and global crises linked to financial capitalism over the last few decades. Financial engineering has already produced several generations of relatively sophisticated, so-called exotic, derivatives that are often combined with other assets to diversify the risk and create personal or institutional investments with original risk/return profiles. These instruments are basically hedging instruments that help to insure economic and financial players against the risk of the future value of other underlying monetary or financial assets, for example commodity or stock prices, exchange rates, interest rates, etc. According to the promoters of these risk management instruments, they offer unprecedented flexibility and efficiency for the long-term hedging of financial liabilities of companies and investors. On the macroeconomic level, they would therefore warrant a better allocation of risks. Nevertheless, the equally unprecedented speculative opportunities that they have created are called into question due to the instability they have brought about on the markets.

Societal domestication

The sociological domestication of derivatives has first consisted in considering them as epitomising or fuelling a wider socio-historical phenomenon that characterises our contemporary societies and economies.

Derivatives and modern risk culture

To begin, as insurance technologies, derivatives illustrate and amplify modern risk culture characterised by Beck, with its anchorage in the future and its characteristic self-referentiality (Green, 2000). Indeed, these products are based on a belief in the calculability of the risks of future values and embody the promise of their possible management. According to Arnoldi (2004), the strength of risk estimation models conveyed by these techniques lies in that they create information from a potential future. Consequently, the risks and market uncertainties subjected to forecasting cease to be mere possibilities and acquire a virtual existence offering a grip on the present action. This virtuality enables them to be elevated to the rank of commodity. Derivatives are, in this regard, emblems of a new form of capitalism that develops according to a self-referential logic by creating markets out of markets; moreover, they 'colonize the future' by developing technologies for an entirely new 'hyper-speculation'. It should be noted that this is not a speculation concerned with the possible evolutions of a security or an asset, but rather with the risk of such speculation itself. In reality they transform and generate new risks, creating new innovations derived from derivatives, as is the telling case of options on volatility. Such options are designed to hedge against the risks of incorrect volatility estimates in the process of calibration of option pricing models by market participants. Risk, viewed as volatility, then becomes the underlying for new derivatives and therefore the asset subject to commodification (Martin, 2005).

Derivatives and the virtualisation of the economy

The virtualisation of the economy thus emerges as the second noteworthy societal trend, spearheaded by derivatives. The rise in the abstract nature of finance is patently obvious in these sophisticated products, which are subject to often complex and very dynamic arrangements in the name of innovation. For Li Puma and Lee (2005), it is the objectivation of abstract risks, carried out by the evaluation models enlisted on these markets, that turns these risks into new objects for exchange and accounts for the original and dramatic character of the culture of circulation instituted by derivatives. Dramatic due to its dynamic nature – that can be measured by the hundreds of thousands of billions of potential dollars traded annually on these markets – and due to the improbable trading equivalences that derivative transactions allow between different sectorial and geographic areas, with varying maturities, thus creating new forms of interdependence across time and spaces. This way, derivative markets connected the Orange County financial crisis in California during the mid-1990s with the UK consumer debt boom, or furthermore indexed US pensions on Japan's inflation rate and yearly overall economic performance!

Derivatives, globalisation and financialisation

In this sense, derivatives can also be recognised as the outstanding financial operators of a third major phenomenon, *i.e.* economic globalisation. For Pryke and Allen (2000), these supposedly specially disconnected derivatives constitute a new 'monetary imaginary' in that they carry out unprecedented equivalences and transfers of value between the future and the present, but also between different geographic areas, thus financially connecting together everyday realities distant in time and space. These authors therefore explicitly elaborate on Simmel's founding approach, by focussing on the way in which the monetary institution involves original forms of sociability based on distance. In this respect, the rise in the abstract nature and the virtualism which is sanctioned by their use, in turn generate more of a hyper-connected financialisation instead of a finance that is disconnected or dis-embedded from the real economy. The logic behind the systemic spread of collapses during the recent financial crises has also exposed the many geographical, sectorial and inter-temporal connections, as well as the intervention of derivative products in those arrangements responsible for these transmissions of risk. Derivatives transform the day-to-day experience of entire sections of our economies and anchor finance at the heart of our societies by thoroughly transforming our concepts of ownership, capital and currency (Bryan et al., 2009).

In methodological terms, the contributions of this initial form of domestication, which we have labelled as societal, are based essentially on the exegesis of diverse second-hand data that attest to the market lifecycle of these products. Being macro-sociological in scope, they provide an understanding of the cultural and even civilisational transformations of financial capitalism to which these products contribute, which include modernity and the risk society, the virtualisation of the economy, globalisation and financialisation. However, a second approach that appropriates derivative products as sociological objects of study consists of subjecting them to an approach that is decidedly more ethnographic. It does so by heading more resolutely to the heart of these products, their most tangible expressions and into the social spaces where they are being dealt with daily, thanks to the introduction of empirical devices that multiply the captured images of the product. This approach opens the 'black boxes', as the expression goes. The social studies of financial products here illustrate the methodological eclecticism that characterises the Social Studies of Finance in general (cf. the introductory chapter of this collection).

Ethnographic domestication

The scripts and the people

The ethnographic project that empirically examines these highly abstract products in detail has uncovered their eminently scriptural and distributed form across multiples mediums and in various spaces (Martin, 2005). They comprise a dispersed, hybrid and protean corpus that *describes* them (contractual wording, legal definitions, standards published by the ISDA, etc.), *prescribes* them (theoretical models, *pricers* integrated into trading floor screens, marketing materials, rules for hedging operations, codes of conduct, etc.) and *inscribes* them (instantaneous confirmation between negotiators, reporting lines in computerised *back office* systems, entry in financial statements, etc.). This polygraphic reality is the correlate of the multitude of actors and forms of expertise that are involved in the formation of a derivative market. The linguistic work at the centre of the negotiations of these products (Lenglet, 2006) and the multiplicity of heterogeneous codes encountered inside a bank during the engineering process of these same products (Lepinay, 2011) have been documented. These scripts and codes consist of diverse financial scenarios, various legal precepts, accounting constraints and heterogeneous financial objectives, which give shape to the product as they manage to work compatibly together in practice. Among these scripts, modern financial theory constitutes a register of meaningful language that is especially 'performative', in Callon's sense of the term (1998) [cf. Introduction]. Indeed, financial theory has proved to be capable of designing products and of being translated into calculation tools, accounting terms, legal statements or pedagogical stories for public use, which altogether provide these products with substance and allow them to be understood and appropriated by a wide network of heterogeneous actors who then go on to ensure their circulation (Martin, 2005; MacKenzie, 2006). The case study on the option market and the now famous Black–Scholes formula, created in 1973 and awarded a Nobel prize in 1997, is even used today as a textbook case illustrating this phenomenon of performativity in economic theory, which is able to shape a financial product and committed market players, and to guarantee the socio-technical alignments necessary for the formation and the liquidity of a market dedicated to this product (MacKenzie and Millo, 2003).

According to some interpretations, on the subject of scripts and codes, the religious register – originally consubstantial with stochastic mathematics that are at the core of theoretical *pricing* models – is repressed to obscure the share of arbitrary belief that justifies unbridled speculation on these markets (Maurer, 2002). Instead an illusion of mastery and expertise is favored, which is more in line with the values and rational-legal legitimacy targeted by the actors and regulators of these markets who resort to mathematical formalism (Godechot, 2001).

Ethnographic domestication, based on oral histories and/or systematic chronic monographs of particular markets, has also made it possible to highlight that the success of these markets has been supported by the full commitment of some influential, individual or collective, entrepreneurs. Such enterprising market actors intervene by developing institutions or disseminating materials that are useful for the cognitive and practical appropriation of derivatives by other targeted market participants, though in parallel, they also do so to plea their economic usefulness and moral legitimacy before potential regulators and society at large. Bernstein (1992) has voiced this idea with regard to several academic or Wall Street figures; while MacKenzie and Millo (2003) have pointed it out for certain personalities in the regulated options market in Chicago. On the over-the-counter (OTC) derivatives markets, both Morgan (2008) and Martin (2002 and 2005) highlighted it with regards to the former governor of the US Federal Reserve, Alan Greenspan, in addition to some major banks, and also international professional associations made up of market players such as the ISDA. Conversely, some actors or scripts at times prove to be threatening or should be kept at a distance for the full deployment of these markets. For example, the International Accounting Standards Board (IASB) met with strong resistance from banks and ISDA regarding its financial standardisation venture, which aimed to enforce the appearance on company balance sheets of any undertakings on the derivative markets as measured at their 'fair market value' (Martin, 2005). Such standardisation would, in their view, induce an artificial and pro-cyclic misevaluation of the performance of those companies resorting to derivatives, and would consequently discourage their use.

The animated worlds of the product

Socio-technical networks surrounding and finally embodying the product and the market are prone to proliferate, especially due to the connectionist features of derivatives. These products unify and establish original collective entities. Nevertheless, various factors, including the uncertainties of the markets themselves, contribute towards turning them into shifting and conflicting social spaces. The formation of the American housing bubble and its subsequent explosion have revealed the extensive and sometimes unexpected networks of interdependence that derivatives have woven. Complex financial arrangements (risky macro-credit portfolios, synthetically replicated by credit derivatives to disperse risk on the market) were created to enable hedging and support the proliferation of these mortgages. These arrangements required the alignment of (sometimes purposefully created) actors and institutions around conventional views and calculative practices concerning the circulation and evaluation of these products, which happened to be perilous from an epistemological point of view. Indeed, the formation of the bubble and its explosion could be interpreted as an issue of cognitive sociology, revealing the spread of chronic bias in the calculation and interpretation of risk by investors and ratings agencies (Mackenzie, 2012). The international spread of the financial crisis notably occurred through socio-technical networks that underpinned the US mortgage system, based on the notorious risky tranche of subprimes targeted at modest income households. Langley (2006) has thoroughly described the extensive proliferation of networks that had linked American lower-middle class suburbs to various financial bodies and institutional investors across the Atlantic via these financial arrangements, since characterised as toxic. On the regulated derivatives markets, MacKenzie and Millo (2003) have also explained how the market community and its risk estimation conventions had to be reconfigured following the 1987 crisis. Regarding the notorious CDS derivative market, called into question during the 2008 financial crisis, Morgan (2008) who had previously explained the social and political dynamics that favored the boom and the governance regime of these markets, also went on to similarly analyse the repositioning of the social world of these markets following the internal and external legitimacy crisis that had shaken them (Morgan, 2012).

Conclusion: sociology as reflected by the financial product

What lasting teachings do these products bring to sociology? Undeniably, the social sciences have not come away unscathed from their domestication of other exotic objects, such as the Trobriand Islands, the seventeenth-century Protestant sects, the Chicago ghettos, or the Saint-Jacques scallops in Saint-Brieuc bay! And so, what about financial derivatives?

The first general lesson for the sociology of markets is based on calling into question the duality of embedding and dis-embedding. Being especially abstract and specialised, these products require the construction of a partially unprecedented community of actors, conventions and artefacts. The importance of social, cognitive and political dynamics in the creation of a derivative market reveals that it is at least as equally *embedding* as it is *embedded* in the social substratum that preceded it. Moreover, the sociological domestication of these products has shown that the condition for the possibility of finance's apparent autonomy or detachment from the real economy is, paradoxically, super-connectionism. This refers in particular to the ability of those promoting these markets to enlist a growing number of players and to colonise increasingly distant social sub-spaces, which they first subdue and then come to depend upon, enabling the market's vitality. Without the potential bad debtor, there is no credit risk. Without virtual credit risk, there is no derivative. Without credit derivatives, there is less credit, which consequently penalises the creation of businesses or access to private property for lower-income households... therefore calling into question the American dream that is so foundational to social integration.

A second fundamental lesson we can here summarise is that through, on one hand, their dual promise of security and prosperity and, on the other hand, via the remarkable financial globalisation that they perform, these products renew and reawaken financial capitalism while at the same time weakening its foundations (Bryan and Rafferty, 2006). The remarkable strength of these products and their promoters is obvious in light of their survival, despite the crises of legitimacy and efficiency that they have undergone following various crashes. Our interpretation is that they significantly account for finance's power over society, especially that of some powerful and engaged financial actors such as major private banks. Not simply because they increase their wealth (as they can incidentally also ruin them), but due to the civilisational project they offer contemporary capitalism. Nevertheless, this is done at the cost of creating tension in certain historical and institutional foundations of financial capitalism, such as ownership and currency. These drifts aggravate the contradiction between ownership and control, splitting even further the capacity for internal and external control attached to the ownership of an underlying asset. They dissipate and amplify the pecuniary right attached to ownership by staking it on speculative derivative transactions that will not implicate their holding. Moreover, these drifts challenge the nature and stability of the monetary institution, turning currency into the object, and not merely the instrument, of exchange in the case of options or currency swaps for example, but also through credit derivatives. All derivative products, more generally speaking, become *de facto* new forms of currency in their role as operators of equivalence and circulation between all types of assets.

Speculators on derivative markets strive to achieve opacity and flexibility in the use of these fetishised instruments that are crucial to this civilisational project. In return, they demand transparency, predictability and discipline from the rest of the economy that they index, *a priori* for its own well-being.

References

Arnoldi, J. (2004). Derivatives virtual values and real risks. *Theory, Culture & Society*, 21(6), 23–42.

Bernstein, P. (1992). *Capital ideas. The improbable origins of modern Wall Street*. New York: Maxwell Macmillan International.

Bryan, D. and Rafferty, M. (2006). *Capitalism with derivatives: A political economy of financial derivatives, capital and class*. Basingstoke, Palgrave MacMillan.

Bryan, D., Martin, R. and Rafferty, M. (2009). Financialization and Marx: Giving labor and capital a financial makeover. *Review of Radical Political Economics*, 41(4), 458–472.

Callon, M. (1998). Introduction: The embeddedness of economic markets in economics. In M. Callon (Ed.) *The laws of the markets* (pp. 1–57). Oxford: Blackwell Publishers.

De Goede, M. (2005). *Virtue, fortune and faith: A genealogy of finance.* Minneapolis: University of Minnesota Press.

Godechot, O. (2001). *Les traders. Essai de sociologie des marchés financiers.* Paris: La Découverte.

Green, S. (2000). Negotiating with the future: The culture of modern risk in global financial markets. *Environment and Planning D,* 18(1), 77–90.

Langley, P. (2006). Securitising suburbia: The transformation of Anglo-American mortgage finance. *Competition & Change,* 10(3), 283–299.

Lenglet, M. (2006). Des paroles aux actes: usages contemporains de la performativité dans le champ financier. *Études de communication,* 29, 39–51.

Lepinay, V.-A. (2011). *Codes of finance. Engineering derivatives in a global bank.* Princeton: Princeton University Press.

LiPuma, E. and Lee, B. (2005). Financial derivatives and the rise of circulation. *Economy & Society,* 34(3), 404–427.

MacKenzie, D. (2006). *An engine, not a camera. How financial models shape markets.* Cambridge: MIT Press.

MacKenzie, D. (2012). Knowledge production in financial markets: Credit default swaps, the ABX and the subprime crisis. *Economy & Society,* 41(3), 335–359.

MacKenzie, D. and Millo, Y. (2003). Constructing a market, performing theory: The historical sociology of a financial derivatives exchange. *American Journal of Sociology,* 109(1), 107–145.

Martin, D. (2002). Dispositifs de défiance et fluidité des échanges sur les marchés financiers de gré à gré. *Sociologie du travail,* 44(1), 55–74.

Martin, D. (2005). *Les options fondamentales de la finance moderne. Domestication sociologique d'un produit financier.* Unpublished PhD, Université Toulouse le Mirail.

Maurer, B. (2002). Repressed futures: Financial derivatives' theological unconscious. *Economy & Society,* 31(1), 15–36.

Morgan, G. (2008). Market formation and governance in international financial markets: The case of OTC derivatives. *Human Relations,* 61(5), 637–660.

Morgan, G. (2012). *Constructing financial markets: Reforming over-the-counter derivatives markets in the aftermath of the financial crisis.* Oxford: Oxford University Press.

Pryke, M. and Allen, J. (2000). Monetized time-space: Derivatives–money's new imaginary? *Economy & Society,* 29(2), 264–284.

21

THE WORK OF FINANCIALISATION

Eve Chiapello

Financialisation is defined in this contribution as a specific process for transforming the world, by practices, theories and instruments that originated in the financial sector and are now being used to reassess all sorts of questions, some of them theoretically far removed from that world (social, environmental, educational and cultural questions). This approach through technicalities, devices and valuation processes (Chiapello, 2015) makes it possible to propose a new definition of financialisation, and to focus on the 'work of financialisation'. Indeed, financialising requires considerable efforts, 'investments in form' (Thévenot, 1984), into systems of visibility creation, metrics, databases, development of theoretical conceptualisations, production of a large number of policy documents and laws, preparation of contracts, and setting up new organisations. All these activities mobilise the efforts of a large number of public and private actors interacting in many national and international arenas. The purpose of this chapter is to propose a descriptive language to account for this distributed process. After resituating the concept of financialisation as used here in the literature, I propose to identify a certain number of basic operations that mark the stages along the road to financialisation, bringing out a gradual increase in financialisation, which can vary in intensity.

An approach to financialisation

The concept of financialisation has been used for slightly over a decade to designate a collection of changes in our economic system that began to emerge in the 1970s and have been accelerating since the late 1990s (Boyer, 2009; Erturk et al., 2008; Epstein, 2005; Krippner, 2005; Van der Zwan, 2014). The term has been used to describe changes in the governance of large firms subject to demand for shareholder returns (Aglietta and Rebérioux, 2005), the growing capture at macro-economic level of resources by providers of capital, to the detriment of labour (Duménil and Lévy, 2001), a growth in financial activities by non-financial firms (Baud and Durand, 2012), changes in the forms of government financing with a rise in indebtedness on the financial markets (Streeck, 2014; Lemoine, 2016), development of savings products for households, faster accumulation of wealth for personnel working directly or indirectly for the financial sector (Godechot, 2012; Lin and Tomaskovic-Devey, 2013), and so on. All this research emphasises the rising power of actors in finance who manage and handle money professionally and act (mainly, but not exclusively) on the financial markets. These actors now have more influence than previously on the decisions made and the policies applied by other economic agents: households, states, non-financial firms both large and small, non-commercial organisations, and public services.

These different articles all take an approach to financialisation that I call 'externalist', stressing the role and power of financial actors, i.e. mainly the asset management industry and all categories of investment funds. These are the actors that keep the financial markets in operation, and organise a financing circuit for the economy in which they play the leading role, collecting savings and investing in the purchase of various types of assets. It is this investment financing circuit that has grown substantially with financialisation; it must be distinguished from the credit circuit, which is based on traditional banking intermediation[1] and also from the tax and public spending circuit.

Rather than concentrating on financial actors, I propose a slight shift in focus, towards the socio-technical arrangements that enable them to create these financing circuits in which they are the principal operators, the forms of knowledge and knowhow they use in these operations, and the techniques – primarily financial and legal – in which they are experts and on which their legitimacy is founded. My approach can be called 'internalist' in the sense that what matters most is *what* is done, said, and made, rather than *who* is doing, saying, and making. This approach focuses on the techniques, management instruments, devices and instruments (Chiapello and Gilbert, 2013 and 2016; Lascoumes and Le Gales, 2004) that equip the action, have substantial influence on situations, and partly escape the underlying intentions and aims. Financialisation in the 'internalist' sense can be seen as a 'colonisation' of situations by 'financialised' forms of reasoning and calculation (Chiapello, 2015), involving financial flows management techniques specific to the financial industry.

This approach interacts easily with the 'externalist' approach that concentrates on financial actors, because it is through the implementation of a range of specific practices and instruments that financial actors are gaining power and become increasingly likely to capture resources. Nonetheless, techniques and ways of thinking clearly have a specific appeal and a capacity to circulate in partial independence of the professions whose core knowledge they constitute. This is what makes the analytical distinction between the two approaches interesting and particularly relevant when rather than directly concerning the financial world, an investigation concerns social spaces where very few financial professionals are to be found, and where the traditionally important knowledge and knowhow relate to other types of expertise (educational, social, medical, environmental, etc.). Financialisation of these areas can also be observed in the arrival of approaches and techniques specific to finance, even when no financial actors are involved and there is no significant change in financing circuits.

Financialisation in the internalist sense is reflected in the spread of a financialised technical culture[2] that tends to see everything from the point of view of an investor, i.e. from a capitalist angle, as described in Marx's formula M-C-M. In this view, money should be invested in order to generate more money, a financial return for the investor, and the activity (the goods produced and sold) that makes financial growth possible is only a means to greater wealth. It is only worth buying a thing, or investing for it, if it produces future revenues that are higher than the amount invested, if it can be considered as 'capital'. The capitalist (or, here, the investor) is the person who bears the risk of the circulation of capital (investment) to recover the gain (the return); he analyses any outlay as an investment associated with an expected return and a risk. This culture carries embedded forms of valuation, calculation methods, and decision-making rules, and it is possible to trace the adoption and incorporation of these formats and ways of thinking into new socio-technical arrangements in a very diverse range of sectors (Chiapello, 2015). In this article the term 'the work of financialisation' is used to refer to the efforts made by actors to distort practices, and incorporate into them these financialised forms of thought and action.

The work of financialisation

This section proposes to identify the different stages or operations in this work of financialisation. This should also enable us to measure how advanced the financialisation is: is it simply a metaphorical financialisation ('weak financialisation'), or have new financial circuits been created that operate under financialised rules and have connections with private investors ('strong financialisation')?

Three types of operation are required to construct these new financing circuits: first, the work of *qualification and interpretation* of the world using the words and perspectives of an investor; second, the activity of *making assets and liabilities* through financial quantification work; and finally, the activity of *structuring monetary flows* around these new assets and liabilities. I illustrate these stages based on questions which would appear to be far removed from the financial world, such as social and environmental issues.

Qualification and interpretation of the world using the words and perspectives of an investor

This first stage concerns work that is chiefly discursive and ideological, consisting of relabeling social and environmental questions in terms of investment, capital, returns and risks in order to present the decision as a choice between alternative investments, a consideration of the comparative expected returns and associated risks.

One way to do this is to call the thing to be protected or encouraged 'capital', a precious commodity because it should generate returns in the future, and thus worthy of care and expenditure. For example, 'human capital' is used to designate the stock of people's skills and knowledge, 'natural capital' to designate the environment. Social questions then become questions of investment in 'human capital'. Another way is to redefine things that are to be avoided and problems encountered as 'risks', which thus affect future returns. This is observed in references to 'environmental risks' and 'climate risks'. This language indicates probable losses, suggesting that it is necessary to both reduce and cover the risks – potentially using financial techniques.

Making assets and liabilities

The second activity in the work of financialisation is giving physical embodiment to these concepts of capital, i.e. making assets, and symmetrically, turning risks into liabilities. In this case the work consists of producing figures and models, then monetary valuations of these new objects. This creation of visibility lends credibility to the theory that they are worthy of investment, and also means they can be included in reports, calculation of optimisations and investment decisions.

The work of quantification requires upstream explicitation work (Linhardt and Muniesa, 2011; Muniesa, 2014) setting the boundaries of the risk and capital, the types of returns, the expected services and benefits, and the associated risks. This explicitation work is based on input from the specialists in the public issue being addressed. The concept of 'ecosystem services', intended to capture the value of nature, is one illustration of this process. It shares the financial framework's view that the value of a thing relates to the services it provides and is thus very useful to support the work of financialisation. Thanks to this conception, nature can be made into a 'natural capital' whose worth is measured by the 'returns' it generates. This perspective was initially based on descriptions and inventories drawn up by natural science specialists (ecologists and naturalists). During the 1990s and 2000s, the concept became established in the political arenas: one key step was the *Millenium Ecosystem Assessment* launched by Kofi Annan in 2000 (Tordjman and Boisvert, 2012). The reports resulting from this international process have proposed classifications and lists of services provided by nature: regulating services (air quality, water quality, etc.), provisioning services (wood, food, etc), cultural services (aesthetic and leisure services), and supporting services such as the provision of habitat. This initial stage of explicitation then led to work on more detailed definitions and non-financial quantification of these services, drawing on knowledge from the natural sciences.

In a second phase, this enormous production of knowledge and creation of visibility began to fuel more detailed financial assessments seeking to assign a value to each type of service, drawing on different actors and forms of expertise, not without attracting resistance and criticism from the actors of the first stage. Going further than the earliest attempts at giving natural capital a monetary value,[3] the development of methods, organised data collection, and a general monitoring apparatus made it easier to put a financial value on specific ecosystems and to transform them into assets. This was the work undertaken by TEEB (The Economics of Ecosystems and Biodiversity), an international initiative launched in 2007 with notable financial backing from the European Commission, and now hosted by the UNEP (United Nations Environmental Program). Having proposed a general methodology, it is now trying to disseminate it, and assist states in their valuation operations and the creation of new policies based on these values.

Once at this stage, the work of financialisation of social and environmental questions is well advanced: there is a narrative using the language of investment and its returns, capital and its risks, and various methods and sources of financial quantification that can assign values and incorporate them into calculations. But these elements are not enough to ensure that the rhetoric of investment will in fact attract private investors. That is the role of financialisation activities, which we shall now examine.

Structuring monetary flows

This stage requires mobilisation of specific competences, principally legal and financial, to bring about change in the legal and regulatory frameworks and elaborate cleverly structured financial operations. Creating a financial circuit largely proceeds from the work of law-writing, defining entities, which receive funds that are managed under certain criteria by certain people, signing contracts with other entities that organise monetary exchanges and lay down the terms for such transactions. How can funding be provided for the maintenance, protection or growth of the newly identified assets (human, natural, intangible, etc.)?

Creating financial securities. The first possibility is turning these assets or liabilities into merchandise that can be sold, i.e. financial securities, under the same principle as the principles governing formation of a company limited by shares. Industrial firms that need to finance their material investments had found it convenient to issue shares, which are rights to future profits. For the new social and environmental assets, they need to sell rights to future income generated by the assets. This gave rise to the markets for social impacts (Barman,

2015; Chiapello and Godefroy, 2017) and environmental impacts. Negative effects were transformed into 'pollution rights', while positive effects became 'carbon credits'. Other liabilities (probable debts) that can be calculated by insurance techniques, potentially carried in insurers' balance sheets or implicitly guaranteed by the state have also recently been turned into securities (such as 'catastrophe bonds') to capture the funds that can cover them.

Note that government action is vital if these securities, newly devised through shrewd legal and financial engineering, are to be purchased and thus to provide new resources. The public authorities can make their purchase compulsory in some situations (the 'polluter pays' principle), or ensure scarcity in such instruments (carbon emission rights), which determines their price and therefore the amounts invested in the cause. They also have to take care to manage investors' expectations of returns, i.e. make sure that there will actually be future monetary flows that can end up in their pockets.

Creating returns. One example of the creation of returns is France's *Contrats à impact social* (social impact contracts), modelled on the UK's Social Impact Bonds (SIB). They were first tried out in 2016 to provide financing for a social sector suffering from lack of public funding. These contracts encourage financial investors to put money into projects, which are, by definition, non-profitable – such as support programmes to prevent re-offending of prisoners. The trick is considering that if the social activity is well-managed, then the induced costs for the community will be lower (fewer re-offenders means less public expenditure in the future). It may thus be in the community's interest to promise the investor a return if the entity financed achieves its social objectives. Another way to create returns is to offer tax incentives for social and environmental investments.

Reducing risks. The reasoning used by investors closely associates returns and risks, which are in fact two sides of the same coin, since they are both indicators describing the same cash flows expected of an investment. Whenever products are structured in a way that generates returns, there are invariably conditions, and therefore risks, attached. A commitment by the state to lease a building constructed via a Public–Private Partnership for 40 years is a secure return, as is an immediate tax break or a waiver of income in a concession, while the signature of a Social Impact Bond in which payouts are conditional on achievement of social objectives suggests slightly greater risks. Portfolio theory has rationalised this investment choice, considering that for a high risk a high expected return is required, and conversely a low expected return should be associated with more certainty. The engineering work consists of creating acceptable risk-return balances that can attract investors.

In this work, certain measures exist entirely to manage the question of risk, for example the guarantee systems granted by the public authorities, or increasingly by guarantee funds (an option that allows the state to limit its exposure to the amount of the fund, and offers the financial industry funds to invest).

Similar to company shares, these new financial instruments, investments or contracts that grant conditional rights to potential future income can provide funding for the target causes. And also like shares, the investors may want liquidity, i.e. want to be able to resell these contracts or securities, often in order to reduce their risks.

Creating liquidity. Offering liquidity to potential investors can thus be part of the work that must be done to make these new financing circuits operational, and this requires a specific sort of engineering. Organising marketplaces or exchanges is one possible solution, but the products traded there must be known, regularly valued, and comparable so that participants can invest and divest, and manage their portfolios. This work has traditionally been done by specialised professionals (auditors, ratings agencies, data brokers, financial analysts, etc.). The creation of new assets means they need to create new metrics and collect new data.

Another way to create liquidity is to use the legal instrument of the investment fund, for which the relevant professionals are financial actors. Funds manage money by creating pockets that confine the risk to the amounts invested, which are managed by appointed fund managers in accordance with various objectives. This creates liquidity through a form of securitisation that groups several investments of a non-liquid nature, for example investments in small and medium enterprises, into a single investment vehicle. This vehicle purchases shares, makes loans, and signs contracts, which cannot be simply sold on. However, shares in the vehicle are sold to investors, giving them rights to future profits. A first type of liquidity can be organised inside the fund itself: some funds choose not to invest all the money collected, and retain a certain percentage in order to be able to reimburse a share-owner if requested. A second type of liquidity is created by trading shares in these funds on specific marketplaces: although the providers of capital cannot buy and sell the investments made by the funds, they can buy and sell their own shares in the funds.

For social issues, one example of this type of financing system is the European Investment Bank's (EIB) Social Impact Accelerator (SIA), which was established in July 2015 and raised €243 million to fund social enterprises. The SIA is a fund of funds, with plenty of public finance input, that invests the money collected in 'impact investing' funds in various European countries. These impact investing funds are supposed to raise additional money from private investors and to contribute funding for enterprises with social objectives, either directly or indirectly via other funds specialised in specific themes or geographical areas. The public authorities hope that their initial contributions to such funds of funds will act as a 'leverage' for private investors and extend their action, as government involvement is supposed to be reassuring.

Financialising an issue, an organisation, an activity or a public policy thus consists of transforming the language and instruments that organise it, and importing practices and ways of thinking that come from the financial world. This transformation may remain at the first stage (weak financialisation) or progress through all three stages and connect with the world of private finance by constructing alternative financial circuits (strong financialisation). This description appears to match the case of social and environmental questions where the work of financialisation is in progress, but it also covers the action that has been necessary for listed firms (whose shares are largely owned via a range of funds) or firms owned by Private Equity funds, which have as a result also been 'financialised'.

The same three stages of financialisation are detectable. Listing or sale to investment funds is possible because the enterprises concerned are considered as objects of investment whose purpose is to produce returns for the shareholders (instead of places of socialisation, activities that supply jobs, or places where products or services are made, for example) (stage 1). The development of financial valuation techniques and a world of professional experts in such valuation offers the required expertise for estimating the value of these investments, consultants and analysts such as in-house teams who can identify untapped reserves of value, growth potential, and stage 'corporate products'. They paint a glowing picture of the gains on such and such a sale or acquisition project, backed up by their calculations and simulations (stage 2). Finally, other actors create the connection with the world of finance (stage 3): in the case of private equity finance, and more broadly the worlds of mergers and acquisitions, banking intermediaries act as brokers, lawyers and tax specialists organise international operation structures that make use of tax laws to increase returns; in the case of listed firms, other merchant bankers, with the help of service providers from various fields (legal, accounting, etc.) give out advice for IPOs, set share issue prices, organise sales, etc. Finally, the investment funds become purchasers and the stock markets organise the liquidity of shares. The credit circuit, meanwhile, rather than directly funding firms as is the case in traditional financial circuits, instead funds the financial holding companies that make acquisitions, enabling new shareholders to use the leverage effect to increase returns further.

Conclusion

The work of financialisation is built on the practices and techniques of financial actors, and tries to meet their demands in terms of returns, risk and liquidity. It also requires considerable efforts and investments in metrics, databases, development of theoretical conceptualisations, policy and law-writing, preparing contracts, and formation of new organisations. This activity mobilises efforts by professional groups who specialise in the techniques applied – and are also the people who have found support and prospered thanks to financialisation (financiers, lawyers, auditors, consultants, assessors). Its rise has given them an opportunity to gain legitimacy by showing that their knowledge can serve causes other than money, and for some, an opportunity to extend their market and sell their services. The third stage, when operational financial circuits are created, is the stage that most needs their involvement.

The first stage essentially engages economic expertise, using theories of value applied to the objects concerned and making public policy recommendations, while the second stage particularly mobilises specialists in the issues concerned (biodiversity, global warming, social questions,[4] etc.), who strive to produce appropriate metrics that are then adopted by economists and financiers. The number and range of actors and skills required for the work of financialisation and the fact that they do not all have the same access to the places where policy is made also explain why – depending on the spaces and issues addressed – financialisation is a heterogeneous, uncertain process.

For a given case of local organisations or issues currently in the process of financialisation, the level of financialisation can be assessed by examining whether there is only a discourse, or there is a discourse plus valuation methods and offers of expertise, or new financing circuits that have been constructed. On social questions, for example, the existence of a few Social Impact Bonds that have managed to attract a few investors is an indication of strong financialisation at local level. At worldwide level, however, greater nuance is needed: a few successful experiments will not necessarily become generalised, and may simply be a reinforcing factor for stages 1 and 2.

At systemic level, the financialisation of an issue must be considered in the early phases or weak when it is essentially discursive. A large body of grey literature exists, metrics are proposed, standards have been developed, consultants are proposing their services but in practice, and apart from a few much-hyped experiments, the financial volumes involved are low and the social or environmental impacts are tiny, or debatable. This is currently the case for Social Impact Bonds (much has been written about them, but there are still few), or concerning anti-global warming policies for REDD+[5] projects which prevent deforestation in very small areas. Both of these cases have failed to attract many financial investors, who are reluctant to get involved in projects of this kind. These financial innovations are widely discussed but make very little difference to the problems they are intended to solve. In many respects their role appears essentially ideological, with financialisation presented as an answer to social and environmental questions rather than one of their causes. To the financial industry as a whole, the extremely small-scale activity of certain funds dedicated to such questions can look like a form of social washing or greenwashing. The experiments that have succeeded, whatever the involvement and authenticity of the actors implementing them, can be accused of being no more than proofs of concept whose job is to support the ideological work and general legitimacy of financial activities.

However, a weak level of financialisation can also be considered as the first step towards much greater financialisation as the innovations tried out become more common and the new financial circuits become better established. Private equity funds have developed significantly in certain countries, becoming key actors in business handovers, while other countries are more reticent. Extending financialisation is clearly the aim of some of the actors whose input supports stages 1 and 2. The progress or otherwise of financialisation depends on the issues, the national spaces, the channels used and the resistance triggered by these projects. In social questions, strong financialisation would mean a significant rearrangement of the welfare state – for example, a substantial shift towards a funded pension system (which would provide income for investment funds). In the case of France, despite significant developments in the arrangements that would allow this shift, it has not (yet) taken place. Financialisation is not inevitable. It is, however, supported by dominant groups of actors who have an interest in its development, either to gain legitimacy or profit, while other actors seek to enrol them in their social or environmental causes.

Notes

1 With financialisation, the credit circuit has become extensively hybridised with the financial circuits. On the one hand the banks have developed asset management activities and are offloading their loans via securitisation. On the other hand, as research on shadow banking shows, the financial sector contributes to monetary creation and issuance of credit.
2 I proposed a first description of this financialised technical culture based on three identified conventions of valuation that are specific to financial methods (Chiapello and Walter, 2016, p. 1) the actuarial convention, which uses discounting to present value, 2) the mean-variance convention central to portfolio management techniques, which considers that any value can be expressed in terms of expectation (returns) and standard deviation ('risk'), 3) the market-consistent convention, which identifies value with market price.
3 Generally considered to date back to an article published in *Nature* in 1997 by ten authors (R. Costanza et al.) entitled 'The value of the world's ecosystem services and natural capital' (vol. 287, pp. 253–260).
4 For the financialisation of firms, management expertise is mobilised.
5 Reducing emissions from deforestation and forest degradation.

References

Aglietta, M. and Rebérioux, A. (2005). *Corporate governance a drift. A critique of shareholder value.* Cheltenham: Edward Elgar.
Barman, E. (2015). Of principle and principal: Value plurality in the market of impact investing. *Valuation Studies*, 3(1), 9–44.

Baud, C. and Durand, C. (2012). Financialization, globalization and the making of profits by leading retailers. *Socio-Economic Review*, 10(2), 241–266.

Boyer, R. (2009). Feu le régime d'accumulation tiré par la finance : la crise des subprimes en perspective historique. *Revue de la régulation*, 5. DOI: 10.4000/regulation.7367

Chiapello, E. (2015). Financialisation of valuation. *Human Studies*, 38(1), 13–35.

Chiapello, E. and Gilbert, P. (2013). *Sociologie des outils de gestion*. Paris: La découverte.

Chiapello, E. and Gilbert, P. (2016). "L'agence" des outils de gestion. In F.-X de Vaujany, A. Hussenot and J.-F. Chanlat (Eds.) *Théories des organisations. Nouveaux tournants* (pp. 177–198). Paris: Economica.

Chiapello, E. and Godefroy, G. (2017). The dual function of judgment devices. Why does the plurality of market classifications matter? *Historical Social Research*, 42(1), 152–188.

Chiapello, E. and Walter, C. (2016). The three ages of financial quantification: A conventionalist approach to the financiers' metrology. *Historical Social Research*, 41(2), 155–177.

Duménil, G. and Lévy, D. (2001). Costs and benefits of neoliberalism. A class analysis. *Review of International Political Economy*, 8(4), 578–607.

Epstein, G. (Ed.) (2005). *Financialization and the world economy*. Cheltenham: Edward Elgar Publishing.

Erturk, I., Froud, J., Johal, S., Leaver, A. and Williams, K. (Eds.) (2008). *Financialization at work. Key texts and commentary*. New York: Routledge.

Godechot, O. (2012). Is finance responsible for the rise in wage inequality in France? *Socio-Economic Review*, 10(2), 1–24.

Krippner, G. (2005). The financialization of the American economy. *Socio-Economic Review*, 3(2), 173–208.

Lascoumes, P. and Le Galès, P. (Dir.) (2004). *Gouverner par les instruments*. Paris: Presses de Science Po.

Lemoine, B. (2016). *L'ordre de la dette. Enquête sur les infortunes de l'État et la prospérité du marché*. Paris: La découverte.

Lin, K.-H. and Tomaskovic-Devey, D. (2013). Financialization and U.S. income inequality, 1970–2008. *American Journal of Sociology*, 118(5), 1284–1329.

Linhardt, D. and Muniesa, F. (2011). Trials of explicitness in the implementation of public management reform. *Critical Perspectives on Accounting*, 22(6), 550–566.

Muniesa, F. (2014). *The provoked economy: Economic reality and the performative turn*. London: Routledge.

Streeck, W. (2014). *Buying time: The delayed crisis of democratic capitalism*. London: Verso.

Thévenot, L. (1984). Rules and implement: Investments in forms. *Social Science Information*, 23(1), 1–45.

Tordjman, H. and Boisvert, V. (2012). L'idéologie marchande au service de la biodiversité? *Mouvements*, 70(2), 31–42.

Van der Zwan, N. (2014). State of the art. Making sense of financialization. *Socio-Economic Review*, 12(1), 99–129.

22

CIRCUITS OF TRUST AND MONEY

The resilience of the Italian *Credito Cooperativo*

Valentina Moiso

Introduction

This chapter focuses on the client–operator relationship in a *Bank of the Credito Cooperativo* system (BCC; Mutual Bank thereafter), a bank characterized by a strong link with the territorial identity, interlocked with a particular activation of trust in the *face-to-face* client–operator interaction in the branches. Following the mutuality rules, all the BCC banks have to respect territorial boundaries. Moreover, they have few decisional levels and a simple organizational structure. These elements facilitate the 'embeddedness' of operators in the social and economic context in which they operate. The possibility for clients to become members, a low standardisation, a contained use of ITC in risk assessment and in sharing information on financial products, are the main features that configure the situated interactions between client and operator.

This specific configuration was more widespread in the overall Italian banking system since the reforms starting in the 1990s: its *persistence* in the BCC system can be seen as a form of *resilience* of the way of *doing slow finance* – in terms of designing and selling financial products and services for families – facing the structural changes requested within the framework of the Basel constraints. In other words, this configuration persists while at institutional level the BCC system is changing its organizational arrangement in order to respect the criteria in terms of capital reserve and more generally of risk management, stability and liquidity. Some BCC banks had problems in mastering unpaid credit after the economic crisis in 2007, while some banks of the system have been dimensionally growing in the last few years, which is now important in order to maintain autonomy. In fact, Law 49/2016 (implementation is on-going) has established the creation of a holding to which each bank should be joining in the near future, and the degree of freedom in operability allowed to each bank is directly linked to their degree of risk. Therefore, a reform process of the whole BCC system is on-going, and the effects on the relationship, care and evaluation of the clients are impossible to know at the moment: in the following years, the resilience in the BCC's way of doing *slow finance* will be under pressure. But what exactly does this way mean, what are its features in terms of risk control from the point of view of the banks and from the side of clients?

A qualitative research was carried out in the last 10 years to examine closely the decisions of a sample of Mutual Bank clients with a mortgage during and after the financial crisis. In 2007–2008 their monthly mortgage repayments rose because a variable interest rate was used for the calculation of the interest amount. Mutual Bank clients made decisions in a singular way with respect to the other people in the sample, who had a variable interest rate mortgage in a bigger commercial bank.[1] The results suggested that the resilience in the client–operator relationship strategy itself plays a key role in making the bank comply with the prudential norms on credit risk management (see Moiso, 2011 and 2015). In the branches of these banks, specific configurations based on social and mutual elements perform (see Callon and Muniesa, 2005) a form of domination on the client who gets indebted, designing a *Zelizer circuit* of money (Zelizer, 2010; see also De Blic and Lazarus, 2007; Mizruchi and Stearns, 2005). In our research we don't pursue the goal of disclosing such domination, but rather to take into consideration the moral explanations actors give to their actions, in line with their ability to evaluate (Boltanski and Thévenot, 2006). Moreover, the financial crisis facilitated a sort of objectification of the decisions about the mortgage: when the interest rate rose, clients had the possibility to change a component of their mortgage, e.g. to change the type of interest rate from variable to fix rate. We have reconstructed the economic socialization in a context in which trust and asymmetry of power are interlocked, taking into account actors' evaluations (Bourdieu and Boltanski, 1976; Godechot, 2017; Guérin et al., 2014; Knorr Ketina and Preda, 2005; Lazarus, 2009; Vargha, 2011). In the next paragraphs we go deeper into the feature of the BCC system and the Zelizer circuit we analytically found.

The Italian *Credito cooperativo*: mutualistic banks sustaining the local economy

The *Credito Cooperativo* is a group of locally embedded Italian banks with mutualistic goals. In fact, they are cooperative banks[2] established at the end of the 1800s with Christian inspiration in order to include in the banking system people normally excluded from it, such as agricultural workers in the countryside and the working class in the cities. The client risk assessment finalized to access to credit was made through so-called social assessment. This is a method based on the interpersonal knowledge among members of the same community in which the bank operated: not only on the embeddedness of the operators within the social and economic context and the information they can obtain thereof, but also on the social control and the will to maintain their own shared reputation from the point of view of clients. This method was still being carried out until the last few years, taking into account that the BCCs have legal boundaries to respect, which also impacts on the nature of their financial operations. Ninety-five percent of the credit operations have to be granted at local level, on the territory in which the bank operates, and mainly to its members.

The *Credito Cooperativo* has played a crucial role in the Italian banking system – especially for maintaining the link with local communities when larger Italian commercial banks are more concerned with being international global players (Barca, 1997; De Cecco, 1984). More generally, the territorial extensiveness of some banks has been an Italian feature until the 2000s: popular treasuries, popular banks and rural banks are the principal examples of these institutions, all of whom have been non-profit: "the local banks had to compete to maintain a complex equilibrium between the specific social need of the local communities and the national choices in terms of policies" (Conti and Ferri, 1997, p. 430). This role was more evident after the 1980s, when the application of Directive 77/780/CEE in the Italian context, especially through the government's Amato Low (1992), started deregulation in the Italian banking sector. Today, the system continues to play an important role in the Italian banking system. It consists of 313 banks with a remarkable extensiveness on the territory:[3] 4,270 branches, 15 percent of the total in Italy, present in almost all of the Italian provinces (*Province*) and in 33 percent of the towns. The rhetoric in the presentation of these banks is focused on *difference*, not only in terms of care, individualization of the service and client satisfaction, but overall as being the *local bank*, consistently with tradition. In fact, the BCC system finances more than 20 percent of handicraft and family businesses,[4] two well-known and extremely important sectors for the Italian economy, and around 10 percent of the families.

In the Mutual Bank surveyed in our case study, the number of members has increased during the last year, supporting the bank's strategy of enlarging its area of influence in the urban context, also merging with other smaller institutes. This was not a simple operation, given its strong rural roots and the difficulty to maintain the *difference* while the number of clients multiplied more than fivefold, raising the figure to 50,000. The last board meeting involved over 15,000 members, an almost unique case for cooperative participation in Italy.

The community atmosphere

In the Mutual Bank, financial transactions with families are conducted in a low-standardised way. In the research, in particular, the social assessment and the consulting about a debt were analyzed. The social assessment of creditors is a non-standard method based on the relationship between client and operator and on the capability of the operator to retrace the social and economic context in which the client lives, in order to gain access to information on their creditworthiness (the capacity to pay off a debt) which was not otherwise available (Ferrary, 2003; Moro and Howorth, 2009). This practice was widespread in the Italian banking sector until the liberalization reforms of 1990s, since it was progressively replaced by more advanced and standardised IT systems of risk assessment in the bigger banks, the so-called *credit scoring* (Poon, 2009). In the BCCs, in parallel to the persistent link with the territory, the social assessment has also persisted, only partially integrated within the new techniques.

The Mutual Bank has access to standard and shared information systems on the clients' debt story existing in Italy (the database of CRIF, the Italian central risk agency), which the bank can consult upon receiving complete consent of the client. The main client information source for the Mutual Bank is the client himself who, during the interaction with the operator in the local branch, provides his personal coordinates, together with social and economic information to the operator. *Coordinates*, because this information is the true reference point through which the operator is able to place each client on his creditworthiness *map*. What is the *family tree* – as the operator calls it – of the client? Is there someone who is able to informally help him in case of troubles? Is the client trustworthy, without any bad propensities, does he have the reputation of a responsible person in the networks of its peers and colleagues? Does he/she have a stable job position, taking into account the working contract, the robustness of the economic sector or the firm in which he/she works, impacting his/her capacity to receive a stable income? To give an answer to these and similar questions, the face-to-face interaction with the client remains crucial. During this interaction, the client – comfortably seated in an office without any noise from other clients at the desk, in a branch where the director is in the next room with glass walls or even talking to him or her directly – experiences what would only be achievable by so-called *private* wealthy clients in a branch of an Italian commercial bank.

In a certain sense, clients are forced to enter into such interaction: credit information is only partially available on-line, and the conditions are less costly for those clients who decide to become members of the cooperative. In that way, numbers, costs, possibilities, rates, generally all the information about the financial transaction is given directly *face-to-face* first, without any IT devices, and without recurring to detailed information forms written in "expert" language. In fact, the operator is the expert who transmits such information to the client, once translated in a language that is clearly understandable to him. Financial information is not hidden or obscure: the operator talks about financial data, markets, types of rates and historic trends, which are issues for experts, but using familiar and non-technical words, translating them in understandable matters. He performs a consulting operation. Indeed, the relationship between client and operator is not intimate or friendly but totally professional. Operators in the branch have a high turnover, and they have to avoid any unprofessional behavior whatsoever such as, they told us, drinking tea or coffee in front of the clients.

In other words, these features allow us to analytically represent the client–operator relationship relative to the management of a mortgage using the concept of Zelizer's circuit. The sociologist Viviana Zelizer has conceptualized *circuits* as structures through which commercial transactions are enacted also by means of social elements, which were usually indicated as incompatible in economy (Zelizer, 2010; Zelizer et al., 2017):

> Each distinctive social circuit incorporates somewhat different understandings, practices, information, obligations, rights, symbols and media of exchange. I call these circuits of commerce in an old sense of the word, where commerce means conversation, interchange, intercourse and mutual shaping. They range from the most intimate to quite impersonal social transactions.
>
> *(Zelizer, 2010, pp. 314–315)*

The interaction between client and operator in the Mutual bank is characterized by a *community atmosphere* (see Moiso, 2015). The bank represents itself as a member of the community that is doing what it is able to do – finance – in the most effective and efficient way not for its profit but also for the wellbeing of all its members, in a mutualistic way. On the other hand, the Mutual Bank client recognizes such expertise and because of that trusts the operator not as an individual but as an expert of the given territory. Here, we use the term *trust* as an expectation of cooperative behavior (Mutti, 1987).

In our specific case study, the crisis confirmed the trust between client and operator. During the financial crisis of 2008, while interest rates of mortgages at variable rates dramatically increased, the mortgage repayments of a number of Italian families increased and the weight on the family budget became unbearable. Mutual Bank clients were distressed the same as everyone else. However, compared to the others, with regard to those involved in the research, they did not lose their trust in the operators, but indeed, they told us they intensified their contacts with them. The operators were not criticized as guilty parties because they were not responsible for governing the global financial market in the clients' view; they were still the experts, and the interaction with them was conducted in order to construct a representation of what was happening on the financial markets so as to be able to decide what to do with the mortgages. Compared to other banks involved in the study, Mutual Bank clients did not change their interest rates from variable to fixed, which was at its maximum amount during the crisis.

Conclusion

The moral approach to the economy of the BCCs is based on the self-representation as *different banks*. By using the results of a qualitative case study, we can see: i) the reasons why we can consider a BCC bank as different; ii) how this difference is performed; iii) through which type of social relationships and relating to which values. To sum up, in our case the *difference* is not intended in a critical way or in ethical terms, as in other entities which represent themselves as critically alternative to the traditional financial system.[5] The distinctive feature deals with being a mutualistic bank devoted to the local development: the profit goal is not denied but is recognized as possible for the clients-members who live in the same territory where the bank operates. The *clients-members* are *different* compared to simple clients because their membership allows them to pay less for financial services, to have lower interest rate on debts, and overall to maintain a distinctive relationship with operators in the branches. The client's trust in the operator is based on the common belonging to the same cooperative and on the belief in the professional expertise ensured by the same cooperative. Precisely the less standardized and low ITC mediated way to work makes the bank's representation more cooperative and less commercial. All these elements converge to create positive expectations on the operators' behavior in the clients.

We have also to consider the other side of trust in this kind of dyadic interaction between who is searching for money (the client) and who is in charge of assessing the risk before allowing access to credit (the operator): the client–operator relationship is asymmetric in term of expertise, available information, power of money control. In the context of this relationship, for example, the Mutual Bank can make the client choose a mortgage at variable rate, given that the bank prefers this kind of mortgage for reasons linked to the ways it itself has access to funding. This is only one of the multiple examples we could give concerning a relationship in which the role of advisor and that of seller are played by the same person at the same time.

This asymmetric but trustworthy relationship is at the basis of the mechanism through which Mutual Bank manages to respect the Basel constraint in terms of client risk management, by assessing the client risk and by orienting the behavior of the client. In the bank rhetoric the client–operator relationship is framed in the mutualistic field, but given the asymmetry and the control performed by the operator, we can understand it as an implicit domination over the client. We can suppose that the client internalizes this domination through the economic socialization experienced in the branches, during the repeated interactions with the operators. The domination emerges from the situated interaction of actors who perform an economic transaction framed in terms of mutualistic meanings.

The data of the Mutual Bank, as for BCCs in general, in terms of unpaid debts, show a better performance compared to that of commercial banks after the financial crisis (Bonaccorsi di Patti and Felici, 2008), consistent with other cases in the literature (Ferrary, 2003). In fact, the BCCs are more linked to the real and local economy for statutory norms: in our case they perform a social evaluation not in a personal or patronizing way; they were better equipped to foresee and avoid the risk of default related to individual behaviors or social and economic local trends. It seems that in the Mutual Bank we analyzed, a Zelizer circuit takes place, in the sense that the financial transition is strictly interlocked with situated shared meanings and social structures in which the relationship between client and operator is framed (see Zelizer, 1989). A circuit in which – it could sound paradoxical – trust, control of client orientation and domination, risk assessment and management, effectiveness of financial transactions for every actor involved are often well aligned.

Notes

1 The research lasted for 16 months with some interruptions since 2009. An ethnography was carried out in branches, 70 interviews were conducted with clients and operators who sold the mortgage to each client and, for most of them, acted as advisors for managing the mortgage.
2 They have to grant 70% of the profit to the non-divisible capital reserve.
3 Data from 2017 available on www.creditocooperativo.it, last accessed 4th December 2017.
4 Data referred to the total credit in euros.
5 In Italy some entities operating in the field of ethical finance have constructed their identity based on the idea of offering a critical alternative to the traditional financial system, as in the case of the MAGs – Mutua AutoGestione (Mutual self-management), which aim at creating "economic models based on the cooperation, self-management and basic associationism alternatively to the traditional economic system and it wants to give support to no-profit enterpreneurship based on values such as co-management, no-speculative reinvestment of profits, democratic organization, inclusion of disadvantaged, transparency, democracy, respect for the environment and participation" (www.mag4.it, last accessed 4th December 2017).

References

Barca, F. (1997). Compromesso senza riforme nel capitalismo italiano. In F. Barca (Ed.), *Storia del capitalismo italiano dal dopoguerra fino ad oggi*. Roma: Donzelli.

Boltanski, L. and Thévenot, L. (2006). *On justification. The economies of worth*. Princeton: Princeton University Press.

Bonaccorsi di Patti, E. and Felici, R. (2008). *Il rischio dei mutui alle famiglie in Italia: evidenza da un milione di contratti*. Occasional papers, 32. Roma: Banca d'Italia.

Bourdieu, P. and Boltanski, L. (1976). La production de l'idéologie dominante. *Actes de la recherche en sciences sociales*, 2(2–3), 4–73.

Callon, M. and Muniesa, F. (2005). Economic markets as calculative collective devices. *Organization Studies*, 26(8), 1229–1250.

Conti, G. and Ferri, G. (1997). Banche locali e sviluppo economico decentrato. In F. Barca (Ed.), *Storia del capitalismo italiano dal dopoguerra fino ad oggi*. Roma: Donzelli.

De Blic, D. and Lazarus, J. (2007). *Sociologie de l'argent*. Paris: La Découverte.

De Cecco, M. (1984). The Italian banking system at a historic turning point. *Review of Economic Conditions in Italy*, 1, 51–68.

Ferrary, M. (2003). Trust and social capital in the regulation of lending activities. *The Journal of Socio-Economics*, 31(6), 673–699.

Godechot, O. (2017). *Wages, bonuses and appropriation of profit in the financial industry: The working rich*. London: Routledge.

Guérin, I., Morvant-Roux, S. and Villarreal, M. (Eds.) (2014). *Microfinance, debt and over-indebtedness*. London: Routledge.

Knorr Ketina, K. and Preda, A. (Eds.) (2005). *The sociology of financial markets*. Oxford: Oxford University Press.

Lazarus, J. (2009). L'épreuve du crédit. *Sociétés Contemporaines*, 76(4), 17–39.

Mizruchi, M. S. and Stearns, L. B. (2005). Money, banking, and financial markets. In N. J. Smelser, and R. Swedberg (Eds.), *The handbook of economic sociology* (pp. 284–306). Princeton: Princeton University Press.

Moiso, V. (2011). I fenomeni finanziari nella letteratura sociologica contemporanea: l'emergenza di nuove prospettive. *Stato e Mercato*, 92, 313–342.

Moiso, V. (2015). Les particuliers, les banques et la confiance: un cas d'étude en Italie. *Critique Internationale – Revue Comparative de Sciences Sociales*, 69(4), 79–97.

Moro, A. and Howorth, C. (2009). The role of trust in accessing short-term credit. In G. Bracchi and D. Masciandaro (Eds.), *Dopo la crisi. L'industria finanziaria italiana tra stabilità e sviluppo. Fondazione Rosselli – Quattordicesimo rapporto sul sistema finanziario italiano* (pp. 421–452). Roma: Bancaria Editrice.

Mutti, A. (1987). La fiducia. Un concetto fragile, una solida realtà. *Rassegna italiana di sociologia*, 28, 223–247

Poon, M. (2009). From new deal institutions to capital markets: Commercial consumer risk scores and the making of subprime mortgage finance. *Accounting, Organizations and Society*, 34(5), 654–674.

Vargha, Z. (2011). From long-term savings to instant mortgages: Financial demonstrations and the role of interaction in markets. *Organization*, 18(2), 215–235.

Zelizer, V. (1989). The social meaning of money: "Special monies". *American Journal of Sociology*, 95(2), 342–377.

Zelizer, V. (1994). *The social meaning of money*. New York: Basic Books.

Zelizer, V. (2010). *Economic lives: How culture shapes the economy*. Princeton, NJ: Princeton University Press.

Zelizer, V., Bandelj N. and Wherry, F. (Eds.) (2017). *Money talks: Explaining how money really works*. Princeton: Princeton University Press.

23

JUSTIFICATION AND CRITIQUE IN THE CREDIT RATING SYSTEM

Reaffirming the power of agencies[1]

Benjamin Taupin

The last few decades have brought to light a paradox related to the activity of credit rating. Credit rating agencies have been consistently criticised, though this appears to have done little to call into question this pillar of the contemporary financial industry. Furthermore, as Timothy J. Sinclair has remarked, this inconsistency was amplified following the arrival of the 2008 financial crisis:

> It is intriguing that, despite the worst financial crisis since the 1930s and the identification of a suitable culprit in the rating agencies, proposed regulation should be so unsubstantial, doing so little to alter the rating system that has been implemented in the US since 1909 and in Europe since the mid-1980s.
>
> *(Sinclair, 2010, p. 8)*

The paradoxical reaffirmation of the power of credit rating agencies during crises

Criticism has been directed towards credit ratings on several occasions in the past, at any time agencies have been recorded as neglecting their mission to assign a rating determining the creditworthiness of an issuer or a debt issuance. This was notably the case during the sovereign debt crises (for a detailed study on this, see Sinclair, 2005), including the financial crisis in Mexico (1994–1995), the Asian financial crisis (1997–1998), Argentina's default in 2001 and the Icelandic financial crisis in 2008, but also in the *corporate debt* domain at the beginning of the century with the collapse of Enron, Worldcom and Parmalat. As Langohr and Langohr (2008, p. 189) have described,

> Enron was given a good credit rating by S&P and Moody's until four days before its collapse, Worldcom until three months before, and Parmalat until 45 days before.

The 2008 subprime crisis undoubtedly increased this criticism. As of 2007, agencies were criticised for their role in the financial crisis, in particular for having assigned high grades to US mortgage-backed securities, and other financial instruments, which were later on revealed to be toxic assets. They were equally vilified, soon after, for not having foreseen the complications within those financial corporations which they had graded at the top end of the 'investment' scale (in other words low-risk) only a short time before their collapse (Lehman Brothers, American International Group, etc.). Consequently, Senator Carl Levin, then Chairman of the Permanent Subcommittee on Investigations for the American Senate (United States Senate, 2010 and 2011), aptly declared in relation to the agencies' role in the crisis: "I don't think either of these companies have served their shareholders or the nation well" (Senate Panel, 2010). Finally, criticism was also generated concerning the pressure agencies exercised over state governments and their budget policies, through the evaluation of their sovereign debt.

The other side of the credit rating paradox stems from a notable lack of change in the order governing the rating industry. Following the US mortgage crisis, the Securities and Exchange Commission (responsible for regulating the financial markets in the United States) announced an end to the self-regulation of agencies (SEC, 2008), and the European Union equally sought to intervene in the activity through proposing supervision through the CESR (Committee of European Securities Regulators, who moved aside for the European Securities and Markets Authority (ESMA), on 1 January 2011). Despite the criticism it has attracted, the regulative framework for credit rating activity was not really modified (see Table 23.1). In fact, the successive reforms introduced by the American and European regulators instead settled for minor changes related to improving transparency, preventing conflicts of interest and the regulatory use of credit ratings by public authorities. As such, the section of the *Dodd-Frank Wall Street Reform Act* adopted in 2010 in the United States which anticipated control credit rating more strictly was rendered partially meaningless (Eisinger and Bernstein, 2011).

TABLE 23.1 Events involving credit rating agencies and regulatory measures adopted between 1994 and 2011

Date	Events
1994	Orange County bankruptcy, largest municipal bankruptcy in U.S. history that credit rating agencies had failed to predict.
1997	Asian Crisis, credit rating agencies' shortcomings underlined.
2001	Enron bankruptcy, credit rating agencies' shortcomings underlined.
2004	Basel II re-establishes the use of private credit ratings for public regulative use.
2006	Credit Rating agency Reform act of 2006 'to improve ratings quality for the protection of investors and in the public interest by fostering accountability, transparency, and competition in the credit rating agency industry'. Enacted on 29 September
2007	Subprime Crisis, credit rating agencies' shortcomings underlined.
2007	SEC Final Rule: Oversight of Credit Rating Agencies Registered as Nationally Recognized Statistical Rating Organizations. Credit rating agencies have to apply for registration as NRSROs.
2008	SEC report (July) highlighting credit rating agencies' deficiencies
2009	SEC Final Rules: Amendments to Rules for Nationally Recognized Statistical Rating Organizations (2 February and 23 November). Additional disclosure and con ict of interest requirements on nationally recognized statistical rating organizations in order to address concerns about the integrity of the credit rating procedures and methodologies at NRSROs. In particular, rule 17g-5, known as the 'anti-rating shopping' rule is adopted.

(Continued)

Date	Events
2009	16 September, European regulation 1060/2009 on credit rating agencies. For the first time, agencies have to register to operate in the European Union.
2010	The *Dodd-Frank Wall Street Reform Act*, including some improvements to the regulation of credit rating agencies. Creation of a Securities and Exchange Commission office to oversee the agencies and their ratings. The credit rating agencies regulation includes enhancement in the following fields: conflict of interest mitigation, rating and methodologies disclosure, review of ratings and methodologies and corporate governance.
2011	Because of budget constraints, in part resulting from a Republican House decision, the implementation of Dodd-Frank was seriously weakened.
2011	The European Central Bank rejects the idea of creating a credit rating agency.

Comparing the succession of events during which agencies demonstrated their inadequacy to accomplish their mission, alongside the analysis of their actual power, raises questions concerning agencies' resistance to criticism. Undeniably, with each rating crisis, the role of agencies has been paradoxically strengthened. Following the *Penn Central Transportation Company* crisis in 1970, the Nationally Recognized Statistical Rating Organization (NRSRO) regulations were adopted, and following the Asian financial crisis and the collapse of Enron in 2001, the Basel II regulations were adopted. These two regulatory systems strengthened the power of rating agencies; the former by crediting private companies with the responsibility of issuing ratings used for regulatory purposes, while the latter increased this power by designating, for example, the grades assigned by leading agencies as international references for calculating banks' prudential ratios. Any event that might have been viewed as a threat to agencies has in fact contributed to strengthening their role.

This paradox between the criticism of the activity of credit rating on one side, and the lack of significant changes to its regulation on the other, raises the following question: what has rendered the regulation of credit rating so resistant to critique and change?

Following the agencies' wrongdoings, the controversy surrounding credit ratings increased, triggering a debate in which various ideas for suitable regulation were compared. Below we present a number of comments sent to the SEC within the context of public consultations on credit rating, which it conducted during this period:

When failings by rating agencies triggered contestation, the SEC began considering stricter regulation for agencies and the credit rating industry. The SEC submitted its propositions for public input. According to the pragmatic sociology approach (Boltanski and Thévenot, 2006), it would appear that the diverse justifications expressed in these comments represent *tests* applied to accepted ideas about the credit rating regulation currently in force. By adopting a perspective inspired by this sociological approach, the current chapter proposes to examine this justification effort so as to analyse institutional legitimacy within the credit rating industry.

Three types of institutional maintenance activities

The comments sent in during the public consultations have been thoroughly processed (Taupin, 2012a). They showed that the compromise underpinning the organization of

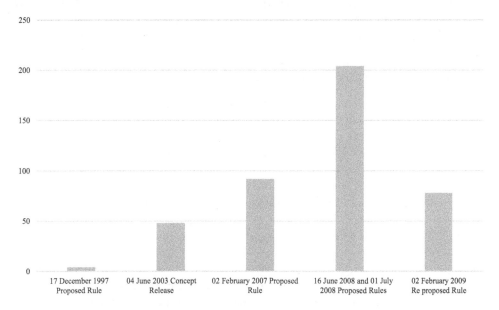

250

200

150

100

50

0

| 17 December 1997 Proposed Rule | 04 June 2003 Concept Release | 02 February 2007 Proposed Rule | 16 June 2008 and 01 July 2008 Proposed Rules | 02 February 2009 Re proposed Rule |

FIGURE 23.1 Number of comments addressed to the SEC

credit rating is established between the market, industrial and fame worlds (Boltanski and Thévenot, 2006). The examination of the justifications also revealed that an institutional justification work preserved institutions in three different ways, all of which are characterised by varying degrees of complexity.

The first justification work is the simple task of confirmation, in which actors repeat or reproduce the existing regulatory setup or quite simply refuse to take part in the controversy. In general, the comments from the 2003 consultation were punctuated with references to the suitability and the relevance of the current organisation ("*The NRSRO system is designed, appropriately in our view* [...]"; "*The current system of oversight of credit rating agencies functions reasonably well.*"). The actors confirmed that the system had worked well for years ("*credit ratings is a concept that has served markets well for over 25 years*"). They described the existing system without questioning the representations that they had formed of the reality. The idea of increasing the regulation of credit rating was considered to be irrelevant as the actors did not seem to think there was a problem.

However, during the period examined, this action was not the only type of work perpetuating the compromise. Following the subprime crisis, an unveiling process started though it did not succeed at triggering a challenge to the regulation of credit rating. Two types of work carried out during this unveiling should be identified. The first type, which is similar to the one described by Patriotta et al. (2011), stems from the process of test formatting displayed by criticisms expressed against ratings. Consequently, the absence of civic objects (related to collective well-being) or domestic ones (which create a family-like connection) in the justification work is observed. The second type of work originates from the compromise's circular nature, which prevents the tests from undermining the compromise underlying the regulation of credit rating. The justification work presents a situation in which stakeholders have actually referred to the orders of worth without modifying the existing social configuration. Through this process, the source of institutional maintenance lies in immunising the institution through the repetition of criticism, in line with the operating principles of the compromise's circular nature. These two types will be examined in further detail in the following sections.

Operations of qualification depending on the test format

Following the crisis of justification, the view of the regulation conveyed by the compromise was compared with the failures observed in agencies. At this stage in the research, *reality tests* are involved (Boltanski, 2011). Within the justifications, arguments are put forward and favoured in order to allow the regulatory order to respond to any criticism. Thanks to the *reality tests*, the principles used to establish legitimacy come to light with much greater clarity. A *rise towards generality* was thus observed, which unveiled the situation's compromise; more specifically, a strong tropism bringing together fame, market and industrial worlds (Boltanski and Thévenot, 2006), in line with the following configuration: "the market is efficient and creates confidence" and "transparency renders the market efficient" (Taupin, 2012a and 2012b). These comments thus show a propensity towards shaping criticisms by adopting a testing format that fits the current compromise. As such, the debate surrounding the conflict of interests in credit ratings was handled via the intervention of tests respectively stemming from the market, industrial and fame worlds (Boltanski and Thévenot, 2006), rather than, for example, through the creation of tests relevant to the civic world (based on creating a sense of responsibility) or the inspired world (based on innovation). The actors thus prevented criticism from situating the debate within a world that was extraneous to the compromise. The irresponsible behaviour by credit rating agency analysts is not considered at the level of the civic world. The explanation favoured here is that the agencies experienced difficulties in meeting the rise in demand for ratings, in terms of volume. The way in which the debate was handled brought about criticism that not only confirmed the validity of the higher principles on which regulation is founded, but which equally attempted to strengthen its underlying principles by disengaging the debate from any elements foreign to the compromise (Nachi, 2006). In order to resolve the issues of credit ratings, such as the conflict of interests, it is necessary to improve transparency, favour competition and achieve performance.

In a similar fashion, the majority of actors oppose the exclusion of nationally recognised private ratings (e.g. NRSRO) from the regulations, as such a change is thought to be an operation that would seriously destabilise the ratings production system. According to the 'common good' sustained by the existing compromise, the act of withdrawing the NRSRO ratings from the regulations would correspond with depriving market actors (investors, insurers, brokers) of what they consider to be their credible market tool. Consequently, all aspects of the 'common good' assembled together within the compromise are embodied in NRSRO ratings (the industrial world, the world of fame and the market world). The use of credit rating standards issued by a public agency therefore cannot be considered legitimate without there being a questioning of or, at least, a modification made to the compromise.

The circular figure of institutional maintenance work

According to Boltanski (2011), no assumptions are made concerning the outcome of the justification work when *reality tests* are conducted. Such an operation is just as likely to come to an end following an actual reconfiguration of the compromise, as it is to end following a conclusion of the controversy without any change. An unveiling therefore does not necessarily lead to calling the current compromise into question. In this case, preservation does not result from the strength of the compromise obtained via the justification process but from the justification process *per se,* which by preventing the debate from concluding via a self-sustaining logic, leads to the perpetuity of the *status quo.* The compromise here has a particular nature: observably it is precisely the composite character of the harmonising situation which, through its sophistication, renders the situation perpetual. This process is outlined by the notion of the circular figure of the compromise.

Due to this composite characteristic of the compromise, 'in such a case the critique can never be completely clarified, because it is impossible to return to a higher common principle' (Boltanski and Thévenot, 2006, p. 282). The critique plunges itself into a test format from which it can no longer escape, resulting in absolutely no radical challenges being made to the arrangement. As such, there is no danger to the compromise and instead it comes away strengthened, as this emphasises the orders of worth of which it is composed.

Thus, when criticisms targeting the individualistic character of the rating system arise, they become established (*ex ante*) in reference to the industrial worth, market worth and fame-based worth formula without ever before having succeeded (*ex post*) in truly rising to one of them as they are in fact all foreign to each other. The *ex ante* mechanism corresponds with the process of converting tests to the format of the current compromise as outlined by the circular figure. This nature enables the *ex post* procedural component of institutional preservation to be outlined, identifying the competition, transparency and performance within one single compromise. These three worths are treated as equivalent, as one can indifferently cast aspersions that the 'competition is not performing well', that 'performance is not linked to competition', that 'transparency is not practical' or again that 'the market is not transparent'. However, the imprecision of the 'common good' defended by the compromise does not advance the debate very far; if one seeks to expose the agencies' lack of competitiveness, then objections are made that it is the best performing system because it is also the most transparent. For example, financial agents like brokers or investors justify the current oligopoly by upholding the idea that having only three ratings to consult (Moody's, S&P and Fitch) is optimal for their decision making. On the contrary, if we attack the lack of performance, then it will be argued that the system is competitive and transparent. Consequently, confronted by the lack of performance from private ratings corporations, the idea of creating a rating agency that is not undermined by conflicts of interest linked to their remuneration system is swept aside as it no longer appears to be a solution that maintains credible free competition. At the core of the current compromise, this indicates the features of the *complex figure* as outlined by Boltanski and Thévenot (2006, p. 282).

Circularity as an escape from the limits of justification

With the qualification process in compliance with the test format, the field of credit rating initially illustrates the work of maintenance resulting from the characteristics of a standard compromise. Second, the circular nature of the compromise shows the process that helps, in this specific setup, to avoid any tests internal to the compromise from attaining their target. In this sense, those investors opposing the reform affirm, for example that, admittedly, the production of credit ratings was not efficient (it failed to rate products issued from structured finance at their objective value), though they equally underline that the entire market community places their trust in these ratings. The test is diverted by reference to one of the dimensions that is not under attack in the composite arrangement. As called to mind above, this leads to a form of circularity in the questioning whereby, turn for turn, the efficient nature of the ratings is asserted in order to counter the lack of trust in the industry, or conversely, it is maintained that the ratings' lack of efficiency is regrettable, but acceptable, as the market has confidence in this method for ratings production. In our view, this consequently explains the paradox which postulates that in order to resolve the issues of credit ratings, actors seek to improve the transparency, to favour competition and to raise efficiency, despite the current framework having specifically led to an oligopolistic situation, repetitive ratings errors and a lack of clarity within the ratings system. Indeed, in a universe in which public justification prevails, the circular nature of the compromise enables one to step back from the logical consistency in those arguments put forth, in order to either challenge or justify the existence of the compromise.

This characteristic relates to the idea of the private arrangement described by Boltanski and Thévenot. a private arrangement does not require a new equivalence to be established:

> [t]he concession that is made in a private arrangement consists precisely in avoiding recourse to a principle of justice: people come to terms among themselves – that is, locally – to bring a disagreement over worth to an end without exhausting the issue, without really resolving the quarrel.
>
> *(Boltanski and Thévenot, 2006, p. 128).*

The private arrangement, contrary to the compromise, has value at a local level. It is the place to express a convergence of private interests, independently of any reference to the constraints of justification, and is generally used in justification situations related to the private sphere. Even though it is not valid in our case on a local level, the circular nature of the compromise as observed in credit rating is comparable to the liberation from constraints of justification that characterises the private arrangement.

Conclusion

In conclusion, this analysis enables a new interpretation to be carried out with regard to the events produced within the rating industry. Without judging the reliability of ratings or on capacity of agencies to issue "accurate" ratings, we have noted that the notion of the "right way to issue a rating" remains unchanged despite the critical incidents observed. Our research points out how, under the guise of this change, if one examines the justification work carried out by actors, the principles that both guide and found the actions of these actors within the rating industry seize upon opportunities created by new events to reaffirm their existence. Little or no questioning of the basis of legitimacy is observed, and the mechanisms that support the status quo are solid (Ouroussoff, 2010). Contrary to certain appearances (the restructuring of Wall Street, through the *Dodd-Frank Wall Street Reform Act*, was announced as the largest financial reform since the 1929 crisis), the pillar of modern finance that is credit rating is not in the process of being thoroughly reformed.

Note

1 This chapter sets out arguments that I have published elsewhere (Taupin, 2012a) in an extended version.

References

Boltanski, L. (2011). *On critique: A sociology of emancipation*. Cambridge: Polity Press.

Boltanski, L. and Thévenot, L. (2006). *On justification. Economies of worth*. Princeton: Princeton University Press.

Eisinger, J. and Bernstein, J. (2011). From Dodd-Frank to Dud: How financial reform may be going wrong. Retrieved from http://www.propublica.org/article/from-dodd-frank-to-dud.

Langohr, H. M. and Langohr, P. T. (2008). *The rating agencies and their credit ratings: What they are, how they work and why they are relevant*. Hoboken: Wiley.

Nachi, M. (2006). *Introduction à la sociologie pragmatique*. Paris: Armand Colin.

Ouroussoff, A. (2010). *Wall Street at war, the secret struggle for the global economy*. Cambridge: Polity.

Patriotta, G., Gond, J.-P., and Schultz, F. (2011). Maintaining legitimacy: Controversies, orders of worth and public justifications. *Journal of Management Studies*, 48(8), 1804–1836.

SEC [Securities and Exchange Commission] (2008). *Summary report of issues identified in the Commission Staff's examination of select credit rating agencies*, July.

Senate Panel (2010). Ratings agencies rolled over for Wall Street. Retrieved from http://www.mcclatchydc.com/2010/04/22/ 92709/senate-panel-ratings-agencies.html#.

Sinclair, T. J. (2005). *The new masters of capital: American bond rating agencies and the politics of creditworthiness*. Ithaca: Cornell University Press.

Sinclair, T. J. (2010). Credit rating agencies and the global financial crisis. *Economic Sociology, the European Electronic Newsletter*, 12(1), 4–9.

Taupin, B. (2012a). The more things change...Institutional maintenance as justification work in the credit rating industry. *M@n@gement*, 15(5), 528–562.

Taupin, B. (2012b). Maintaining the regulative order in the credit rating agency industry. In I. Huault and C. Richard (Eds.), *Finance: The discreet regulator. How financial activities shape and transform the world* (pp. 85–108). Basingstoke: Palgrave MacMillan.

United States Senate (2010). *Exhibits. Hearing on Wall Street and the financial crisis: The role of credit rating agencies. United States Senate Permanent Subcommittee on investigation*, 23 April.

United States Senate (2011). *Wall Street and the financial crisis: Anatomy of a financial collapse. United States Senate Permanent Subcommittee on investigation*, 13 April.

24

THE FUNCTION OF FINANCE

An ethnographic analysis of competing ideas

Alexandra Ouroussoff

According to the vast majority of academics and journalists, the central organising principle of capitalism is market competition. Conservatives, Liberals and Marxists are united in their assumption that competitive exchange regulated by supply and demand is the momentum through which global capital moves. It is taken as given that actors at the highest levels of the capitalist structure share this view. Making a profit, after all, entails the conscious adaptation of economic and institutional processes to the needs of the market. Once we accept that markets are competitive, we cannot but hold that actors caught up in the processes of profit-making recognise and respond to the external exigencies of the price mechanism. Quite aside from this point of logic, the correspondence between subjective experience and objective conditions is daily affirmed by practitioners on radio, television and in newspapers.

Taking a historical view, however, we know that consensus of opinion may be only apparent. This phenomenon is well documented by historians, usually with respect to divergence rooted in social class. Here, however, I will be examining twenty-first-century capitalism, not from the perspective of those who do not share in the wealth enjoyed by elites, but rather from the perspective of economic elites whose practical experience and corresponding views throw into question the presupposition that the economic system in which we live and work is by and large determined by market competition. The dynamic I describe below emerged from ethnographic fieldwork among executives in charge of 13 corporations listed on the New York, London or Tokyo Stock Exchanges, and credit analysts employed by two of the three major U.S. based credit rating agencies. In this chapter I focus on the perspective of executives responsible for developing and implementing long-term corporate strategy, and senior credit analysts who specialise in assessing risk to the larger corporations on investors' behalf.[1]

These elites take the view that the principles now determining international capital flows are incommensurable with a competitive market. Nor, it should be emphasised, do they fall under the concepts of monopoly capitalism as defined by classical theory. Perhaps the most surprising aspect of my finding is that these new principles, which I explain below, cannot be deduced from classical economic texts. From a methodological standpoint, the difference between the subjective perception of my fieldwork participants and the standard view of the economy is so profound we can usefully think of the former as a positive heuristic in that it draws our attention to new institutional dependencies and processes we would otherwise be unlikely to observe. Most importantly, the perspective of my elite participants brings to light recent changes in the economic goals served by finance.

A good place to begin the analysis is with their understanding of the relationship between the economy and objective nature. As we know, according to classical theory, production and distribution arranged through the behaviour of prices liberate us from direct dependence on the natural world. Moreover, the mediating process – the will to compete to satisfy our material needs – leaves us free to choose with whom to enter into relations of exchange and free to withdraw from these relations whenever we please. By contrast, the perspective of my fieldwork participants rests on the proposition that our dependence on nature is mediated by processes of production and distribution over which, as individuals, we have no control. For them, the idea of dependence rather than choice stands as the *a priori*.

Living in an urban environment, as an individual, I have no means of producing food to sustain myself or my family for a single day, let alone a year. I depend for my livelihood on the external sphere of production and services. We all, in fact, depend for food on farmers who in turn depend on fertilisers, tractors, and pesticides; bakeries depend on ovens and bread tins; schools and universities rely on desks, chairs, computers and paper. After deliberating with an artist friend who makes her own paper, we decided it would not be possible to make even a single sheet of paper independently of the sphere of production and distribution we call 'the economy'. One could, in principle, strip bark from a tree, pulp it with a stone and soak it in water. The problem is the pulp crumbles into many particles and has to be sieved before being dried out. It would, she thought, be possible to make a sieve out of horsehair if you or a neighbour owned a horse. But even then, it would take some time to acquire the skill to weave the hair and you would have to find some way of making a frame. Fortunately, there is an abundance of paper on the market and so our dependency is not something we feel or concern ourselves with.

However, this aggregate dependency that we do not experience as relevant to our lives is my fieldwork participants' point of departure. A central question exercising their minds is how to use a corporation's resources to gain control over a market and to ensure – let us take the case of a paper manufacturer – that every purchase of a paper product contributes to the profit of that same company.[2] Just as individuals depend on corporations, corporations in turn depend on one another. The following example shows how market dependency is integrated into the economic infrastructure.

Corporation X, listed on the New York stock exchange, employs over 900,000 people. It manufactures 50 products, most of which incorporate one of two raw materials. Along with another corporation, the company controls production and distribution of one of these raw materials – a metallic element. Now, the metallic element (which I cannot name because it would identify the company with whom I have signed a strict confidentiality agreement) is one component of a product manufactured by Company X that will be essential for the production of the next generation of computers. Because computers will not be able to be made without it, as computer manufacturers go into production, the demand for the component is virtually guaranteed. Thus, manufacturers' dependency on the component will create the potential for vast profit with minimum risk of loss.

The principle is not limited to manufacturing and extractive industries. Executives in charge of banks and other financial institutions also strive to expand their control over demand for financial services as a means of achieving profit. In the United States, for example, the massive reduction in the number of banking organisations since 1979 has been characterised by takeovers of existing banks as opposed to, for example, bank failures.[3] What is new here is not that some executives succeed in creating conditions in which demand can be controlled and the risk to profit radically reduced. What is new is the perception among many executives, credit analysts and investor groups that the underlying dynamic defining continuity in the economy has ceased to be competitive.

The primary function of credit rating agencies

For historical reasons yet to be fully understood, the task of transforming the underlying dynamic from a competitive to a non-competitive market system has fallen to the three U.S. based credit rating agencies, Moody's, Standard & Poor's and Fitch.[4] According to the standard view, agencies' role is limited to providing investors with information about the risk to a wide range of investment entities, including corporations, sovereign states, municipalities as well as the securities and securitisations they issue.[5] In terms of the perspective presented here, however, during the late 1970s, the primary function of credit analysts shifted from passively assessing the risk generated by competitive markets, to creating the conditions that make accurate measurement feasible. That is to say, since the late 1970s their more important task has been to mediate a transformation in the principles governing capital formation.

To grasp the scope of the enterprise it is necessary to bypass the agencies' method of assessing risk to securitisations, the usual focus of enquiry into the systemic importance of rating agencies, and begin instead with an analysis of the criteria used by credit analysts to establish equivalences from one corporation to another for comparative purposes.

First and foremost, ratings criteria distinguish between companies whose future earnings will be able to withstand unforeseen events on the one hand and, on the other, companies whose growth potential will, over time, be affected by changes in economic conditions. Using Standard & Poor's notation: Triple A, Double A, A, BBB, i.e. investment grade, represent a gradual decrease in the relative *known* risk to future earnings growth. Companies rated BB or below are considered speculative, or non-investment grade. To quote a senior credit analyst, 'Triple A is the safest investment with almost no chance of default. A Triple A is 5% risk – virtually risk free. We guarantee 95% risk free.'[6] We might ask, what factors permit some companies to withstand changes in future economic conditions and what is the basis of analysts' faith in their guarantee?

The significance of these questions lies in the economy's dependence on ratings produced by just three rating agencies. It is not broadly recognised that for corporations at least, financing in general depends on the quality of the overall corporate rating. The amount of debt executives can raise, the cost of the debt (the cost of risk to bond issues, for example) as well as which assets or pools of assets can be securitised, hinges on detailed assessment of the issuing company's anticipated profitability and the risks attached to these profits.[7]

To quote Frederick, a senior credit analyst, 'An "A" rating gives them [corporate executives] tremendous financial flexibility. They can attract all the capital they would need for investment purposes. If I want to acquire ten billion to finance buying another company, no problem at all, but below "A", availability may be compromised.' Jan explained further, 'Some companies can finance internally, [nevertheless] they want to know they have firepower behind them. If you do a pure cost analysis, debt is more effective.'

By focusing on the values underpinning analysts assessment of corporate viability, we can begin to make sense of the widespread confidence in the accuracy of their calculations which in turn explains why, to attract international capital, companies have no choice but to ask and pay for a rating.

If we listen to what credit analysts say to one another, as opposed to the official rhetoric, the ideal company at the summit of the evaluative hierarchy is the pure global player specialising in tightly related products or services. This is followed by more diversified global corporations with worldwide integrated strategies. Specialisation and grouping of products respectively are closely associated with a corporation's ability to control markets, a condition of predictive accuracy. Corporation X for example, rated investment grade, is a pure player with control over one of the many millions of products vital to the global economy. According to ratings criteria, executives in charge have succeeded in creating conditions in which future loss can be accurately predicted.[8]

Similarly, Goldman Sachs' investment grade rating (A, long term) denotes that its executives have demonstrated their capacity to achieve predictable profit. Regardless of economic sector, the evaluative criteria favour those companies in a position to secure profit through market control of products or services seen as key to the smooth functioning of the global economy.

The principle is clearly reflected in the strategic achievements of the three corporations with triple A status. Microsoft's success, according to Standard & Poor's, is a consequence of its market position in corporate OS software and its very high customer retention due to the fact that thousands of corporations are locked into Microsoft's technical architecture, making switching costs excessively high. Johnson and Johnson, the pharmaceutical company, controls the market for sutures.[9] And ExxonMobil is part of an oligopoly of five oil companies which, according to a report published by the U.S. General Accounting Office, manipulates prices by artificially controlling supply.[10] In April 2016, after 80 years of triple A status, ExxonMobil was downgraded to AA+ following a dramatic fall in the price of oil.[11]

Although criteria used to assess the relative strength of a company take into account the business cycle, the company's past performance, anticipated demand for its products, the risk entailed in its strategy and the capacity of executives to implement it, credit analysts themselves emphasise the importance of the last two factors as determinants of future risk, relative to other data. This is especially true for the largest companies whose activities determine risk for their sector or sectors. As Edward put it, 'A change in priorities for a major (corporation) changes business risk for the whole sector...they have a key role in defining international market conditions.'

Since investment capital is raised on the prediction, that is to say the rating, companies in a position to determine risk for their sector or sectors find it easier to finance their strategic pursuits: the higher the rating, the lower the cost of capital. An investment grade rating will lower the cost of bank loans on the one hand and, on the other, raise the price a company receives for new securities.

Viewed thus, ratings work to produce a dynamic hierarchy of corporations capable of generating known loss. From the analysis presented here, credit analysts' confidence in their predictive accuracy as well as their use of the term 'guarantee' is based on the quite reasonable assumption – affirmed by classical economic theory – that the major source of immeasurable risk is market competition, and the best way to reduce it is by strengthening the non-competitive market domain. As long as we continue to analyse the impact of ratings from the narrow perspective of individual companies, we lose sight of their aggregate effect: to ensure a steady flow of low cost capital into those companies for whom determinate probabilities relating to profit have already been established.

Determinate probabilities, then, find their material basis in the impetus towards market control. It is worth recalling that were agencies' criteria consistent with competitive principles, they would be directing low cost capital towards those companies best able to withstand competitive pressures. However, as a director of one of the major credit rating agencies put it to me, 'None of the normal markets wants risk.' In as far as the direction of international capital flow is determined by ratings, it follows that the price mechanism has lost its traditional allocative role of bringing in line supply and demand of global capital. In its place we find highly centralised, standard assessments determining the allocation of capital according to criteria based in well-defined values which, as we have seen, favour a non-competitive market system.

Explaining investor dependency on credit ratings

This analysis helps us to understand investors' dependency on ratings which, as we now know, survived the 2008 bank crisis without issue. It appears investors accepted agencies' explanation for their failure to accurately assess risk to sub-prime mortgages, which many argue precipitated the 2008 financial crisis and the world recession that followed. Agencies' position was that, at the time, no one knew the size and global reach of the sub-prime mortgage market. No one held these data in aggregate. For them, the sub-prime crisis counts, therefore, as a rare *external* event, and does not ultimately reflect their ability to accurately assess risk during 'normal times'.

Academics specialising in credit rating agencies (see, Darbellay, 2013; Longohr and Longohr, 2008; and Sinclair, 2005), as well as political bodies, (the U.S. House Committee on Financial Services, for example) hold investor dependency on ratings to be a consequence of the globalisation of financial markets, the increase in complexity of financial products, and the incorporation of ratings into laws and financial regulation.[12] An implicit yet powerful assumption underlying these explanations is that while investor dependency can be explained in terms of agencies' superior access to a wide range of comparative data, these data are, in principle, accessible to all market participants.

The conviction that market participants have equal access to data is crucial for the preservation of the free market ideal that achieves efficiency and equilibrium through the spontaneous interaction of many thousands of independent investment decisions. For this reason, following the 2008 bank crisis, academics argued for the elimination of ratings from laws and financial regulation which, they said, constrained investors' freedom to choose alternative investment strategies. This argument, however, confers a determination on regulatory bodies that is left unexplained. I will return to this point below.

The now generally accepted view that eliminating ratings from laws and financial regulation will restore investors' freedom, fails to take into account agencies' privileged position with regard to the world's largest corporations. As we have seen, analysts' capacity to calculate accurately future profitability and the risk attached to these profits, is contingent on access to corporate strategy. For the large, internationally oriented companies, however, strategy is a security issue and is not in the public domain.

The impasse is easily explained once we recall that Standard & Poor's, Moody's and Fitch have been rating bonds issued by major American corporations since the turn of the last century.[13] Bond ratings have always taken into account the overall corporate rating that requires assessment, over time, of executives' capacities to develop and implement viable strategy. These assessments are partially but crucially based on lengthy discussions with executives, who are called upon to justify their strategic decisions. On the basis of personal interaction, ratings agencies have, over the decades, established a reputation for trustworthiness with respect to the security of commercially and politically sensitive data.[14]

Exclusive access to the strategic priorities of the largest U.S. corporations, without which any international comparison would be invalid, goes a long way to explaining the power ratings exert over investors.[15] It also accounts for the willingness of foreign corporations' executives, looking to access international capital, to submit details of their strategic priorities to American agencies. To put this into the language of the non-competitive market model, close relations between credit analysts and American corporate executives permit the major rating agencies to control a vital commodity – that is, data – on which investors collectively depend.

In light of this, it comes as little surprise to find that following the banking crisis, investors rejected a proposal put forward by the United States Securities & Exchange Commission (SEC) to eliminate all references to ratings from its rules. Seventy-nine percent of all respondents favoured the continued use of ratings.[16]

To quote one respondent: 'The removal of such a benchmark would likely create confusion for investors who would face multiple opinions and decreased comparability of risk.' And from another respondent: 'Ratings establish a floor below which investment cannot be made.... Eliminate the floor and you eliminate investor protection.'[17]

The use of ratings, it should be emphasised, goes far beyond the SEC. Ratings are used to circumscribe the discretionary powers of money managers investing on behalf of fiduciaries including pension funds, mutual funds and insurance companies. I have yet to find a study elucidating the sheer range of financial institutions that permit fund managers to invest only in investment grade entities. I think I have said enough, however, to show that investor confidence in ratings is not easily dislodged and perhaps, as this analysis suggests, for good reason.

To return briefly to the argument that were ratings to be eliminated from laws and financial regulations this would significantly diminish the power of ratings over investors, leaving them free to make their own investment choices. If the source of ratings' power resides in their credibility, in investors' conviction that they accurately measure the cost of risk, then it is far more likely that the incorporation of ratings into SEC rules, the Basel Accords and other regulations *follows from* investors' confidence in credit ratings. A world where investors give positive value to measurable risk and reiterate that value in the certainty of their expectations is likely to develop activities and processes designed to eliminate uncertainty. The decision of regulatory bodies to incorporate ratings would have been a logical and rational response to investor trust in the capacity of agencies to do just this.

Competing indigenous perspectives

The fact that important elite groups act on non-competitive market principles and recognise their actions as such, enables us to distinguish between two groups of financial actors: a) those actors for whom the essential dynamic lies in the movement of international capital towards consolidation, stability and risk free profit, for whom the recent explosion of securities and securitisations is an important source of funding and liquidity that serves to fuel the expansionist aims of the strongest companies.[18] And b) those financial elites for whom the core dynamic is driven by competitive market exchange; for this group, international capital flows are determined by the price mechanism. Primary and secondary financial markets also contribute to capital formation – in this case, however, by spontaneously directing investment to companies best able to resist competitive pressures.

As we can see, in both the non-competitive and competitive conceptions of the market system there is a strict correspondence between the function of finance and what are perceived to be the real needs of the economy.

For those familiar with recent ethnographies of finance, it will be evident that criteria for selecting field sites and processing observations fall under the second set of premises whereby the market system is competitive. I examine below how the presupposition that market actors are responding primarily to the price mechanism can act as a negative heuristic, diverting attention from institutional processes that might otherwise throw this dominant paradigm into question.

As an exemplar, I have chosen Horacio Ortiz's article 'The limits of financial imagination: free investors, efficient markets and crises', published in *American Anthropologist* because, in contrast to other studies of financial institutions, Ortiz sets out to analyse concepts shaping our understanding of the organisation of the financial industry.[19] His ethnographic analysis of managers investing in credit derivatives for ACME, a major French investment management company, exposes the distance between the liberal ideal of financial markets, where individuals acting in open arenas invest money on their own account, and the markets' actual constitution where the overwhelming majority of financial trades are carried out not by owners of the money, but by employees of the investment institution acting on the owners' behalf.

Ortiz demonstrates how fund managers' maximising activity is circumscribed by strategies defined in relation to an assumption of market efficiency. He describes their method of calculating the price of risk to investment entities (according to standard formulae), and the various ways in which their calculations affect and are affected by supply and demand, and he places these activities in the context of competitive struggles between fund managers over investment funds, fees, salaries and bonuses.

In addition to providing rich institutional context, Ortiz analyses the discrepancy between the fund managers' concept of the 'efficient market' in which the law of supply and demand leads to an optimal allocation of credit, and its objective distribution, which serves to reinforce vast inequalities between debtor and creditor nations.

Notwithstanding Ortiz's commitment to contextualising individual fund managers' activities, he appears unaware that the way he conceptualises 'the context' is itself circumscribed by the presupposition that exchange between individual maximising agents is the economy's mode of integration and this institution's sole source of profit, objectively speaking.[20] We come to know in some detail the activities of a number of individuals, named, fund managers (Marie, Thierry, etc.), their relation to one another and to the various brokers with whom they trade. From the outset of Ortiz's study, the function of the investment institution is associated with the activities of these individuals.

The actual directors of ACME, that is to say, the people in charge of developing and implementing long-term strategy, escape both description and theoretical understanding. Instead, Ortiz commutes the directors, their function, their power and their subjectivity into an abstract ideal – ACME, the company's legal entity.[21]

The methodological problem is that Ortiz' totalising theory, that is, the ideas that for him define 'the context', does not allow for the possibility that people occupying different positions in the institutional structure may perceive the structure and function of the institution and their relationship to the economy differently. The presupposition that fund managers and their directors share the same totalising theory precludes this possibility.

It could well be the case that, had Ortiz been able to imagine an alternative set of premises, he would have found that the directors' views coincide with the views of the elites I studied. From their perspective, the investment activities of fund managers, although essential to the success of the business, are nevertheless a subset of a higher goal: to expand the quantity of capital that investment presupposes. From this standpoint, the ultimate source of profit does not reside in calculating risk to return on investment entities; it resides instead in directors' capacity to increase the quantity of capital handed over to them in the first place. The economic logic is far from opaque. A larger capital base generates more profit than a smaller one.

And it should not come as a surprise to find that for directors, autonomy and real creative intelligence are expressed not through calculating risk according to standard formulae, but through activity designed to expand the capital base. Fund managers, by contrast, fall into a category similar to that of factory workers whose tasks are heavily determined by processes that serve the higher goal of profit maximisation.

We have, of course, no way of knowing whether ACME's directors share this vision because Ortiz has relegated them to an abstract domain that stands in antithesis to the well-defined individual fund managers. In other words, Ortiz seems to have committed the old Hegelian error identified by Marx in 1844: that of implicitly commuting the directors – their power and their subjectivity – into an independent abstract entity, ACME, whose relation to individual fund managers is purely contractual.[22]

The same error underscores many ethnographies taken to represent the best of this new field. In studies by Zaloom (2006), Riles (2011), Maurer (2002), and Lepinay (2011), the weight of the dominant totalising framework is unrecognised as such. These studies unwittingly serve to affirm that competitive exchange between individuals and/or corporations regulated by supply and demand is the momentum through which capital moves and, moreover, that this mode of exchange carries a primary value for all participants. As I have shown, whether or not it can be demonstrated in some objective sense that competitive exchange defines the underlying dynamic, this dominant paradigm conceals the experience of capitalist elites who conceive of the global economy on the basis of market dependency and control and not that of market competition.

Notes

1 The first stage of fieldwork, 1999–2001, was funded by the then Department of Accounting & Finance, London School of Economics. Between 1999 and 2002, fieldwork focused on 13 corporations operating on three continents in five sectors: pharmaceuticals, extractive industries, manufacturing, high tech communications and, to a more limited extent, two international investment banks. All the companies are listed on the New York, London and, in one case, the Tokyo stock exchanges. Eleven are investment grade. Between 2002 and 2006, my focus shifted to two major U.S. based credit rating agencies. Between 2009 and 2010, I returned to discuss the banking crisis with two credit analysts and the chief economist of one of the agencies.

2 Since I do not have the alternative of producing my basic needs directly for myself, I have no choice but to enter into exchange with the external sphere of production and services. In an economy where my relationship to nature is mediated by companies competing to satisfy my needs, my freedom to withdraw demand from one producer or service provider in favour of another masks my antecedent dependency and fundamental lack of autonomy. In a non-competitive market economy, concentrations of economic power (otherwise impeded by competition) raze our freedom to withdraw demand, leaving companies in a position to take unfair advantage of our antecedent dependency if they so decide: what Milton Friedman called 'market coercion'.

3 See Forbes.com/sites/steveschaefer/2014/12/03/five-biggest-banks-trillion-jpmorgan-citi-banamerica/ # 2a39fae41d43

4 In 1998, the U.S.-based Fitch Ratings was acquired by Fimilac, a French holding company listed in Paris (though their headquarters remained in New York). In 2014, the U.S.-based Hearst corporation bought control of Fitch. As of November 2016, Fimilac retains 20 per cent of the company.

5 Probably the most sophisticated exposition of the history of credit rating agencies from the perspective of the dominant interpretive framework can be found in the entry 'Rating Agencies', *The Oxford Handbook of the Sociology of Finance* (Martha Poon, 2012). One task of this framework is to protect the idea that the function of ratings is limited to "producing and selling a type of information that plays an essential role in debt markets." It is this assumption that importantly establishes the exogenous viewpoint from which Poon's analysis of credit ratings and their history is made.

6 According to rating agencies' official position, each rating is merely an opinion about the credit worthiness of a borrower or debt instrument. This claim is backed by the U.S. courts, which afford agencies first amendment protection (see White, 2010). In the internal discourse of credit analysts, however, 'investment grade' means that all the determining circumstances that relate to profit have been identified and their prediction is, therefore, accurate and objective. This conviction is shared by many investors (see p. 221 of this chapter). The main point here is that investment choices are shaped by the collective conviction that ratings for investment grade entities are accurate and objective; note that this is not the official position of either the agencies or the courts.

7 See, for example, *Securitizations and the effect on credit quality*, report by Standard & Poor's (2005).

8 For a full analysis of the principles supporting the guarantee for predictive accuracy, see Ouroussoff (2010, Chapter 2).

9 So far only China has invoked anti-trust laws against Johnson & Johnson, The Shanghai People's Court held the corporation liable for enforcing vertical monopoly agreements on distributors of suture products. See F.B. Daniels LLP September 17th 2013, lexology.com.

10 *Effects of Mergers and Market Concentration in the U.S. Petroleum Industry*, United States General Accounting Office, May 2004.

11 S&P strips ExxonMobil of its coveted triple A rating. *The Financial Times*, 26 April 2016.

12 See also, Oversight of the credit rating agencies, post Dodd Frank. Hearing before the subcommittee oversight investigations of the committee on financial services, U.S. House of Representatives 112th congress first session, 27 July 2011 serial no. 112–51, page 5.

13 By the end of the 1920s, nearly all bond issues in the U.S. were rated by Moody's, Standard & Poor's or Fitch. See White (2010).

14 Concerned about the selective disclosure of material information by corporations and its adverse effect on market integrity, the United States Security and Exchange Commission brought in 'Regulation Fair Disclosure' (2000) prohibiting U.S. public companies from disclosing non-public information selectively (United States. Security and Exchange Commission: 17 CFR parts 240, 243 and 249 R in 3235-AH82). However, Section 100(b) (2)(iii) of the regulation allowed corporations to disclose non-public information to credit rating agencies for the purpose of determining or monitoring credit ratings, as long as the ratings were publically disclosed. Following the financial crisis in 2008, The Dodd-Frank Act (2010), removed this exemption (Section 939b). But since public companies are permitted to make selective disclosures to any person who agrees to keep the information confidential, the amendment can be by-passed by a simple confidentiality agreement (see U.S. Securities and Exchange Commission, Section 101. Rule 100: General rule regarding Selective disclosure June 4, 2010). This raises a question as to why regulators consent to non-public disclosure of information by corporations to credit rating agencies. One can speculate they are well aware of its importance to ratings accuracy and the financial interests of investors. I would further speculate that regulators are unlikely to be aware of the implications for capital formation. How they do, in fact, understand the economic implications of non-public disclosure of information is clearly a subject for further empirical research.

15 Even the largest financial institutions depend on ratings. It is worth recalling that following the 2008 financial crisis, Calpers, the world's largest pension fund with its own team of highly trained financial analysts, successfully sued all three rating agencies in connection with losses caused by agencies' failure to accurately assess risk to mortgage-backed securities.

16 See Baklanova (2009).

17 Notwithstanding the views of respondents, The Dodd Frank Act (2010) required the SEC to remove references to credit rating agencies from its regulations. But even a cursory look at rating agencies' annual reports shows this move did not affect profits.
18 The availability of an efficient secondary market for securities is one of the more important factors inducing investors to acquire new issues of securities.
19 See Ortiz (2014).
20 In Ortiz's perspective, any increase in the volume of funds follows from the quality of investment decisions made by individual investment managers. The driving principle is competition between investment companies at the level of investment practices.
21 In law, a company is an abstract legal entity or an 'artificial legal person' separate and distinct from its shareholders, directors and employees. When Ortiz writes, for example, 'Acme did nothing different than other economic actors', he is using the legal definition, standard practice among economists, sociologists and lawmakers.
22 For Hegel, the monarch is self-originating, grounded in the authority of God while directors are self-originating, grounded in the authority of the Law (Company Law). Thus, like Hegel's monarch, the personalities of the directors are abstract. They have no history, no material existence, and no content (Marx, 1975, p. 108).

References

Baklanova, V. (2009). Regulatory use of credit ratings: How it impacts on the behavior of market constituents. In J. J. Choi and M. G. Papaioannou (Eds.) *Credit, currency, or derivatives: Instruments of global financial stability or crisis?* (pp. 65–103). Bingley: Emerald Group Publishing Ltd.

Darbellay, A. (2013). *Regulating credit rating agencies*. Cheltenham: Edward Elgar Publications, Ltd.

Friedman, M. (1962). *Capitalism and freedom*. Chicago: The University of Chicago Press.

Hayek, F. A. (1979). *Law, legislation and liberty: A new statement of the liberal principles of justice and political economy*. London: Routledge & Kegan Paul.

Lépinay, V. (2011). *Codes of finance: Engineering derivatives in a global bank*. Princeton: Princeton University Press.

Longohr, H. and Longohr, P. (2008). *The ratings agencies and their credit ratings*. Chichester: Wiley.

Marx, K. (1975). Contribution to the critique of Hegel's Philosophy of law. In K. Marx and F. Engels, *Collected Works*, Volume 3. New York: International Publishers.

Maurer, B. (2002). Repressed futures: Financial derivative's theological unconscious. *Economy & Society*, 31(1), 15–36.

Ortiz, H. (2014). The limits of financial imagination: Free investors, efficient markets, and crisis. *American Anthropologist*, 116(1), 38–50.

Ouroussoff, A. (2010). *Wall Street at war: The secret struggle for the global economy*. Cambridge: Polity Press.

Poon. M. (2012). Rating agencies. In K. Knorr Cetina and A. Preda (Eds.) *The Oxford handbook of the sociology of finance*. Oxford: Oxford University Press.

Riles, A. (2011). Collateral expertise: Legal knowledge in the global financial markets. *Current Anthropology*, 51(6), 795–818.

Sinclair, T. (2005). *The new masters of capital: American bond rating agencies and the politics of creditworthiness*. Ithaca: Cornell University Press.

White, L. J. (2010). Markets: The credit rating agencies. *Journal of Economic* Perspectives, 24(2), 211–226.

Zaloom, C. (2006). *Out of the pits: Traders and technology from Chicago to London*. Chicago: Chicago University Press.

25

AT THE VERY HEART OF FINANCIAL DOMINANCE

The case of LBOs

Isabelle Chambost

The creation of the neologism 'financialization' symbolises the way in which current-day and so-called 'financial' capitalism acts as a system, subordinating different spans of society by imposing its normative referents and its balance of power, capturing the essential of created value and instituting mechanisms of financial annuities (Dumesnil and Levy, 2011). In his concretely apprehensive concern for this process, Dore (2002, pp. 116–117) has defined it as:

> the increasing dominance of the finance industry in the sum total of economic activity, of financial controllers in the management of corporation, of financial assets among total assets, of marketed securities […], of the stock market as a market for corporate control in determining corporate strategies, and of fluctuations in the stock market as a determinant of business cycles.

Thought provoking as it is, due to the continuum it introduces between the regulation of the economy by financial markets and the relevant impacts on companies' operations, this definition nevertheless struggles to specify the complex and contingent nature. The variety of capitalisms, the existence of different forms of mediation, of a micro-economic, political or institutional nature (Gospel and Pendleton, 2005), all make it difficult to identify the consequences specific to financialisation. Analysing this subject also implies grasping the junction points and interpenetration points figuring between two systems too often considered separately: the production sphere and the financial sphere.

We propose to analyse the way in which financial domination is divided into financial apparatuses (Foucault, 1980, p. 194), by studying in turn their discursive, material (network of financial, legal, remunerative and governance-based techniques) and political dimensions. We seek to define how these measures result from a progressive construction, attached to the diverse strata of power relations within this microcosm of finance (Benedetto-Meyer et al., 2011). Financial domination is indeed founded on the naturalisation and reification of finance – the markets – which contribute to its power and from which its anonymous character may be de-constructed. In order to do so, we have relied on the analysis of domination carried out by Metzger (2012, p. 24), based on the 'continuum' existing between 'those who do not have access to the creation of apparatuses', 'those who dispose of capacities for action that govern over the actions of others in the longest-lasting and furthest-reaching ways and who also have available well-thought-out practices permitting them to adapt their means for action', and those who 'interpret and conceive the apparatuses', the objectives of which have previously been decided. More broadly, this analysis offers as its aim to expose the way in which different relations of power become connected and, then, reinforcing their dominance (Bourdieu, 1990).

Our analysis will be based on companies acquired by private equity funds. Through analysing the support from governments and financial theorists, along with the strategies and power relations played out between the different professions involved – investors, lenders, analysts and representatives of legal and accounting professions – we will demonstrate how a system of apparatuses, particularly effective in its ability to align the operations of a company and those of its production system to a logic based on financial valuation, is indeed built.

Some empirical precisions

Within the context of an IRES (*Institut de Recherches Economiques et Sociales* – French Social and Economic Research Institute) study, this research, conducted in 2007 before the financial crisis, is based on 21 semi-structured interviews carried out with employees and trade unions representatives, all of whom were paid employees of companies acquired by private equity funds. At this time, acquisition operations by private equity funds were particularly well viewed and received very little criticism in relation to their economic and social consequences, except those put forth by 'The LBO Collective'.[1] Characterised by a huge tendency for debt, this period, which also boasted strong speculative intensity, recorded some of the most significant operations in both numbers and figures. This research equally called upon 12 interviews carried out between 2007 and 2013 with private equity fund managers, business lawyers and financial directors from targeted companies, as well as enlisting data from non-participant observations carried out during exchange days organised by professionals from this field and, finally, a longitudinal study, between three to seven years long, of documents (notably strategic plans, loan contracts and financial statements). This secondary analysis took place during the period following 2007, marked by debt renegotiations by funds notably in anticipation of 'the wall of debt', created by 2006 and 2007 acquisitions.

From the financial sphere to the production sphere: the characteristics of this dominance

The construction of economic legitimacy based on risk categorisation

From the so-called economy of debt (*'économie d'endettement'*), in which companies' share-ownership was marked by strong familial control, which concerned both SMBs and major companies, the French economy opened itself up during the 1980s to the financial markets, both progressively and essentially with regard to major companies. The 1990s were characterised by the government's disengagement from companies which had been nationalised in 1981, and by the forming of '*noyaux durs*' (core groups of shareholders) or 'cross-holdings' involving banks, insurance firms and industrial companies. At the end of this decade, with the objective of financing their growth and repositioning strategies, these major companies sold the cross-holdings they possessed on the stock market and undertook to 'refocus their core activities', leading to the divestment of 'non-strategic' activities. For the capital of major French companies listed on the stock market, this move facilitated the rise in importance of foreign investors, principally of Anglo-Saxon origin, who represented more than 40 per cent of several companies featured on the CAC 40 index at the end of the 1990s.

This transformation of French capitalism was rapid and brutal, moving from an 'economy based on a financial core'[2] to an 'economy based on a financial market' in which the investor was a major actor (Morin, 1998). It however overlooked numerous companies, such as in particular traditional small and medium-sized companies, and following the burst of the 'dot-com bubble', the entire grouping of SMBs, which were considered not attractive enough for either bankers or investors on the financial markets.

Within this context, private equity funds, which had appeared in the United States and reached Europe through the United Kingdom around the mid-1990s, began to develop further through the acquisition of SMBs seeking shareholders – in the case of business transmission for example – in addition to carrying out those activities deemed 'non-strategic' by the major groups. Despite the absence of official statistics, the figures issued from various professional organisations figuring at the national and European level show that between 2002 and 2007 France experienced an extremely rapid development of this type of financing, positioning the country in second place behind the UK (Bédu and Montalban, 2009).

Published a few months before the events of September 2008 and at a time when the banking sector sensed their eminent arrival, the report *Private equity et capitalisme français* (Private equity and French capitalism) by the *Conseil d'Analyse Économique* (Economic Analysis Council)[3] specified in its introduction (Glachant et al., 2008, pp. 9–10):

> The crisis of the financial markets will [...] provide [private equity] with a major role in the restructuring of the productive fabric of major developed economies [...]. Thousands of medium-size companies, which make up a large share of the productive framework of our country, today do not have any and tomorrow will have even fewer, financing sources other than those of private equity.

This conclusion refers to the analysis of the report '*Private equity and LBO*' by Gottschalg (2007), conducted for the European Parliament, which analysed the motivations governing the transfer of activities towards private equity funds. According to this report, the reasons put forth were divided between the fact that these activities no longer figured at the core of the profession (53 per cent), financial issues (26 per cent) and financing growth (21 per cent).

By its own name, their professional association, the '*Association Française des Investisseurs pour la Croissance*' (French Association for Investors in Growth), testified to their ability to underline their 'social utility'. Private equity funds were as such presented as funds capable of withstanding and managing any risks which might be linked to the nature of the productive project (size, innovation, etc.). In truth, the companies that they acquired were financially 'neglected' due to a composed categorisation of risk which was based on an estimation of their degree of liquidity. As analysed in the following, private equity funds put into place financial apparatuses which allowed for the transformation of a non-listed company into a 'liquid' investment, that is to say re-saleable for investors with strong capital gains prospects. To do this, risks are taken notably through resorting to heavy debt, which is potentially transferred to other investors, owing to the potential for debt securitisation for example, with the risks principally transferred over to employees.

Labour under financial influence

The rupture linked to the acquisition of a company by a private equity fund enables any impacts on work to be captured and identified (Chambost, 2013), notably corroborating the research of Sauviat (2002) and Brochard (2008), and which can be summarised as:

- A strong progression of productivity, leading to an overload of work and a clear degradation in the conditions of labour, provoking a permanent feeling of being understaffed;
- The increase in the reversibility of remuneration which has a tendency to strengthen individualism and a feeling of injustice when faced with the enlisted criteria, combined with a lack of recognition and profound misunderstandings;
- A loss of motivation and fear for the future.

According to the circumstances, the violence exerted is reproduced according to various registers. Directors will seek to break up work collectives constituted in order to establish bilateral relations with employees, operating according to registers of recognition *versus* guilt. Among employees, divisions are performed through the increased use of different statuses according to the value and the specificity of recognised skills. Among the most 'recognised' employees, the emphasis placed on the individualisation of remunerations and intensifying workloads provokes a competitive environment and reinforces individualism.

Presenting themselves as the saviours of the company and/or as financers capable of guaranteeing their development, private equity funds often establish from the outset power relations through the implementation of restructuring. This restructuring helps to reinforce the idea of previous economic failures and also the need for complete commitment from those employees not made redundant. Establishing a climate of uncertainty creates fertile ground for implementing a high-tension environment and situations of permanent 'destabilisation' (Spurk, 2012). This is fuelled by the want to maintain out of reach, any elements which enable the logics at work to be understood.

The rupture connected to the acquisition of the company by a private equity fund appears as it were equally involved in exercising the economic prerogatives of work councils and union representatives, in that which concerns both information-consultation and employee negotiations. The violence thus emerges in a more conflictual form. The simple fact of wanting to respect legally defined rights – using experts for example – becomes, in itself, a form of opposition. The continuum of situations is thus established between two cases. The 'better' one is a henceforth formal character of direction-employee representatives' relations. But this situation may be combined with a lack of willingness to negotiate and the implementation of strategies to bypass representatives by the company management, who seek to establish bilateral relations with its employees. And it can lead to a complete denial of legal rights until their hindrance (so called in France *'situation d'entrave'*[4]), allied with particularly violent confrontations.

The very clear focus on financial performances, in particular the famous EBITDA, is coupled with a problematic understanding of the system as a whole. Employee representatives collide with an apparent lack of clarity, an opacity that is as much spatial as it is temporal. Often distant from the decision-making centres, they encounter barriers to enter into contact with the relevant spokesperson, as well as face very rapid rotation of managers and the shortening of temporal horizons. The information communicated by directors remains delimited within the legal perimeter of the company, offering no persuasive evidence whatsoever on account of the financial arrangements carried out. The information on the purposes of reimbursing debt or of reselling the company is even often only obtained thanks to expert advice and/or legal actions in the courts.

The work council and the trade unions representatives face the circumventing of their rights about the employment conditions or wages bargaining. But their attempts to understand the financial system are even more violently quelled. This situation is representative of the subtle construction of a dominating system corresponding to a 'social field' within which various 'professional logics' clash (Benedetto-Meyer et al., 2011; Bourdieu 1990).

At the heart of the construction of financial measures: the playing field of the private equity finance industry

The private equity industry has developed thanks to favourable legislative, institutional and macro-economic contexts. It implicates and turns a profit for numerous actors thanks to the legal-financial arrangements at work by which high productivity can be guaranteed and all the risk transferred over to companies. This system of financialisation apparatuses is analysed, in the following, through their political, discursive and material dimensions.

The power relations between the initiators: the fund managers, the investors and the lenders (bankers)

Created at the beginning of the 1970s in the United States, the private equity industry was further developed in the US during the 1980s, thanks to fiscal and monetary measures implemented by the Reagan government. Figuring within the world of financial intermediation, the private equity industry belonged to the category of management practices labelled 'alternative', long considered to be minor activities, with regard to the more established professions such as portfolio managers responsible for securities listed on the financial markets. Geuens (2011) has provided a particularly heavily documented insight, to date, into this oligopoly and the relations existing between the private equity actors in this social field and the members of various governments, both American and European.

A quest for legitimacy for management practices qualified as 'alternative'

The qualification of 'alternative' refers to the disconnection of these management practices from the stock market indexes and their necessity to call upon low-cost debt, making their activity reliant upon interest rate levels. The institutional legitimacy of private equity dates back to 1979, a time in which the *Department of Labor* authorised US pension funds to invest in all types of investments (Montagne, 2006), including risky investments, on the grounds of the diversification principle. Even though they attracted the same categories of investors (as traditional asset management practices), private equity management nevertheless remained marked by its 'artisan' character, linked to the absence of modelling and its difficulty in being rolled out on a large scale. It therefore developed an entire rhetoric that targeted major funds collectors, such as pension funds or insurance firms, and was centred around its aptitude for freeing up profitability thanks to the control it exercised over the directors of those non-listed companies for which it held securities (Froud et al., 2008) (cf. the following).

The private equity industry is structured over two levels and analysing them provides information on the segmentation of existing authority figures, their games and their issues.

On the 'upper' level, relations are developed between those providing capital (limited partners) – institutional investors, but also wealthy private investors and foundations – and the funds' manager (general partners) who manage said capital – often former directors of industrial groups or commercial banks – and are part of private equity firms. On the 'lower' level, this private equity fund manager takes measures for investing the received capital, in the acquisitions and resales of companies in relation to the lenders (bankers).

The funds manager at the centre of power relations

The extent of the relationship between those providing capital and those providing their skills in management is defined by contract when the fund is first created, for a limited duration normally set at ten years. During the first five years the manager raises and invests capital which he gives back during the following five years, with the addition of any capital gains realised with the re-sale of companies. The capital is thus 'blocked' for five years, i.e. the holding duration of a company by the fund.

The power relations between fund managers and capital providers have given way to abundant financial literature, concerning the lack of 'transparency' that managers demonstrate in relation to their remuneration amounts and more broadly to the effective profitability of their investments (Cumming and Walz, 2010; FSA, 2006). As far as sharing in the accumulated profit, the manager's remuneration includes two components: first, fees related to the amount of capital being managed (2 per cent), and second, a part of the capital gains realised on the re-sale of companies (20 per cent), which is supposed to represent the higher amount, so that the interests of the manager are 'aligned' with those of the investors. Owing to an event in which capital raising may reach significant amounts, the first, less incentivising component can nevertheless be revealed as superior (Froud et al., 2008). In a different way, this literature testifies more broadly to the conflicts that occur in sharing the profits gained by this financial industry, notably through evading existing legislations.

In the United States private equity funds have developed to a global extent outside of the legislation controlling the activities of financial investors. Owing to their development at the end of the 1970s, private equity firms claimed they were not obliged to conform to the *Securities Act* (1933), as they do not intervene on the financial markets, and engaged in effective lobbying to ensure that they did not have to register as 'investment advisers' or conform to the *Investment Company Act* (1940) (Cheffins and Armour, 2008). It was not until the *Dodd-Frank Act* (2010) that certain exemptions related to information were eventually lifted. In France, the obligations in terms of public information remain very low. Furthermore, from the point of view of taxation, the remuneration of fund managers has always been considered as capital incomes instead of wages (which are always more taxed). And it's only recently that the tax deduction of interest expenses of the company loans has been restricted a little bit.

A fund managers/investors agreement based on expected profitability rates

The intended profit level to be freed up is the response to a rhetoric: the five-year block of the capital from the limited partners must find a financial compensation. It is thus 'expected' or required, that annual profitability rates will be around 20 to 25 per cent. From the investors' perspective, it is of course normal to request profitability superior to that likely to be obtained on the financial markets due to the relative 'illiquidity' of investments in private equity funds. From the perspective of private equity firms, these rates are likely to be achieved due to the control enacted over acquired companies, control that is academically channelled by the famous normative text by Jensen, the father of agency theory, in *The Eclipse of the Public Corporation* (1989). Within this text he advocates for more active involvement from shareholders and puts forth how the use of debt as well as remuneration expressed through objectives of shareholder value creation (or incentives), can act like disciplinary tools. In a more pragmatic way, the use of financial engineering techniques founded on sizeable debt and combined with fiscal optimisation techniques helps to 'mechanically' raise shareholder profitability, especially during low-interest rate periods.

A fund managers'/lenders' agreement: based on the securitisation of risks related to the non-payment of loans

During company acquisitions, fund managers thus minimise the capital really provided (to around 20 to 30 per cent of the company's value), seeking instead to maximise the sums borrowed. Considering their sizeable weight, these sums are spread across various loan categories which are characterised by the degree of risk involved – taking into account the conditions of repayment – and the associated conditions for remuneration. For debts considered high-risk, the required interest rate level allows for remuneration that is largely superior to the nominal amount of the debt. This debt used to be managed, at least up until the crises, by French banking departments specifically dedicated to this industry, and was subject to significant securitisation.

More broadly, when they are not participating per se as departments within investment banks, private equity firms call upon the diverse advisory professions fulfilled by these banks – or their subsidiaries – in order to control and reduce the risks incurred. Thanks to their primary activity (commercial bank, financial analyst, client relations for commercial banks), banks are indeed liable to spot potential business opportunities and to set about evaluating them. For these activities, remunerations can represent from 5 to 6 per cent of the sums at stake (Fenn et al., 1995). For the smallest firms, the plan involves more accounting professions that are more specialised in medium-sized businesses such as expert accounting and auditing firms, as well as tax consultants and business lawyers. The development of the presence of lawyers, positioned 'at the intersection between different components of the powerful elite' (Vauchez, 2012), is therefore representative of the training strategies implemented by lenders and directors in the framework of their relations with fund managers.

Financial measures working towards the financial liquidity of the production process

Given the low sums provided in capital by private equity funds, the arrangements enacted lead to a situation in which the company must itself pay for its own acquisition through the repayment of debts entered into. In order to evade the relevant criminal bans,[5] debts are not directly shouldered by the target company and therefore do not appear on the financial statements of the company housing the production process. The target company is held through a stream of holding companies, consigned to shoulder various portions of the debt according to their degree of risk and also to arrange for those profits raised in the form of dividends to avoid being taxed.

A management practice centred on financial indicators

During the years in which the company is held by the private equity fund, it is managed in line with the repayment of debts, according to the monitoring of quarterly-defined indicators, with the minimum amounts to be paid written into the loan contracts. These indicators (or covenants) are centred on the capacity for generating cash, calculated through the famous EBITDA, enabling recurring interest and debt repayments to be covered. Not attaining these indicators may lead to the possibility of lenders demanding the immediate repayment of debts, thus causing a reversal of power, with the shareholder, in our case the fund manager, being ousted in favour of the lender. In order to anticipate and guard against any potential difficulties, fund managers configure the relations they establish with the director to their own advantage, and if need be delegate advisers responsible for 'backing up' this individual.

The basis for the fund manager's power over directors

The resale value of the target-company becomes an objective from the moment it is acquired by a private equity fund. The company's value is commonly defined as the combination of a multiple – varying according to external economic criteria – and an indicator of economic profitability. From the moment of acquisition, the shareholder-fund manager and the (future) shareholder-director set the targeted amount for this indicator come the end of a five-year period, on the basis of a business plan to be implemented, which is divided into financial and accounting objectives for each quarter.

This way, the private equity fund manager is guaranteed to have the shareholder-director's full commitment to this process, and furthermore that of the entire directional team. Attaining these performance objectives determines whether or not the shareholder-director's position is maintained within the company and impacts upon his remuneration. The commitments are legally sealed by a 'shareholder pact', a contract susceptible to be instantly broken in the case of the objectives not being attained. If this should occur, then the director receives his 'thanks'. He loses not only his position but also the capital that he had invested, at times quite substantial in comparison to his personal income, as well as the hope of touching any of the very sizeable profits. It is as such interesting to observe the existence of training processes that steer towards modifying ever so slightly the balance of power relations when directors adopt financial measures working, with this appropriation, toward reinforcing financial dominance (Barneto and Chambost, 2014).

The total abstraction of the company's forms of production and a spotlight on its resale

For the fund manager, the company boils down to a 'model' drawn up on a spreadsheet, integrating the business plan of the director and the financing conditions. One of his principle skills consists of getting the model 'to turn', in order to determine a price range according to accounting, fiscal and financial hypotheses, by visualising the projected flows over the five years in which he holds the company. The valuation fully configures the company's operation – over a horizon limited to five-years holding by the fund – according to the scheduled attainment of these specific performance objectives (Chambost, 2013).

The company must as such generate results according to the quarterly rhythm imposed upon it, by reducing/adapting to the costs (resorting to precarious contracts, externalising and subcontracting, etc.), by accelerating incomings and limiting outgoings, in order that these funds be paid in the form of dividends to holding companies responsible for repaying various loans. The investments, both tangible and intangible, are extremely limited. Assets considered to fall 'outside the core of the profession' are sold off and external growth, through the acquisition of other companies likely to provide very rapid EBITDA growth, is implemented, even if disastrous mid-term effects are revealed to be possible.

It is thus expected that the company's resale price, multiplied thus by this indicator, enables part of the debt to be repaid all while guaranteeing substantial capital gains. These gains are so well guaranteed that company resales can take part during a speculative bubble and lead to the installation of a second LBO by the new acquiring party. Intrinsically, this industry therefore operates via speculative cycles, supported by low-interest rates and an abundance of liquid assets.

Conclusion

Starting with the emblematic case study of companies acquired by private equity funds, this chapter has sought to analyse the modalities behind the construction of financial apparatuses, according to their nature (rhetorical, political and material), and connecting them to diverse professional logics. The aim thus being to analyse the domination at work thanks to the analysis of the continuum existing between those who do not have access to the creation of apparatuses, those who dispose of capacities for action that govern over the actions of others and those who interpret and conceive the apparatuses revealing the division of financial labour at work while also situating the respective power/relations. The financial apparatuses can be distinguished according to their capacity of working towards 'liquidity' for the company in the way they perfectly match with its productive process which they spell out and prescribe its future, across a horizon that is dramatically restricted. It is therefore important to underline the oppositions between fund managers and directors that ultimately work towards reinforcing financial domination. The company director's appropriation of the operations of financial apparatuses only reinforces the power maintained by them.

Concerning this latter point it is interesting to analyse the consequences of the crisis that arose in 2007, in the midst of a speculative cycle. This crisis led to the acquisition of companies by private equity funds at excessively high prices and through resorting to equally sizeable debts. This 'wall of debt' led to compromises – loan renegotiations with lenders and capital injections by the private equity funds – in addition to shifts in power on behalf of lenders and to the rise in capital for some of them. Despite very few fiscal modifications, the foundations of this financial industry nevertheless do not seem to have been, to date, particularly impacted.

Notes

1 The collective group was created in 2006 by unionists of the *Caisse des dépôts et consignations* (CDC), a famous financial state institution, and employees of a company that the CDC owned through a LBO. They were joinded by economists, sociologists, statisticians, lawyers, judges, etc.
2 Based on crossed intra and inter-group shareholdings and on close relationships between banks and industry.
3 This Council, reporting to the French prime minister, delivers economic analyses for the government and makes them publicly available.
4 Under French law this situation is a criminal offence.
5 According to the French commercial code a company can't buy itself.

References

Barneto, P. and Chambost, I. (2014). L'appropriation par les dirigeants des dispositifs financiers : une étude exploratoire de la relation dirigeants-investisseurs. *La Revue du Financier*, 206, 4–25.

Bédu, N. and Montalban, M. (2009). Une analyse de la diversité géographique des opérations de *private equity* en Europe : le rôle des configurations institutionnelles. In C. Dupuy and S. Lavigne (Eds.), *Géographie de la finance mondialisée* (pp. 111–124). Paris: La Documentation Française.

Benedetto-Meyer, M., Maugeri, S. and Metzger, J.-L. (2011). Introduction. In M. Benedetto-Meyer, S. Maugeri and J.-L. Metzger (Eds.), *L'emprise de la gestion : la société au risque des violences gestionnaires* (pp. 11–39). Paris: L'Harmattan.

Bourdieu, P. (1990). *The logic of practice.* Cambridge: Polity Press.

Brochard, D. (2008). Logiques de gestion du travail, environnements conventionnel et concurrentiel : des politiques de rémunération sous influences. In T. Amossé, C. Blonch-London, and L. Wolff (Eds.), *Les relations sociales en entreprise* (pp. 376–398). Paris: La Découverte.

Chambost, I. (2013). De la finance au travail: sur les traces des dispositifs de financiarisation. *La Nouvelle Revue du travail*, 3. Retrieved from http://nrt.revues.org/1012

Cheffins, B. and Armour, J. (2008). The eclipse of private equity. *Delaware Journal of Corporate Law*, 33(1), 1–67.

Cumming, D. and Walz, U. (2010). Private equity returns and disclosure around the world. *Journal of International Business Studies*, 41(4), 727–754.

Dore, R. (2002). Stock market capitalism and its diffusion. *New Political Economy*, 7(1), pp. 115–121.

Dumesnil, G. and Levy, D. (2011). *The crisis of neoliberalism.* Cambridge: Harvard University Press.

Fenn, G., Liang, N. and Prowse, S. (1995). *The economics of private equity markets.* Staff study #168, Washington, Board of Governors of the Federal Reserve System.

Foucault, M. (1980). The confession of the flesh. In *Power/Knowledge: Selected Interviews and Other Writings* (pp. 194–228). New York: Pantheon Books.

Froud, J., Sukhdev, J., Leaver, A. and Williams, K. (2008). *Ownership matters: private equity and the political division of ownership.* CRESC *working paper*, n°61.

FSA (Financial Services Authority) (2006). *Private equity: A discussion of risk and regulatory engagement.* Discussion paper, November.

Geuens, G. (2011). *La finance imaginaire. Anatomie du capitalisme : des « marchés financiers » à l'oligarchie.* Bruxelles: Aden.

Glachant, J., Lorenzi, J.-H. and Trainar P. (2008). *Private equity et capitalisme français.* Paris: La Documentation Française.

Gospel, H. and Pendleton, A. (2005). Corporate governance and labour management: An international comparison. In H. Gospel, H. and A. Pendleton (Eds.), *Corporate governance and labour management* (pp. 59–83). Oxford: Oxford Press University.

Gottschalg, O. (2007). *Private equity and LBO*, Policy department economic and scientific policy. European Parliament, November.

Jensen, M. C. (1989). Eclipse of the public corporation. *Harvard Business Review*, 67(5), 61–74.

Metzger, J.-L. (2012). Le changement perpétuel au cœur des rapports de domination. *SociologieS.* Retrieved from http://sociologies.revues.org/3942

Montagne, S. (2006). *Les fonds de pension entre protection sociale et spéculation financière.* Paris: Odile Jacob.

Morin F. (1998). *Le modèle français de détention et de gestion du capital. Analyse, prospective et comparaisons internationales. Rapport pour le Conseil Analyse Economique.* Paris: Les éditions de Bercy.

Sauviat C. (2002). Nouveau pouvoir financier et modèle d'entreprise: une source de fragilité systémique. *Revue de l'IRES*, 40, 39–72.

Spurk, J. (2012). Le consentement fatal: pouvoir et domination aujourd'hui. *SociologieS.* Retrieved from http://sociologies.revues.org/4248

Vauchez, A. (2012). L'avocat d'affaires: un professionnel de la classe dirigeante? *Savoir Agir*, 19, 39–48.

26

THE INTERNATIONALIZATION OF THE MUTUAL FUND SECTOR AND THE ORIGIN OF THE FINANCIALIZATION

A historical process of production rules

Caroline Granier

The financialization process has been facilitated by the internationalization of the asset management sector. This sector is organized around companies administratively and financially promoting and/or managing the portfolios of institutional investors (mutual funds, pension funds, insurance companies, sovereign wealth funds, hedge funds). These management companies operate as independent companies or as subsidiaries of banking or insurance or other financial services groups. Other actors, such as custodians/depositaries and distributors, are in charge respectively of the safekeeping of portfolio assets and of selling funds' shares. Management companies are today characterized by their ability to invest money collected from everywhere in every part of the real economy and by their location in the globalized network of financial centres. This geographical expansion of the asset management industry can be viewed as one of the sources of the domination of finance and it has been the result of an historical process of production and adaptation of rules.

In this chapter, we focus on the expansion of the mutual funds (or open-ended funds) industry. The main characteristic of these funds is their liquidity in that their shares can be bought and redeemed at any time. The principles of fund governance established by the 1940 US regulation and its subsequent amendments have been adapted in European countries since the 1940s. While there are still institutional differences between countries, the fund management sector organized around this common set of rules has been becoming globalized under the leadership of the European directives called UCITS (Undertakings for Collective Investment in Transferable Securities). In fact, directives facilitate the selling of funds in several countries and the international division of labour within and beyond the European frontiers. The principles of fund governance have been finally transmitted to companies in the real economy. Then while the US regulation was enacted to avoid financial companies from having too much control on the real economy after the 1929 crisis, in the end, it has led to the domination of finance over the real economy. The expansionist dimension of the financial sector that we describe in this chapter can be seen as a part of the more general process of capitalism expansion underlined by Harvey (1982). It is also the consequence of the on-going search for liquidity by financial actors (Corpataux et al., 2009).

The first section is dedicated to the description of the US regulation of mutual funds. In fact, it could be seen as the model for both the design of the fund sector and the design of what is now known as corporate governance principles. The second section describes the process of adaptation of the fund governance and practices in Europe. It also shows how the directives aiming at building the single market have created a globalized fund market. The third section evaluates the consequences of UCITS directives for the location of funds' activities and for the competition between financial centres. The fourth section concludes by underlining what is at stake for the fund management sector with the Brexit vote.

The principles of fund governance: the origin of corporate governance principles

The activity of promoting and managing mutual funds is regulated in the United States by the Investment Company Act (ICA) of 1940. It was enacted after the abuses encountered in the closed-end fund (fund with non-liquid or non-redeemable shares) sector that contributed to the 1929 crash. The 1940 Act and its subsequent amendments have defined fund governance principles and practices such as transparency, independence of monitoring agents (directors), protection of shareholders' rights (such as the 'one share-one vote' rule), the focus on the core business and the outsourcing of the other activities. These rules have contributed to the design of the well-known corporate governance principles and practices that characterize the current financialization period.

The transparency principle was common to all the regulations in the stock markets after 1929 (i.e. the 1933 Securities Act and the 1934 Securities Exchange Act). The ICA forced fund promoters to disclose information about the organization, the portfolio and the net asset value (i.e. the price) of the funds in a document called a prospectus. The transparency principle was associated to the fact that savers were considered as autonomous and full investors: they were able to read and understand the information written in the prospectus and consequently they could choose (and were responsible) which funds they wanted to invest in. Besides, they were endowed with voting rights that were equivalent among investors. Concerning the investments, the 1936 Internal Revenue Code was modified in order for diversified funds not to be taxed (Roe, 1991): the US fiscal policy has promoted the diversification rule.

The delegation of financial management existed before 1940. In fact, any person could become a fund promoter but because some of them did not have the knowledge of the financial markets, they delegated the portfolio management to other entities (called investment advisors) with the appropriate ability (Senn, 1958). The ICA did not question this behaviour but to limit the number of fund promoters, the ICA introduced a minimum threshold of equity for funds. In addition to the ICA, the 1940 Investment Advisers Act required fund managers to be registered with the Securities and Exchange Commission (SEC). In accordance with the 1933 Glass-Steagall Act, banks could not become advisers.

The distribution of funds' shares to the savers was through an underwriter who can sell the shares to the savers or be a kind of wholesale seller to security dealers (Faffa, 1963). The administrative tasks (or back-office tasks) such as the fund accountancy, the writing of reports and prospectus can be delegated to a party who acts as administrator. A dedicated party called a custodian is in charge of the safekeeping of the shares; in this way, the assets of the different stakeholders in the fund activity are separated. This functional segmentation has favoured a logic of delegation and henceforth the focus on core business and the outsourcing behaviour.

The monitoring of fund manager behaviour was given to the board of directors or to the trustees (if the fund is constituted either under the corporation status or the trust status), at least 40 per cent of whom were not affiliated to the advisers or the distributors. As defined by the 1940 Act, affiliated people were people who belonged to the same family as the adviser or a holder of at least 5 per cent of the capital of the adviser; the 1970 amendment enlarged this definition to persons who were partners, shareholders of the adviser company or members of the adviser company, and raised the threshold of independent members to 75 per cent. The audit committee of the fund was also characterized by this principle of independence. The 1970 amendment also introduced a due care constraint and a fiduciary duty to the adviser.

Finally, since the ICA, mutual fund governance has been characterized by a duality of functions that has become the golden rule over the financialization period: management on the one side, independent monitoring on the other side. According to Jeffers and Plihon (2001) and Montagne (2001 and 2006), the form taken by current corporate governance comes from the governance of pension funds and the constraints associated to the trust status. But as Montagne (2001) underlines, the activity of pension funds over the globalization period has been increasingly characterized by the delegation of portfolio management to management companies that also manage mutual funds. Rules governing mutual funds have been transmitted to pension funds and finally to companies. This transfer of rules has been facilitated by the two legal forms taken by the US mutual funds, the trust (i.e. the most common form of pension fund) and the corporation (i.e. the representative entity of the financialization period), and by the influence of agency theory in corporate governance. It is worth noting that Jensen who is one of the main contributors to the agency theory defended a PhD dissertation about the performance of mutual funds.

The process of adaptation of fund governance in Europe

Open-ended funds were introduced in the 1930s in Great Britain and Switzerland and after WWII in Germany, France and Belgium (Senn, 1958).[1] The typifying form of the continental model was the contract, although the corporate form was also developed in some countries such as France. As funds organized contractually were not legal entities, they were necessarily dependent on a management company that actually had a legal form. Most of them were banks or subsidiaries of banks. This contractual form gave the monitoring function to actors called depositaries that had to be legally distinct from management companies. But they could belong to the same financial group as the management companies; in other words, the independence rule for the monitoring function in force in US did not really apply. Depositaries also had the role of custodian. Finally, funds' shares were mostly distributed through the already constituted network of bank branches. Consequently, the fund activities in continental Europe were mainly organized around the model of universal banking. Open-ended funds constituted a way for banks to find a new source of income and to diversify their activities, while collecting more savings in the framework of a universal banking system.

In most countries, a national regulation of fund activity has followed the creation of the first open-ended funds and some countries such as Luxemburg and Germany have begun to set up a favourable status (i.e. the holding status in Luxemburg) and rules (lower restrictions by the 1969 Foreign Investment Law in Germany) in order to attract foreign promoters. But the enlargement of the fund market in Europe was really facilitated by the construction of the single financial market. The single market aimed at allowing all financial actors (banks, insurance companies, UCITS, investment services firms) to operate in a harmonized legal and regulatory framework and in a competitive environment in order to decrease operational requirements and costs for companies seeking to expand their activities. This harmonization relies on existing regulation in the European countries.

Concerning the fund market, the first UCITS directive was enacted in 1985 and offered a passport to open-ended funds domiciled in European countries, i.e. the possibility to be sold in any European country if they respected common rules about transparency, organization and savers' rights.

The 1985 directive allowed the standardization of a prospectus by editing an important number of disclosure rules. The 2001 directive simplified these rules and recommended the disclosure of: a short presentation of the fund, its objective, its strategy in terms of risk, its past performances, fees and commissions, distribution details, contact for receiving additional information. The 2009 directive goes further in this process of simplification by introducing a standard format for the prospectus (i.e. any prospectus can be read in the same way, graphs and scales are used to facilitate the reading of risk and performances). In other words, information is now codified for savers to be autonomous and full investors. Their rights as investors are protected through the investment policy afforded by the directives and the development of voting policy disclosure. To guarantee the possibility for savers to buy and sell shares at any time, the 1985 directive only authorizes investments in the most liquid shares, i.e stocks and bonds. In 2001, the range of possible investments was enlarged to derivatives and monetary markets' shares. Besides, the 2010 execution directive that is associated to the 2009 UCITS has encouraged management companies to establish shareholding voting right policies and to disclose them to their savers.

According to the 1985 directive, the funds had to be managed by a company that did not offer any individualized portfolio management services, i.e. a company with a dedicated funds management structure in charge of the administrative and financial management of funds. The individualized services were instead regulated by the 1993 Investment Services Directive and then by the 2004 MiFID (Markets in Financial Instruments Directive). The 2001 UCITS III directive loosened this constraint by recognizing the possibility for UCITS management companies to undertake individualized portfolio management services as well. It also recognized the separation of the administrative and financial functions and regulated the delegation of these functions to a third party. In other words, the directive facilitated the focus on core capabilities of companies (either the administrative or the portfolio management function) and the outsourcing of the other functions.

In accordance with the previous rules in force in most European countries, the behaviour of the management companies is monitored by depositaries. Until the 2014 UCITS V directive, the monitoring by depositaries varied according to the legal form of the fund (contract or corporation). Among their monitoring functions, depositaries have to control the price calculation and the compliance with the investment restrictions. This activity has remained mostly in the scope of banking groups all the more so as the 2014 directive restricts this activity to national central banks, credit institutions and legal entities authorized to provide depositary activities and subject to prudential supervision and CRR/CRD IV (Capital Requirements Regulation and Directive) capital adequacy requirements. Among the two functions that can be exercised by depositories, only the activity of safekeeping can be delegated to another entity.

The 2014 directive introduces some constraints on variable remuneration of fund managers and some incentives to align the interests of portfolio managers with those of savers. More specifically, the variable remuneration has to be composed of shares of UCITS actually managed by the company. In other words, the fund governance is also influenced by the governance rules applied to companies, since this incentive rule looks like the stock options plans granted to corporate managers. Such a rule does not exist in the US.

The construction of the financial single market: the globalization of the savings market and the issue of location

UCITS is nowadays recognized as a 'global brand' and as a global standard of investors' protection. It is currently possible to sell shares of UCITS not only within but also beyond European borders. Lipper FMI lists at least 60 countries in the world. Nonetheless, one country is difficult to penetrate: the US. In fact US regulation has acted as a barrier to the penetration of European managers in the US by imposing additional administrative constraints with the 2010 Dodd-Franck Act. Consequently, European promoters can only easily sell their funds to a particular group of US investors, the tax-exempt investors that are mainly institutional investors (Christian, 2012).

While it is difficult to enter into the US market, the EU directives have allowed US promoters to find a new source of income whereas their funds domiciled in the US were characterized over the 1997–2007 period by a decrease of their attractiveness to American savers (Ferreira et al., 2014). In fact, the increase of their size has led to a decrease of their performance. Henceforth US promoters take advantage of the UCITS market and nowadays they appear to be among the main promoters of UCITS funds sold in several countries in Europe and the world (Cumming et al., 2013).

The European directives have led not only to a global standard of rules but also to a hardening of the competition between financial centres. Historically, financial activities tied to stock markets have been concentrated in few cities (i.e. financial centres) whereas banking services were more dispersed. Financial centres are associated to geopolitical interests: for a state, the higher the ranking of its financial centre, the higher its recognized financial power (Capelle-Blancard and Tadjeddine, 2007). In addition, financial activities offer advantages for a city such as higher paying jobs, tax revenues and economic growth. Then the attractiveness of fund activity is of great interest for European financial centres.

To sell their funds to European investors, management companies must have a subsidiary or a branch located in the EU. But their country of establishment can be different from the country of the fund domiciliation. Before the 2009 directive, management companies had to have the main administrative activities located in the country of fund domiciliation. The 2009 UCITS directive offers all fund managers a passport, i.e. the possibility of centralizing their management activities in one particular location. In other words, it is now possible for management companies that promote funds domiciled in Luxemburg to delegate the administrative management to an entity localized in Luxemburg while they are located in GB. Besides, by establishing a framework for the delegation of the financial management of the fund's portfolio, the 2001 directive has favoured the separation between the country of the management company and the country of the delegated management company. According to the nationality of fund promoters and/or the investment policy of the funds, the portfolio management can be located in any city in the world; for example, a UCITS fund investing mainly in the US is more likely to be managed from the US, in order to take advantage of the geographical proximity between managers and companies (cf. the literature of the home bias behaviour of fund managers). French promoters have more incentives to manage UCITS funds from France if they want to profit from economies of scale thanks to their other range of funds. This centralization process is also facilitated by the possibility given by the 2009 directive to merger funds and to create master-feeder structures.

Nonetheless, the responsibility of the overall activity is that of the management company that delegates activity. The monitoring function is the only function that does not (yet?) have a passport: the depositary still has to be located in the same Member State as the UCITS (country of domiciliation).

Finally, we assist the achievement of an international division of labour between centres in the world. Luxemburg, Dublin and Paris are the main places of domiciliation of UCITS funds. The first two cities constitute the main hubs for cross-border funds, i.e. funds sold in several countries. Consequently people dedicated to administrative and monitoring functions are localized in these centres. The financial management is more dispersed and could be located in the main financial centres: London, Paris, Frankfurt but also New York and Tokyo. It is actually possible for a French management company to promote funds domiciled in Luxemburg or Ireland, to delegate a part of the management of the fund portfolio to an entity located in London and to sell them in France and in Asia. Nonetheless, this international division of labour is counterbalanced by some local resistance such as the behaviour of home-institution bias from households (McQueen and Stenkrona, 2012), i.e. the preference for domestic institutions.

Concluding remarks

The internationalization of the mutual fund sector is characterized not only by the cross-border flows of money but also by the globalized market for savings' collection and the network operations around the financial centres. It has been a result of a historical process of production rules. Financial firms today are characterized by outsourcing, geographical expansion and organization around networks, just like any other companies. The same governance rules apply to companies in the real economy. Consequently the internationalization of the financial industry can be viewed as one of the sources of the domination of finance and now it goes hand in hand with the financialization process.

Besides the increased competition in the fund market resulting from the construction of the single market, there is also the issue of the competition between financial centres. The attractiveness of financial activities is considered as key strategy for economic growth and for the affirmation of the power of states in the world. The Brexit vote leaves open the question of the future of the City that is currently one of the main locations chosen, along with Paris, for fund financial management.

For UK asset managers, Brexit could lead to a decrease in the demand for their funds from foreign investors,[2] as they would no longer allow to access to the European market and the associated fund protection. Nonetheless, this decrease could be counterbalanced by the fact that some UK management companies already offer funds from one of the European offshore centres. Their strategy would be close to the one followed by US managers. For foreign management companies that have chosen to be located in London in order to take advantage of the European market, Brexit could lead them to set up more funds in other European countries and to move their branches out of the UK.

Notes

1 But closed-end funds had existed in Great Britain since the nineteenth century.
2 See *Financial Times* website, 3 July 2016, Newlands C., Marriage M. and Mooney A. 'Brexit: asset managers retreat from the City of London', https://www.ft.com/content/080f6a48-3fa0-11e6-9f2c-36b487ebd80a, and 20 July 2016, Marriage M. and Newlands C. 'Asset managers assess impact of Brexit', https://www.ft.com/content/bd2f8996-4e8a-11e6-8172-e39ecd3b86fc.

References

Capelle-Blancard, G. and Tadjeddine, Y. (2007). Les places financières: désintégration, suburbanisation et spécialisation. *Revue d'Economie Financière*, 90(4), 93–115.

Christian C. D. (2012). Offering UCITS to US institutional investors: A post Dodd-Frank overview. *The Investment Lawyer*, 19(8), 3–14.

Corpataux, J., Crevoisier, O. and Theurillat, T. (2009). The expansion of the finance industry and its impact on the economy: A territorial approach based on Swiss pension funds. *Economic Geography*, 85(3), 313–334.

Cumming, D., Imad'Eddine, G. and Schwienbacher, A. (2013). Harmonized regulatory standards, international distribution of investment funds and the recent financial crisis. In R. Cressy, D. Cumming, and C. Mallin (Eds.) *Entrepreneurship, finance, governance and ethics* (pp. 175–211). Dordrecht: Springer.

Faffa, J. (1963). *Les sociétés d'investissement et la gestion collective de l'épargne*. Paris: Editions Cujas.

Ferreira, M. A., Keswani, A., Miguel, A. F. and Ramos, S. B. (2014). The determinants of mutual fund performance: A cross-country study. *Review of Finance*, 18(2), 561–590.

Harvey, D. (1982). *The limits to capital*. Chicago: University of Chicago Press.

Jeffers, E. and Plihon, D. (2001). Investisseurs institutionnels et gouvernance des entreprises. *Revue d'Economie Financière*, 63(3), 137–152.

McQueen G. and Stenkrona A. (2012). The home-institution bias. *Journal of Banking & Finance*, 36(6), 1627–1638.

Montagne, S. (2001). De la 'pension governance' à la 'corporate governance': la transmission d'un mode de gouvernement. *Revue d'Economie Financière*, 63(3), 53–65.

Montagne, S. (2006). *Les fonds de pension: entre protection sociale et spéculation financière*. Paris: Odile Jacob.

Roe, M. (1991). Political elements in the creation of a mutual fund industry. *University of Pennsylvania Law Review*, 139, 1469–1511.

Senn, J. P. (1958). *Les sociétés d'investissement en droit français et compare*. Paris: LGDJ.

27

CONCEPTUALISING FINANCE *WITHIN* THE CAPITAL-LABOUR NEXUS

Asset management as a new zone of social conflict

Sabine Montagne

If we move beyond the never-ending reductionist labels, over the last twelve or so years it is clear that the sociology of finance and the sociology of credit have both become research areas rich in hugely diverse theoretical and methodological approaches, with both making a contribution to economic sociology. Nevertheless, a lack of anticipation concerning the 2007 financial crisis has led to some in-house criticism. None of the three major forms of sociological analysis that deal with finance – the first studying trading floors and financial instruments, the second being more critical of the globalisation of finance and the loss of government power, and the third which considers the world as a network producing coordination – could have predicted the arrival of the subprime crisis (Fligstein, 2009). Fligstein himself has admitted to being focused on how the ideology of shareholder value was affecting business strategies and how such notions were being diffused. In fact, before 2005, very little research paid attention to the growth of the financial sector, or its role in profits and GNP (Duménil and Lévy, 2011; Krippner, 2005). The financial sector was studied with little importance given to firms and research often side-stepped the role of the government. Moreover, macro-economic phenomena (e.g. the circulation of monetary flows on the global scale) and socio-political processes (e.g. the role of central banks or the circulation of political, economic and academic elites across different sites of power) were not sufficiently made use of in explaining sociologically the deployment of financial activities on either national or global levels.

The consequences borne by corporations that resulted from the 2007 financial crisis, in particular the acceleration of re-localising sites of financial power, were an invitation to no longer limit the study of finance to analysing financial markets (focusing on the trading of financial securities and price formation), but to instead consider finance as a social relation (*rapport social*) that transforms other social relations, in the same way that they also contribute to produce it.[1] This change in register implies an interest in structural objects (macro-social regularities, rules and regulations, thought patterns) and in financial and non-financial agents (employers, employees, politicians, judges). It also implies integrating a historical dimension into the analysis. Concretely, by following the *transformations* of these agents and institutions we can hope to account for the transformations of social identities commonly assembled under the term 'financialisation'. Hence, having studied agents of finance (traders, financial analysts, investment managers) per se in their daily work of allocating capital, and also institutions (stock markets, regulation agencies, central banks) in their work expanding financial markets, it is worthwhile in following up to then observe how these agents and institutions, over time, redefine the identities of other economic agents, but also how, in return, they are themselves produced via these changes (Lemoine, 2016; Montagne and Ortiz, 2013; Moulévrier, 2013).

The present chapter proposes to show how employees of major US companies, a group of agents among the most affected by financial expansion, have been led towards becoming involved in the financial playing field and, eventually, to contributing towards the desta-bilisation of their own employment standards, under the continuous monitoring of their employers. Their widespread access to company pension funds, created by employers under union pressure following the Second World War and, at the time, considered to be a major fringe benefit, backfired on them from the 1980s onwards. The funds at that time served to lead hostile takeover bids which 'restructured' industrial firms, implemented massive redundancies and opened the way for the de-industrialisation of North America for decades to come. By retracing the principal moments that occurred throughout this history, this chapter illustrates the degree to which finance's expansion originated, not from an endog-enous socio-economic dynamic, but rather from a redistribution of economic powers that takes place through interactions with other types of actors, such as unions and employers, legislators and public officials, judges and academics. Each of these groups contributes in different ways to the development of financial activities and, *in the same movement*, to the transformation of the capital–labour nexus. In particular, the emergence of new professional identities, deemed *competent* enough to manage other people's money, cannot be disassoci-ated from the transformation of the identity of the '*white male breadwinner*', from the mas-culine, salaried and unionised employee of major American companies in the 1950s, to the *passive* owner of financial assets. Through the development of a financial sector dedicated to the management of employee savings plans (pension funds, health funds, mutual funds), the legislators, employers and courts put into place new measures for economic governance, in particular a new way of subjecting employees to their own logic in relation to capital.

A structural deprivation

Following the Second World War, trade unions demanded the creation of pension funds, though it was not until later, during the 1970s, that the government decided to begin regu-lating this activity. The purpose of such funds was to provide employees of major companies with an additional pension benefit, as the social security benefits at the time were insuffi-cient for middle class living standards. Contributions to these funds by employers would provide a decisive jackpot for the financial sector involved in asset management. The possi-bility of employee control was consequently evoked numerous times by left-wing reformists in the United States. Yet the literature generally emphasises the difficulties experienced by employees in terms of exercising any influence over the direction of investments made with these funds. Employees were 'distanced', even deprived, as a result of the organisation of the management of these investments and, more specifically, on account of the mediation carried out by financial managers (Aglietta, 1979).

These types of savings instruments seemed to institute, in a *structural* sense, a separation between the purpose of the savings, which the employees may have wished to assign, and the actual methods for managing these savings, instrumentalised by employers and finance professionals. This setup conveniently resulted from the fact that it was an employee savings plan, figuring as part of the capital–labour nexus. The perspective here mirrors that of the Marxist analysis of wage labour, in that the employee is defined not by the correspondence between the product of his labour and his salary, but precisely by the *absence* of a relationship between these two variables. The financialised capital–labour nexus would therefore represent an extension of the Marxist *rapport salarial*: the deprivation of employees from the power that these savings could impart upon them.

To analyse the motivations behind this deprivation, we must simultaneously examine the three objective functions fulfilled by these enslaved savings, as well as the representations (of the employee, employer and *financier*) that they encouraged.

On one hand, these savings were a substitute for wage compensation, of which an unspecified amount relied on the uncertainty of the financial markets and was unable to be subject to union negotiation. The introduction of this form of compensation therefore contributed towards shifting from the Fordist capital–labour nexus, based on the wage and union representation, to a capital–labour nexus devoid of any representation, as it relied on financial market 'forces'. The figure of the employee as a unionised member in his company was challenged by that of the financial securities-holding employee, considered to be an informed investor capable of managing his position on these international financial markets.

On the other hand, such savings provided financial markets with financial liquidity. These frozen savings (Montagne, 2008), over which employees had no real decision-making autonomy, were transformed into short-term, liquid investments in accordance with norms defined by powerful financial intermediaries (Montagne, 2005). They therefore contributed towards developing a specific type of finance, different from both 'private banking' (rich people) and banking finance (regulated by *New Deal* legislations right into the 1980s). Economic literature justified this type of finance due to its presumed ability to optimally allocate savings to economic projects that were beneficial for the greater good, both on the global scale with the placement of capital flows, and on the local scale with the gathering, pooling and redistribution to groups of savings investors.

Finally, these savings represented financial leverage for employers on two accounts. On a microeconomic level, they were a 'jackpot' from which employer-companies could draw in order to wage aggressive financial strategies (supporting stock prices, takeover bids, merger and acquisitions). On the macro-financial level, the financial liquidity allowed them to take control of other firms through recapitalisation, which is based on stock market prices and does not encourage cash payments (takeover bids, Public Exchange Offers). These savings therefore contributed towards shifting the competitive relationships between firms played out on the product markets, towards competitive relationships focused on company ownership. The tendency was therefore to replace the figure of the Fordist industrial company CEO, a stakeholder in the 'Keynesian' political economic compromise and anchored to the *national* territory, with the more universal manager who strives for the global optimisation of the firm's activities portfolio.

We can therefore observe that the distancing of employees takes place on the following three levels: the non-negotiability of financial revenues, exclusion from the processes defining investment norms, and finally disempowerment in terms of controlling territorial redeployments and ownership of employer firms. This analytical description unveils distancing as a process, as though it was a product derived from a somewhat standard process of transformation that involved shifting from Fordist capitalism to financial capitalism. Conversely, this chapter instead opts to provide a political account of the issue, namely an account of the conflicting socio-political processes that have constructed these connections between employees and finance. This perspective leads us to consider that employee disempowerment is a *political project* common to those actors who have strived for the following evolutions to capitalism: financialisation of household revenues, financial liquidity and international competition. Structural distancing is therefore not an accidental mishap; rather, it is a constant concern for actors.

The firm grasp of both employers and *financiers* is particularly visible in the workings of the Prudent Man Rule, which guides the investment of these savings funds (Montagne, 2012). This legal ruling – the purpose of which is to oversee the allocation of savings in the *sole and unique interest* of employees and, in doing so, protect them from potentially being taken advantage of by *financiers* and employers – has been the subject of conflict between these dominating economic fractions who both sought to reorient its definition to their own advantage; with their ideas nevertheless converging on the subject of employee exclusion. Tracing the history of the transformation of this prudent approach, from its definition during the 1960s to the current day, we highlight how the notion of 'in the employees' interests' was repeatedly orchestrated in order to serve the advancement of other economic actors.

The political project: implementing social protection thanks to financial accumulation

During the 1960s–1970s, the US federal government put plans in place to structure corporate social protection, which would still fall within the framework of employment relations and under the control of the employer, but that would involve financial accumulation and therefore demand the involvement of financial agents. Beginning with the Kennedy government in 1962, the US Administration and Congress planned to legislate on private company pension funds. The idea was to promote the development of these funds and to better organise their management so as to guarantee employees additional retirement benefits at the end of their working life.

The administration's initial focus fell on employers, the concern being to encourage their capacity/willingness to make *sufficient* contributions to these funds. Employers were required since 1949 to create such funds if unions demanded them, though they also remained the sole and unique administrators of them, independent of any form of union or regulatory control. This autonomy was justified on the basis that they bore the legal and economic responsibility to effectively deliver the promised benefits. To this end, they also decided upon the contribution level and the type of investment made on the financial markets.

Without questioning the employers' management of these funds, the government nevertheless wished to introduce a form of monitoring of investment methods. The analysis of successive bills (Wooten, 2004) shows that the objective of encouraging employers to contribute sufficient amounts was extended to include the objective of engaging financial professionals to manage the sums amassed. The idea was to delegate financial investment decisions to investment professionals, expressly appointed to steer policies in line with the recognised practices already present in the 'financial community'.

With the federal Employment Retirement Income Security Act (ERISA) passed in 1974, the government's proactive approach thus succeeded in 'making' employers pay (by imposing rules regarding the funding of their pension funds) and in uniting the financial professionals around a set of investment principles. The idea of having a federal "Prudent Man

Rule" for federal investment was therefore progressively accepted. Such prudence should guarantee both the employers' interests (who could make suitable investments from contributions, so that the capital thus accumulated would pay out retirement benefits) and those of the *financiers* (who could invest according to taken-for-granted methods without risk of being personally implicated).

The trial of the 1980s takeover wave

In order to put an end to employers and unions using the money in pension funds for their own benefit, the US Department of Labor undertook to renew the interpretation of an old measure: the 'Exclusive Benefit Rule'. This rule stipulated that the manager must make all his investment decisions in the sole and unique interests of the *beneficiary* of his fund management. This rule seemed to be an appropriate solution towards the banishing of investment practices conspicuously conducted to benefit employers or unions, such as buying equity ownership of competitive or complementary companies (in order to control their business strategies), financing employee loans or financing social housing.

From the 1980s, the Department decided to reaffirm the authority of this rule, already present in law, and to reform its contents by calling upon concepts developed by academics, financial economists and *Law and Economics* lawyers from the University of Chicago. According to this academic theorisation, the interest of the beneficiary resided in a single aim: maximising the return on the finance portfolio held by the funds. It was a matter of separating the financial interests of the beneficiary of a fund, from the other interests exclusive to the employee's situation, such as maintaining one's job or receiving a salary increase. This now 'uncluttered' definition of the interest of the beneficiary would find itself concretely implemented during the 1980s' hostile takeover wave, during which financial *raiders* instituted proceedings against major American industrial companies. These financial attacks would indeed give way to a defensive reaction from targeted firms, who systematically used the money from pension funds to counter any takeover bids that were threatening company managers. Employees approved this strategy implemented by their employers numerous times, believing that they had more to lose in the wake of a change in leadership. The raiders, when they won, most often proceeded to split and sell the acquired company parts. And once sites began closing and there were no more buyers, this consequently led to massive redundancies.

In the context of this temporary alliance between employers and employees, the Reagan government undertook to make illegal any strategies hindering takeover bids. The US Department of Labor instituted proceedings surrounding the funds in question, arguing that the exclusive financial interest of the beneficiaries, the employees of the targeted firms, had not been respected. The Department maintained that the beneficiary's interest in protecting his job was nothing but a false pretence employed by the directors in charge to preserve their power. While financial raiders, such as the Kohlberg, Kravis & Roberts (KKR) firm, have remained notorious for their radical liquidations of major American corporations, it should also be noted that industrial companies were equally active in the instrumentalisation of pension funds. These companies used their pension funds to lead their own takeover bids or to loan money to financial raiders.

The legal strategy of the government, implemented according to the definition of 'exclusive benefit', had a two-tiered effect. It transformed employees into shareholders, on account of their status as beneficiaries of a pension fund, and it also pushed industrial companies to accept a finance-driven logic. The employee savings funds were therefore paradoxically transformed into financial agents, positioned as shareholders encouraged to participate in the redistribution of the ownership rights of American companies and compelled to adopt a shareholder rhetoric that was hostile towards employees. At the same time, during a period destabilised by this new financial playing field, company directors hijacked this new opportunity to circulate ownership rights and anti-wage policy to their own advantage.

Ever-present employer control

While the intention behind the ERISA was to promote professionalised financial management shielded from any conflicts of interest linked to employers, the sustained presence of employer lobbies within Congress tempered the actual impact of the law. Employers conserved the possibility to allow their pension funds to invest in the company's shares and encouraged their employees to increasingly acquire more. The stock market crisis of 2000 and the bankruptcies that followed made apparent the sheer extent of this type of investment.

These practices that flouted not only the principles of financial theory, but also the highly practised logic of risk diversification, placed employees in a situation similar to the one the ERISA legislator had been hoping to avoid: an overly high dependency of employee savings, to the employer-company. History shows that, despite critically analysing the employees' position in relation to these pension funds (which included analyses from highly '*mainstream*' economists), despite legislation expected to remedy the most blatant problems, despite the government's willingness to withdraw the management of these savings plans from the employers' grasp, in the end the employee never becomes the independent financial decision-maker capable of organising the financing for his own retirement or health insurance or children's education on the financial markets, as projected by theorists.

During the legal proceedings that opposed employees against employers, the employer lobbying power within Congress was increased two-fold thanks to local influential power, situated close to judges. An analysis of jurisprudence that we previously conducted allows us to indeed hypothesise the existence of an extremely wide-spread employer influence, which affects the categories of legal reasoning (Montagne, 2013). The way in which judges interpret one of financial theory's fundamental principles, the hypothesis of efficient markets (the creator of which, E. Fama, was recently awarded the Nobel Prize in 2013), constitutes a good example of this potential employer influence. This principle is called upon by judges whenever a case involves evaluating whether the decision to invest or not to invest in listed securities on the stock market was executed at a reasonable price. The litigations that followed the stock market crisis in 2000 offer several examples of how judges tackled this type of examination.

In the cases studied, the judges' reasoning followed two different paths: either the judge retained the principle of market efficiency as the *only* legitimate criteria for evaluating the investment decision, or he considered that *additional* criteria should equally be taken into account and thus privileged these over the notion of market efficiency. What these two judicial decisions have in common is that they both dismiss the plaintiffs. Considering this issue is systematically against employees, should we not hypothesise that such judicial reasoning serves to reinforce financial decisions overseen by employers? Here, it is not a question of the direct influence of employers, but rather of the judges' interiorisation of an additional constraint: the attempt to avoid threatening the existence of employee savings funds, as they are concretely organised, by further burdening them with legal risk.

Conclusion

Reviewing the history of the Prudent Man Rule offers us the possibility of shifting the spotlight onto actors and socio-economic relationships that are non-financial but which, through their strategies and actions, directly contribute towards defining not only the positions of various groups of agents within the financialised universe, but also those exceedingly financial objects that are investment norms. By way of complementing the perspective that entails measuring the effects that financialisation has *on* the capital–labour nexus (Lordon, 2014), this present approach has sought to illustrate the interest to be found in rethinking the basis (both in the sense of 'foundations' and 'purpose') of contemporary finance *within* the capital–labour nexus.

Notes

1 The original French term employed here 'rapport social' (translated as 'social relation') revisits the vocabulary forged by the *Théorie de la Régulation* (The Regulation School) in particular the notions of capital–labour nexus and 'institutional form' (Boyer, 1990 and 2004).

References

Aglietta, M. (1979). *A theory of capitalist regulation. The US experience*. London: Verso books.

Boyer, R. (1990). *The regulation school. A critical interpretation*. New York: Columbia University Press.

Boyer, R. (2004). *Une théorie du capitalisme est-elle possible?* Paris: Odile Jacob.

Duménil, G. and Lévy, D. (2011). *The crisis of neoliberalism*. Cambridge: Harvard University Press.

Fligstein, N. (2009). Neil Fligstein answers questions on the present financial crisis. *Economic Sociology, the European Electronic Newsletter*, 11(1), 41–44.

Krippner G. (2005). The financialization of the American economy. *Socio-Economic Review*, 3(1), 173–208.

Lemoine, B. (2016). The strategic State committed to financial markets: The creation of a French public debt management office. *Revue Française de Science Politique*, 66(3), 435–459.

Lordon, F. (2014). *Willing slaves of capital: Spinoza and Marx on desire*. London: Verso books.

Montagne, S. (2005). Pouvoir financier vs. pouvoir salarial. Les fonds de pension américains: contribution du droit à la légitimité financière. *Annales. Histoire, Sciences Sociales*, 60(6), 1299–1325.

Montagne, S. (2008). Le trust, fondement juridique du capitalisme patrimonial. In F. Lordon (Ed.), *Conflits et pouvoirs dans les institutions du capitalisme* (pp. 221–250). Paris: Presses de Sciences Po.

Montagne, S. (2013). Investing prudently: How financialization puts a legal standard to use. *Sociologie du Travail*, 55, 48–66.

Montagne, S. and Ortiz, H. (2013). Sociologie de l'agence financière : enjeux et perspectives. Introduction. *Sociétés contemporaines*, 92, 7–33.

Moulévrier, P. (2013). Le crédit donné aux pauvres. Droit à l'endettement et financiarisation de l'action sociale. *Sociétés contemporaines*, 92, 89–106.

Wooten, J. A. (2004). *The employee retirement income security act of 1974. A political history*. Berkeley: University of California Press.

28

DEMOCRACY AND THE POLITICAL REPRESENTATION OF INVESTORS

On French sovereign debt transactions and elections

Benjamin Lemoine

Is there a political representation of investors and creditors? Making the collective entity of 'financial markets' or sovereign bondholders a subject of action, capable of political decisions and actions, poses *de facto* a number of challenges for sociological analysis. The analysis offered by the sociologist Wolfgang Streeck (2014) brings the division of the social body back to the centre of debt analysis. Streeck describes the opposition, whether implicit or explicit, between two types of political subjects with disjointed interests and modes of expression in our democratic systems: that of *Staatsvolk* (citizens in general) and that of *Marktvolk* (people of the market, or the *'aristocracy of finance'*). He links these forms of political subjectivity with different registers of public and political expression. The *Staatsvolk* citizen-voters, *'the owners of passports commanding a right to vote'*,[1] express themselves during periodic elections and are attached to the public service and the social State. Meanwhile, members of the Marktvolk – *'the owners of bonds and movable capital commanding a right to sell'*[2] – participate in political life as creditors who buy, trade and sell State bonds during auctions and renew (or not), their confidence in the government depending on its orientations. Auctions and interest rates for sovereign bonds are considered as competing modes of democratic expression objectifying opinion polls and election results. This understanding of the division of the social world through debt has proven controversial.[3]

Critics aimed at Streeck focused on the very possibility of attributing 'market people' and sovereign bondholder, with a social unity, a political homogeneity and an inclination to form a group: in other words in considering it as a 'collective actor' with a class consciousness.[4] This controversy highlights one of the weaknesses in the sociology of public finances: How to refer to the social and political groups concerned, interested and affected by sovereign debt? And where does the coordination of their interests, if any, take place? Is it possible to differentiate between the social classes in their relationship with debt, and treat financial markets as active entities without leaving oneself open to accusations of conspiracy theory (Tooze, 2017)? The obstacles to such an inquiry are unquestionably numerous. The heterogeneity of the 'international financial class' thwarts any attempts to describe it. Likewise, the complexity of the relationship between States and markets – determined by skilfully-measured gifts and counter-gifts, and which, ultimately, cannot easily be said to be favourable to States, balanced, or harmful to citizens – makes it difficult to state with any certainty the social and political interests that are served by debt. In order to avoid being trapped in an alternative between 'conspiracy' on the one hand and a supposed social neutrality of market debt on the other, this chapter shows the importance of investigating the way in which the financialisation of sovereign debt – its sale as standardised contracts in a unified global bond savings market – transforms the capacity for action and reaction among the different social groups and either strengthens or weakens their very existence.

Relying on an empirical investigation of sovereign debt management techniques, commercialisation and evaluation, this chapter describes different scenes where the 'publics' of the sovereign debt are made explicit. Debt transactions and technical operations are analysed as social sites where legitimate citizenship is produced, political representation crafted and the democratic trials are reconfigured. In the first part, I open the black box of the government debt selling machine in order to grasp how an economic policy of a certain social class is produced, consolidated or defeated through the issuing of competitive sovereign debt. Road shows, commercial presentations of a country bond enact political promises on the future of a State, but also a particular *state* of the economy and the social and political order. In the second part, I describe how the interest of creditors, and professional bondholders, becomes manifest, explicit and a public concern during a recent electoral campaign in France. I develop on the omnipresence, in the public sphere, of the 'political risk', i.e. the way financial investors qualify political attempts to change the structures as a 'danger'. I consider 'political risk' as an indirect mode of creditors' political representation.

The political and social laws of Sovereign Bond Market

The redevelopment of French sovereign debt markets during the 1970s and the 1980s responded to a State project. The progressive dismantling of the administrative, regulatory and authoritarian modes of State financing, established after the Second World War (and described at this time as inflationary circuits) aimed at sanctuarising savings, the value of which needed to be protected against the risk of inflation (Lemoine, 2016). Therefore, the post-war arrangement – based on credit administered in the service of a plan for full employment, growth and a significant reduction in inequality through social protection – was considered as the problem itself and, as such, quickly challenged. As early as the 1960s, the French finance administration reasserted the idea that 'sound' financing was to be achieved through the development of bond industry. Cultivating outlets for this type of saving, by creating yield and therefore profitable financial assets, became a priority. The policy of strong borrowing (just as there was a 'strong currency', a *franc fort* policy) required reduced inflation, the end of administered financing and positive real interest rates. The redeployment of private finance and the end of the administrative 'corsets' that constrained it were the result of battles patiently waged within the government. This was also the case regarding openness towards foreign investors, which gave rise to numerous spars within the government's 'right hand' (Bourdieu, 1998). Within the Finance ministry, the Directorate General for Taxation (*Direction Générale des Impôts*), which sought to maintain ways of taxing foreign savings invested in debt, was actually opposed to the Treasury department, which was inclined to promote the attraction of capital, even if that meant lower tax revenues. Similarly, the Treasury department supported the neutralisation of monetary policy, its increased independence from politics and from the Treasury department (later embodied through a dedicated and 'autonomous' organisation, in accordance with the Independent Central Bank's international standard), and the allocation of credit to the economy, which would no longer be centralised and government-led but would allow the market mechanisms and the initiative of the private finance sector to come into play.

The State's 'right hand' promoted a return to economic and fiscal orthodoxy: a disengagement of the public authorities in matters relating to credit and currency in order to favour 'sound money'. The social project of a strong currency, a strong borrowing policy and an 'autonomous' and democratised private finance was driven by this fraction of the state bureaucracy. The State propaganda that was being developed in the 1980s should not be underestimated, based on the idea of a 'fair' society in which savings or financial investment would be accessible to all. An advertising campaign orchestrated by the Treasury department in 1987 lauded a State putting itself at risk on financial markets in the service of the French people and a society that was financialised for the good of all – 'the State gets itself wet for the sake of your liquidity,' chanted the businessman Paul-Loup Sulitzer, cast as spokesman for the project of modernising France through the capital markets (Lemoine, 2016).

Government utopia: inclusion theory and a financialised society

The development of bond markets since the late 1960s – correlative to the financialisation of the economy – also corresponds to a social *utopia*, conceived at the very top of the financial State, to construct a society of 'middle classes' in which social antagonisms would be mitigated by enlisting the whole of society under the banner of savings and debt. Such French Treasury department doctrine echoes US Treasury department discourse stressing the fact that debt has become 'democratised' and debt ownership is not concentrated but, on the contrary, dispersed among the population. Everyone is included and, from the capitalised retirement savings of the American 'grandmother' to Rockefeller's fortune, their interests are united. This doctrine also pretends that government bonds are gradually redistributing income (Cavanaugh, 1996).

But the social and political consequences of debt remain controversial. In the case of France, a quick overview of the social distribution of savings (which are placed in public debt in particular) is likely to put the theory of widespread enlistment into perspective, by revealing the extent to which the public affected by the State's financial debt remains a minority that can be distinguished from the rest of the population. The French national institute for statistics (INSEE) data, although insufficient to make a precise characterisation of the inequalities created by debt, points to a social distribution of savings that divides the French population. In 2009, 35 per cent of French households earned income that did not cover their expenditures.[5] One statistical study by the Central European Bank showed that, in 2013, only 1.7 per cent of French households directly owned French government securities, 37.5 per cent had life insurance or a voluntary pension plan and 10.7 per cent held financial assets in an investment fund (European Central Bank, 2013).

To overcome this debate that cannot be settled abstractly, it is possible to focus on the arbitrating mechanisms that are at play inside public bureaucracies, for instance between policy options and the promotion of savings or taxation as distinct means for financing the State (Cusset, 2015). A systematic investigation into the State's legitimation of debt management is likely to reveal whether a policy favourable to the bondholding class permeates the choices of successive governments. Does the economic apparatus surrounding debt techniques activate and reinforce the 'left hand' (the redistributive side of public policies, represented by so-called social ministries and services), rather than the 'right hand' of the State (a globally 'competitive' monetary and financial State, represented by the Treasury department, the Budget office or the Central Bank)? When it comes to redistribution and social inequalities, what matters is not so much the amount of debt (in absolute terms or in relation to the GDP) but rather the nature of the expenditures that those sovereign loans are funding. In the case of nineteenth-century American debt, during the era of James Adams' bondholding class (Hager, 2016: 59), public debt was accompanied by mechanisms of bottom-up social redistribution and public spending essentially geared towards a 'night-watchman State' that centred on the essential functions of justice and the police. If debt finances tax cuts that benefit holders of wealth, then it leads to redistribution from the poorest to the richest. On the other hand, if debt allows social investments for the poorest and public services where quality is given precedence over lower costs, then the system of financing through taxation is progressive and debt plays its Keynesian, redistributive role, making the State an investor in the economy and the social, for example with real tax rates that are higher than interest payments.

Sovereign bond selling and the making of economic policies

By following Treasury civil servants while they are commercialising their liquid sovereign bonds, the sociologist can understand which form of State and political promises (or socio-economic orders) are sold to investors. French archives from 1987 disclose how the Treasury secretary of that time, Daniel Lebègue, wanted to present its 'collection of bonds' as if the State was a commercial entity as any other. In London, at the Queen Elisabeth II conference centre, devoted to '*New French securities*', he was reminding bankers and investors that 'French Treasury is today in the position of a company that has completely renewed its product range and that is currently presenting its new collection to its potential customers'. Two months before, investors had the occasion to send lists of their expectations and concerns to Treasury officials. After inquiries regarding inflation and 'cost competitiveness'[3] of work, they asked if it was 'possible that French leaves the European monetary system (EMS)'. They were also wondering if civil servants could 'describe' to them what 'a socialist policy' consists in, that appeared quite exotic to US investors. And finally, they were worried about the 'Communist Party participation in the government'. During another road show in New York, a representative of J. P. Morgan was asking, in the title of his slideshow, 'Why invest in France?' The 'economic fundamentals' he was listing were: 'a free trade economy', a 'non-inflationary policy stance' with 'a high unemployment rate', which was considered a sign of 'pressure on low wages'; 'a close and tight fiscal policy', a 'stronger position of French big business', the 'respect of external constraints'. And, finally, the characteristics of French debt products: 'the fourth largest bond market in the world', 'a Triple-A credit rating A', 'liquidity' and 'efficient markets' – that made French bonds quite an interesting investment.

Debt and new democratic trials

Unlike in conspiracy theories, which believe in an almost 'magical' coordination between the actors of finance, it is a question of monitoring the work and instruments that their professionals display effectively in order to unite their claims and influence political decisions. The notion of 'political risk' has recently emerged, even in so-called 'economically advanced' countries like France (which is a new phenomenon), as a natural and 'objective' category in presidential debates. Functioning as a new barometer for public life, the indicators that establish this risk allow journalists to gauge candidates and label their platforms as 'serious' or 'unrealistic'. This political risk is sometimes quantified by estimating the likelihood of a sovereign debt issuer defaulting – a task performed by rating agencies. It may also be reflected in the evolution of interest rates from which State loans benefit and can be seen, for example, in the interest rate gap between France and Germany, which mirrors an unequal level of confidence in the country's capacity to honour its commitments. Finally, it may quite simply materialise in the press, in the form of judgements or concerns about politics from investors, whether individual or collective.

Auctions or elections? Objects of indirect political representation of creditors

The recent French presidential campaign (2017) showed how social groups of creditors influenced the issue of debt during this democratic test. 'Never before has a presidential election sparked so much interest among financial investors', stated a French radio station (France Info),[6] which emphasised the 'political risk' posed by certain candidates, with extreme-right wing Marine Le Pen and on the left, Jean-Luc Mélenchon being in the lead. Concern over political risk, widely covered by the media and shared during the final weeks of the campaign, revealed the financial sector's uneasiness over how long its hegemony might last.

This awakening of investors' concerns came about in France after several decades in which the political programme was aligned between the right and the left in the area of economic and financial governance – i.e. successive political decisions of governments that established the legitimacy of finance and the exclusivity of the markets in the financing of the State's deficits. This structural intricacy between States and markets has given the numerous representatives of finance (investment banks, pension funds, insurance companies, etc.) the ability to decide between good and bad candidates, and therefore indirectly to choose between them: investors' opinion translates into facts, because their confidence and presence (or absence) at debt auctions enables or prevents the implementation of a given political programme. And it is precisely that centrality, which has become structural and objective, of financial investors' opinion in the functioning of our democracies and our State that was challenged during the last French election campaign, with the exception of François Fillon and Emmanuel Macron.

When compared to previous presidential elections, the treatment of debt during the 2017 election campaign was unprecedented. Few were the candidates that had inherited the 'Pébereau framework'[7] for the public problem of debt – which posits that the volume of public spending on the economy and the 'muddle' made of public services are solely responsible for the debt burden, and that political courage is needed to 'cut the fat'. François Fillon and Emmanuel Macron were the only ones to make their election pledges part of such a decision-making script: promote (implicitly or explicitly) austerity programmes and pursue budgetary efforts without radically increasing fiscal resources (because that would amount to hindering France's 'competitiveness'). It is clear that the apprehension of bondholders and potential investors in French debt matched the uncertainty affecting the success of these candidates. The other influential voices, on the other hand, gave a more or less drastic reinterpretation of this traditional 'framework' for the debt problem: a proposal to exit the euro area and return to administered, socialised means of allocating credit to the economy, by re-establishing public monetary creation (as opposed to allocating capital to the economy through the markets), and by emancipating from the European convergence criteria, together with massive fiscal stimulus to the economy, a break with anti-inflationary dogma, the democratisation of political and economic objects whose technocratic legitimacy appeared damaged, and so on. One banker, a primary dealer specialising in sovereign bonds, conceived this gap between candidates 'inside' and those 'outside the framework' as an unrealistic relationship with the principles of the market economy, understood as indisputable:

> There were two candidates, Fillon and Macron, who, in concrete terms, had an equally good understanding of what was happening. Afterwards, one might agree or disagree with what they said. They had an idea of what a budget deficit is, and how a budget deficit is financed. Then we had other candidates who, apart from saying 'We're going to renegotiate Maastricht and we're going to renegotiate everything'... We got a chance to hear from a guy from the National Front, where they had a very vague notion of the financial reality of the French debt.
>
> *(Hercelin, 2017: 59)*

The framework that most of the other candidates wanted to dismiss was presented by Fillon and Macron as an exogenous (that is, irreversible and ahistorical) constraint but also as an unsurpassable infrastructure. Nevertheless, this arrangement is the result of an aforementioned series of political choices, which led to the dismantling of the financial system established in the post-war period. In order to rebuild a market debt from the 1970s, in other words an exchangeable and negotiable product, it was necessary to make a break with the administered management of credit and finance, to depoliticise the monetary question (by making the fight against inflation a goal that sidestepped democratic debate), to protect these choices in organisations outside of political decision-making and to 'free' the financial system from government control. During the electoral campaign, Treasury department officials that still needed to issue debt in auctions and to promote French securities did battle to convince people that the political risk had been neutralised and that the stability of the arrangement was not questionable. Road shows therefore played a vital role in reassuring investors:

> What are road shows? It's where we go out and meet investors from home and abroad. Normally the SVTs (*Spécialistes en Valeurs du Trésor,* or commercial banks distributing the French public debt) spend their time talking about the French economy and what the Treasury's debt issuing policy [is]. This year, there were so many questions about politics that they made an additional little booklet to explain the main political parties and the last election results to major investors. First of all you have to go quite far back, because you see, we have a two-round direct voting system. There are lots of countries where people don't even realise that. The Americans are convinced that every system is like theirs. So we have to explain that if Marine Le Pen comes to power, there'll be legislative elections. She can't just do what she likes, you can't

just change the constitution however you want, and you can't hold a referendum just because you feel like it [...] Next, people have trouble understanding ideas like the Republican Front. [...] You might have almost 8 million people who will vote for you in the regional elections. To become President of the Republic you need 18 millions people to vote for you, actually more like 19 million. And it's a huge jump to get from 8 million to 19 million. [The SVTs] don't give their opinion but they show studies and surveys done on what kind of transfer of votes there might be between Mélenchon and typically between the left, the far left and the far right.

(An investment banker quoted in Hercelin, 2017, p. 54)

The debt order therefore has its sentinels. Internally, the Treasury ensures that political imperatives of the investors are enforced and that demands made by the rest of the State apparatus (the so-called 'spendthrift' ministries) to lower spending are accepted. Externally, and even if the continual flow between the public and private financial sectors make this boundary quite unclear, ratings agencies (Moody's, S&P's and Fitch) quantify the 'sovereign risk' in the form of a rating (a credit score) that takes into account both economic and institutional factors. In other words, these agencies take into account a specifically political risk: for example, by differentiating between the types of regimes, considering constitutional monarchies to be more likely to follow the market debt regulations (and respect the 'natural' right of private creditors) than absolute monarchies, which are more inclined to change it arbitrarily.[8]

Thus, in order to decide the financial value of the State, agencies rely on their expertise to select a small number of criteria (establishing a 'country file') that enables them to gauge the ability and willingness of a State (or a debt issuer in general) to service its debt over the long term. These indicators of the quality of a State consist in general and quantitative factors such as per capita income, growth measured by GDP, inflation, external debt, level of economic development and the country's history of defaulting on its debt. They also take into account qualitative and socio-political indicators that might affect the firmness of a State's commitment to repay its debt, such as the likelihood of a revolution, the electoral results for the far right or the far left, the regularities of the political sphere, the unionisation rate, the stability of the executive authority, the degree of independence of the central banks in relation to the Treasury, a State's 'capacity' to implement structural budgetary reforms, etc.

This is the real meaning of 'debt sustainability': it measures a State's ability to maintain a social distribution of State duties, requiring effort and sacrifices from certain sectors of the population for the benefit of others. In the transaction between 'invested State' and private investors, the public's likelihood to accept a permanent transfer of income towards creditors is checked. One banker recalled a parliamentary hearing with a member of parliament concerned about a budgetary rebellion or a political insurrection by the French people, in which he said that, when it came to the 'political factor', mutual reassurance between State and creditors (played out in the buying and selling sessions) was decisive:

Charles de Courson: 'What would happen if the French people, silver medallists in compulsory levies, revolted and refused to pay their taxes? History is peppered with tax rebellions. The bankers always make the assumption that things will follow their course and never reach breaking point.'

Amaury D'Orsay (Global head of fixed income trading at Société Générale): 'In situations of extremely tense crises, as we have witnessed in Greece and other European countries, the main concern is the European people's capacity to accept reforms and the difficulties that ensue. If we look at the way the markets reacted to the problems in Spain, it seems that they started to anticipate problems when the extreme parties were in a position to win a majority. That is a political crisis that might constitute a problem, but right now investors do not consider France to be in that crisis situation.'[9]

In a more or less objective and quantified way, 'political risk' shapes the particular expectations of financial investors and, with regard to debt, bond investors. The circulation of this theme in the public sphere – in a banal and obvious form – tends to erase the social context of investors' very specific concerns to transform into 'universal democratic values', their opinions and anticipations of profit or loss that are projected onto a particular political offering.

The forms of democracy and the publics that matter

As far as sovereign debt is concerned, class interests are made invisible. The bondholder value – protecting the value of debt securities against inflation and any form of contract renegotiation – is largely denied in formulas with a universal aim ('France's political risk') or in generalisations ('future generations' who are victims of the debt burden) that make social divisions invisible; in other words, which denies the antagonism between French holders of treasury bonds and beneficiaries of government-guaranteed minimums and public structures. A dual challenge then arises in our democracies: how can the real causes of the failure of a given policy be identified when the very environment it depends on for financing is hostile right from the start?[10] Investors' perception of 'political risk' and its clarification are doubly performative. By creating panic, these evaluations can drag financial actors into a downward spiral. Above all, by 'no longer attending' the auctions of government debt that they feel uneasy about (when bondholders are said to be 'voting with their feet'), investors make it very difficult, if not impossible, to implement a political programme. At the same time, their condemnations of those same programmes, driven by personal motives, become established as the objective economic causalities that explain the failure of a policy. Investors' motives thus play a decisive role: the 'political risk' is primarily a risk for finance professionals and not a risk for the economy itself, as if the latter existed in a unique, immutable form.

Conclusion

Political risk constitutes a focal point for the interests of the bondholding class – defending the value of financial securities and stabilising an institutional arrangement that guarantees the sustainability of this bondholding value over time.[11] The interdependence between governments and capital markets, which is at the root of the ubiquity of financial discourse in the media and the public space, establishes a new, invisible and unchallenged criterion for political participation that lies in the holding of financial assets: holdings and savings that make the holders feeling included and like legitimate participants in this parallel electoral system of 'votes thanks to financial securities' (through the participation of actors in the auctions market). The framework of interpretation of sovereign debt in terms of social antagonisms, differentiation or social classes, is reduced as a result of two phenomena: on the one hand, the social and political enlistment of populations as a whole (without any social differentiation) into the debt regime that is perpetuated by institutional marketing practices (through the channelling of savings, or household retirement pensions, see Montagne, 2008); and, on the other hand, the imposition of a universalising and depoliticising rhetoric and state statistical categories of future generations that make room for a representation of the social world that is structured around 'middle classes' made up of groups of individuals who are all equal to one another. But, while financial technocrats tend to represent debt as a neutral instrument or a democratic asset, smoothing out inequalities, this chapter has showed that the social structure of debt holding is mostly non-egalitarian and its political effects depends on state apparatus trade-off. The way the political and media agendas of our democracies now revolve around financial issues, anxieties and concerns – as indicated by the presence, in the public sphere, of the 'political risk' measured by investors during presidential campaigns – is increasing cultural, political and financial costs of access to public life and, also, contributing to the exclusion of the majority.

Notes

1 Reply from Wolfgang Streeck to Adam Tooze, in the *London Review of Books*, 39(2), 19 January.
2 *Ibid.*
3 The German sociologist has been criticised, in a debate that began rather badly, for calling finance professionals 'people' by linking the term Volk with the market (Tooze, 2017).
4 Idem.
5 'Les inégalités entre ménages dans les comptes nationaux', *Insee Première*, n°1265, 17 November 2009.
6 Radio France, 'Le brief éco', 13 April 2017.
7 In reference to the report commissioned by Thierry Breton to Michel Pébereau, president of the board of BNP Paribas, and which discussed the subject of debt from a media and political perspective. See Lemoine (2016).
8 'Are monarchies more creditworthy than other types of sovereigns?' *Standard and Poor's*, 5 August 2015.
9 *Mission d'évaluation et de contrôle, Rapport sur la gestion et la transparence de la dette publique*, déposé par la Commission des Finances, présenté par Busine, J-C., Gorges, J-P., et Sansu, N., enregistré à la présidence de l'Assemblée nationale le 6 juillet 2016: 234.
10 It reminds one of what was once identified in France as a 'wall of money'. Historians interested in periods such as the Popular Front alliance and more generally at times when left-wing parties come to power also discuss these questions.
11 Investors can express their concerns in aggregate form within associations (such as the International Capital Market Association or, more particularly for debt and private banks, the European Primary Dealers Association) where they meet and exchange information with senior civil servants from the financial institutions (treasuries, central banks, financial regulation agencies) of different States.

References

Boltanski, L. (2014). Croissance des inégalités, effacement des classes sociales? In F. Dubet (Ed.), *Inégalités et justice sociale* (pp. 25–47). Paris: La Découverte.
Bourdieu, P. (1998). *Le Mythe de la 'mondialisation' et l'État social européen*. Paris: Raisons d'agir.
Cavanaugh, F.-X. (1996). *The truth about the national debt: Five myths and one reality*. Boston: Harvard Business Press.

Cusset, P.-Y. (2015). Quels effets redistributifs de la dette publique? *Regards croisés sur l'économie*, 17(2), 147.

European Central Bank (2013). *Statistics Paper Series*, 2 (April), 37.

Hager, S. (2016). *Public debt, inequality and power. The making of a modern debt state*. Oakland: University of California Press.

Hercelin, N. (2017). *La démocratie financiarisée. Les urnes à l'épreuve du marché : élection présidentielle*. Unpublished Master thesis. Faculty of Economic Sciences, Catholic University of Leuven.

Lemoine, B. (2016). *L'ordre de la dette*. Paris: La découverte.

Montagne, S. (2008). Le trust fondement juridique du capitalisme patrimonial. In F. Lordon (Ed.), *Conflits et pouvoirs dans les institutions du capitalisme* (pp. 221–250). Paris: Presses de Sciences Po.

Streeck, W. (2014). *Buying time. The delayed crisis of democratic capitalism*. London: Verso.

Tooze, A. (2017). A general logic of crisis. *London Review of Books*, 39(1), 3–8.

29

KNITTING TOGETHER FINANCE AND OUR DAILY LIVES

Jeanne Lazarus

The most commonly evoked link between our daily lives and finance figuring in the media and political discourses, is related to employment and the organisation of work. Sociology and economics speak of the 'financialisation of the economy' to outline these processes. For example, power within companies is increasingly found in the hands of those who hold its capital, meaning banks and especially majority shareholders – read entities such as pension funds – who are not interested in the production side of companies but simply their profitability. Some of them go so far as to distinguish between the real economy and the financial economy, with the first involving production and the second, simple speculation that interferes with 'genuine' economic activities. This approach is flawed in that it does not take into account and does not describe the interlacing of finance with productive activities. It gives the impression that there are spheres which should remain entirely impervious to each other within the same economic universe. Yet, the reality in practice is more complex, and clearly, one of the objectives of social research into finance is to show that finance is an object linked to other human activities, and therefore well anchored in reality.

The influence of finance over everyday money issues is an exemplary illustration of this. One of the most notable evolutions from the last decades has been what certain sociologists have called the 'financialisation of daily life'. José Ossandón (2012), in research devoted to the financial practices of poor families in the suburbs of Santiago, Chile, coined the concept of 'knitting' to show that money which circulates in families is attached in one way or another to the financial world, even for those who do not own a bank account. He shows that these families employ credit by using a card obtained, for example, by an aunty or a neighbour from a major retail store and which aids several households. Poorer households which are used to an informal economy consequently employ such 'formal' tools and through this research we can see how calculations and monetary projections are transformed through the presence of financial institutions. For all that, Ossandón does not describe the unilateral imposition of financial logics, rather he shows that individuals integrate these logics into others by occasionally hijacking them. In return, financial industries propose products that are adapted to the new populations that they wish to influence. This research describes currently occurring developments and does not offer a 'happily-ever-after-ending', which would be the victory of calculated logic over all other types. On the contrary, one can recognise that analysing the effects of introducing 'formal' financial tools requires simultaneously taking into account institutions and practices.

Monetisation

In 1900, the German sociologist George Simmel, in his 700-page text called *The Philosophy of Money*, described what was for him one of the major advances of the nineteenth century: monetisation. He explained as it were the fact that the transformations of modes of production, urbanisation, industrialisation and paid employment had provided money with an ever-increasing role and that it was henceforth impossible to live without money. In the traditional rural world, money was very rare and what was consumed was for the most part produced on the farm. Care for children, elderly people or the sick was undertaken by the family, and as for housing, when families did not own their own home, they rented their lodgings against contributions in kind. In the city on the other hand, lodgings were rented for money, food must be bought and members of the family did not live together, therefore it was occasionally necessary to pay to have the children minded, or to have someone care for the sick or elderly, thus money was necessary to guarantee basic living standards. Simmel describes in great detail these transformations and has analysed the consequences.

Money has numerous qualities: it allows people to agree upon the value of things, it makes exchanges possible between strangers as it is not in the stranger that one must place trust but in the money being exchanged, and most importantly it provides vast freedom in comparison with traditional social bonds, as it breaks the cycle of gifting and counter-gifting. Nevertheless, money is also for Simmel the source of much more questionable processes: it individualises, it turns social bonds insipid, and it makes life meaningless and colourless as it renders everything comparable. If people and things are now only evaluated due to their monetary value, individuals and societies run the risk of becoming cynical and indifferent. The contemporary American sociologist Viviana Zelizer (2010) opposes this description of the effects of monetisation which, in her opinion, demonstrates a description of the world constructed during the nineteenth century, according to which money and family constituted separate spheres and hostile worlds. Instead, shows Zelizer, when a great amount of money is introduced into the domestic home, individuals do not 'adapt' to money but rather they make money adapt to their lifestyle by colouring it with norms, practices and meanings. Money *does* smell.

Monetisation is well documented: the monetary mass in circulation across all the world's economies has greatly increased since the industrial revolution. As has the quantity of money possessed by families. The new notion from the second-half of the twentieth century, and what has been reinforced since the 1970s, is the financialisation of household money. This term implies that domestic money is henceforth almost entirely deposited in financial institutions, banks of course, but also credit unions or insurance firms. In France, 99 per cent of households possess a bank account. Without an account, it is impossible in France to receive your salary or your social benefits; paying your bills, taxes and rent all require having a cheque book or being able to carry out electronic transfers. Banking payment methods are so essential to daily life, to the point whereby the law makes prevision for a 'right to an account' which allows the *Banque de France* to demand a bank to open an account for a person who does not have one.

The financialisation of daily life

So, what are the consequences of this financialisation? The well-known *New York Times* very regularly publishes articles on the best way to manage your money, with these articles allowing us to grasp up to what point mastering how monetary institutions work has become essential to the contemporary lives of individuals. One of the newspaper's favourite subjects is credit scores. This individual score represents the grade attributed to every inhabitant in the United States, by private bodies named 'credit bureaus'. While the famous AAA grades attributed to governments by ratings agencies have become well-known, these individual credit scores have for a long time been the fellow travellers of every United States citizen, though they are less known within countries such as France where banking regulations do not allow this information to be made public. Martha Poon (2009) has demonstrated how since the 1990s the FICO score – *Fair Isaac Corporation* who devised the algorithm enabling the calculation of individual risks using information on the monetary practices of people – has emerged as the unique measurement relating to the quality of borrowers. As such, banks and credit institutions rely on this score to determine whether or not they will decide to lend and more importantly at what rate. This credit score has become an important criterion for judging people across the entire scale of their social life. In order to be hired or to rent an apartment, it is commonplace that Americans are required to provide their score (when employers or rental agencies don't actively search for the information themselves, which is easily accessible in a few clicks and for a few dollars). However, this is not all: as another article in the *New York Times* from 2012 has explained, having a bad score can wreak havoc right down to your love life (Silver-Greenberg, 2012). The article told of the misadventures of several young men and women who were informed by the person they were going out with that they no longer wanted to continue seeing them because of their weak credit score. Indeed, building a life with someone who has a bad rating does have its consequences: borrowing is more expensive, finding housing will doubtlessly be more difficult, and so on; however, beyond the purely economic aspect, the score is in reality interpreted as information about the character of certain individuals. For instance, when it is reported as low, is it not a sign that the person in question lacks self-control? That he/she is irresolute or handles his/her affairs poorly? On top of the traditional social inequalities linked to one's level of education, salary or type of employment, is henceforth added the more or less respectable integration into the financial world. The score creates sub-classes of citizens who cannot access the same goods and services as others, or otherwise only through damaging and more expensive means.

The banking exclusion

The credit score does not exist in the same way in France, in particular because banks do not share their information (Lazarus, 2012b). Scores are therefore internal to banks, which prevents synthetic scores from being constructed that summarise people's status such as is the case in the United States. For all that, France does experience a process of banking exclusion. Georges Gloukoviezoff (2010, p. 4) has described this exclusion as 'the process by which a person encounters such difficulties with their access to and use of banking facilities that he/she is no longer able to lead a normal social life'. This definition allows us to account for the fact that many bank clients, who possess an account, are in fact third-rate clients: they are not invited into the advisers' offices but are served at the counter, their potential problems are treated in a standard manner and often too quickly; the explanations given to them regarding the means of payment and banking services they have available are too brief and hurried for the client to truly be able to grasp them; and finally, they are frequently 'profitable' clients with whom the banks are able to secure a return through practices such as forced selling (for example the advisor to whom they have come to request an extension on their overdraft grants it to them on the condition that they sign an insurance policy) and through extremely high banking fees in the event of non-payment – even if successive regulations have attempted to limit their amount. These excluded banking clients are therefore much more likely than others to find themselves being refused credit, to see their debits rejected, to be listed on the *Banque de France*'s non-payment files, to find their means of payment revoked, to resort to procedures of excessive debt, etc. All these situations have by no means insignificant repercussions on their daily lives: they require multiple and extensive administrative procedures and lead to forms of stigmatisation, for example when it becomes impossible for them to write out cheques to pay bills, rent, school cafeteria fees, etc.

Research on banking exclusion shows two very significant processes. The first is that social difficulties are not just rubber-stamped by banks. Indeed through their practices they also amplify them due to the fees they add during distressed situations, though even before arriving to this point, through the services they propose. The means of payment provided by banks are at the origin of the de-structuring of traditional household management practices: money is de-materialised when it is in a bank account, and it is possible, particularly with cheques, bank cards and automatic withdrawals, to make payments when one does not actually have the necessary funds available. Doing one's accounts with a bank account is much more difficult than doing them with cash: have the cheques I wrote been cashed? Have the withdrawals been accepted? And if one doesn't follow one's account, what happens then? The financialisation of daily life implies a transformation of the representations of money, time and any related practices that banks very often neglect to take into account, acting as though the tools which they make available to people are straightforward.

The second significant result of research into banking exclusion is its clear identification as one of the facets of social exclusion: in order to fully take part in social life it is necessary to be properly integrated into the banking world. This signifies that one possesses an understanding and a minimum amount of knowledge concerning the means of payment that one has available, but equally that one's lifestyle enables one to successfully overcome the 'trials of the bank' (Lazarus, 2012a). It requires being able to offer the bank a description of oneself which the bank is able to understand. The bank expects stability and linearity within one's personal and professional pathways, which enables future revenues to be anticipated and levels of risk to be calculated. Young people and people with non-linear pathways – cases of which are only multiplying within a world of work organised around intense though temporary project-based work, in accordance with the 'new spirit of capitalism' (Boltanski and Chiapello, 2005) – are less easily understood by banks, who do not know how to 'profile' them and as such do not lend easily to them, more often than not putting into place conditions that are less favourable than for others.

Sharing risk

Sociological research concerning the bonds between finance and daily life are nevertheless not limited to relationships with banks. Indeed, the transformations of welfare states since the 1980s have led to what Jacob Hacker has called the 'risk shift', in other words transferring the division of social risks from the collective body onto individuals and their personal finances. The costs related to sickness, ageing, education and unemployment, and more broadly to risks of a non-linear nature stemming from one's personal and professional existence, have progressively been transferred onto households, in accordance with the various calendars and modalities in each country. Yet, across the developed world the sum total of student loans, self-funded retirement plans, and insurance policies of all kinds gain more and more momentum, which forces households to sign contracts with private financial companies in order to obtain services and protection which had previously been borne by the State, at least since the end of the Second World War. This transformation of the social contract has had very concrete effects on the definition of the correct management of the family budget. It has become necessary for members of the middle classes to multiply the choice of contracts, the level of risk or the level of savings by anticipating both their needs and the unforeseeable circumstances which may touch their families. Paradoxically, or not, this process took place during a period of massive destabilisation within the working world and stemmed from the near impossibility of anticipating and planning for the level of resources available across an entire life span. The 'risk shift' also affected the division of wealth: household revenues are less secure and less protected when the financial industry possesses the tools that allow it to make profits in an increasingly continuous manner.

Within this context, an idea was developed that the State had not only a role to protect its citizens by sharing between them and with them the social risks, but also to assist them with this individualisation and '*responsabilisation*', in other words, the development of their ability to take on the responsibility for their financial decisions. For around fifteen years now, initiatives have been increased in order to offer people monetary assistance, helping them to learn how to not only calculate but also to economise with the financial institutions. While the money of the poor has for a long time received particular attention from philanthropists like the public authorities, current initiatives are slightly different in that they are destined for the middle classes and are presented as though stripped of any moral connotation. It is a matter of 'only' rationally presenting the risks incurred and the choices to be made, first, so that people make their decisions with full knowledge of the facts, and second, that they be led towards more 'optimal' choices, according to these financial educators, in other words towards an increased level of saving. The OCED has played a very important role in the development of these ideas since the 2000s. It promotes improvement policies in *financial literacy* for the populations of developed nations, a term that outlines both the financial culture, that is the level of people's understanding, and their behaviours. Being *financially literate* signifies that an individual is able to calculate an interest rate and can claim to do his/her own accounts, to save, to anticipate and never be in overdraft with the bank, all while understanding how to compare credit propositions if the need arises. The tools proposed stem largely from behavioural economics, whether they consist of *nudges* created by Richard Thaler and Cass Sustein (2008), public policy tools that propose to transform 'the architecture of choice', or tools for enhancing self-awareness, used in health education (such as pedometers counting daily steps taken) in much the same way as they are in individual money management. In other words, it is a matter of discovering devices so that people can see where their money is going and can derive from that alone the outcomes related to them transforming their practices and themselves.

Conclusion

The G20 listed financial education among its 'high-level principles' in 2011, and the number of governments having put into place public policies related to financial education has not yet ceased to increase. The OECD counted 45 countries in 2013. Such evolutions are proof of the significance of financialisation in daily life and the importance of it being accounted for politically. For all this, does the answer rise to match the scale of the phenomenon? The financial risks which must be confronted by households regularly increase, so information and education can certainly improve the decisions occasionally taken, however the question remains, should these aspects replace the regulation of financial products targeting private individuals, as well as ideas related to the ways of sharing not only the risks but also the riches?

References

Boltanski, L. and Chiapello, E. (2005). *The new spirit of capitalism*. London: Verso Books.

Gloukoviezoff, G. (2010). *L'exclusion bancaire*. Paris: PUF.

Lazarus, J. (2012a). *L'épreuve de l'argent. Banques, banquiers, clients*. Paris: Calmann-Lévy.

Lazarus, J. (2012b). Prévoir la défaillance de crédit: l'ambition du *scoring*. *Raisons Politiques*, 4(48), 103–118.

Ossandón, J. (2012). The economy of the quota: The financial ecologies and commercial circuits of retail credit cards in Santiago, Chile. Retrieved from http://www.charisma-network.net/finance/the-economy-of-the-quota.

Poon, M. (2009). From new deal institutions to capital markets: Commercial consumer risk scores and the making of subprime mortgage finance. *Accounting, Organization and Society*, 34(5), 654–674.

Silver-Greenberg, J. (2012, December 25). Perfect 10? Never mind that. Ask her for her credit score. *The New York Times*. Retrieved from http://www.nytimes.com/2012/12/26/ business/even-cupid-wants-to-know-your-credit-score.html.

Simmel, G. [1900] (2011). *The Philosophy of money*. London: Routledge.

Thaler, R. and Sustein, C. (2008). *Nudge. Improving decisions about health, wealth, and happiness*. New Haven: Yale University Press.

Zelizer, V. (2010). *Economic lives. How culture shapes the economy*. Princeton: Princeton University Press.

30

MAKING SENSE OF THE ECONOMY

A network of debt networks coordinated by currency

Michel Aglietta

The aim of this collective work is greatly ambitious: to reveal that which is hidden within the nebulous that is finance. And the way in which this book deals with this subject is to consider finance like an industry. Moreover, as this work is founded in practices and because it brings together numerous authors from diverse pathways of research, studies and concerns, the approach it has taken is phenomenological. This is why it refers to 'fieldwork', a mode of investigation familiar to sociology. Conversely, the term field evokes limited spaces, while in contemporary finance the fields, if they exist, are entwined within interrelations that span the globe. It is without doubt necessary to go beyond spatial dimensions in order to redefine this term using a collection of differentiated practices. To that effect, stock markets, mutual banks, private equity and credit rating agencies can all be qualified as fields. This can be stretched to include financial regulation, yet it must be structured as a subset.

Finance does not allow itself to be easily defined. While, indeed, finance does possess distinct territories, it has but one unity. And this springs from the interdependencies that run through all financial practices and which determine how finance takes part in regulating a regime of knowledge, though also how this regulation enters into crisis. Understandably, this book takes a critical perspective towards the so-called neo-liberal approach to finance. This approach is unified by the efficiency hypothesis, which defines a coordination exclusively run by the market. It establishes the compatibility of all the financial practices in this theoretical reference. The fieldwork analysis sets out to show how the practices, which have resulted from this theory, do not comply with the efficiency hypothesis. However, identifying the coordinating element that links all this together can further develop this critical perspective.

Maintaining that finance is governed by the efficiency hypothesis amounts to acknowledging that it is ordered by the logic of equilibrium: if we reject the efficiency hypothesis, then we must also question the coordinating element which allows us to become aware of both the instability of finance and its unity. On the contrary, if we do not reject the efficiency hypothesis, the acknowledgement of economic financialisation does not make sense. The coordinating element at issue here is currency; in short, the system of payments established through monetary obligations, therefore the settlement of debts. Examining currency as debt and the self-referential desire for liquidity as an issue for financial power provides meaning to the contradictions created by the financial system and to the institutions that maintain them.

The economy is a network of debt networks, coordinated by currency

Currency can be defined as an adherence-based relation for the members of one social group to this group as a whole. At this abstract level currency is akin to language. It produces meaning for others. And this meaning is the *value*: an abstract space of measure expressed in accounts that record the transactions taking place between the subjects of the exchange. The operation through which the objects of the exchange acquire a value is the payment. It follows that the value of objects destined to be exchanged does not pre-exist the exchange event. The exchange for currency, that is the payment, is the operator of value.

In a monetary economy of production, commercial relations are structured around debts, since the producers must borrow resources (for example, pay employees) before converting these into new products that aspire to become values. These debts are IOUs (*I Owe You*), more or less transferable depending on the stamp of the issuers.

Because commercial relations are built on debts and because debts are only accepted under the aegis of society, it is normal that the debt relation becomes the system. Whoever talks of debt in a commercial society, refers in reality to the solvency requirement for he who shoulders it. Currency is what enables debt to be dissolved or deferred to a later date in a way that is approved of by society. It is the system of payments that operationalises this social constraint. It is indeed a structural logic in that it does not rely upon reasons for why these debts were entered into.

A system of payment, at the most basic level, has a minimum of three components: a *common unit of account*, which allows for the expression of economic variables (individual price or wealth), a *coinage principal*, which is the condition for the decentralised action of individuals and a *principle for settling balances*, which clearly explains how equivalence in exchanges determines the economic variables. For a settlement to take place, there needs to be a unanimously accepted debt, which settles all other debts. It is the ultimate liquidity, which legitimacy requires the belonging of currency as a system of regulations for sovereignty. Even so, as liquidity is objective, it can still be subject to private ownership. Because liquidity is the absolute form of wealth, he who possesses it is subject to an unlimited desire for wealth. The ambivalence of currency thus results from this and with it the possibility that crises occur in the payment system, which then destroys the stability of renewing the debt structure in the future. This is therefore why every major financial crisis has, at its climatic moment, gone through a crisis of liquidity. In these critical moments, the exclusive and contagious hunt for liquidity by those agents in debt destroys the interdependent chain of compensation and the vulnerability of balance sheets becomes widespread.

Financial cycle and shareholder value: the macro-micro link in financial capitalism

Ever since the aftermath of financial crises began to persist in time, the macro-economy has once more been confronted with the issue of age-old stagnation. Today, the most unique and worrisome expression of this age-old stagnation phenomenon is the breakdown of investment. The productive investment of companies, the most substantial share of all private investment, accounts for close to two-thirds of the downturn. Among all the probable causes for this collapse in investment, the most immediate explanation is the overall weakness of activity. There is undeniably some truth to this analysis. Nevertheless it is not enough to just be aware of the phenomenon. One must examine the heart of the capital accumulation dynamic by enlisting the theory of the *natural rate of interest* attributed to Wicksell.

Within this framework, the interest rate becomes less of a passive reflection of imbalances between savings and investment, and more the product of an interaction between the marginal productivity of investments on one side and the costs and risks of its financing on the other. Historical studies conducted by the Bank for International Settlements going back more than 20 years, and enhanced by numerous academic studies into the historical comparisons of large-scale financial crises, have shown the existence of financial cycles of great importance and with long periodicity (15 to 20 years). These cycles are proof that finance is driven by a logic of *momentum*, and not one based on balancing the intrinsic values of assets which the efficiency of finance would help discover. It follows that the natural rate of interest, which is the marginal net return for capital, is a function of the determinants of this *momentum*, which are the expansion followed by the contraction of private credit and the euphoria followed by the depression of financial and property asset prices. This harks back to Marx's observations concerning phases of over-accumulation, followed by the depreciation of capital. In the wake of the turning point marked by the 2008–2009 crisis (a Minsky moment), a dormant depression was endured in which the natural rate of interest fell too low for investment to be able to pick up again in spite of nominal interest rates being steered towards zero by the central banks.

This financial cycle, which has been observed in nineteenth-century classical capitalism, had disappeared with the arrival of Fordist capitalism following World War II when finance was widely regulated and corporations were directed according to managerial governance, immune to financial market incentives. The financial cycle's return to a macro-scale during the 1980s is not a phenomenon unique to finance, as if it were a field separated from the rest of the economy. At the micro-level there is but one field incorporating the financialisation of non-financial corporations, in other words the transformation of governance principles in relation to the so-called 'Fordist' company. Antoine Rebérioux and myself have highlighted this radical transformation of capitalism's regulation mode since 2004, through studying the drift of financial capitalism (Aglietta and Rebérioux, 2005), without receiving any support from the academic community during a period in which the concept of the efficiency of finance was triumphantly prevailing.

The most important point is that the principle of shareholder value disassociates the natural rate of interest, that is the net marginal return of productive capital across the entire economy, from the financial profitability pursued by shareholders. Its operating mode is EVA – Economic Value Added. This consists of extracting an additional annuity on top of the capital's marginal return. Entering into debt is the main lever for targeting the financial return of equity capital.

Shareholder value, through its organic connection with debt, is a powerful motor for the financial cycle. Indeed, for a rate of return anticipated on the total assets of a given company, shareholder value is increasingly dependent on debt. This results in companies entering into a minimum rate of debt to sustain an EVA target superior to the marginal return of the company's assets. This rate of debt grows with the expectations of shareholders. In addition, debt involves creditors, for whom uncertainty regarding the company's future returns leads to establishing a debt maximum based on a limit of acceptable losses (the value-at-risk). This limit increases with the debtors' level of debt. If therefore the minimum debt amount demanded by shareholders is superior to the maximum debt limit tolerated by lenders, no system of balanced growth is possible for the company. In this area of instability, uncertainty increases until a catalyst event reverses the financial cycle.

Consequently, shareholder value produces latent instability in finance. Moreover, the higher the distribution rate of the dividends (or the buy-back of shares in order to distribute the annuity as capital gains) the more the productive investment is discouraged for a given rate of debt. In order to push back this limitation, financial innovation has to work hard. In the event that lenders can remove credit risk through dispersal channels, as long as the base interest rate can be contained, the limit of the maximum rate of debt can be pushed back. As a corollary, the financial operations generated by these techniques lead to redistributing the annuity between a multitude of intermediaries. And all these countless measures are equally fields for the making of finance.

Conclusion

Finance is far from neutral when it comes to the economy. The macro–micro interdependency in the financial cycle leads us towards thinking about financial stability as a public asset that thus requires economic policies to define it. One of the challenges is notably to understand that policies which fail to take into consideration medium-to-long term financial cycles may limit short-term recessions, but this is at the cost of experiencing more severe recessions later on.

The interdependencies weaved by financial globalisation play a critical role in the duration of expansion phases, in the intensity of crises and in the prolongation of the economic stagnation that ensues. Banks in every developed nation have become interconnected through derivative markets centred on transferring credit risk, through the securitisation of credits and through the various forms of liquidity creation that circumvent traditional interbank loans (CDS, repos, securities lending, exchange-traded funds) and turn illiquid assets into liquid ones. This liquidity, called *shadow banking*, created within the risk transfer markets, evaporates instantly once asset prices turn around. Financial regulation must therefore go well beyond Basel III in order to be efficient.

With the financialisation of non-financial companies figuring on the other side of this phenomenon, a fundamental change to company governance is indispensable in order to drive back the principle of shareholder value and institute methods of governance that involve the company's partners.

Finally, rediscovering the meaning of the long-term entails involving responsible investors, who are capable and willing to redirect the governance of these companies. A responsible investor is one who enlists strategies that incorporate the challenges of sustainability; is a financial intermediary who gathers large amounts of contractual savings; who recognises the interdependencies existing between financial and non-financial evaluations, because his future vision sees far enough ahead for him to understand that degradation in the quality of growth threatens long-term capital returns. By redirecting investments towards horizons of sustainable growth, these actors can help turn around the profitability of productive capital towards a new regime of growth.

Reference

Aglietta, M. and Rebérioux, A. (2005). *Corporate governance adrift. A critique of shareholder value.* Cheltenham: Edward Elgar.

CONCLUSION

What finance manufactures

Olivier Godechot

Why should we approach the study of finance in an alternative way when other disciplines – such as economics and financial theory – which are older, more legitimate and endowed with more substantial backing, have already been tackling this subject for over fifty years? Admirably, despite any misgivings, the rapid and varied development of a collection of studies on finance has nonetheless originated over the last twenty years from a variety of disciplines (sociology, anthropology, political science, history, management sciences, geography). This has resulted from the dynamic academic practice of diversifying and reviving research subjects, though also because of a dissatisfaction with the inadequacy of standard approaches. But that is not all, as it has equally stemmed from a desire to understand a much deeper phenomenon: the sudden emergence of finance in social life.

This research, at times grouped under the heading of the 'social studies of finance' – underlining its multidisciplinary nature and its relationship with the social studies of science – and other times grouped under the heading of 'sociology of finance' – underlining its relation with economic sociology – was notably developed out of several events which included a seminar held in France,[1] regular international encounters, the setting up of an electronic mailing list and the publishing of several special editions of academic journals,[2] in addition to some collective works (Knorr Cetina and Preda, 2004 and 2012). Beyond the paradigmatic, theoretical or methodological diversity of this research, we can find a common approach: to study finance not only as a subject in itself, but also as a symptom of the contemporary financialisation of societies and their transformations. By studying the making of finance, we also study the magnitude of that which finance itself makes. Within these pages, we address the mechanisms and the social practices of contemporary capitalism that are often more visible in finance and are quite commonly disseminated across the rest of the economy from this financial hearth. After presenting research on contemporary financialisation, we demonstrate how the social studies of finance highlight three emblematic trends related to contemporary capitalism. These are, the – depoliticising – institutional policy of market order, a new knowledge regime combining academic knowledge with non-expert knowledge, and finally, the systematisation of 'greed'.

Approaching financialisation

Since the beginning of the 1980s, the financialisation of the world's economy has paradoxically manifested as a trivial phenomenon experienced by the whole world as part of everyday life, while at the same time being a difficult phenomenon to clearly define, measure or explain. First, both the outline and the definition of financialisation are difficult to establish precisely. Common proxies for this phenomenon include an increase in finance's share of the gross domestic product (GDP), profit or wages (Godechot, 2012 and 2013; Krippner, 2005; Philippon and Resheff, 2013; Tomaskovic-Devey and Lin, 2011). One could be led to believe that a large portion of traditional finance (e.g. retail banking) is not relevant to this trend, as this concept brings to mind first and foremost the growing importance of financial markets in our modern-day societies. A provisional Durkheimian definition of financialisation may be the growing amount of social energy devoted to the trading of financial instruments on financial markets. The volume of transactions taking place on the markets would therefore be a good candidate to measure it (Godechot, 2016b). Nevertheless, restricting financialisation to the trade of financial instruments would lead us to miss an important aspect. The depth of the subprime crisis shows that part of the traditional banking system, which includes mortgages (Fligstein and Goldstein, 2010), consumer credit or credit cards (Poon, 2009), has been deeply affected by new ideas stemming from financial markets, for example commodification, securitisation, liquidity, diversification, standardisation, fair value accounting, mathematical pricing models and delta-hedging techniques for arbitrage. Financialisation therefore cannot be limited to the growth of financial markets, but should instead be understood as the spread of the financial market's core logic beyond the bounds of its original sphere.

Second, the causes of financialisation are far from clear. Traditional explanations, in terms of demands for financial services or links between financial services and economic growth, struggle to account for long-term trends (Philippon and Resheff, 2013). Deregulation policies have played a significant role in this movement (*ibid.*), specifically with respect to all the pro-market policies detailed in the section that follows. In the same line, the combination of advances in financial theory and new technologies equally contributed to perform new markets (cf. third section). However, it would also appear that once the initial favourable conditions are aligned, market finance also increases in accordance with endogenous mechanisms (into which more research is still needed), creating as such a phenomenon of path dependency.

Third, the consequences of financialisation have not yet been fully measured. Traditionally, the main issue in economics is finance's contribution to economic growth, financial and economic stability and global crises (Aglietta and Rebérioux, 2004; Artus et al., 2008). A growing section of the research also underlines finance's substantial impact on the increase of inequalities (Atkinson et al., 2011), due to the high-income salaries distributed at its core (Bell and Van Reenen, 2014; Godechot, 2012). It has also contributed substantially to spatial segregation and the increase in salary differences between global cities and hinterlands (Godechot, 2013), as well as to inequalities within non-financial firms (Goldstein, 2012; Lin and Tomaskovic-Devey, 2013), notably due to the promotion of new forms of management and new ways of conceptualising companies, based exclusively on their financial value. Finally, financialisation emerges by activating powerful mechanisms (both within and outside of its own field) that will be further detailed in the following pages of this chapter.

A depoliticising policy: the institution of markets

Market exchange has not always been thought of as a fundamentally apolitical act. As such, during the emergence of the London Stock Market, at the beginning of the eighteenth century, transactions for certain securities took place preferentially between members of the same party, either the *Whigs* or the *Tories* (Carruthers, 1996). In the context of consecutive political rivalry at the time of the Glorious Revolution, these two parties, whether by safeguarding it or conquering for it, indeed sought to maintain their control over the principal institutions lending money to the State and, in doing so, either establish or defend their own power over the State. The initial political dimension of financial exchange, especially visible in England during the eighteenth century, was nonetheless obscured by the effectively symbolic work of depoliticisation. De Goede (2005) provides a striking example of this process by revisiting the narrow and fragile threshold that financial markets established in the United States between gambling – unlawful and often forbidden – and financial speculation – which was considered lawful. Consequently, US stock market representatives succeeded in establishing, in the eyes of the authorities, a contrast between two very similar practices. The first being bets placed on prices that took place in certain cafés known as *bucket shops*, that were thought to exploit an irrational passion for gambling and destabilise the markets, and the second being futures trading on the stock markets by speculators, who were presumed to conduct sound calculations and therefore stabilise prices through their actions. De Goede thus proposes the groundwork for a Foucauldian history of financial markets which, through re-politicising institutions that present themselves in a naturalised and depoliticised manner, thus demonstrates the very contingent, political and *in fine* amendable nature of financial markets.

Financial markets are hence paradoxically political. They deny their political character by highlighting the primacy of financial interest and the non-partisan nature of their equilibria (above all guided by the principles of economics). However, in parallel, the principle financial maxim – that prices represent the value of securities – is no less than a political affirmation that implies furthermore a specific social order (Ortiz, 2013, 2014a and 2014b). The paradoxically (a)political market order is not only the result of the endogenous dynamic of the financial sphere, it also owes its existence to policies related to the creation or the deepening of financial markets.

Montagne (2006) accordingly retraces the very specific legal conditions within the framework of which US pension funds, one of the pillars of contemporary financialisation, have been able to prosper. In actual fact, they depend upon a type of contract that is hardly representative of classical liberalism, known as a *trust*, which originates from the feudal world and that deems the beneficiary (the employee) a minor. The State's imperative to protect this individual as such leads less towards a freeing-up of the contract, than it does towards the surveying of *trustees*. In particular, the 1974 Employee Retirement Income Security Act (ERISA) urges pension funds to follow 'good financial practices' and forbids them to take into account any additional interests (such as retaining the recipients' employment) other than the financial interests of their employee recipients. This Act *in fine* moves less towards giving employees control over finance, than it does towards sealing off finance within itself.

Quite paradoxically, pro-market policy has not always been promoted solely by financial circles but also quite often by coalitions. Such coalitions were formed between social movements, finance groups and progressive governments – desiring to open up financing possibilities for those most in need or to improve market competition. Fligstein and Goldstein (2010) consequently illustrate how the development of *Mortgage Backed Securities* was initiated by the Johnson administration in the context of its *Great Society* project. The

US government had discovered that this type of security, backed by major governmental mortgage agencies (Fanny Mae and Freddie Mac), could be an innovative solution for promoting access to property for those on the inferior fringes of the middle class, without fuelling the then-threatening inflation. As Krippner (2011) has shown, the dismantling of the *Glass-Steagall Act* – which since the 1930s separated investment banking from commercial banking – and more specifically, the dismantling of one of its emblematic measures, the *Q Regulation* – which limited interest rates on loans and deposits – were also brought on by social movements led by progressive actors such as Ralph Nader. Across the Atlantic in France, the major market transformation was carried out during the 1980s by the socialist government who, following the failure of stimulus policies, opted to promote market socialism (Lagneau-Ymonet and Riva, 2012).

So, in spite of all this, are financial markets wholly embedded in institutions and institutional policies – including those that strive for dis-embeddedness (Gayon and Lemoine, 2014)? Fligstein initiated this particular research programme by illustrating that traditional company governance, notably distinguished by its promotion of the multi-divisional firm and managers who originate from finance departments, owes a lot to legislation changes in the 1950s that limited vertical and horizontal integration in the name of competition (Fligstein, 1990). Numerous studies have shown that the multi-divisional firm model, whose privileged objectives were diversification and expansion, ceded its place to an organisational model focused on creating shareholder value (Fligstein, 2001) and entirely centred on its core business activities, with the aim of maximising the company's stock market value. The firm was therefore split into as many profit centres as there were elementary units, with the value of each being measured in light of its potential resale on the market. A symptom of this transformation was the increasing power attributed to finance directors heading up companies and their appointment as chief financial officers (CFO), replacing chief operating officers (COO) (Zorn, 2004; Zorn et al., 2005). Clearly present at the outset of this movement is an institutional source, namely the transformation of the US tax system at the end of the 1970s (Zorn, 2004). The movement continued however thanks to the promotion of the shareholder value creation ideology, the 1980s hostile takeovers and the heightened role of financial analysts in determining prices (Zorn et al., 2005). It also owed much to a logic endogenous to the economic field of the 1980s, which reunited and opposed three types of actors against one another. First off, the firm CEOs wanting to defend their power and their remuneration. Next, the *corporate raiders* who through leveraged buyout transactions – enabled thanks to the development of *junk bonds* – took control of major companies (or threatened to do so) in order to brutally restructure them. And finally, institutional investors, notably pension funds, preoccupied with avoiding certain transactions that could affect them negatively, such as *greenmailing* – when firms buyback shares from raiders for prices higher than those on the market (Heilbron et al., 2014). The diffusion of the shareholder value ideology, which favours less the shareholder than it does those said to represent them (Goldstein, 2012; Jung and Dobbin, 2016), owes more to the 'field logic' than to a single actor, even if that actor happens to be the State itself (Heilbron et al., 2014).

Approaching finance, its origins and its development, via its institutional embeddedness avoids turning financialisation into a self-emerging phenomenon that materialises out of thin air. Even though institutions do not provide an explanation for everything, they certainly play the role of founder and initiator. Moving beyond this initiator's role, policy from state institutions during the financial cycles of deregulation–crisis–reregulation (Abolafia, 1996), notably that of the central bank (Fligstein and Goldstein, 2010; Krippner, 2011), has also been found to be stunningly short-sighted and incapable in the US of predicting the formation of a bubble or of softening the blow after it has burst. This is also the case with policy from governments, who only succeed in putting into place effective, less costly and restrictive rescue plans once the banking industry has managed to collectively coordinate itself under the leadership of its key players urged on by their declining health (Woll, 2014).

A new regime of knowledge

The *Social Studies of Finance* not only examine how modern finance has taken root institutionally, they also consider the new regime of knowledge that finance encourages, which is characterised by a strong, but also transformative interaction between professional and academic knowledge. It is less a question of contesting such professional and academic knowledge, than it is of taking it up as subjects for study; and doing so consequently enables researchers to show how finance itself is structured and transformed by financial science.

The *Social Studies of Finance* (SSF) are therefore the principal grounds on which a research programme studying 'performativity'[3] has been established, first launched by Michel Callon in 1998. According to Callon, the at times ritual criticism of neo-classical economics found in economic sociology articles is both unproductive and inaccurate. On the contrary, the utopian idea of *homo œconomicus* has re-emerged as 'economics, in the broad sense of the term, performs, shapes and formats the economy, rather than observing how it functions' (Callon, 1998). This revival of John Austin's concept has flourished in the field of SSF, to the point where several authors have considered it a key theme. The research produced as a result of this movement has shown that scientific statements are no longer just observations but, much like the celebrant's words 'I now declare you husband and wife', they also have the ability to transform the reality about which they speak.

In line with this perspective, Muniesa (2000, 2007) established a genealogy related to a minor innovation, which occurred on the Paris Stock Market: the introduction of a *fixing* auction at market close.[4] This auction resulted from the crossing over of two quite distinct areas of activity. On one side, there were the market engineers, anxious about potential end-of-day manipulations with regard to establishing the closing price, a reference for many market agreements. On the other side, researchers from the academic world concerned with either financial theory or auction theory, who were comparing the quality of prices in various market structures. Organising a fixing auction for the market close, ten minutes after the end of continuous trading, appeared to be an elegant solution for establishing market equilibrium – *à la Walras*. It produced 'good quality' prices, founded on the accumulation of all sale and purchase offers made over a substantial period of time, and it was a very good response to the practical problem of price manipulation. It was enforced contrary to an alternative solution used on other stock markets, that of calculating an average of the prices 30 minutes before close, a solution considered by stock market experts to be more artificial and less revealing in terms of market forces. The field of economics therefore acted as a source of inspiration and, combined with market engineering, thus contributed towards performing the organisation of financial transactions.

MacKenzie (2006), examining the fate of the Black Scholes formula in the financial industry, analysed another even more distinct case of the performativity of economics. In 1973 Black and Scholes published a theoretical solution to a then canonical academic issue in financial economics, that of the value of an *option*, a type of contract offering the right – but imposing no obligation – to buy a particular share on a given date. By modelling share prices as a Log-normal random walk, the two economists showed that the price of an option is a function of several elements, which included its duration, the interest rate, the price and the volatility of the share in question. When the two theorists began testing the formula on past data, they found it incorrectly described the relations between prices. However, a short time after the formula was published, prices began to behave just like it had indicated.

The various stages of this example of 'performativity' have been explained in detail by MacKenzie. In the mid-1970s, the price listings were sold off by one of the formula's creators. These listings described the theoretical value of options in relation to the evolution of current market prices. They were subsequently used by *traders* on the market to locate expensive and cheap options, allowing them to engage in arbitrage by selling off the former and buying up the latter. This 'performing' of the market in line with the formula, insists MacKenzie, does not correspond to a situation whereby the market adopts the 'only genuine solution' to the problem of pricing. The formula relied on noteworthy approximations and simplifications, in particular the hypothesis of the Log-normality of prices, that is to say the very weak probability of extreme variations. The crash of 1987 during which the market fell by more than 20 per cent in a single day would have been improbable according to the modelling used above. Financial theory, which deals with the pricing of complex financial products and portfolio allocation, therefore overturns the rationale of scientific discovery. In essence, it transforms financial reality to a much greater extent than it uncovers the relations that structure it.

Such 'performing' is not limited to canonical theories of financial science. Certain seemingly insignificant technical mechanisms of representation can play a determining role in the action. Zuckerman (1999, 2004) as such underlines the impact of categories employed by actors. In his work, financial analysts are seen to perceive firm value through economic sectors. Categories are therefore all the more meaningful to analysts in that they constitute a framework for their professional specialisation. Multi-sector firms, incoherent from the perspective of categorical division, are therefore often monitored by analysts coming from vastly different specialisations. This incoherent network position generates fewer, less favourable and more contradictory valuations; consequently prompting the undervaluation of a company's securities on the stock market, in addition to triggering stronger volatility and higher transaction volumes when results are announced.

It is impossible though to reduce the scientific research programme analysing the regime of financial knowledge to the study of the performativity of academic financial theory. For one reason, it is not always performed with success (Jung and Dobbin, 2016). In certain cases, even counter-performativity could be mentioned (MacKenzie, 2006), particularly that of the anomalies revealed by behavioural finance. Even just the naming of anomalies (such as the 1st of January effect, which is the likelihood of a price rise occurring on this date) can lead to their disappearance (simply through the exploitation of opportunities for arbitrage). For another reason, the programme of performativity often forgets to include cultural, social and institutional reasons that can lead to different theories being adopted. The programme of performativity can therefore be expanded via a study of financial reasoning in all its diversity (Tadjeddine, 2000).

Smith (1999) is without doubt one of the first sociologists to propose a detailed analysis of financial beliefs and behaviours through the development of a gallery of flamboyant profiles that feature financial participants. He distinguishes six diverse categories of true believers who think the market is systematically governed by forces. First up are the 'Fundamentalists', who believe that economic forecasts, in particular those related to dividends, are what determine prices. Next, there are those partial to the theory of 'Insiders' who believe prices are determined by major players who have access to privileged information, which leads them to lie in wait for any related rumours. The Cyclist-Chartists make their predictions on the basis of 'resistance lines', straight lines they trace between the *extrema* (maxima and minima) of prices. Then there are the proponents of the Trader style, who follow their *feelings* trying to sense the market's movements, while Efficient Market Believers consider that the only thing that matters is accurately replicating the global market in their portfolios. Finally, the 'Transformational Idea Adherents' seek out economic ideas likely to radically change the world, like for example the 'new economy'.

Less specific with regard to the spread of possible beliefs and their ways of functioning, within my own research (Godechot, 2001, 2016a) I have examined a variety of financial practices identified in trading rooms involved in the commercialisation and arbitrage of sophisticated derivatives, and have established connections between these and individual career paths in finance, the capital owned by actors and, lastly, the structure of the positions they occupy in the room. Social and educational background, in addition to the means of initiation into financial activities, which often occurs via a mentor, produce ways of seeing the market that are not only persistent, but that also represent a system of likes and dislikes – that never runs dry of tireless controversies – similar in a way to the debates commonly found amongst IT users: Mac or PC, Windows or Linux, etc. As it were, three financial strategies that are easily identified via a questionnaire – mathematical arbitrage, chartist analysis and economic analysis – stand opposed to one another in that they create opposition between individuals who either come from different educational backgrounds or who hold different positions in the trading room or who maintain different market perspectives. Followers of mathematical arbitrage here find an alternative way of continuing the preparatory school where they developed an enchanted relationship with academic knowledge. Like the followers of economic analysis, they often find chartists to be inept, and the two compete to provide explanations for its wholly unfounded use. They are however also quite often opposed to macro-economic analysis as, according to them, it lacks precision. Followers of this latter analysis in contrast highlight the limited character of arbitrage; i.e. the small wins, which deep down are not based on a global understanding of the market, but only on the very narrow relations between various securities from the same family. Finally, the followers of chartist analysis, often hailing from working class backgrounds, hold in high regard the counter-cultural side of this pagan-like knowledge. Although its methods generally lead to ambiguous recommendations, they believe charts enable them to outdo even those financial actors using the most legitimate forms of knowledge (Godechot, 2008a). This description of these three opposing camps jostling around within one space – connected by a continuum of hybrid positions much like a 'bazaar of rationality', where everyone brings what they have to offer and positions themselves in relation to what others are offering, seeking to both associate and differentiate themselves from one another – allows us to think differently about rationality; and not just as an *a priori* given for social actors, like economists' models make it out to be, but as a structural process for acquiring and constructing reasoning (Godechot, 2016a). The guiding principle of this bazaar of rationality is therefore, either consciously or unconsciously, 'economic', as it incites individuals to take up those techniques for which they feel the most affinity, for which they possess the most capital and the necessary predisposition. Concerning the nature of the market, this debate between supporters of different methods in one way shows that the market is a reflexive institution. The market is neither fundamentalist, nor chartist, nor does it conform to mathematic efficiency. It is instead the product of this clash between differing points of view (Godechot, 2008a).

If knowledge is at this point constitutive of contemporary finance, we can therefore deduce that the financial crisis itself is also a matter of knowledge. As has been convincingly demonstrated by Donald MacKenzie (2011) in relation to the *subprime* crisis. The most toxic financial products, the MBS-CDOs – debt obligations backed by mortgage portfolios – were potentially born from two types of knowledge, one relative to mortgage securitisation (for the first stage of securitisation) and the other relative to corporate bonds securitisation (for the second stage of securitisation). Banks and ratings agencies, however, entrusted the valuation of mortgage products to services involved in the securitisation of corporate bonds, who in doing so transposed logical reasoning specific to the valuation of corporate bonds portfolios across to MBS-CDOs. However, in contrast with corporate portfolios, there are no price series for mortgage portfolios enabling the autocorrelation of defaults and anticipated repayments to be calculated. To make up for this lack of information, the banks and ratings agencies adopted an arbitrary level of correlation (a 'Gaussian Copula') of 0.3, which corresponded to the mean autocorrelation for defaults by firms within the same sector. The avalanche of defaults following the 2007 interest rate rise shows that this conceptual decision, the product of a conceptual and social division of labour in asset valuation activities, seriously underestimated the autocorrelation of defaults, leading as a result to the most serious financial crisis since the Great Depression.

The systematisation of 'greed'

The unilaterality of the challenges uniquely faced in finance – namely, providing profit for corporations and bonuses for employees – in addition to the degree of technicality involved in economic calculations and transaction arrangements, and the lively competition that rules over markets, all contribute towards developing the autonomous separation of this field from others, in addition to establishing highly rationalised practices. Numerous authors (Abolafia, 1996, pp. 14–37; Godechot, 2001; Zaloom, 2006, pp. 111–125) have examined this Weberian process of behaviour rationalisation and questioned whether the financial world was not in some way contributing to bringing the fictional being of *homo œconomicus* (Callon, 1998) into actual existence, thanks to work spaces equipped with computing systems, the continuous accounting of business activity and, most importantly, due to strong monetary incentives. Studying incentives is a good way of understanding rationalisation, because their impact is without doubt more striking in this sphere than elsewhere. However, carrying out such a study means avoiding two pitfalls. The first involves considering rationalisation to be so powerful that it will ultimately culminate in the arrival, at the heart of the financial markets, of a perfect and accomplished *homo œconomicus*, wholly validating the scientific approaches (*mainstream* economics) founded exclusively on this hypothesis, even if done so for 'ill-founded reasons', eventually rendering any development of alternative approaches redundant. The second pitfall consists of believing that all incentives have been rationally calibrated in order to produce behaviours aligned in favour with the shareholder's interests.

Emphasising more or less this dimension, ethnographic studies show that compensations, in particular bonuses, constitute the gravitational centre of financial activity (Abolafia, 1996;

Godechot, 2001 and 2016c; Ortiz, 2014a; Roth, 2006; Zaloom, 2006). High remuneration indeed greatly steers behaviours, though without achieving the equilibrium described by neoclassical economics. Indeed, on the whole the extremely elevated compensation levels present in finance illustrate that neither the financial securities market, nor the financial labour market are efficient. If salaries were to follow the predictions provided by principal-agent models, then they would consist of a much lower fixed salary, even a negative salary (< 0), so that the utility in these financial roles would be equivalent to that encountered in non-financial professions that require the same skills (Godechot, 2011 and 2016c). The fact that certain employees are able to acquire the power to *hold-up* a corporation constitutes a better explanation for the level of wages than the idea of optimal incentives to work hard (Godechot, 2016c). Studying an exemplary case concerning hold-ups allows us to stylise how salaries are actually determined. In 2000, two trading room managers working for a major bank obtained €10 and €7 million in bonuses by brandishing the credible threat to leave and take the teams they managed with them to a rival bank. This case illustrates the logic of the hold-up, namely that having control of transferable assets provides the means to threaten the company with damages if they refuse a renegotiation that favours the employee. This technique is even more frequent considering that protection against it is relatively inefficient. It leads us to observe the financial industry's labour market in a different way; as though it was less like a market representing people and individual skills, and more like a market of corporate assets collectively produced and carried off by people who organise their transfer (Godechot, 2014).

Studying compensation is also important for understanding financial behaviours. Following the crisis, the wider public and most economists emphasised the fact that remunerations could encourage risk-taking and help to explain the crisis (Cheng et al., 2015). To this well-known element, perhaps overestimated in the public debate, we can add another that remains underrated (Godechot, 2008b). *Bonuses* not only lead to excess risk-taking (with only the positive amount of the profit being rewarded, while negative amounts carry no penalties), they also lead to the deformation of risk measurement or more precisely the politicisation of risk measurement in financial corporations. Indeed, as long as the equivalent of 100–200 per cent of the bulk of fixed salaries is distributed each year in the form of bonuses and as long as these bonuses depend on accounting measures based on the revenues net of the costs of risk, then the temptation to underestimate the risks incurred so as to maximise bonuses will remain great, and even more so when they involve new financial products that are difficult to value. Moreover, in major banks, risk management departments do not fully assume their supervisory role. To begin with, faced with this role, *front office* staffs enjoy great legitimacy and a powerful ability to impose certain risk measurements on other parties, to inherently favour their own position. Second, bonuses for risk management departments often depend at least indirectly on the percentage of the bonus pool duly granted to the *front office*. Finally, those in risk management often have their sights set on *trading* professions. They must therefore monitor people for whom they would very much like to work for in the future. This therefore means not being too overzealous, so as to avoid upsetting them.

This greed-based logic also fuels the two additional logics discussed above: the depoliticising institution of markets and the transformational overlapping of academic and professional knowledges. The article by Jung and Dobbin (2016) articulates how the partial performing of the neoclassical academic theory of firms, which promotes a depoliticised firm uniquely at the service of its shareholders, owes much to the remuneration conditions of portfolio managers handling pension funds. Paid in the form of bonuses, they promote the elements of this theory in line with this form of extremely short-term compensation, and abandon all others.

Conclusion: the advance of finance

This overview of social studies research centred on finance, which is undoubtedly incomplete, aims to illustrate the *advance* of finance, in the dual sense of the term. On one hand, illustrating the progress finance has made and, on the other, the lead it has taken ahead of other economic sectors and more generally the rest of society. A comprehensive evaluation of the social effects of this advance has, as yet, only just begun. While mainstream economics generally tends to underline any shared benefits, other social sciences, which are more critical, often focus exclusively on the costs. Although finance subjects (certain) people to new constraints, it also liberates (others) from traditional dependencies (Fontaine, 2014). As a final example of this, the development of *credit scoring* in the US clearly demonstrates how transforming the way credit equivalences are established can alter the types of actors who are either favoured or disfavoured. The credit score system indeed replaces a method of credit distribution founded on affiliations with specific categories (i.e. gender, race, age) and local social reputations, with one instead founded on one's personal debt and repayment history (Fourcade and Healy, 2013; Poon, 2009). Furthermore, the academic debate *a propos* the costs and benefits of the *advance* of finance is but a subset of the political and social debate surrounding this same issue. Policy choices reflect a reorientation in relation to this subject. After three decades of policies stimulating the advance of finance, now, following the 2008 financial crisis, societies instead seek to contain it without, for the moment, having found the necessary solutions.

Notes

1 Originally, the expression Social Studies of Finance (*Etudes Sociales de la Finance*) was used in France to group together a collection of social science approaches dealing with financial markets, which offered alternatives to the dominant financial and economic theories. This entry via science and technology studies, inspired by research from Callon and Latour, was a strong initial component but not the only one. Later, certain authors had a tendency to identify the Social Studies of Finance in relation to this unique approach.
2 Notably issue 52 of *Politix* (2000), issue 21 of *Réseaux* (2003), issues 146–147 of *Actes de la Recherche en Sciences Sociales* (2003), issue 63-1 of *L'Année sociologique* (2013), and finally the issues 92 and 93 of *Sociétés Contemporaines* (2013 and 2014).
3 Developed in a collection of works published in 1962 by the philosopher Austin (*How to do things with words*), the concept of 'performativity' describes the characteristic of language that is its influence over the reality it describes.
4 *Fixing* here refers to a discrete call auction wherein the auctioneer has taken time to gather together all the sales and purchasing orders before establishing the price. It sits in opposition to continuous trading, where as soon as an offering price equals the sales price, a transaction is concluded.

References

Abolafia, M. (1996). *Making markets. Opportunism and restraint on Wall Street*. Cambridge: Harvard University Press.

Aglietta, M. and Rebérioux, A. (2004). *Dérives du capitalisme financier*. Paris: Albin Michel.

Artus, P., Betbèze J.-P., de Boissieu, C. and Capelle-Blancard, G. (2008). *La crise des subprimes*. Paris: La documentation française.

Atkinson, A. B., Piketty, T. and Saez, E. (2011). Top incomes in the long run of history. *Journal of Economic Literature*, 49(1), 3–71.

Austin, J. (1962). *How to do things with words*. Oxford: Clarendon Press.

Bell, B. and Van Reenen, J. (2014). Bankers and their bonuses. *Economic Journal*, 124, F1–F21.

Callon, M. (1998). Introduction: The embeddedness of economic markets in economics'. In M. Callon (Ed.), *The laws of the markets* (pp. 1–57). Oxford: Blackwell Publishers.

Carruthers, B. (1996). *City of capital. Politics and markets in the English financial revolution*. Princeton: Princeton University Press.

Cheng, I.-H., Hong, H. and Scheinkman, J. (2015). Yesterday's heroes: Compensation and risk at financial firms. *Journal of Finance*, 70(2), 839–879.

De Goede, M. (2005). *Virtue, fortune and faith: A genealogy of finance*. Minneapolis: University of Minnesota Press.

Fligstein, N. (1990). *The transformation of corporate control*. Cambridge: Harvard University Press.

Fligstein, N. (2001). *The architecture of markets: An economic sociology of twenty-first-century capitalist societies*. Princeton: Princeton University Press.

Fligstein, N. and Goldstein, A. (2010). The Anatomy of the mortgage securitization crisis. In M. Lounsbury and P. M. Hirsch (Eds.), *Markets on trial: The economic sociology of the U.S. financial crisis: Part A. Research in the sociology of organizations, vol. 30* (pp. 29–70). Bingley: Emerald Group Publishing Limited.

Fontaine, L. (2014). *The moral economy. Poverty, credit, and trust in early modern Europe*. Cambridge: Cambridge University Press.

Fourcade, M. and Healy, K. (2013). Classification situations: Life-chances in the neoliberal era. *Accounting, Organizations and Society*, 38(8), 559–572.

Gayon, V. and Lemoine, B. (2014). Maintenir l'ordre économique. Politiques de désencastrement et de réencastrement de l'économie. *Politix*, 105, 7–35.

Godechot, O. (2001). *Les traders. Essai de sociologie des marchés financiers*. Paris: La découverte.

Godechot, O. (2008a). Stratégies financières autour d'une table. *Regards croisés sur l'économie*, 3, 144–156.

Godechot, O. (2008b). Les bonus accroissent-ils les risques? In P. Artus, J.-P. Betbèze, C. de Boissie and G. Capelle-Blancard (Eds.). *La crise des subprimes* (pp. 203–218). Paris: La Documentation Française.

Godechot, O. (2011). Le capital humain et les incitations sont-ils les deux mamelles des salaires dans la finance? *Revue d'économie financière*, 104, 145–164.

Godechot, O. (2012). Is finance responsible for the rise in wage inequality in France? *Socio-Economic Review*, 10(2), 1–24.

Godechot, O. (2013). Financiarisation et fractures socio-spatiales. *L'Année sociologique*, 63(1), 17–50.

Godechot, O. (2014). Getting a job in finance. The role of collaboration ties. *European Journal of Sociology*, 55(1), 25–56.

Godechot, O. (2016a). Back in the bazaar: Taking Pierre Bourdieu to a trading room. *Journal of Cultural Economy*, 9(4), 410–429.

Godechot, O. (2016b). Financialization is marketization! A study on the respective impact of various dimensions of financialization on the increase in global inequality. *Sociological Science*, 3, 495–519.

Godechot, O. (2016c). *Wages, bonuses and appropriation of profit in the financial industry*. London: Routledge.

Goldstein, A. (2012). Revenge of the managers: Labor cost-cutting and the paradoxical resurgence managerialism in the shareholder value era, 1984 to 2001. *American Sociological Review*, 77(2), 268–294.

Heilbron, J., Verheul, J. and Quak, S. (2014). The origins and early diffusion of 'shareholder value' in the United States. *Theory and Society*, 43(1), 1–22.

Jung, J. and Dobbin, F. (2016). Agency theory as prophecy: How boards, analysts, and fund managers perform their roles. *Seattle University Law Review*, 39, 291–320.

Knorr Cetina, K. and Preda, A. (2004). *The sociology of financial markets*. Oxford: Oxford University Press.

Knorr Cetina, K. and Preda, A. (2012). *The Oxford handbook of the sociology of finance*. Oxford: Oxford University Press.

Krippner, G. (2005). The financialization of the American economy. *Socio-Economic Review*, 3(1), 173–208.

Krippner, G. (2011). *Capitalizing on crisis: The political origins of the rise of finance*. Cambridge: Harvard University Press.

Lagneau-Ymonet, P. and Riva, A. (2012). *Histoire de la Bourse*. Paris: La Découverte.

Lin, K.-H. and Tomaskovic-Devey, D. (2013). Financialization and US income inequality, 1970–2008. *American Journal of Sociology*, 118(5), 1284–1329.

MacKenzie, D. (2006). *An engine, not a camera. How financial models shape markets*. Cambridge: MIT Press.

MacKenzie, D. (2011). The credit crisis as a problem in the sociology of knowledge. *American Journal of Sociology*, 116(6), 1778–1841.

Montagne, S. (2006). *Les fonds de pension entre protection sociale et spéculation financière*. Paris: Odile Jacob.

Muniesa, F. (2000). Un robot walrasien. Cotation électronique et justesse de la découverte des prix. *Politix*, 13(52), 121–154.

Muniesa, F. (2007). Market technologies and the pragmatics of prices. *Economy and society*, 36(3), 377–395.

Philippon, T. and Resheff, A. (2013). An international look at the growth of modern finance. *Journal of Economic Perspectives*, 27(2), 73–96.

Poon, M. (2009). From new deal institutions to capital markets: Commercial consumer risk scores and the making of subprime mortgage finance. *Accounting, Organization and Society*, 34(5), 654–674.

Ortiz, H. (2013). La 'valeur' dans l'industrie financière: le prix des actions cotées comme 'vérité' technique et politique. *L'Année sociologique*, 63, 107–136.

Ortiz, H. (2014a). *Valeur financière et vérité: enquête d'anthropologie politique sur l'évaluation des entreprises cotées en* Bourse. Paris: Presses de Sciences Po.

Ortiz, H. (2014b). The limits of financial imagination: Free investors, efficient markets, and crisis. *American Anthropologist*, 116(1), 38–50.

Roth, L.-M. (2006). *Selling women short: Gender and money on Wall Street*. Princeton: Princeton University Press.

Smith, C. (1999). *Success and survival on Wall Street. Understanding the mind of the market*, Lanham: Rowman and Littlefield Publishers.

Tadjeddine, Y. (2000). Les prises cognitives de la rationalité. Une typologie des décisions spéculatives. *Politix*, 13(52), 57–71.

Tomaskovic-Devey, D. and Lin, K.-H. (2011). Income dynamics, economic rents, and the financialization of the economy. *American Sociological Review*, 76(4), 538–559.

Woll, C. (2014). *The power of inaction: Bank bailouts in comparison*. Ithaca: Cornell University Press.

Zaloom C. (2006). *Out of the pits: Traders and technology from Chicago to London*. Chicago: University of Chicago Press.

Zorn, D. (2004). Here a chief, there a chief. The rise of the CFO in the American firm *American Sociological Review*, 69(3), 345–364.

Zorn, D., Dobbin, F., Dierkes, J. and Kwok M. S. (2005). Managing investors: How financial markets reshaped the American firm. In K. Knorr Cetina and A. Preda (Eds.), *The sociology of financial markets* (pp. 269–289). Oxford: Oxford University Press.

Zuckerman, E. (1999). The categorical imperative: Securities analysts and the illegitimacy discount. *American Journal of Sociology*, 104(5), 1398–1438.

Zuckerman, E. (2004). Structural incoherence and stock market activity. *American Sociological Review*, 69(3), 405–432.

INDEX

Italics are used for figures and **bold** for tables.